藍より青し

AI YORI AOSHI™

VOLUME 10

STORY & ART
BY
KOU FUMIZUKI

HAMBURG // LONDON // LOS ANGELES // TOKYO

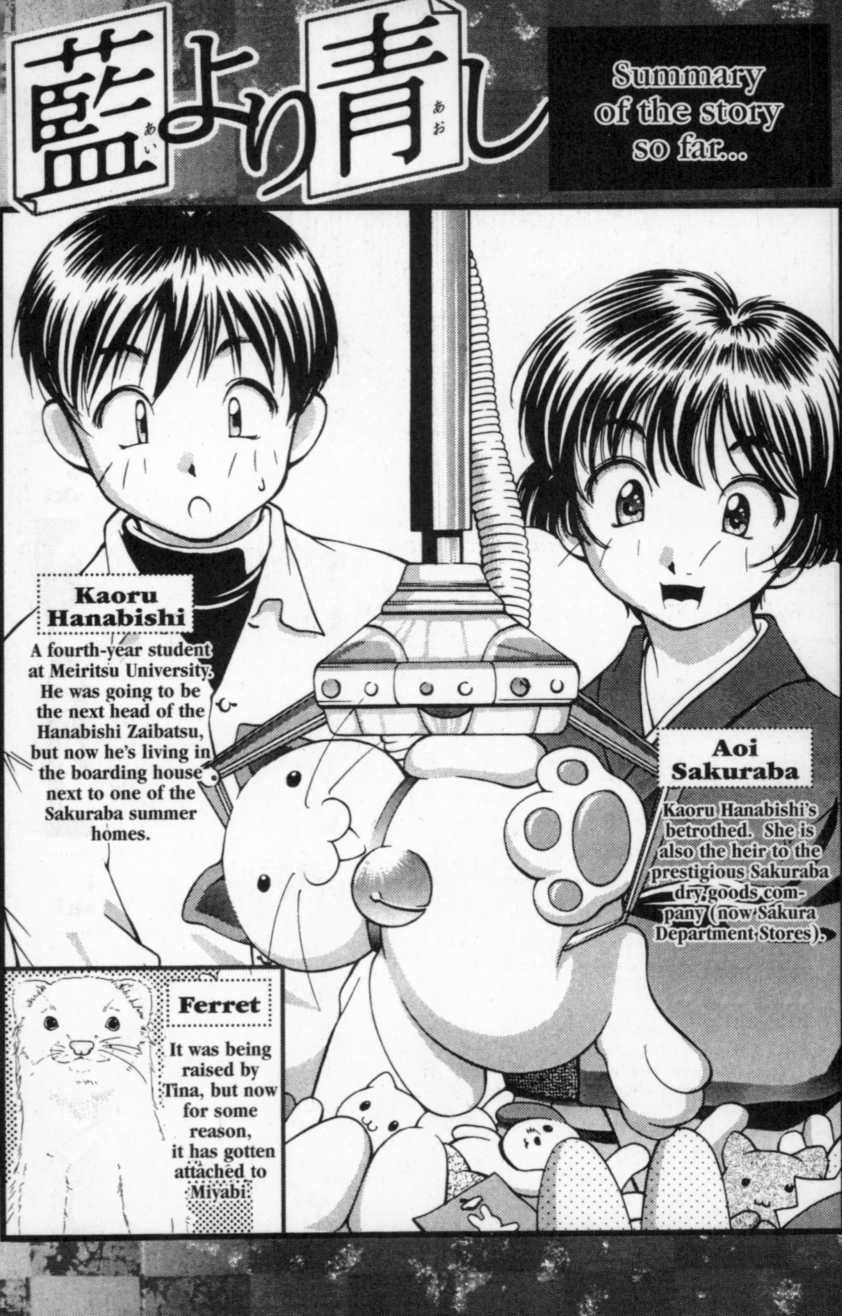
藍(あい)より青(あお)し
Summary of the story so far...
Kaoru Hanabishi
A fourth-year student at Meiritsu University. He was going to be the next head of the Hanabishi Zaibatsu, but now he's living in the boarding house next to one of the Sakuraba summer homes.
Aoi Sakuraba
Kaoru Hanabishi's betrothed. She is also the heir to the prestigious Sakuraba dry goods company (now Sakura Department Stores).
Ferret
It was being raised by Tina, but now for some reason, it has gotten attached to Miyabi.

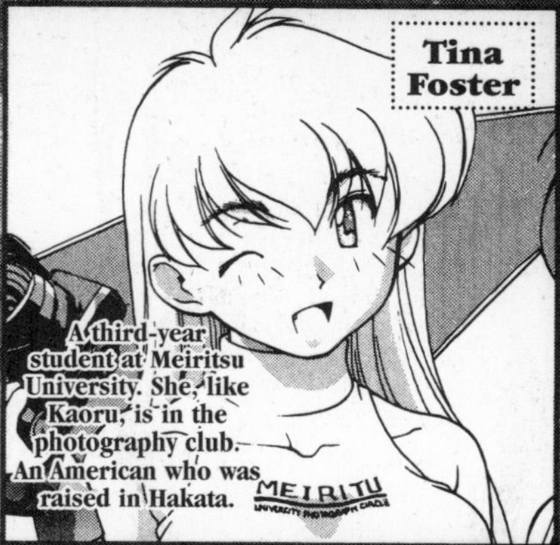
Tina Foster
A third-year student at Meiritsu University. She, like Kaoru, is in the photography club. An American who was raised in Hakata.
MEIRITU
UNIVERSITY PHOTOGRAPH CIRCLE

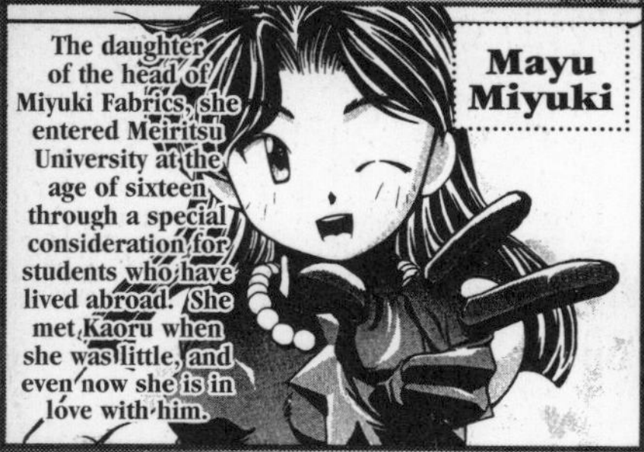
Mayu Miyuki
The daughter of the head of Miyuki Fabrics, she entered Meiritsu University at the age of sixteen through a special consideration for students who have lived abroad. She met Kaoru when she was little, and even now she is in love with him.

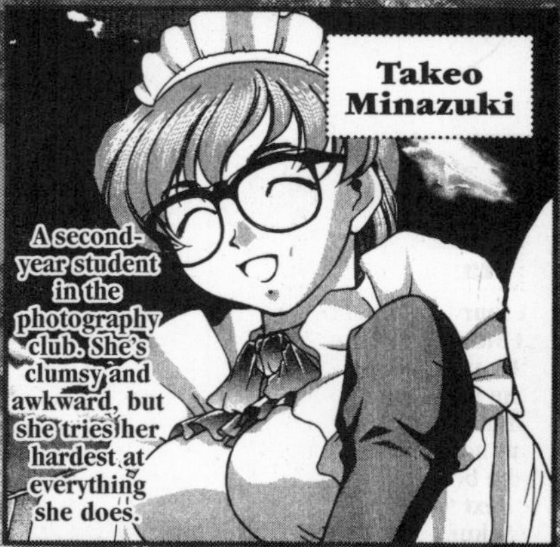
Takeo Minazuki
A second-year student in the photography club. She's clumsy and awkward, but she tries her hardest at everything she does.

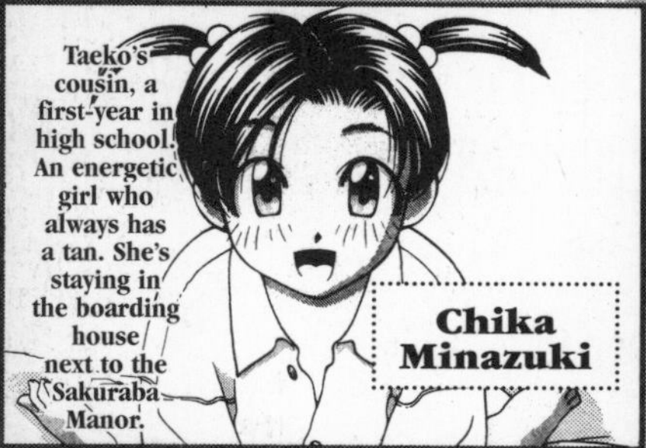
Chika Minazuki
Taeko's cousin, a first-year in high school. An energetic girl who always has a tan. She's staying in the boarding house next to the Sakuraba Manor.

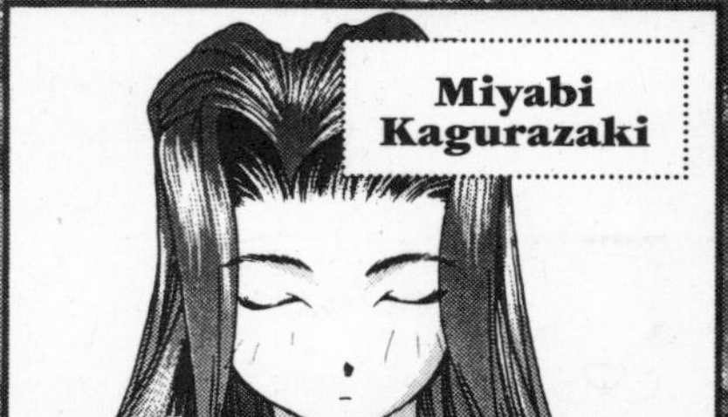
Miyabi Kagurazaki
Aoi's guardian from when she was young. She manages the lives of Aoi and Kaoru.

Kaoru Hanabishi was torn away from his mother when he was very young and raised as the heir of the Hanabishi Zaibatsu; however, he found he was unable to endure the harsh responsibilities placed on him, and he ran away from home to live by himself. He continued life in this fashion right up until the arrival of Aoi Sakuraba, who had been his betrothed and who loved him for eighteen years. Kaoru was blown away by her devotion, but her request for him to go back to the Hanabishi was the one thing he could not do. Aoi recognized the pain this caused Kaoru, so she decided to leave her own family, the Sakuraba, instead. Rather than lose her daughter, Aoi's mother conceded to allow the two of them to live together.

The couple moved to a Western-style house that had previously been one of the Sakuraba's summer homes, and they now share the estate with Aoi's guardian, Miyabi Kagurazaki. There is a catch, though—while Aoi and Miyabi live in the main house, Kaoru has to live in the boarding house adjacent to it.

Then, Tina Foster and Taeko Minazuki, members of Kaoru's photography club, moved in to the boarding house. But Aoi, to avoid any scandal involving the Sakuraba family, must behave not as Kaoru's betrothed, but as the landlady of the boarding house.

After a while, Mayu Miyuki, who has returned to Japan from England, and Taeko's cousin, Chika Minazuki, gather around Kaoru, but even so, Kaoru's and Aoi's feelings for each other grew deeper and deeper.

Ai Yori Aoshi

藍より青し 10

CONTENTS

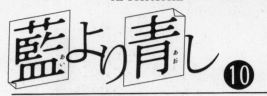

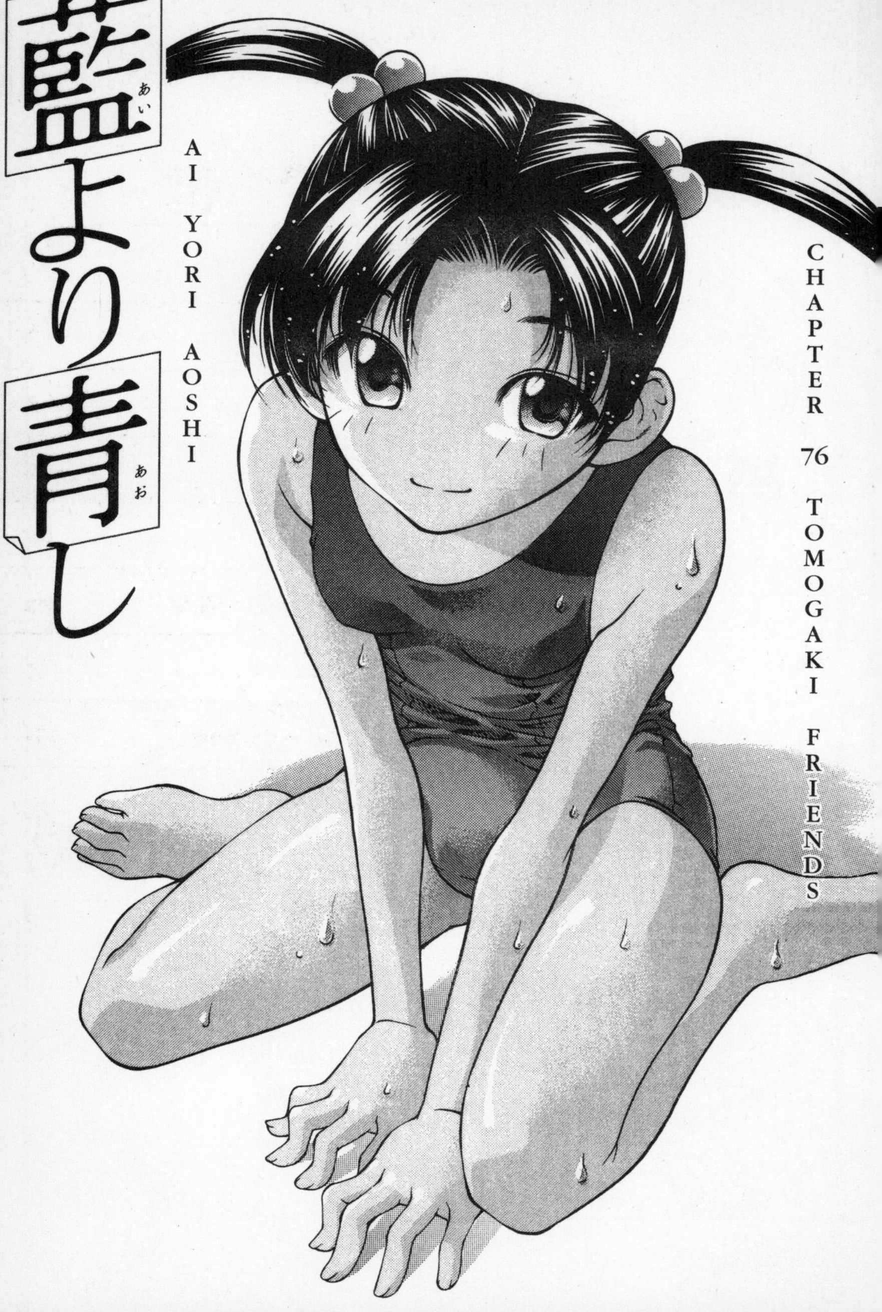
藍より青し
AI YORI AOSHI
CHAPTER 76
TOMOGAKI FRIENDS

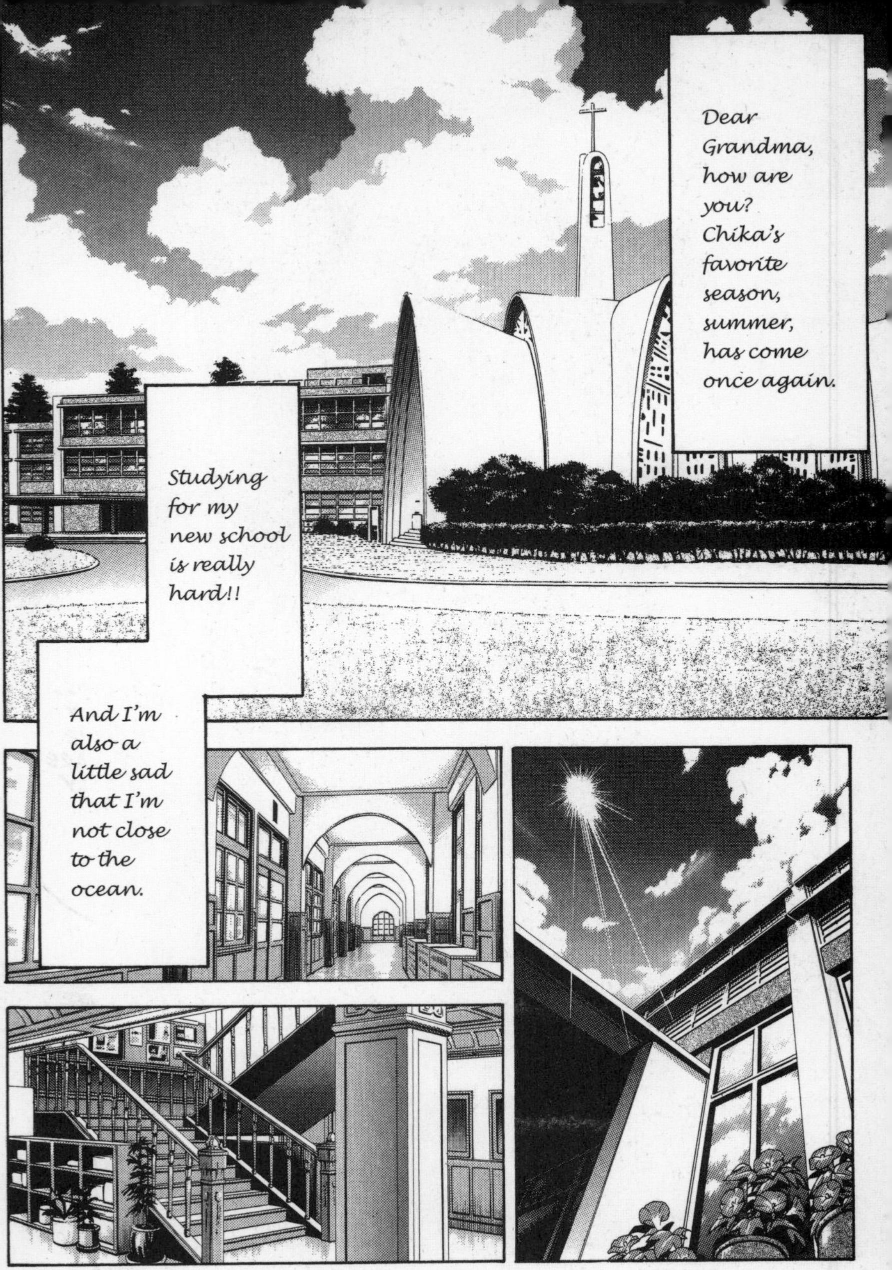
Dear Grandma, how are you? Chika's favorite season, summer, has come once again.
Studying for my new school is really hard!!
And I'm also a little sad that I'm not close to the ocean.

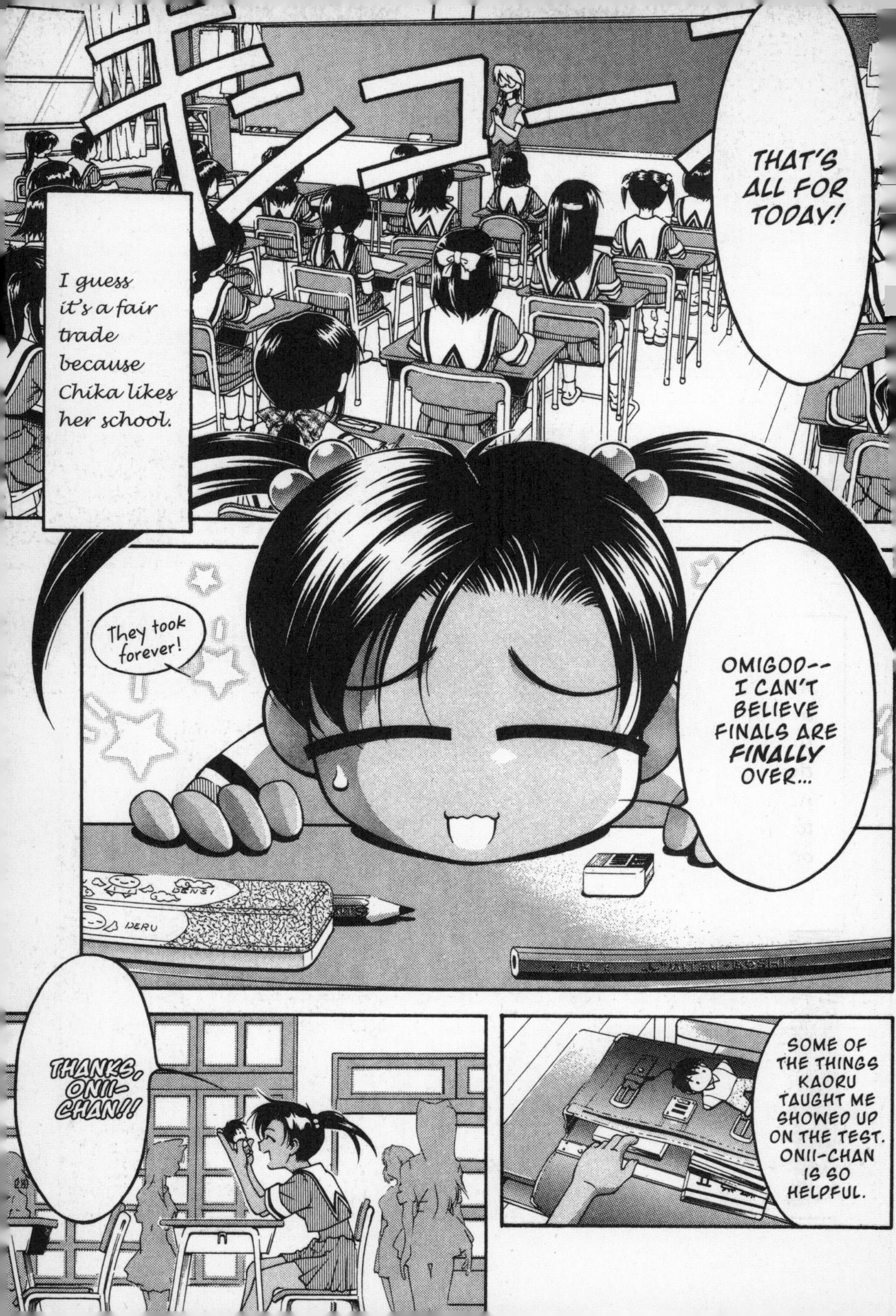
THAT'S ALL FOR TODAY!
I guess it's a fair trade because Chika likes her school.
OMIGOD-- I CAN'T BELIEVE FINALS ARE FINALLY OVER...
They took forever!
SOME OF THE THINGS KAORU TAUGHT ME SHOWED UP ON THE TEST. ONII-CHAN IS SO HELPFUL.
THANKS, ONII-CHAN!!

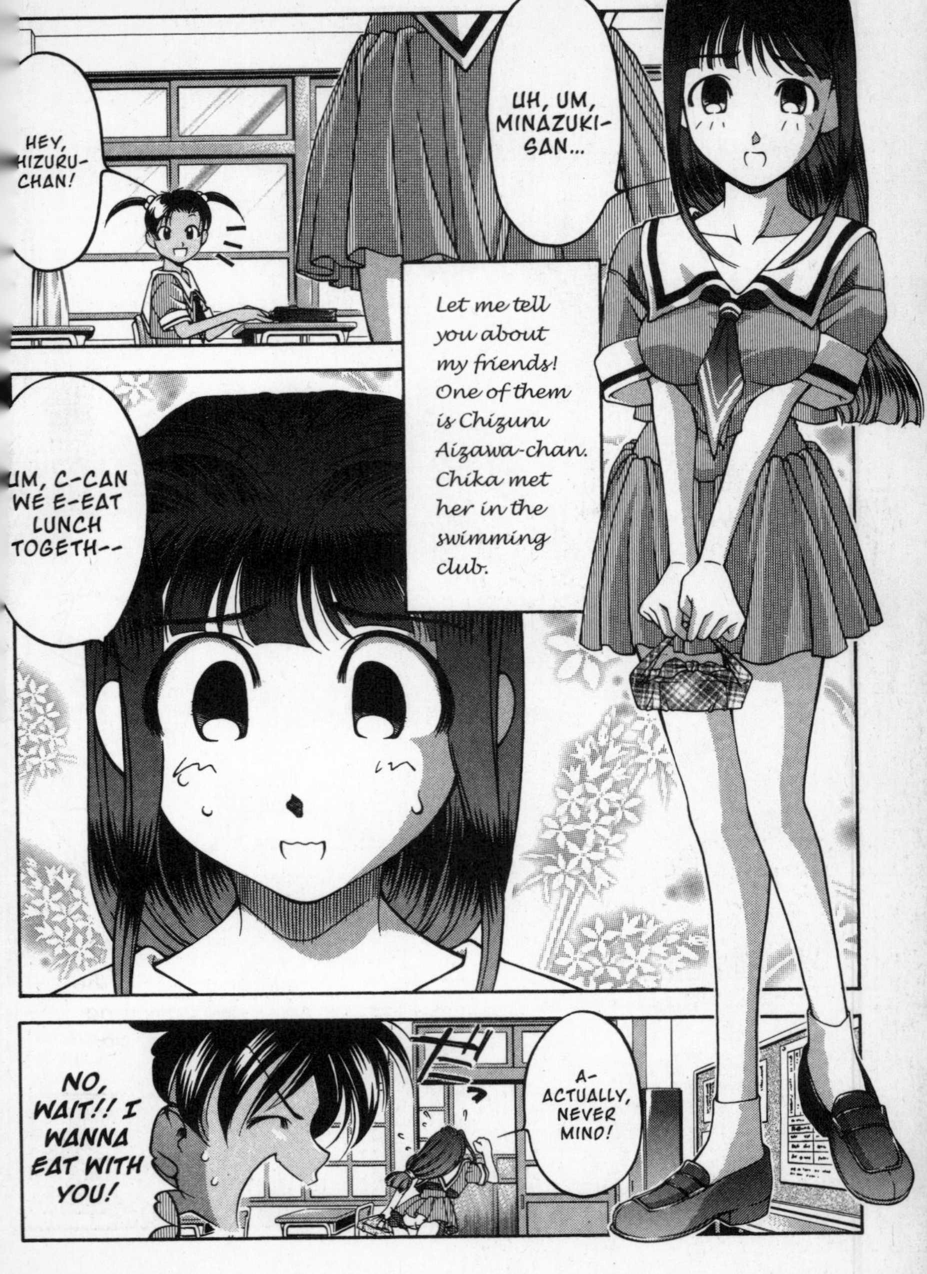
UH, UM, MINAZUKI-SAN...
Let me tell you about my friends! One of them is Chizuru Aizawa-chan. Chika met her in the swimming club.
HEY, HIZURU-CHAN!
UM, C-CAN WE E-EAT LUNCH TOGETH--
A-ACTUALLY, NEVER MIND!
NO, WAIT!! I WANNA EAT WITH YOU!

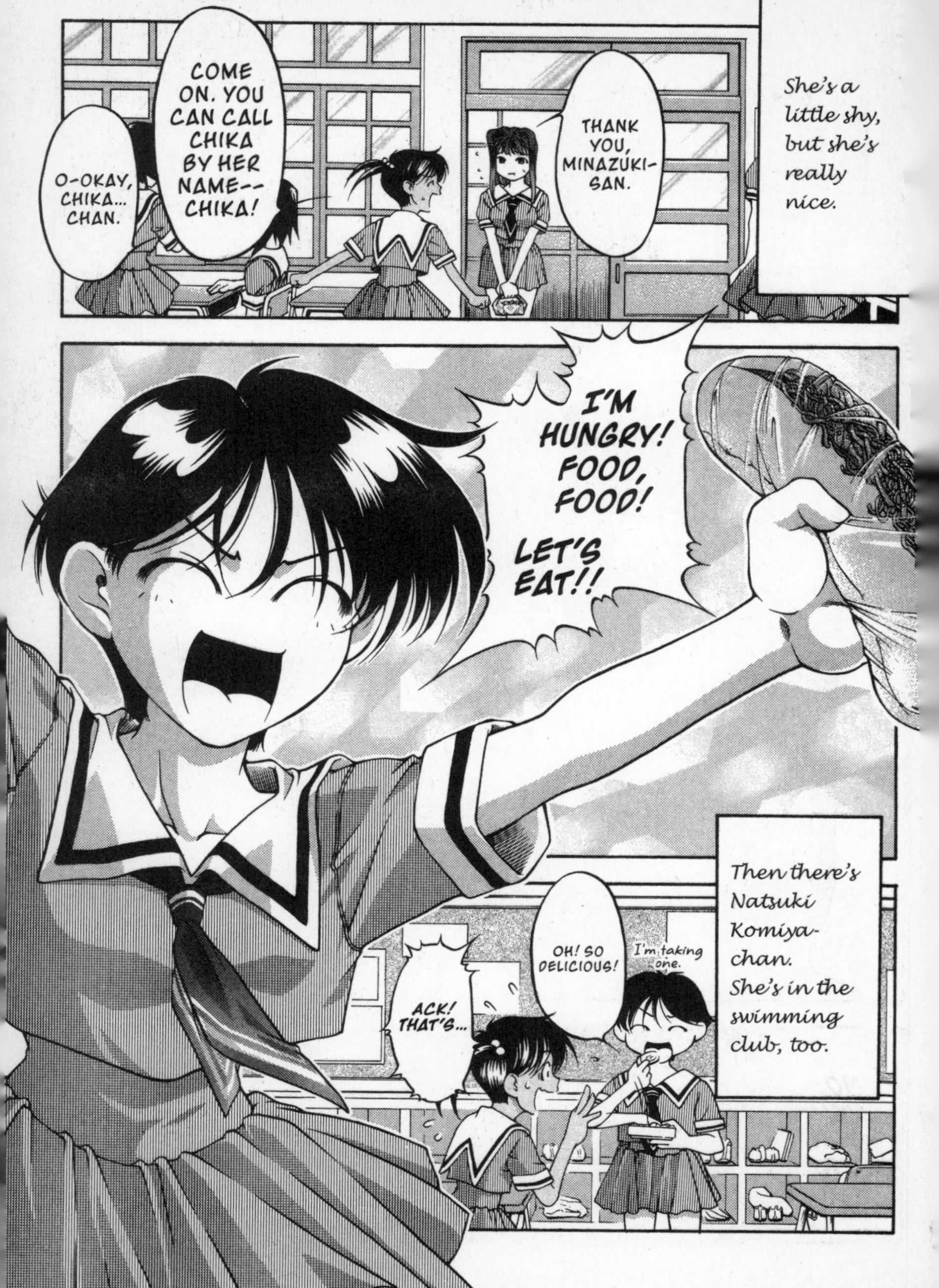
She's a little shy, but she's really nice.
THANK YOU, MINAZUKI-SAN.
COME ON. YOU CAN CALL CHIKA BY HER NAME--CHIKA!
O-OKAY, CHIKA... CHAN.
I'M HUNGRY! FOOD, FOOD!
LET'S EAT!!
Then there's Natsuki Komiya-chan. She's in the swimming club, too.
I'm taking one.
OH! SO DELICIOUS!
ACK! THAT'S...

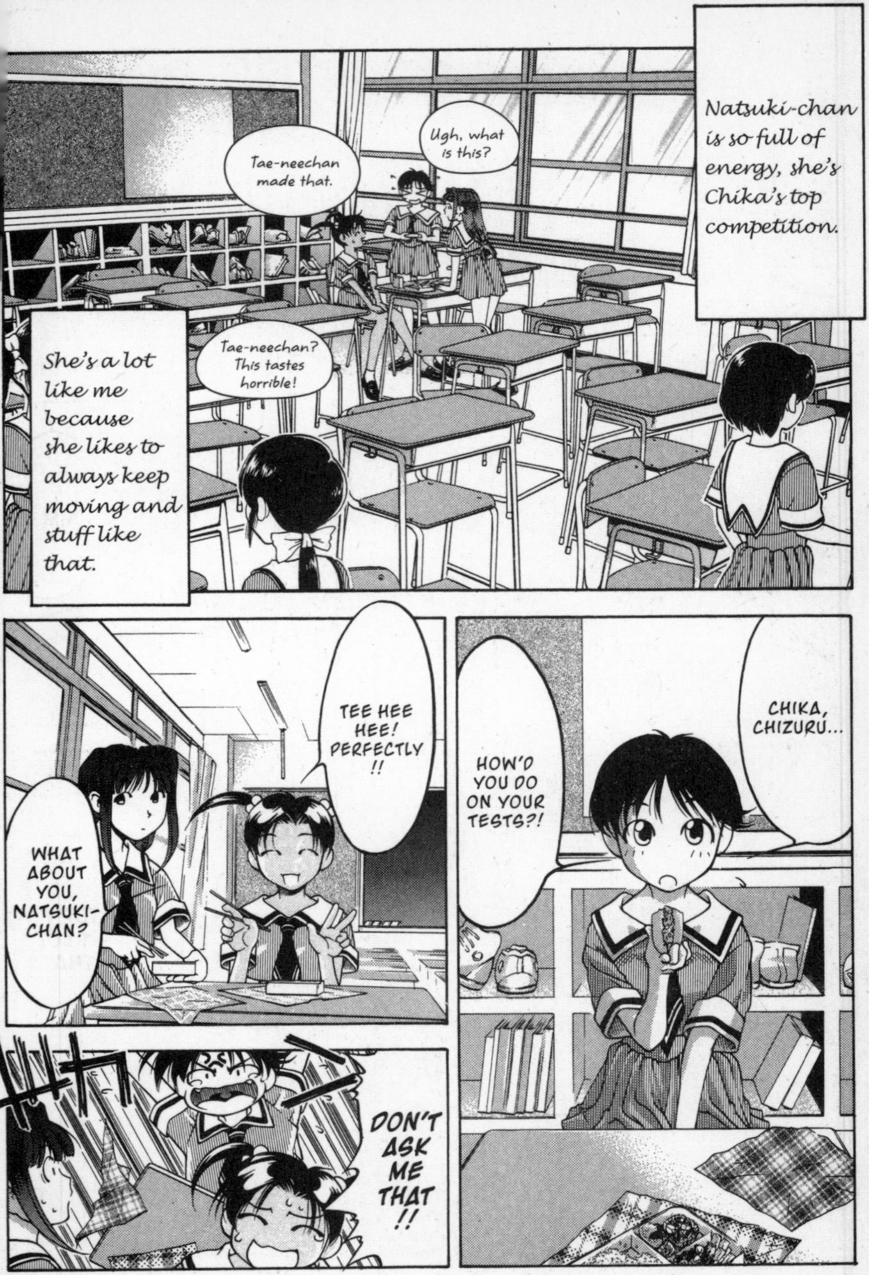

Natsuki-chan is so full of energy, she's Chika's top competition.
Ugh, what is this?
Tae-neechan made that.
Tae-neechan? This tastes horrible!
She's a lot like me because she likes to always keep moving and stuff like that.
CHIKA, CHIZURU...
HOW'D YOU DO ON YOUR TESTS?!
TEE HEE HEE! PERFECTLY!!
WHAT ABOUT YOU, NATSUKI-CHAN?
DON'T ASK ME THAT!!

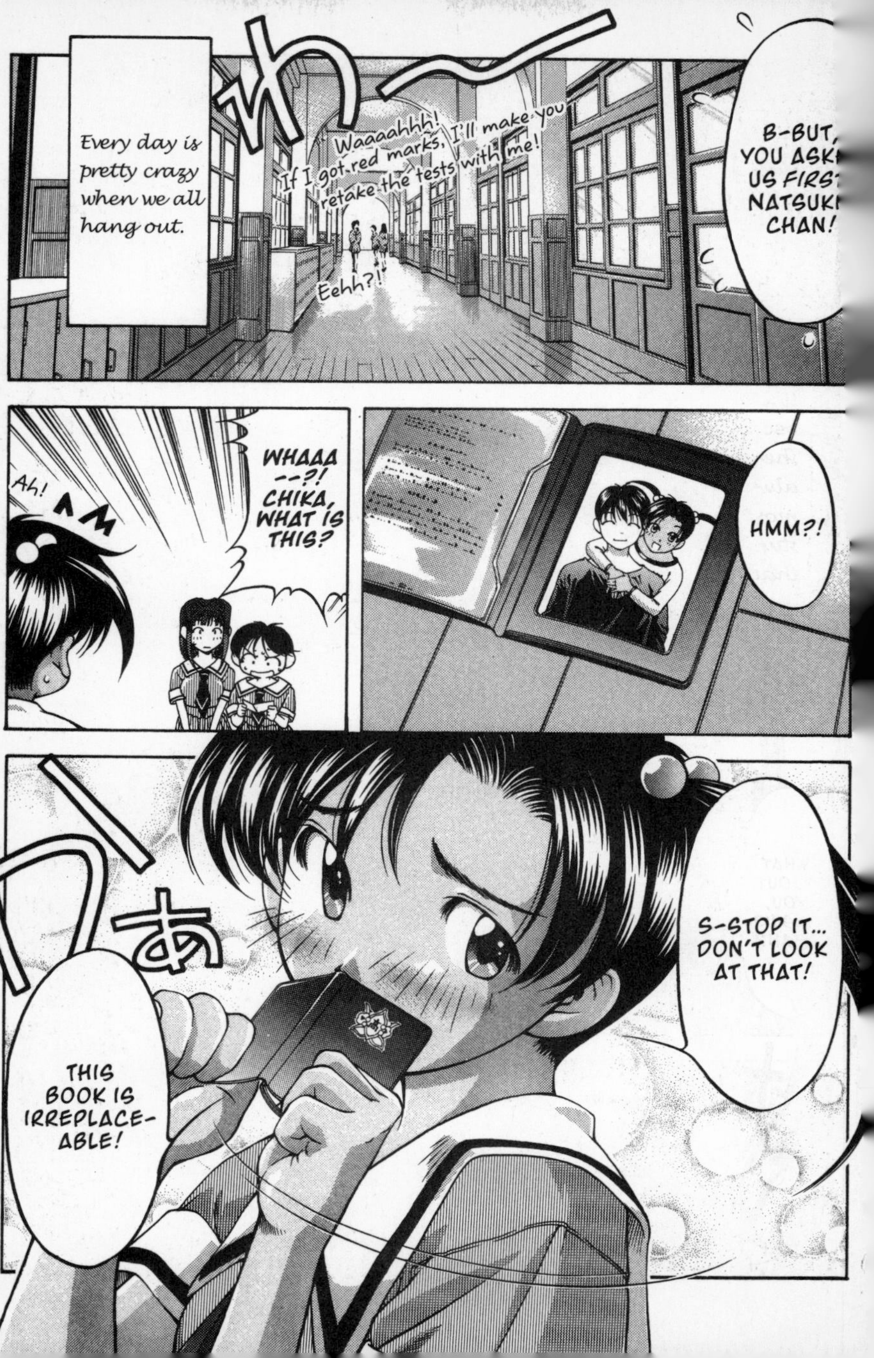
B-BUT, YOU ASK US FIRS NATSUK CHAN!
わ〜
Waaaahhh! If I got red marks, I'll make you retake the tests with me!
Every day is pretty crazy when we all hang out.
Eehh?!
HMM?!
WHAAA--?! CHIKA, WHAT IS THIS?
Ah!
S-STOP IT... DON'T LOOK AT THAT!
やぁ
THIS BOOK IS IRREPLACE-ABLE!

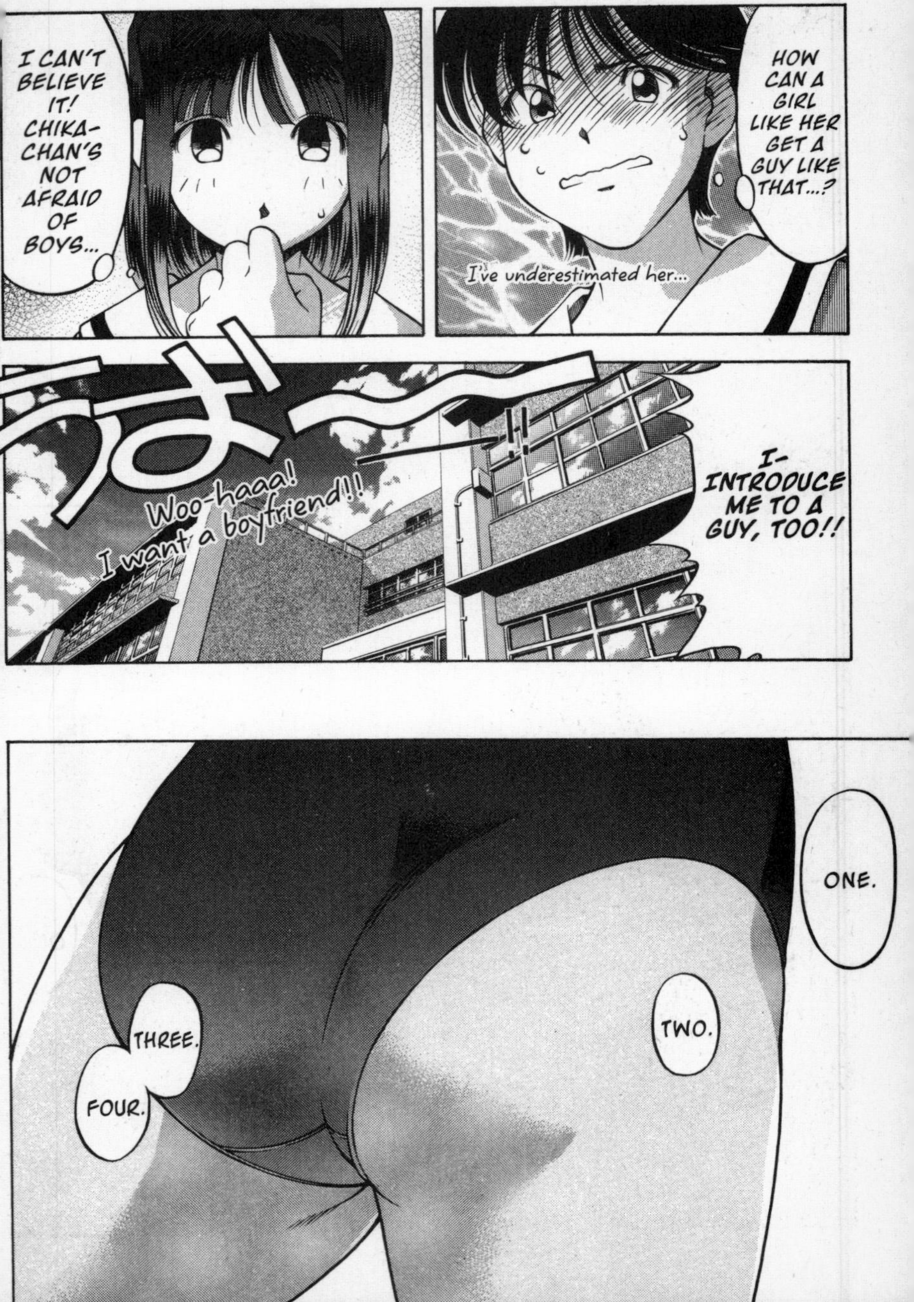
HOW CAN A GIRL LIKE HER GET A GUY LIKE THAT...?
I've underestimated her...
I CAN'T BELIEVE IT! CHIKA-CHAN'S NOT AFRAID OF BOYS...
I-INTRODUCE ME TO A GUY, TOO!!
Woo-haaa! I want a boyfriend!!
ONE.
TWO.
THREE.
FOUR.

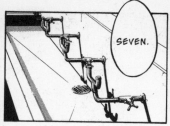

SEVEN.

FIVE.
SIX.

EIGHT.

THREE

FOUR.

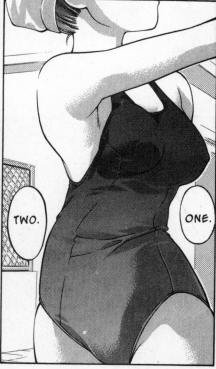

TWO.

ONE.

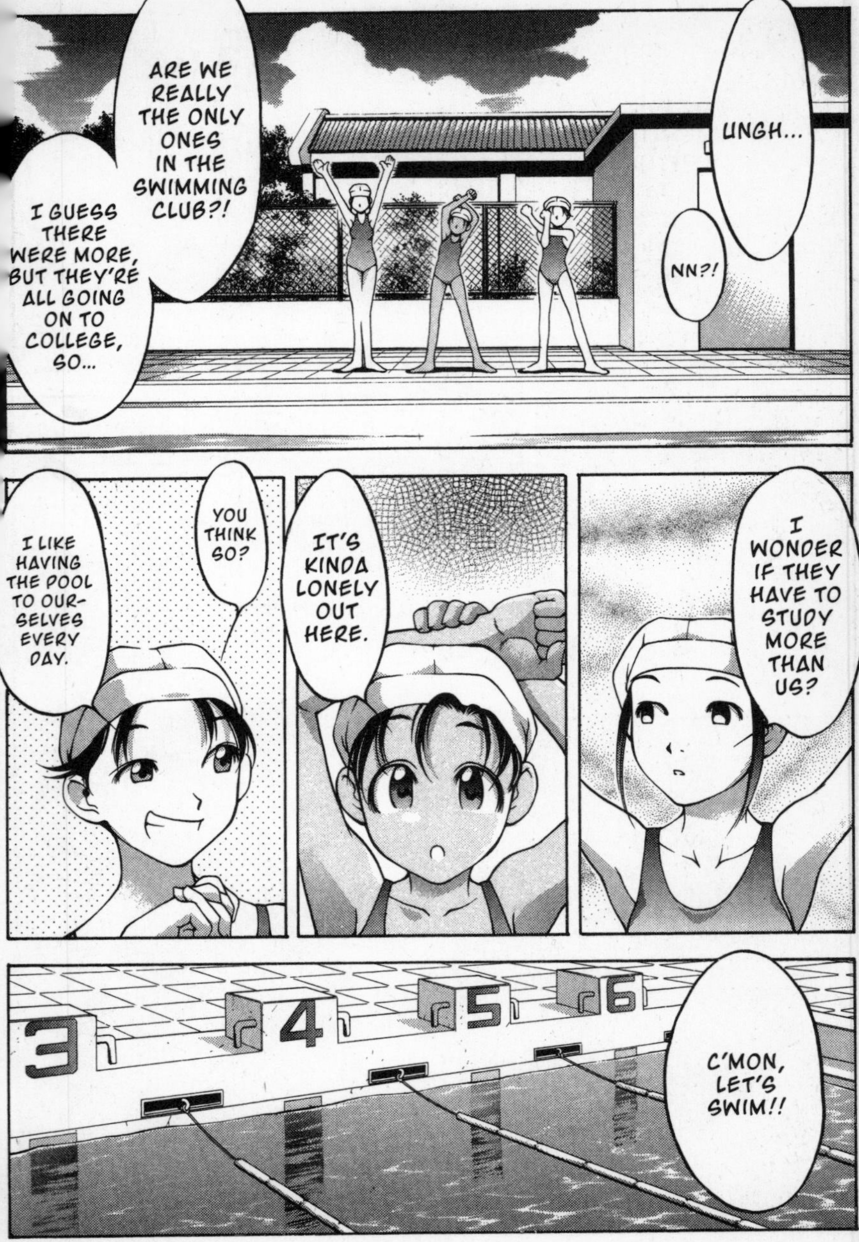
UNGH...
NN?!
ARE WE REALLY THE ONLY ONES IN THE SWIMMING CLUB?!
I GUESS THERE WERE MORE, BUT THEY'RE ALL GOING ON TO COLLEGE, SO...
I WONDER IF THEY HAVE TO STUDY MORE THAN US?
IT'S KINDA LONELY OUT HERE.
YOU THINK SO?
I LIKE HAVING THE POOL TO OUR-SELVES EVERY DAY.
3
4
5
6
C'MON, LET'S SWIM!!

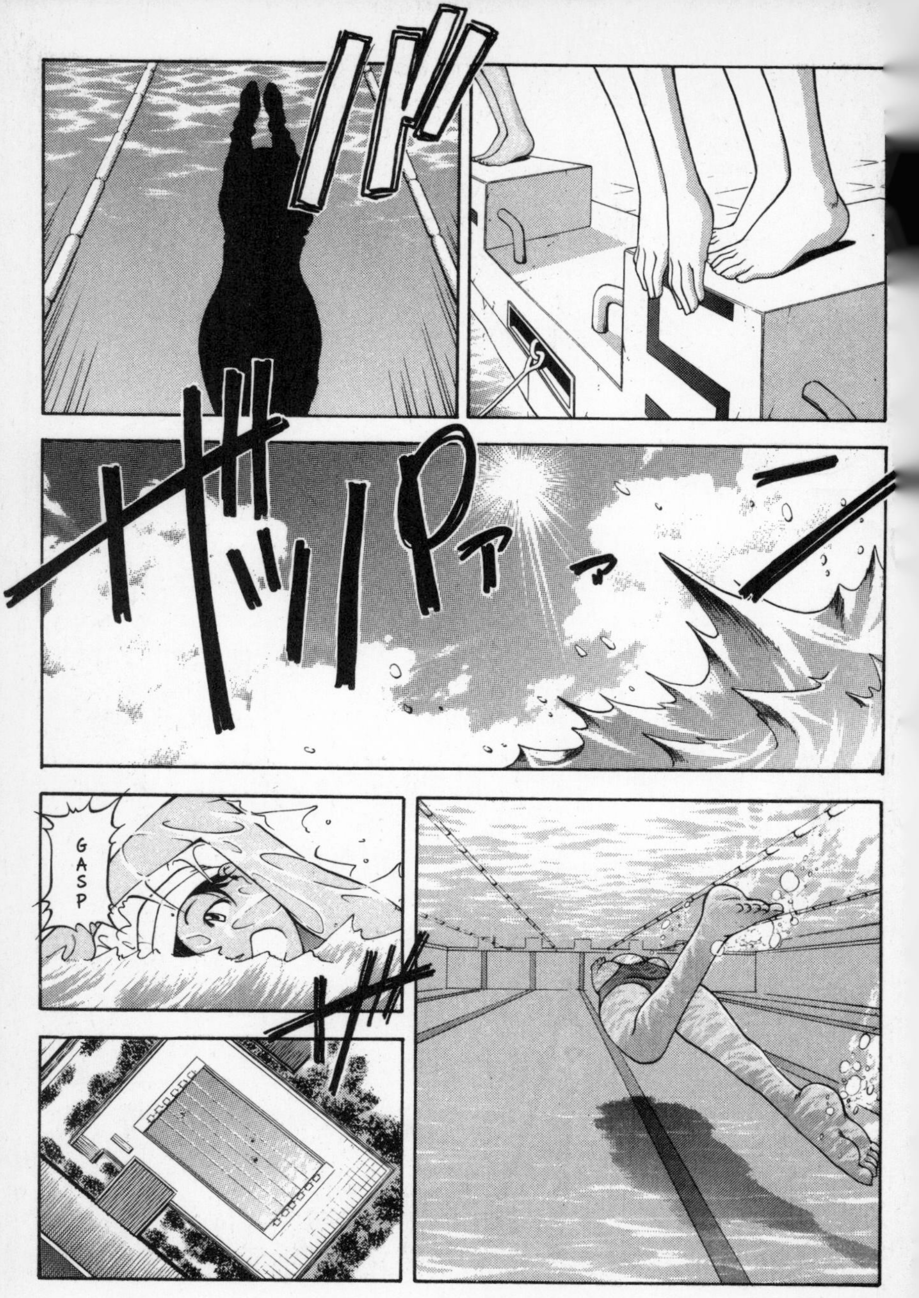
GASP

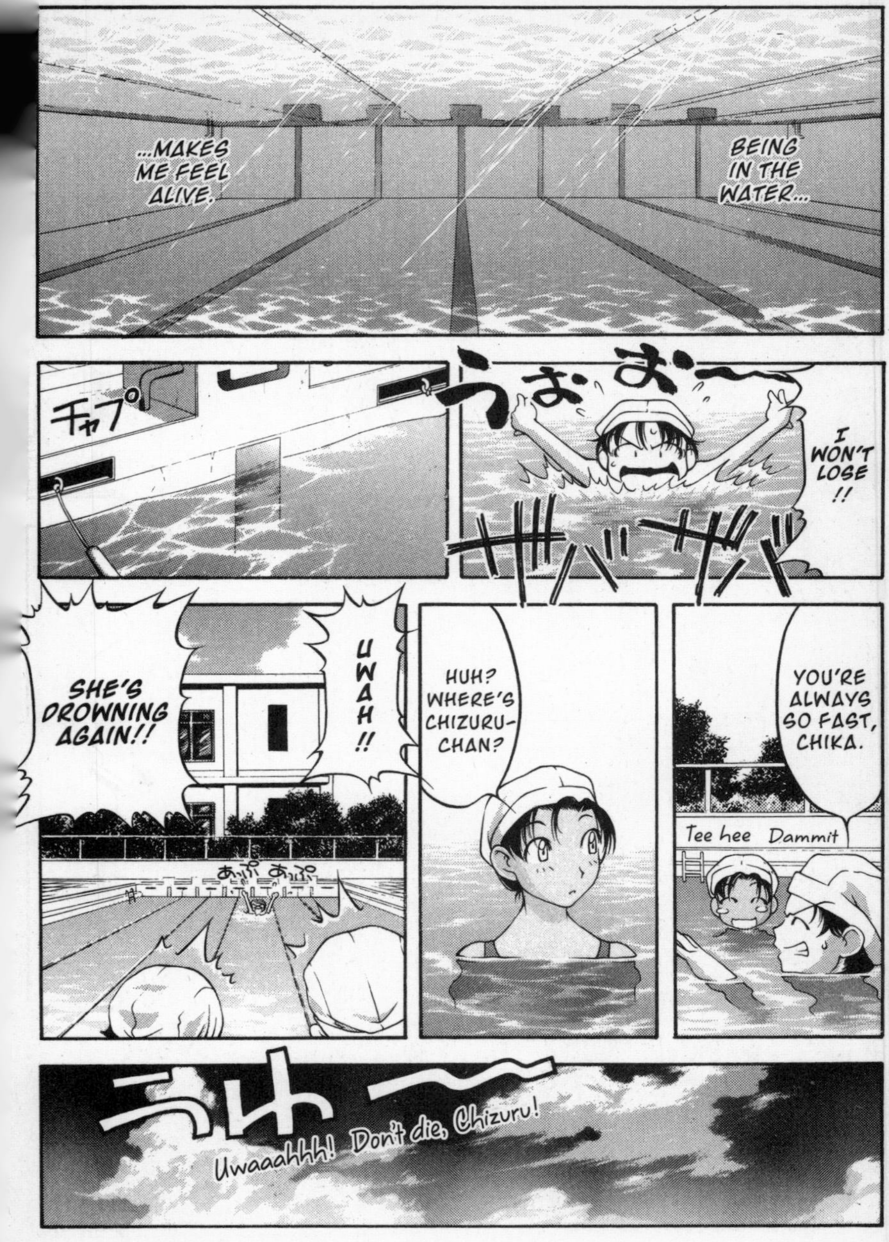
BEING IN THE WATER...
...MAKES ME FEEL ALIVE.
うぉぉ~
I WON'T LOSE!!
ザバザバ
チャプ
YOU'RE ALWAYS SO FAST, CHIKA.
Tee hee
Dammit
HUH? WHERE'S CHIZURU-CHAN?
UWAH!!
SHE'S DROWNING AGAIN!!
あっぷ あっぷ
うわ~~
Uwaaahhh! Don't die, Chizuru!

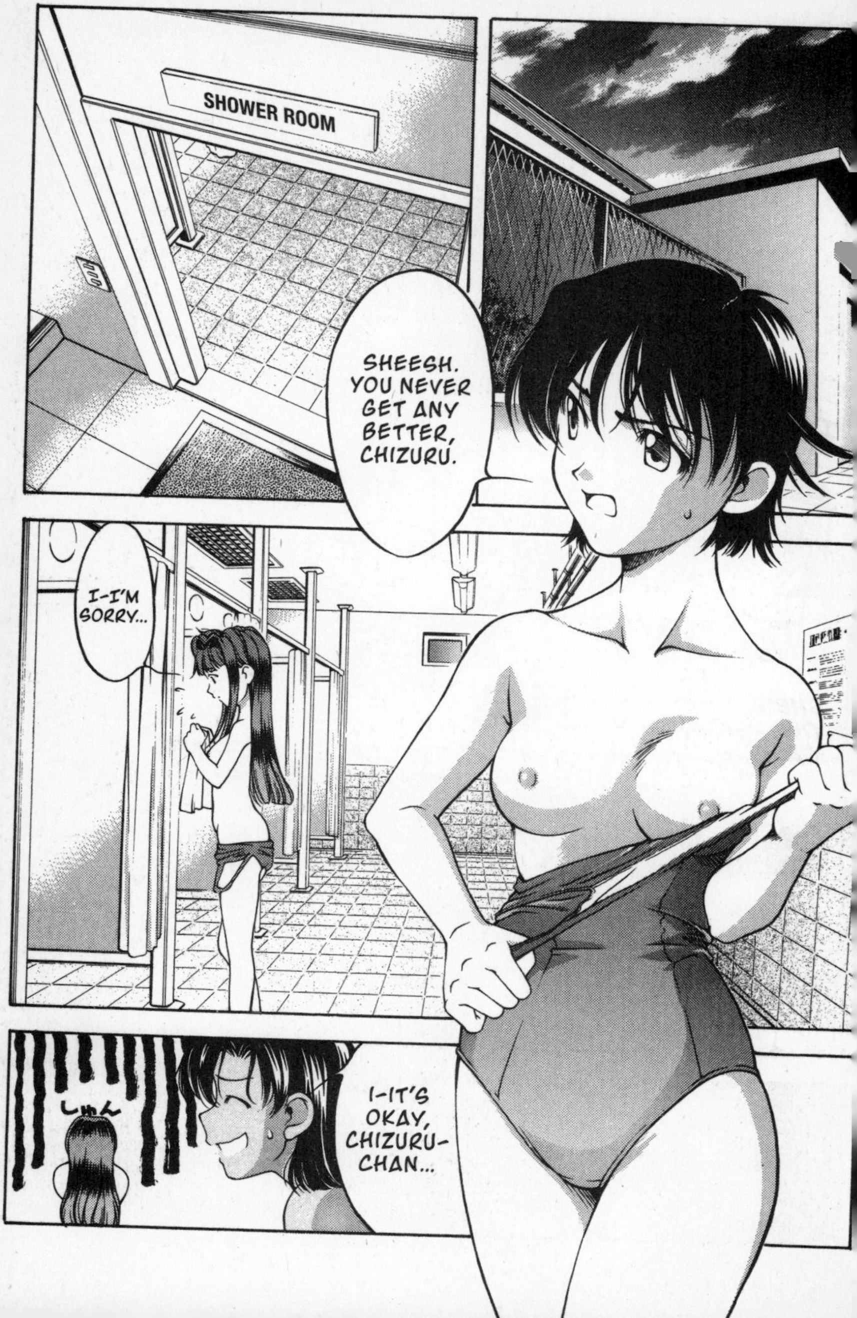
SHOWER ROOM
SHEESH. YOU NEVER GET ANY BETTER, CHIZURU.
I-I'M SORRY...
I-IT'S OKAY, CHIZURU-CHAN...
しゅん

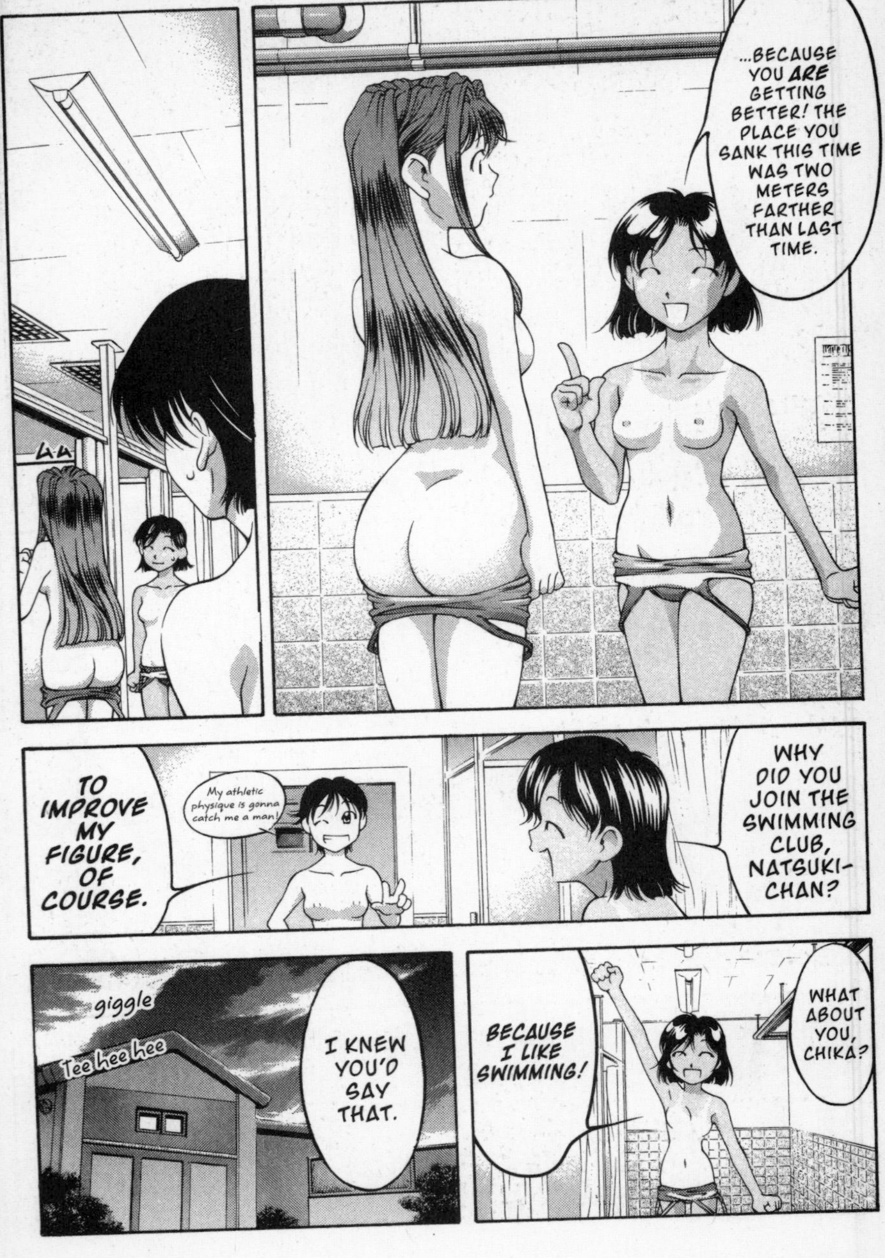
...BECAUSE YOU ARE GETTING BETTER! THE PLACE YOU SANK THIS TIME WAS TWO METERS FARTHER THAN LAST TIME.
WHY DID YOU JOIN THE SWIMMING CLUB, NATSUKI-CHAN?
My athletic physique is gonna catch me a man!
TO IMPROVE MY FIGURE, OF COURSE.
WHAT ABOUT YOU, CHIKA?
BECAUSE I LIKE SWIMMING!
I KNEW YOU'D SAY THAT.
giggle
Tee hee hee

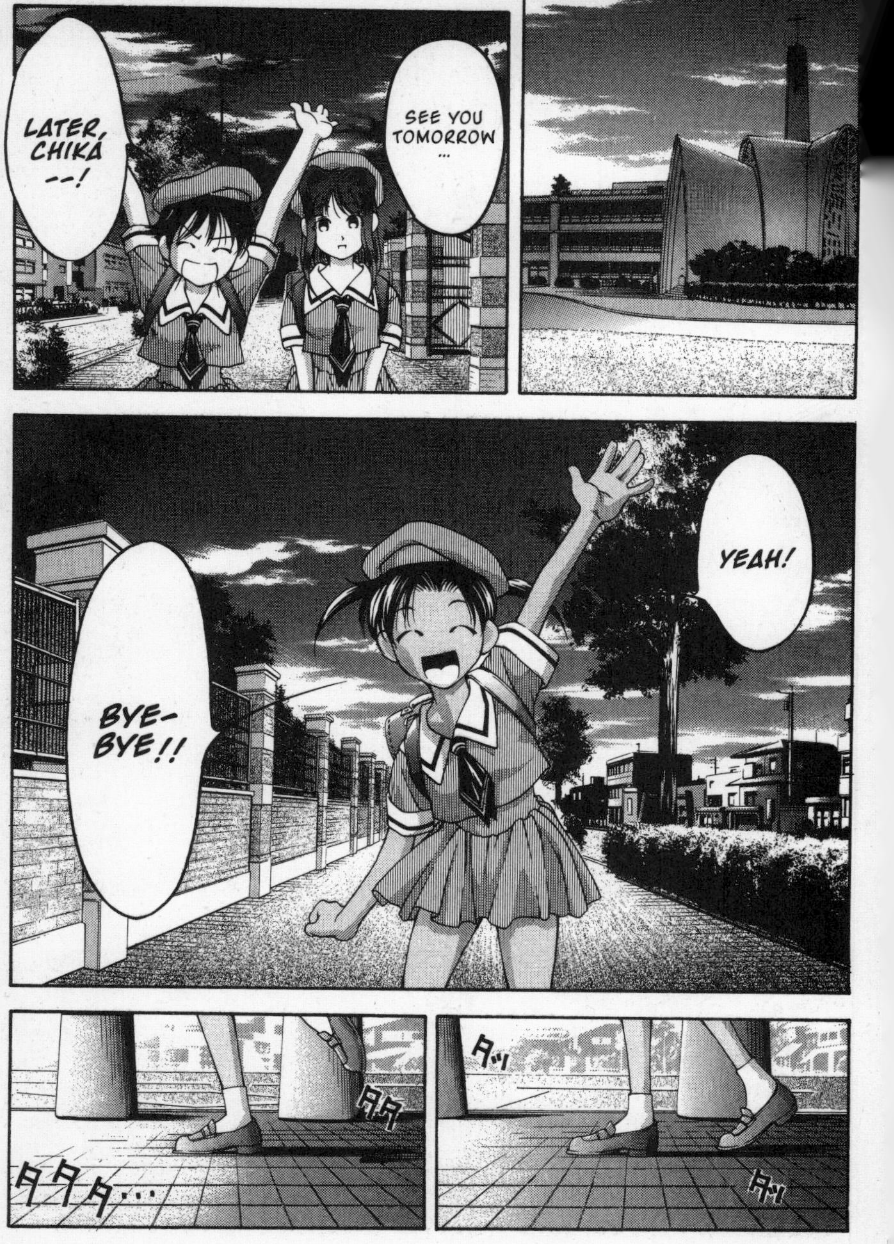
SEE YOU TOMORROW ...
LATER, CHIKA --!
YEAH!
BYE-BYE!!
タッ
タッ
タタ
タタタ...

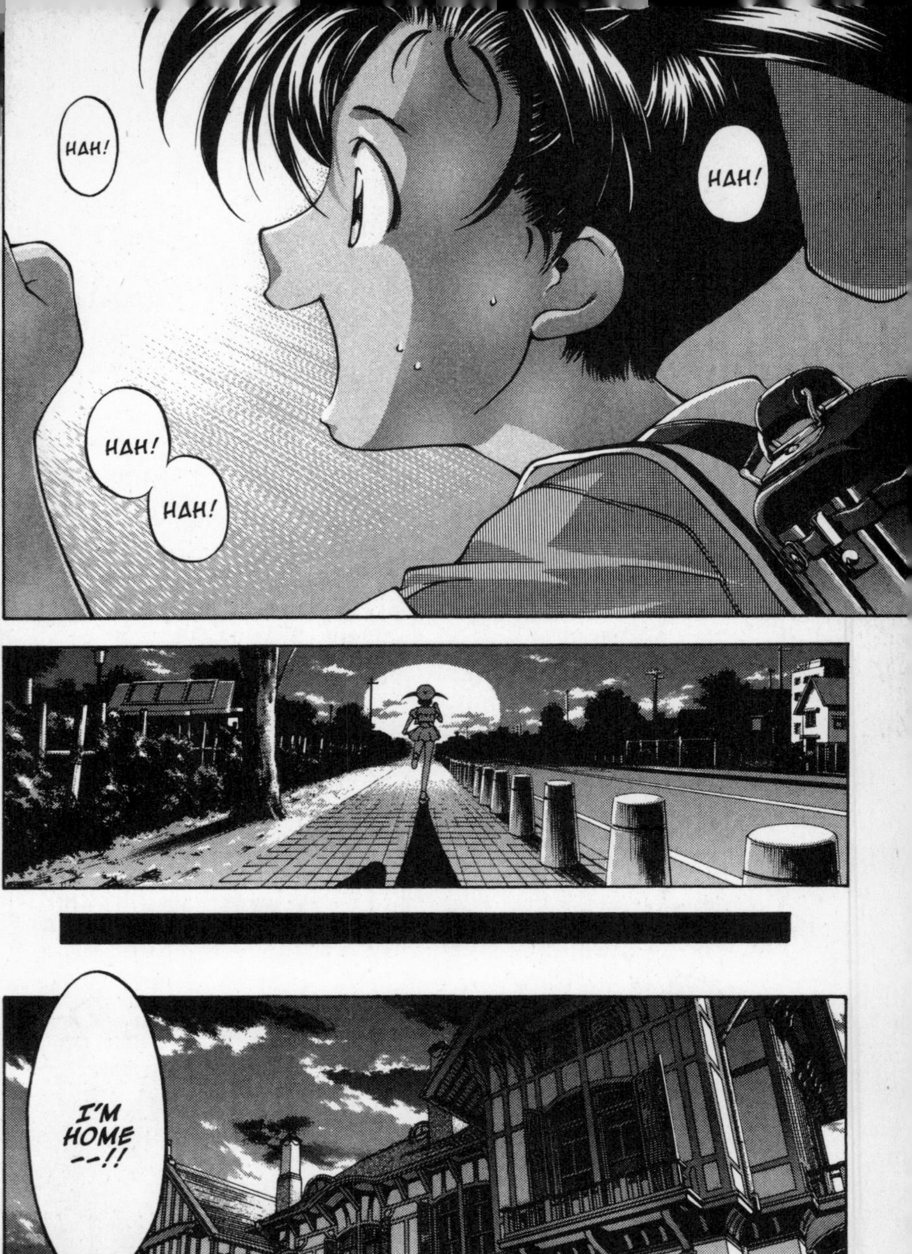
HAH!
HAH!
HAH!
HAH!
I'M HOME --!!

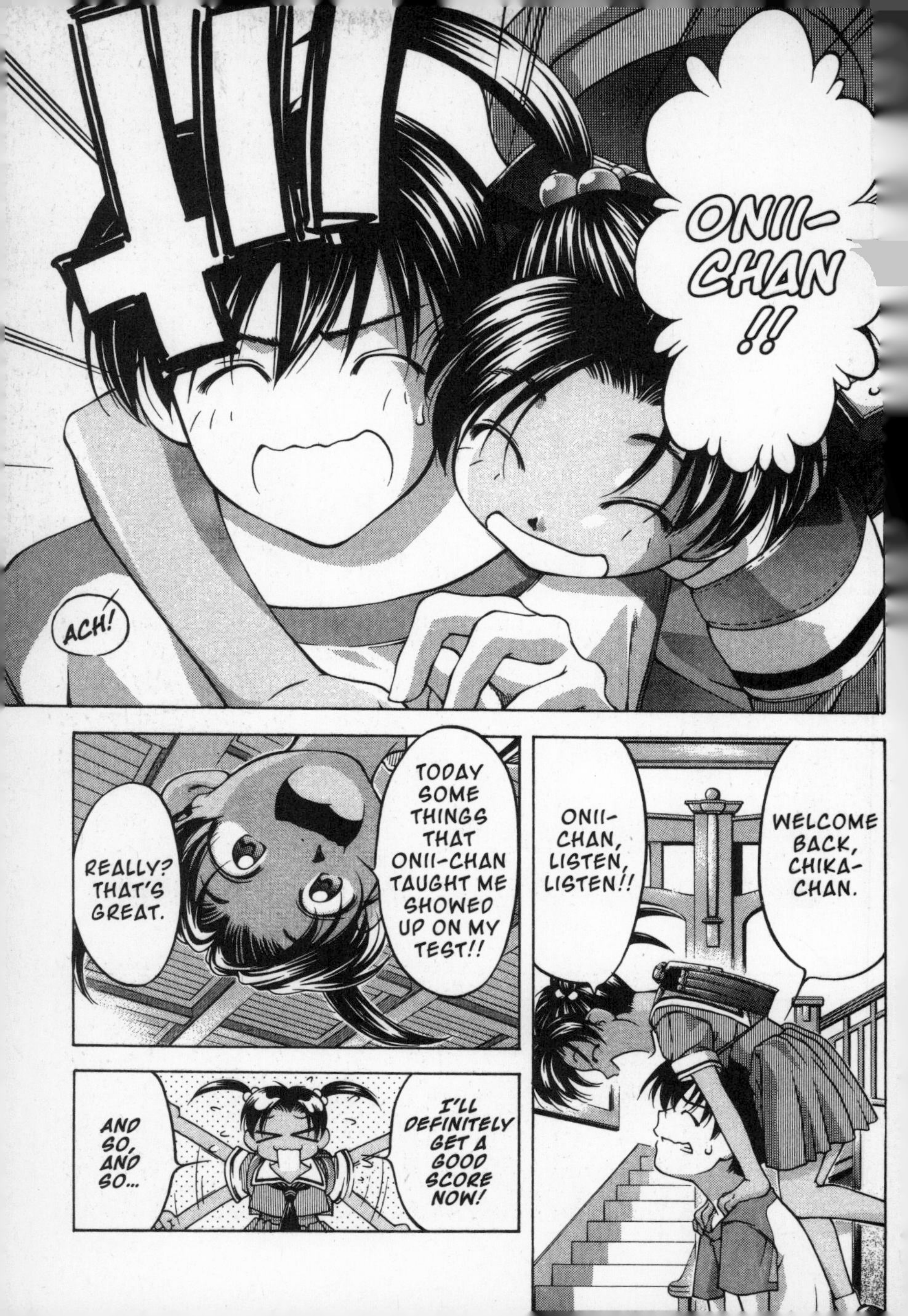
ONII-CHAN!!
ACH!
WELCOME BACK, CHIKA-CHAN.
ONII-CHAN, LISTEN, LISTEN!!
TODAY SOME THINGS THAT ONII-CHAN TAUGHT ME SHOWED UP ON MY TEST!!
REALLY? THAT'S GREAT.
I'LL DEFINITELY GET A GOOD SCORE NOW!
AND SO, AND SO...

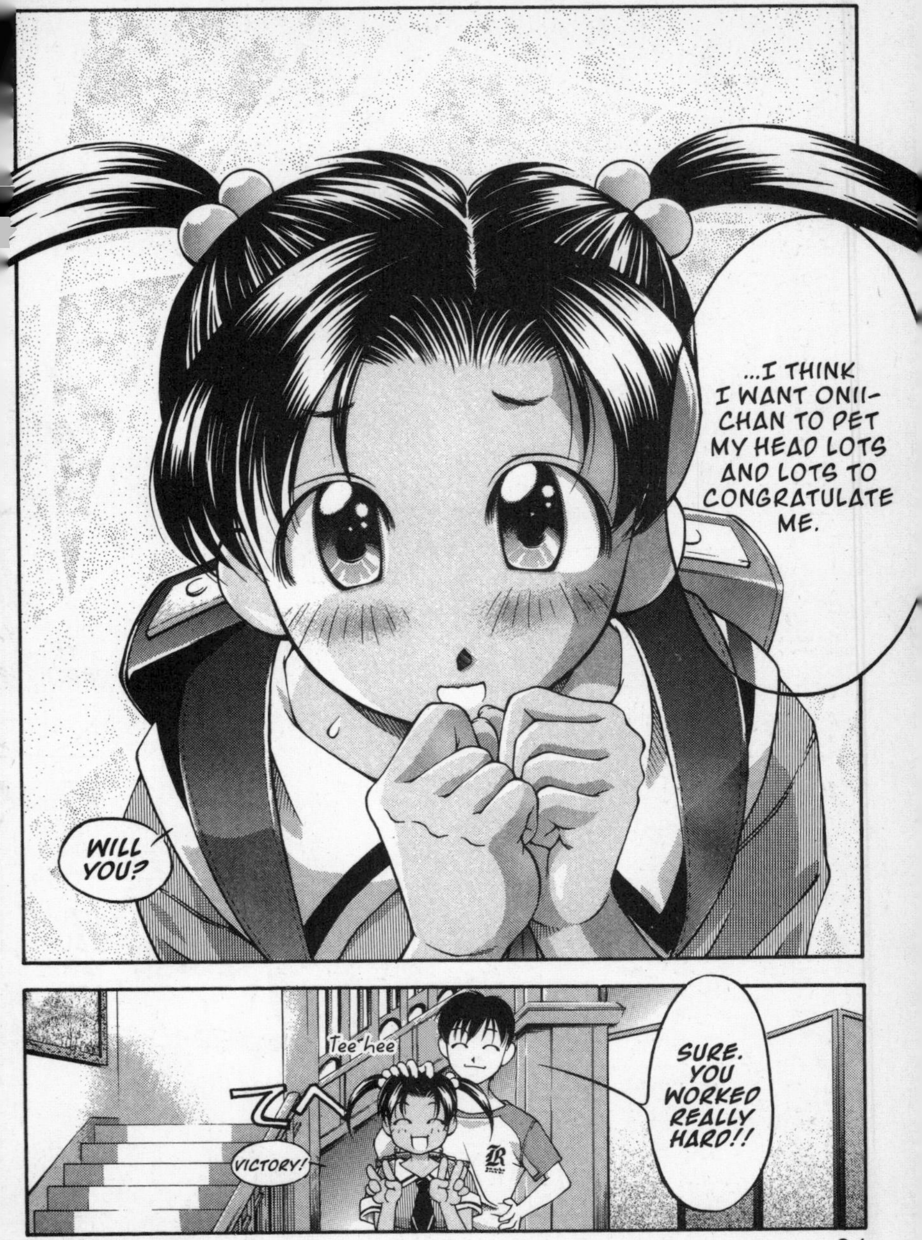
...I THINK I WANT ONII-CHAN TO PET MY HEAD LOTS AND LOTS TO CONGRATULATE ME.
WILL YOU?
SURE. YOU WORKED REALLY HARD!!
Tee hee
VICTORY!

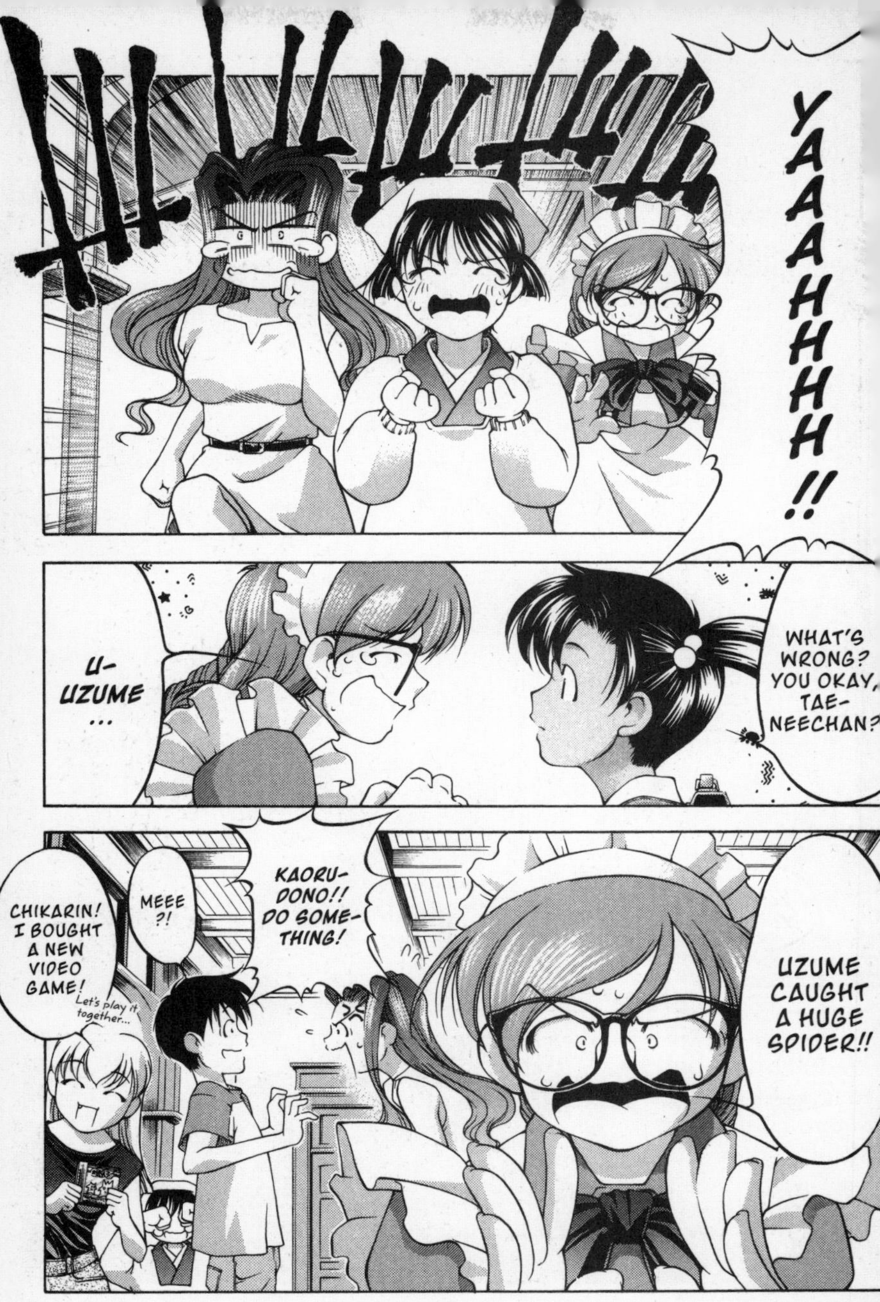
YAAAHHHH!!
WHAT'S WRONG? YOU OKAY, TAE-NEECHAN?
U-UZUME ...
UZUME CAUGHT A HUGE SPIDER!!
KAORU-DONO!! DO SOME-THING!
MEEE ?!
CHIKARIN! I BOUGHT A NEW VIDEO GAME!
Let's play it together...

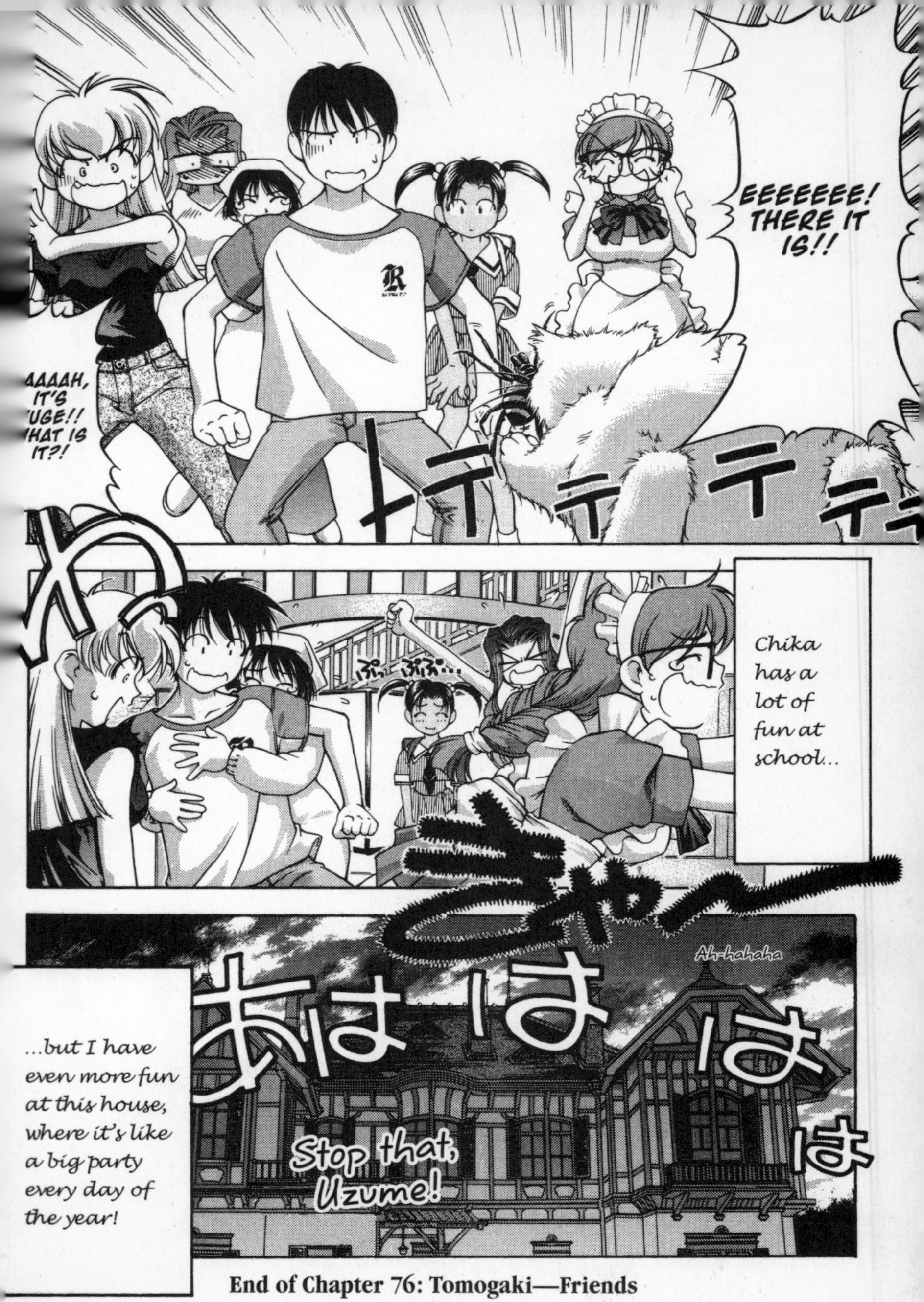
EEEEEEE! THERE IT IS!!
AAAAH, IT'S UGE!! HAT IS IT?!
Chika has a lot of fun at school...
ぷっ ぷぷっ...
きゃ〜
...but I have even more fun at this house, where it's like a big party every day of the year!
あははは
Ah-hahaha
Stop that, Uzume!

End of Chapter 76: Tomogaki—Friends

藍（あい）より青（あお）し

AI YORI AOSHI

S-STOP IT...DON'T LOOK AT THAT!
やぁ
THIS BOOK IS IRREPLACE-ABLE!

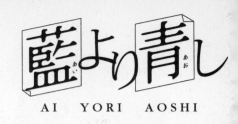

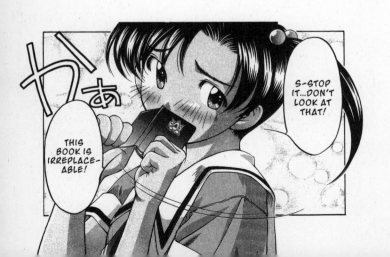

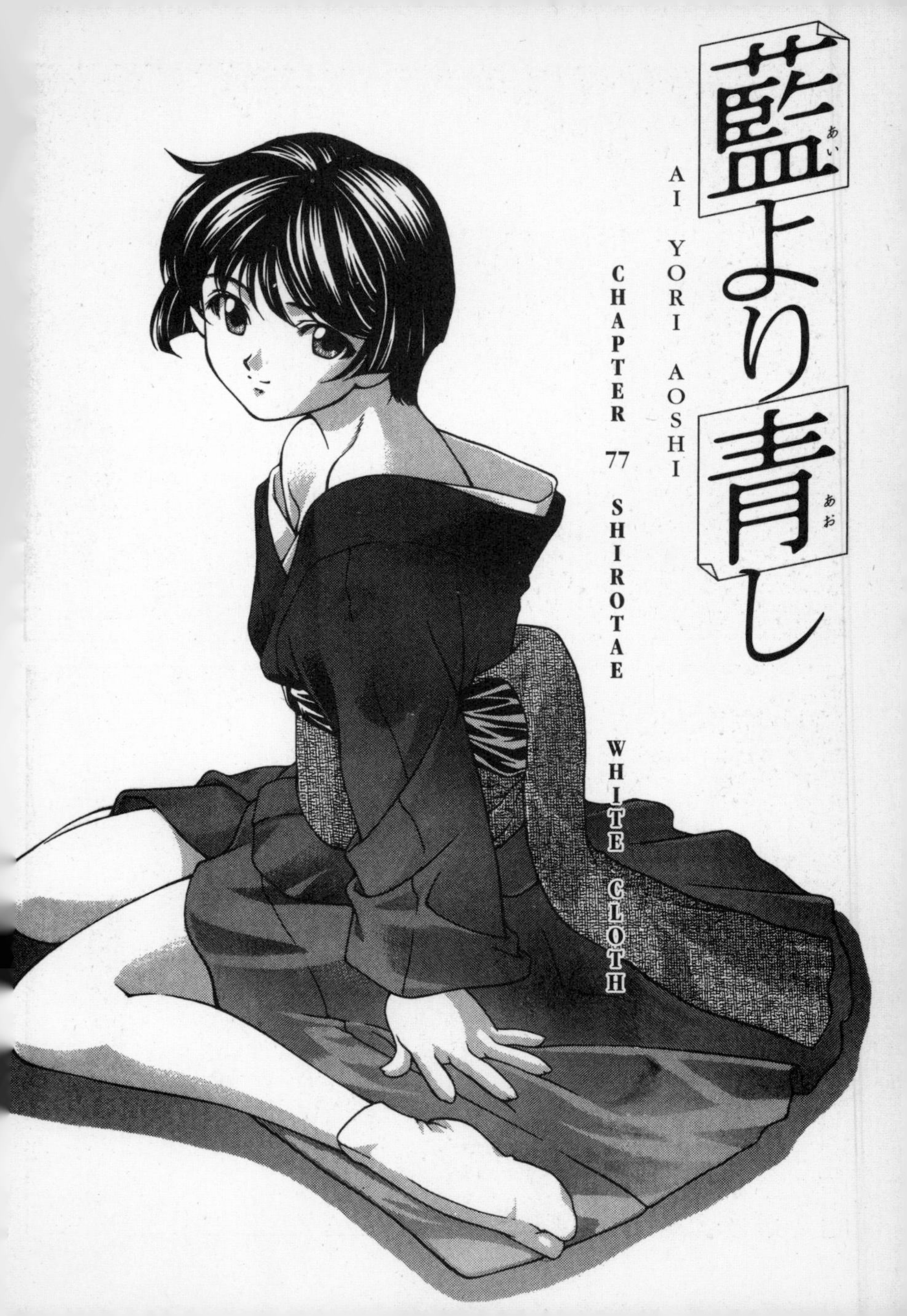
藍(あい)より青(あお)し
AI YORI AOSHI
CHAPTER 77 SHIROTAE
WHITE CLOTH

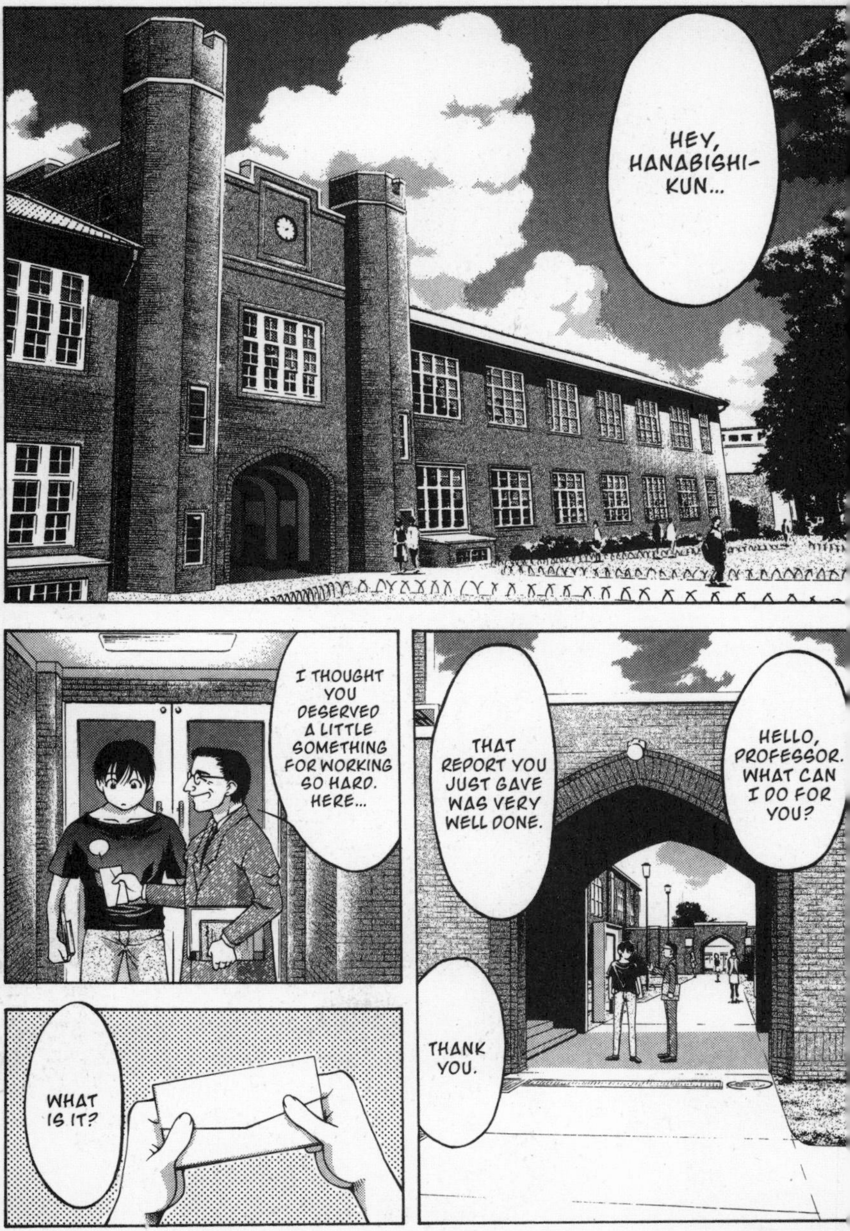
HEY, HANABISHI-KUN...
HELLO, PROFESSOR. WHAT CAN I DO FOR YOU?
THAT REPORT YOU JUST GAVE WAS VERY WELL DONE.
THANK YOU.
I THOUGHT YOU DESERVED A LITTLE SOMETHING FOR WORKING SO HARD. HERE...
WHAT IS IT?

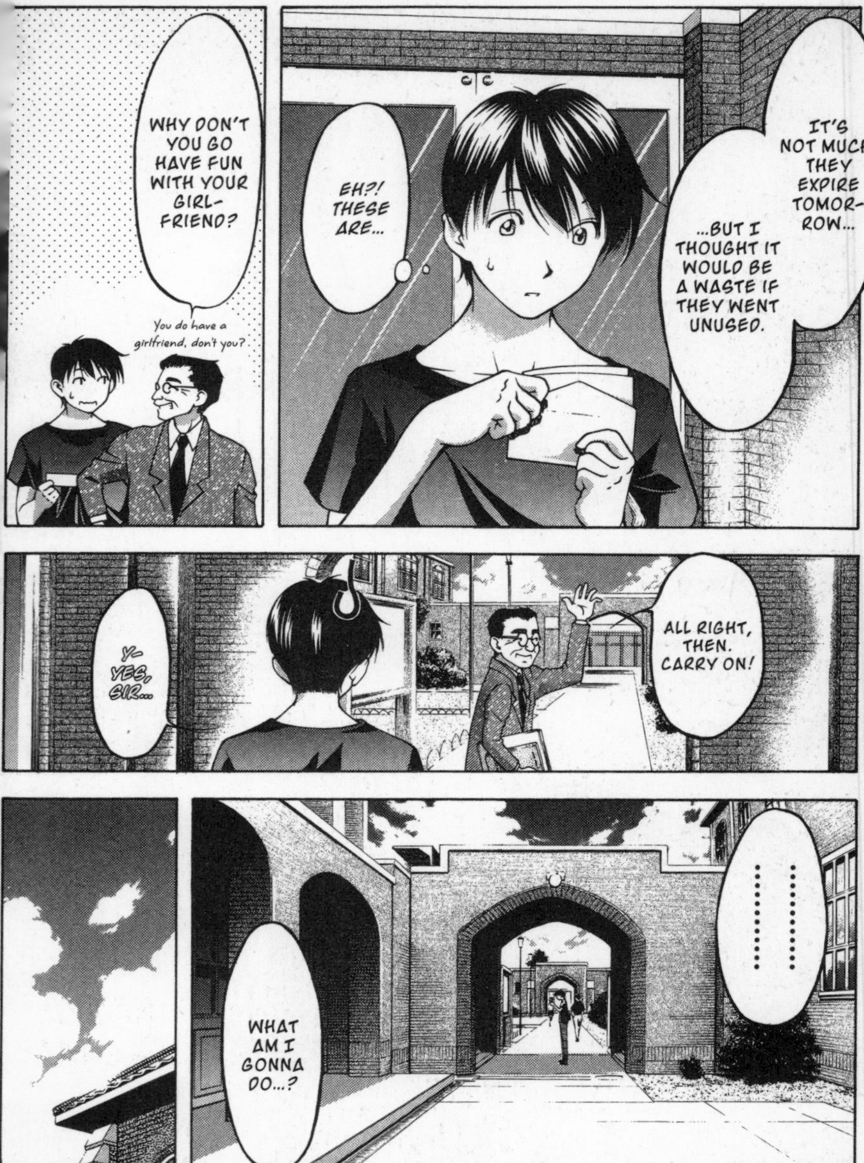
IT'S NOT MUCH. THEY EXPIRE TOMOR-ROW...
...BUT I THOUGHT IT WOULD BE A WASTE IF THEY WENT UNUSED.
EH?! THESE ARE...
WHY DON'T YOU GO HAVE FUN WITH YOUR GIRL-FRIEND?
You do have a girlfriend, don't you?
ALL RIGHT, THEN. CARRY ON!
Y-YES, SIR...
......
WHAT AM I GONNA DO...?

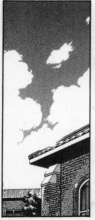

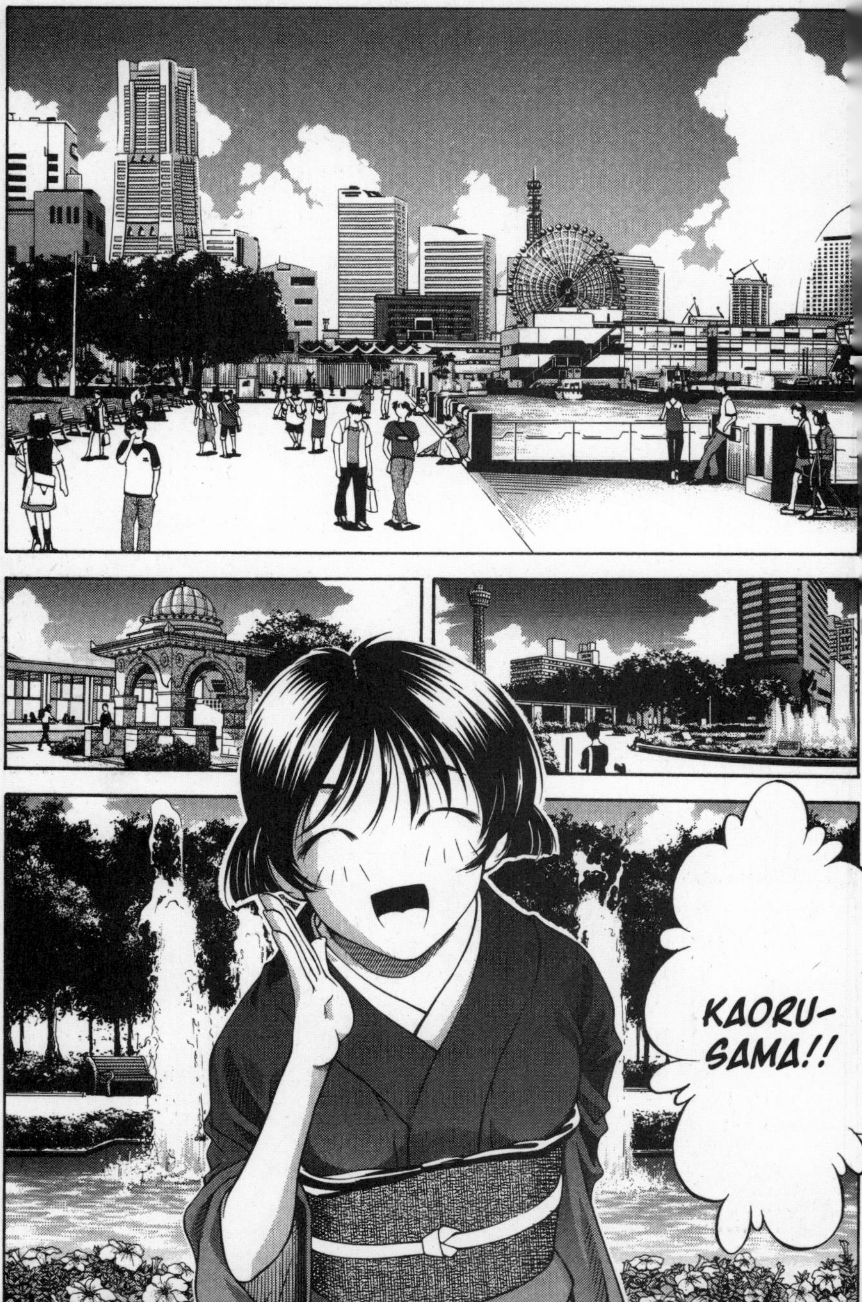
KAORU-
SAMA!!

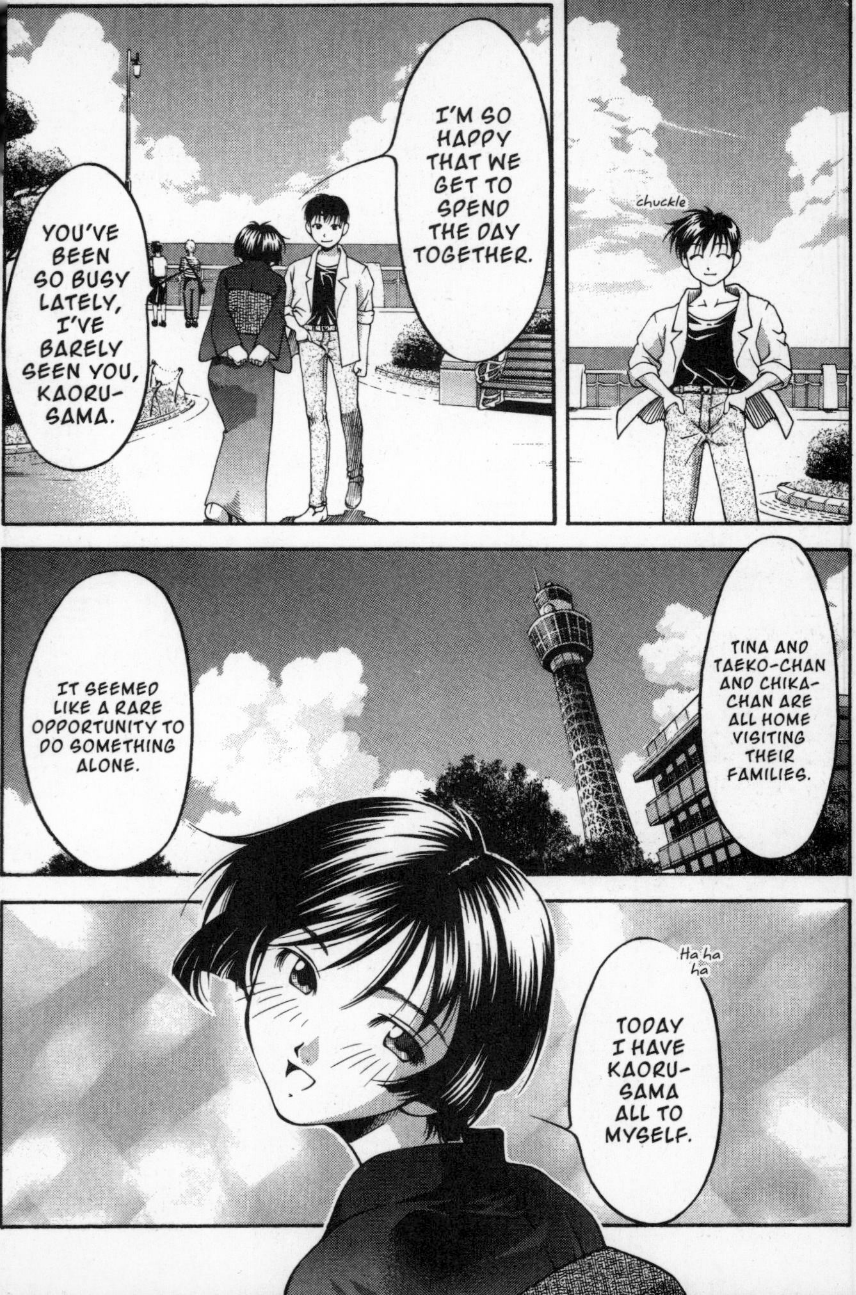
chuckle
I'M SO HAPPY THAT WE GET TO SPEND THE DAY TOGETHER.
YOU'VE BEEN SO BUSY LATELY, I'VE BARELY SEEN YOU, KAORU-SAMA.
TINA AND TAEKO-CHAN AND CHIKA-CHAN ARE ALL HOME VISITING THEIR FAMILIES.
IT SEEMED LIKE A RARE OPPORTUNITY TO DO SOMETHING ALONE.
Ha ha ha
TODAY I HAVE KAORU-SAMA ALL TO MYSELF.

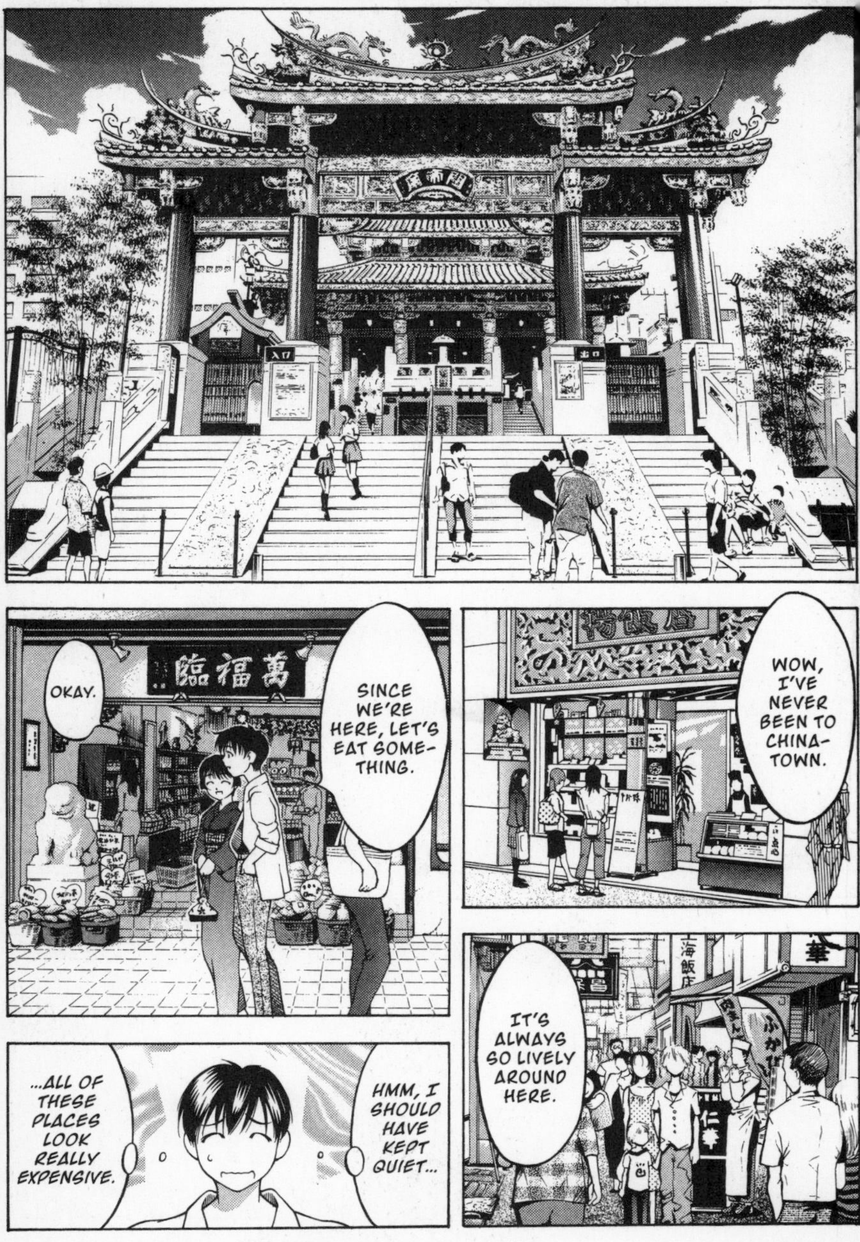
WOW, I'VE NEVER BEEN TO CHINA-TOWN.
SINCE WE'RE HERE, LET'S EAT SOME-THING.
OKAY.
IT'S ALWAYS SO LIVELY AROUND HERE.
HMM, I SHOULD HAVE KEPT QUIET...
...ALL OF THESE PLACES LOOK REALLY EXPENSIVE.

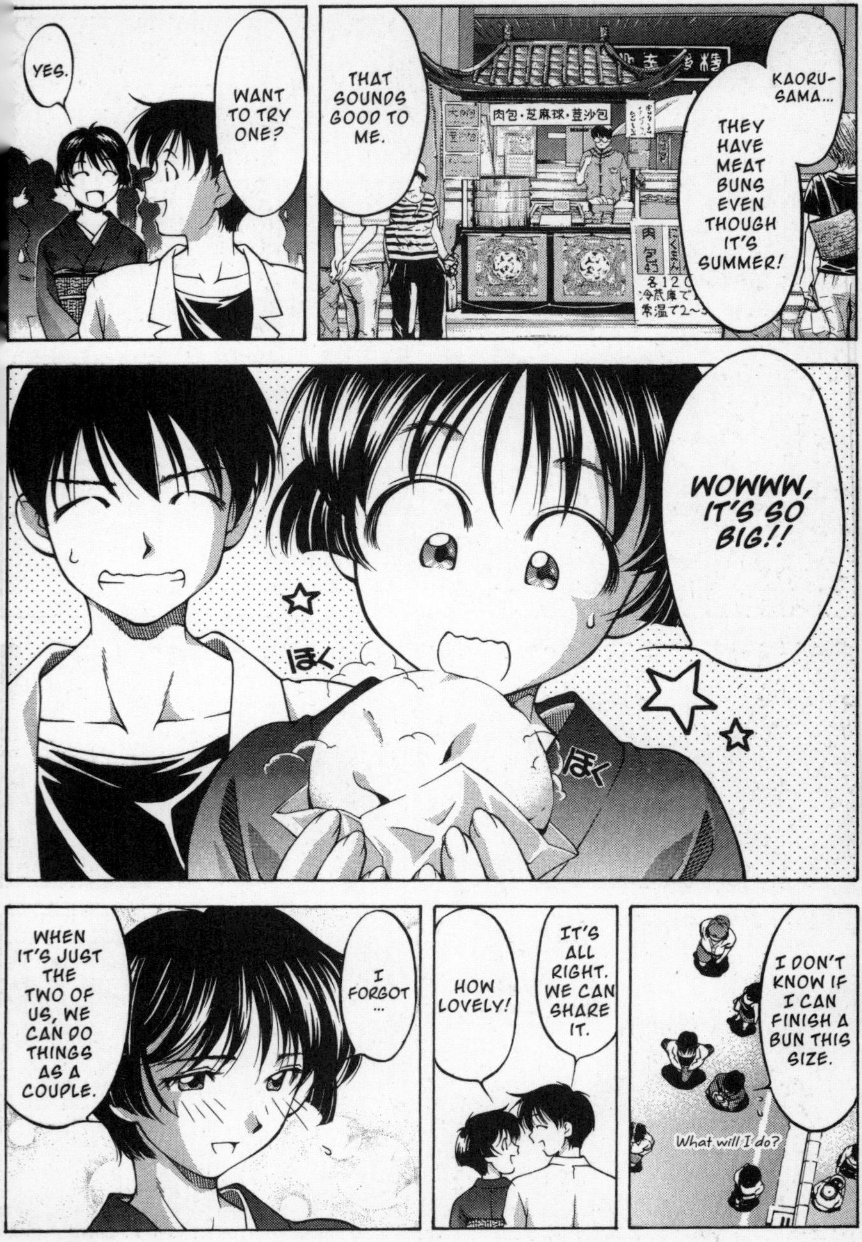
KAORU-SAMA...
THEY HAVE MEAT BUNS EVEN THOUGH IT'S SUMMER!
肉包・芝麻球・荳沙包
THAT SOUNDS GOOD TO ME.
WANT TO TRY ONE?
YES.
WOWWW, IT'S SO BIG!!
ほく
ほく
I DON'T KNOW IF I CAN FINISH A BUN THIS SIZE.
What will I do?
IT'S ALL RIGHT. WE CAN SHARE IT.
HOW LOVELY!
I FORGOT...
WHEN IT'S JUST THE TWO OF US, WE CAN DO THINGS AS A COUPLE.

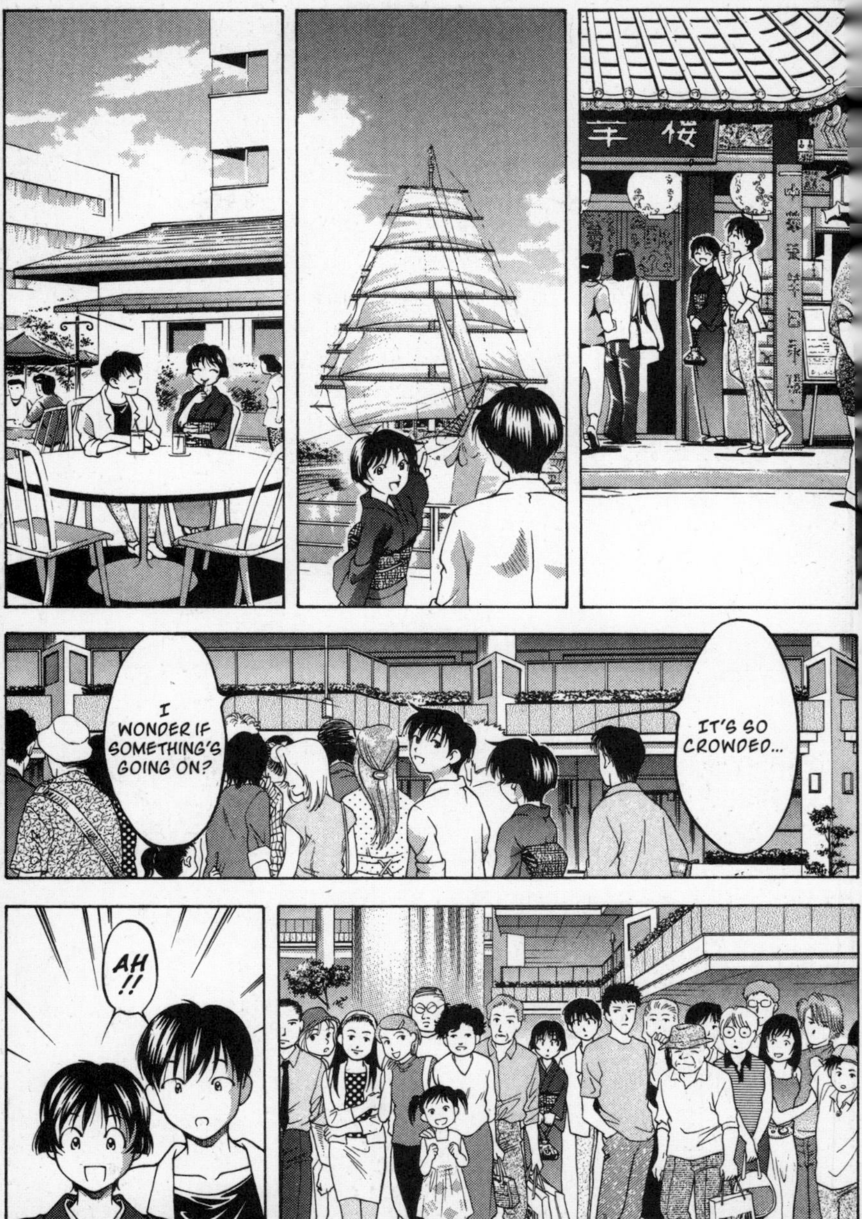
IT'S SO CROWDED...
I WONDER IF SOMETHING'S GOING ON?
AH!!

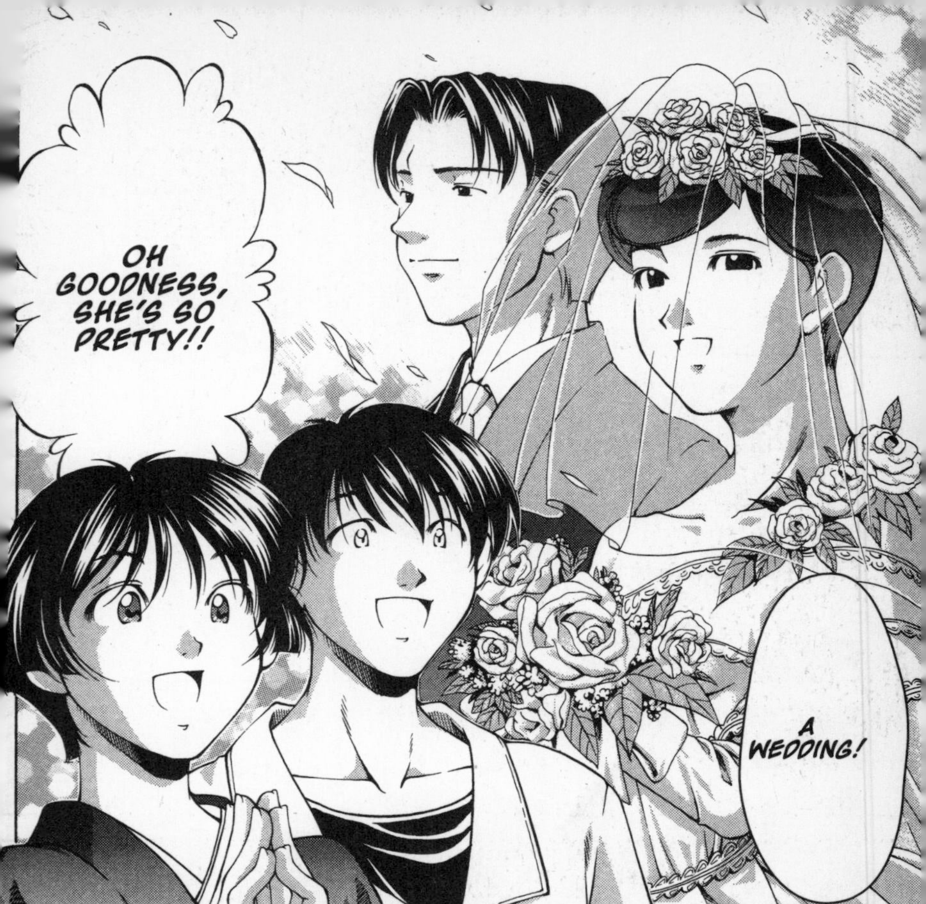
A WEDDING!
OH GOODNESS, SHE'S SO PRETTY!!
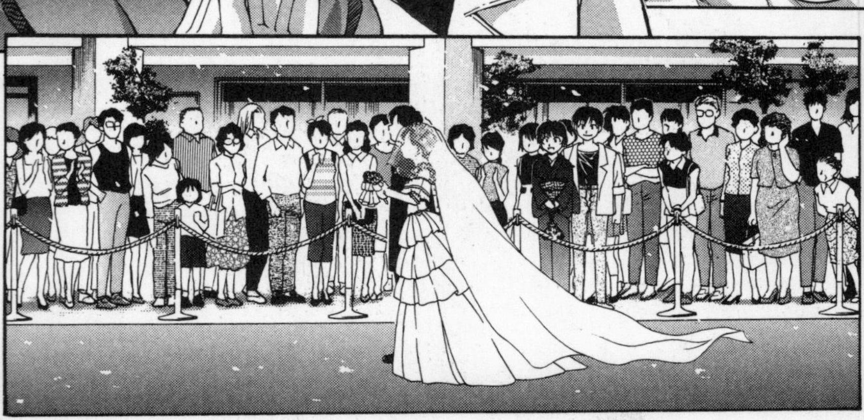

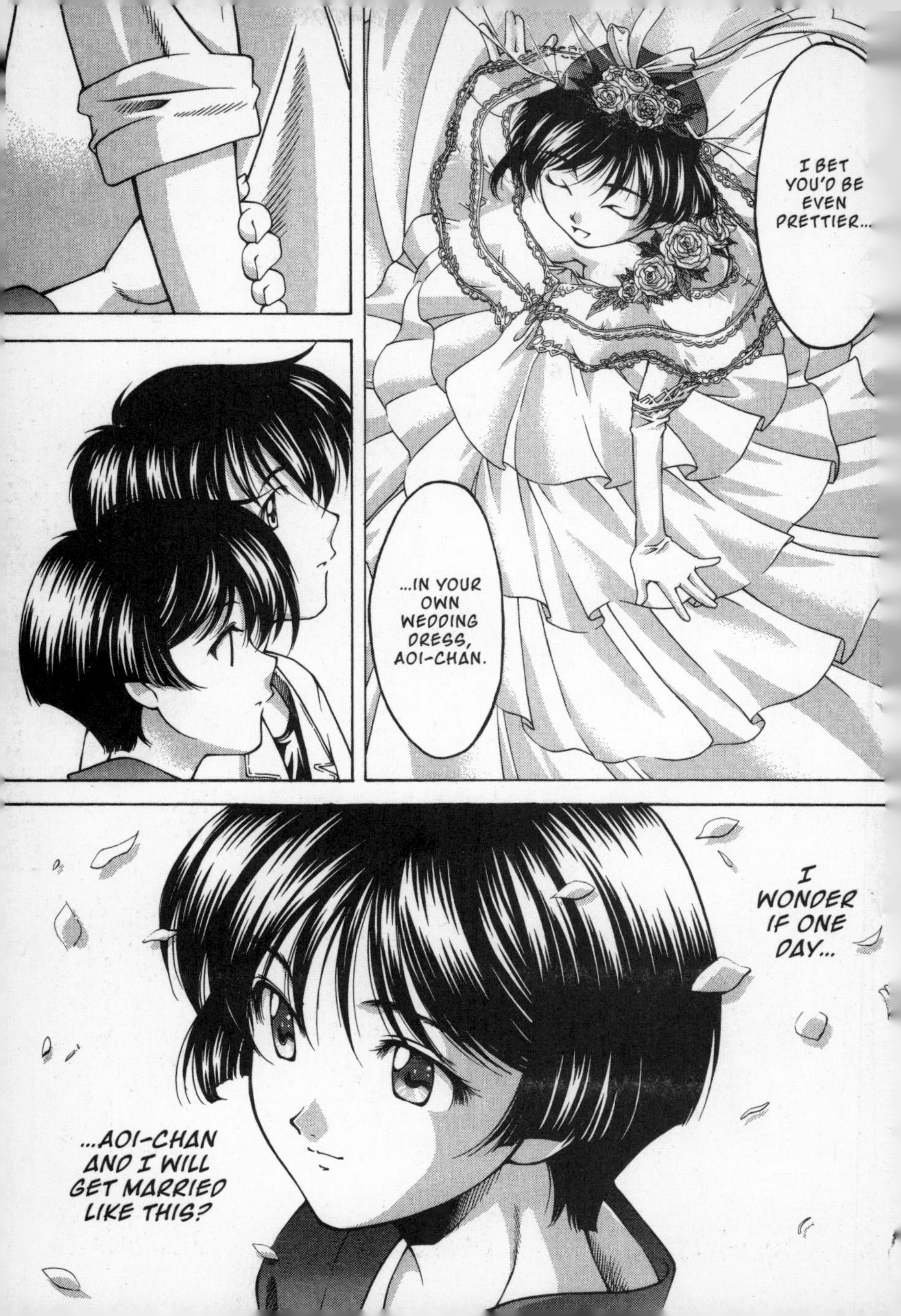
I BET YOU'D BE EVEN PRETTIER...
...IN YOUR OWN WEDDING DRESS, AOI-CHAN.
I WONDER IF ONE DAY...
...AOI-CHAN AND I WILL GET MARRIED LIKE THIS?

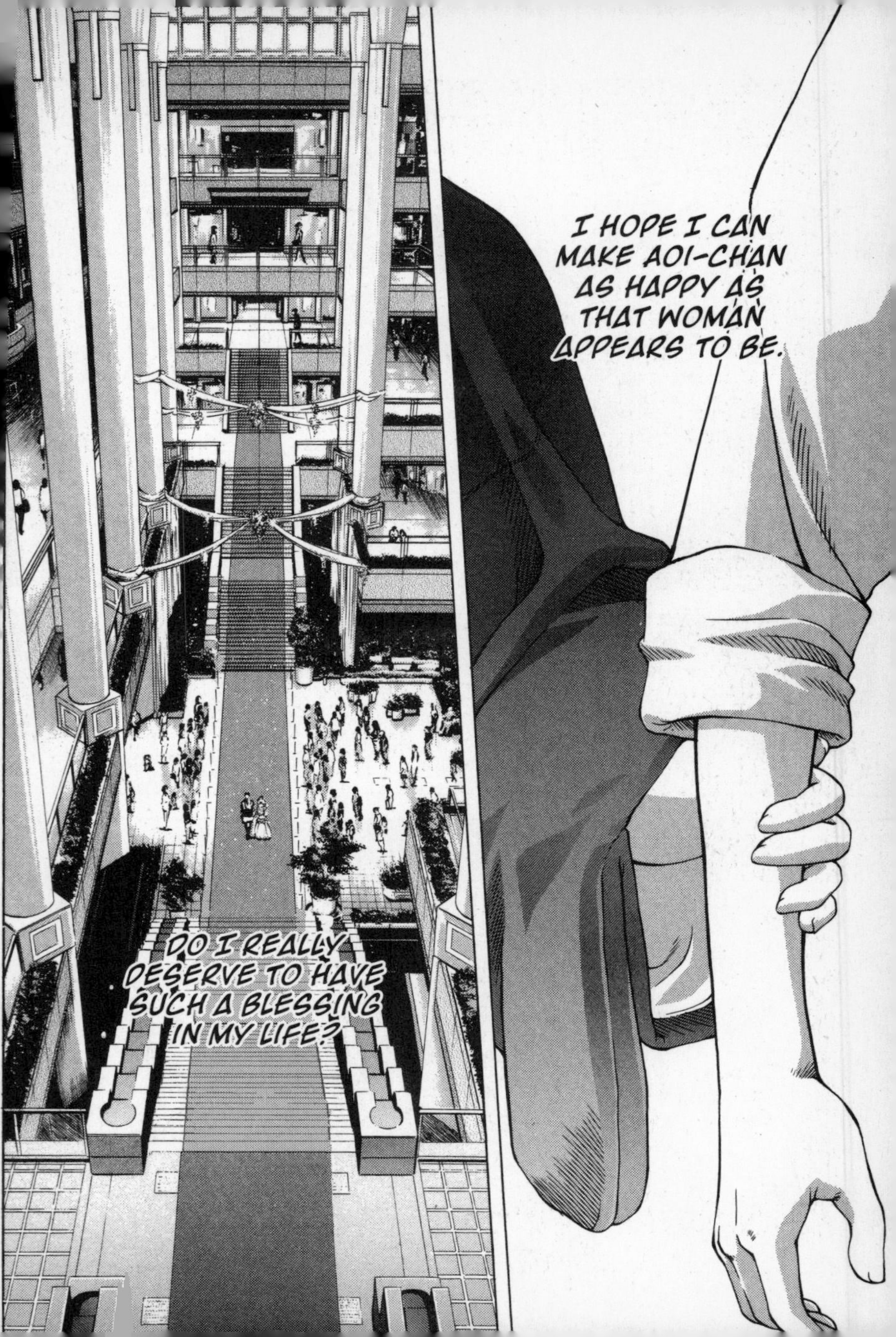
I HOPE I CAN MAKE AOI-CHAN AS HAPPY AS THAT WOMAN APPEARS TO BE.
DO I REALLY DESERVE TO HAVE SUCH A BLESSING IN MY LIFE?

I'M SORRY THAT I MADE YOU WAIT, KAORU-SAMA.

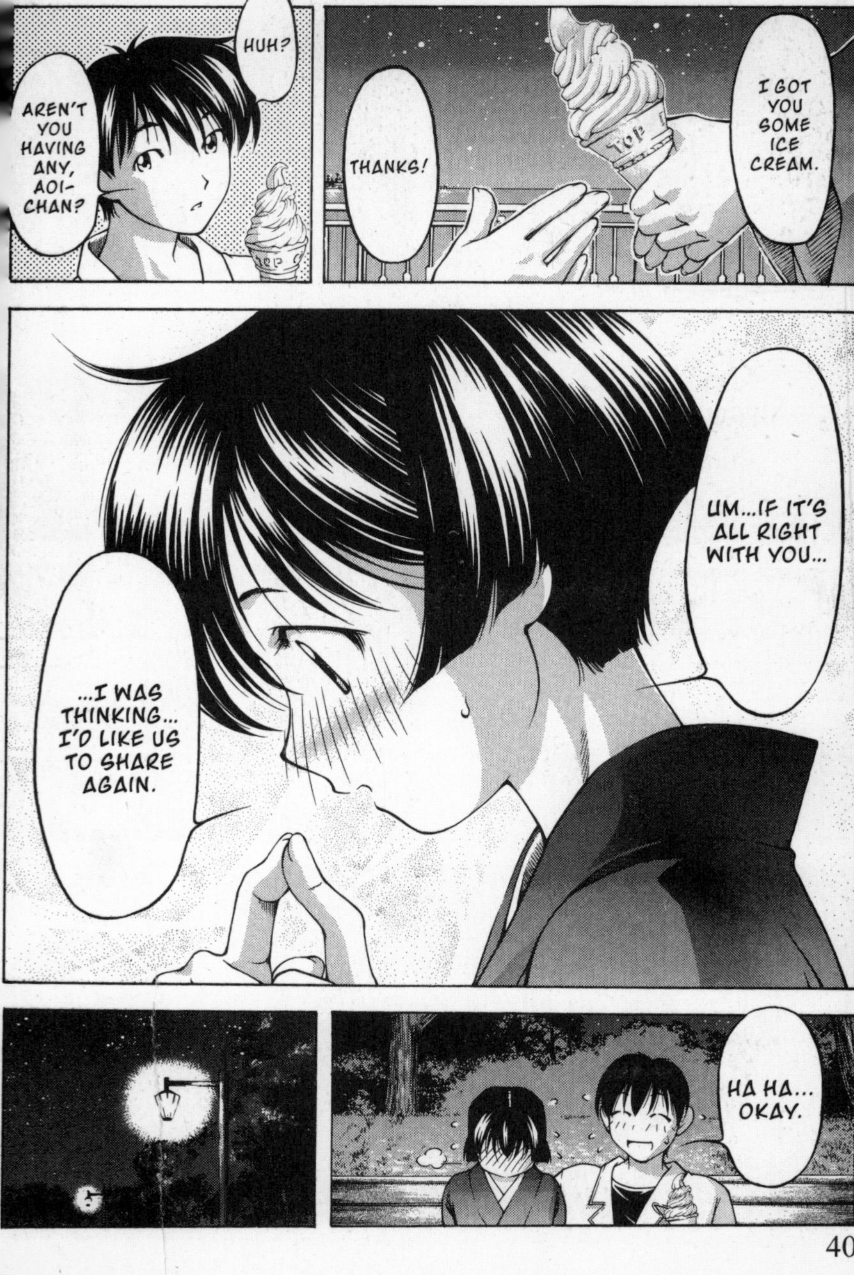
I GOT YOU SOME ICE CREAM.
THANKS!
HUH?
AREN'T YOU HAVING ANY, AOI-CHAN?
UM...IF IT'S ALL RIGHT WITH YOU...
...I WAS THINKING... I'D LIKE US TO SHARE AGAIN.
HA HA... OKAY.

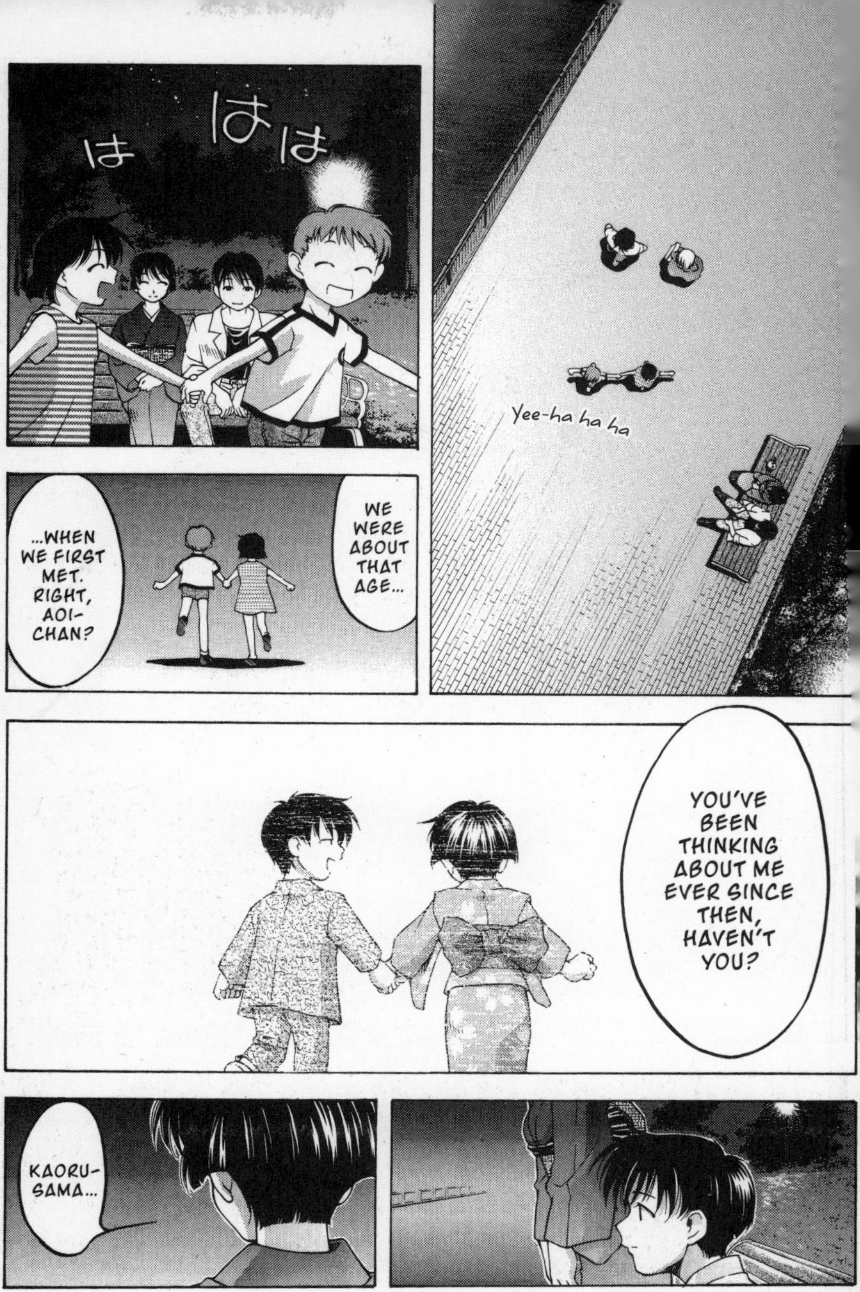

Yee-ha ha ha
はは
は
WE WERE ABOUT THAT AGE...
...WHEN WE FIRST MET. RIGHT, AOI-CHAN?
YOU'VE BEEN THINKING ABOUT ME EVER SINCE THEN, HAVEN'T YOU?
KAORU-SAMA...

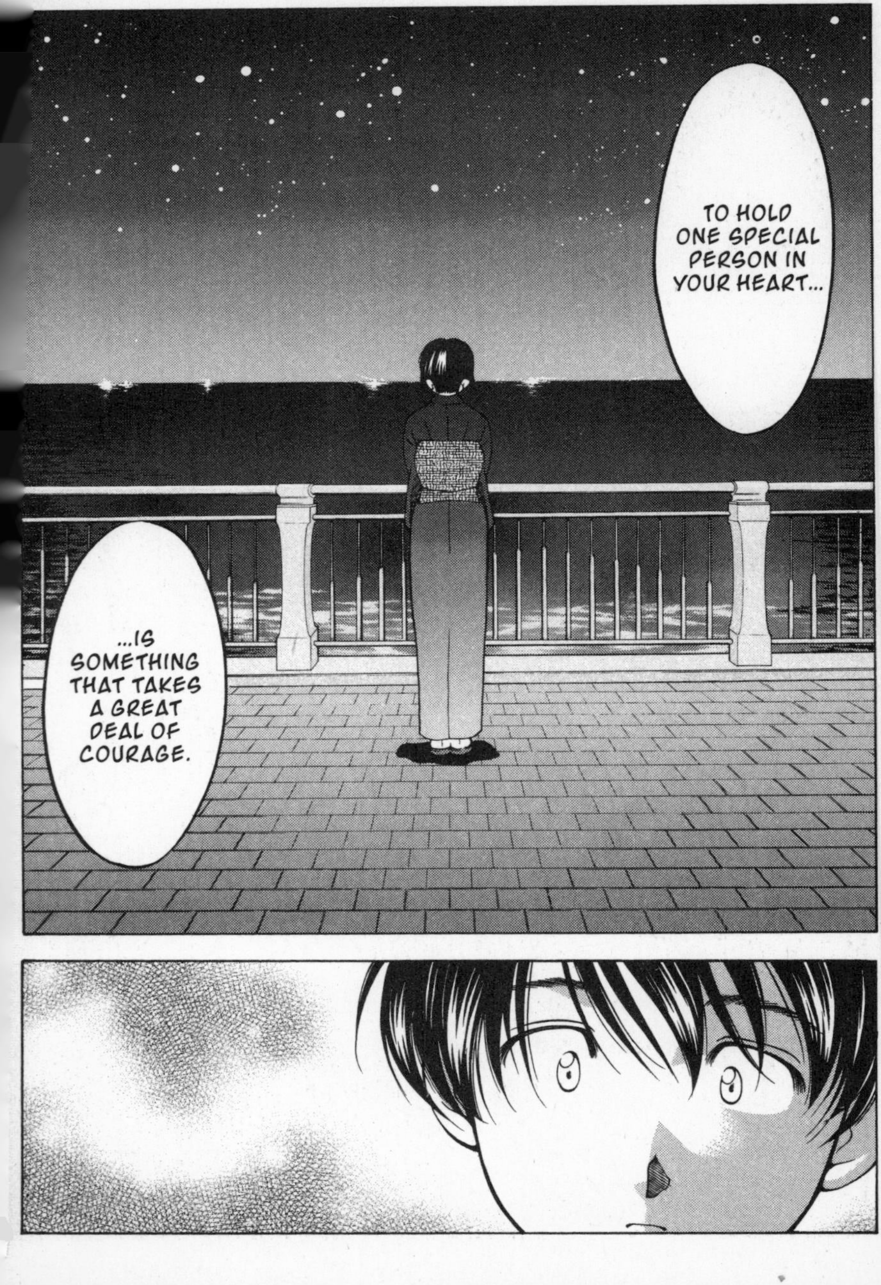
TO HOLD ONE SPECIAL PERSON IN YOUR HEART...
...IS SOMETHING THAT TAKES A GREAT DEAL OF COURAGE.

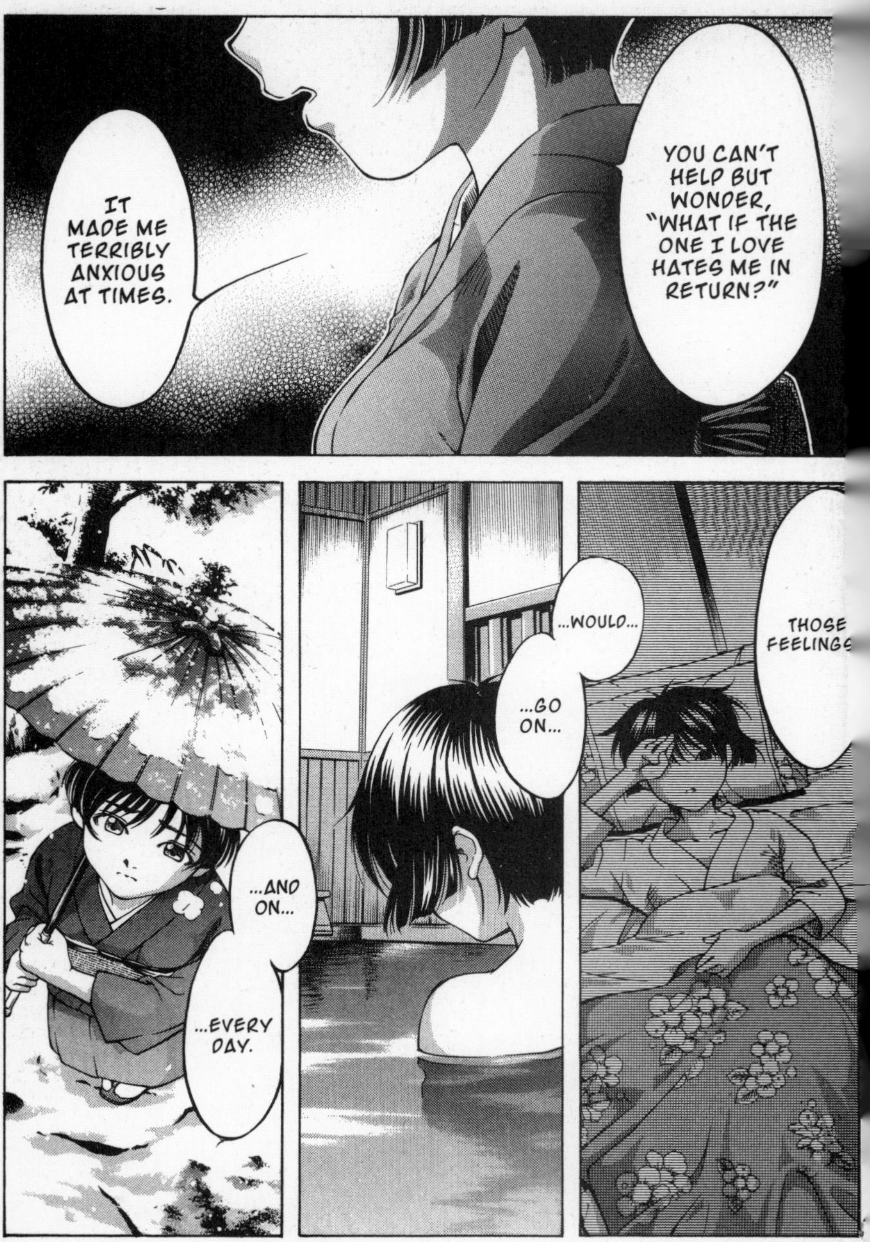
YOU CAN'T HELP BUT WONDER, "WHAT IF THE ONE I LOVE HATES ME IN RETURN?"
IT MADE ME TERRIBLY ANXIOUS AT TIMES.
THOSE FEELINGS
...WOULD...
...GO ON...
...AND ON...
...EVERY DAY.

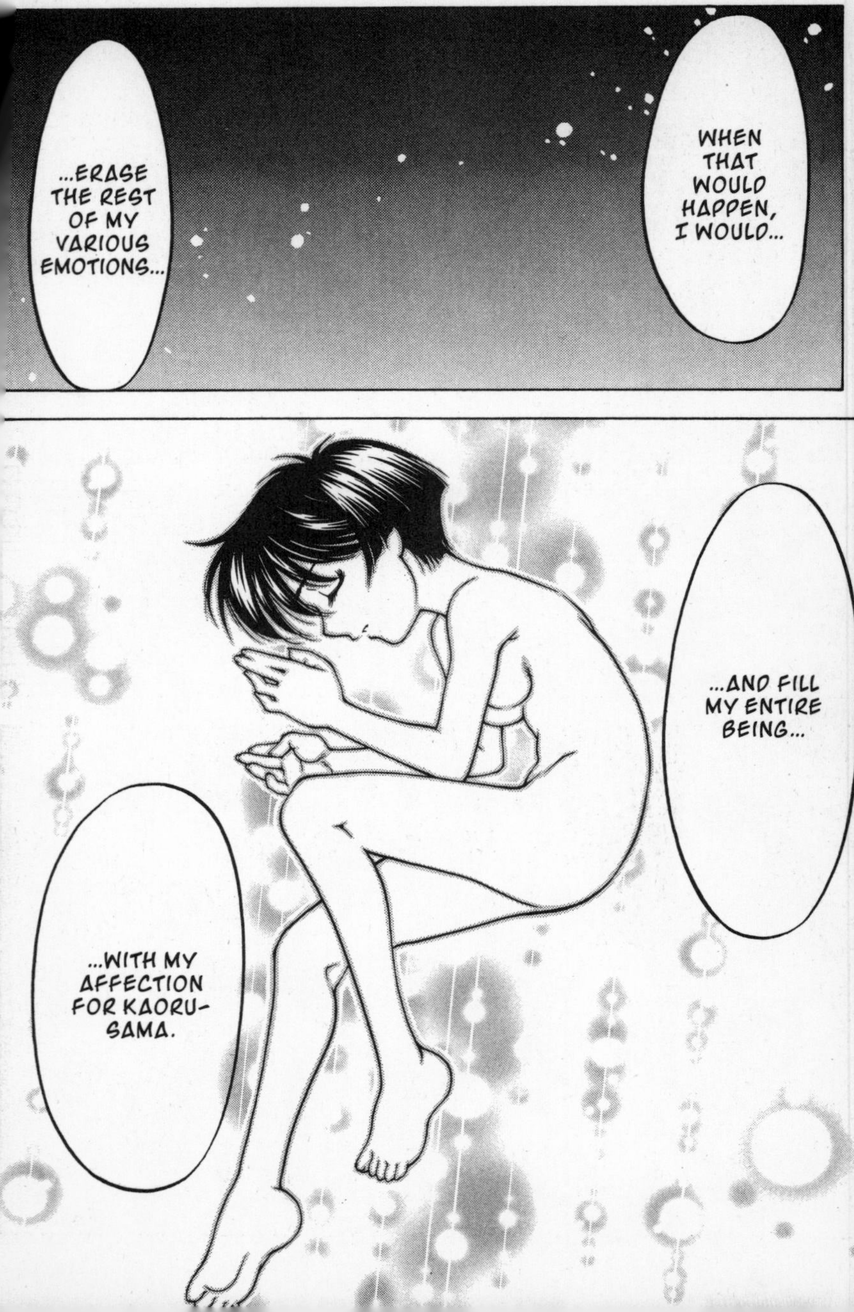
WHEN THAT WOULD HAPPEN, I WOULD...
...ERASE THE REST OF MY VARIOUS EMOTIONS...
...AND FILL MY ENTIRE BEING...
...WITH MY AFFECTION FOR KAORU-SAMA.

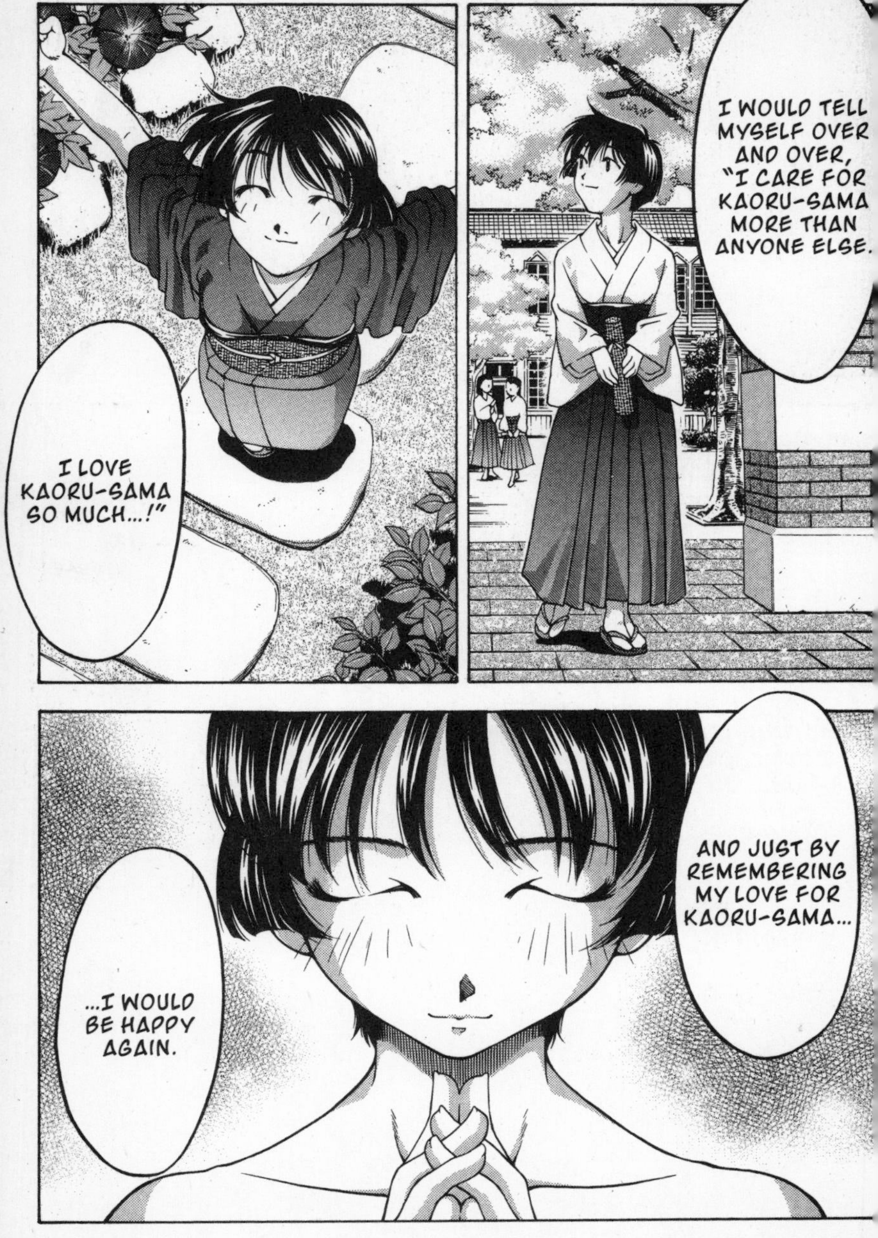
I WOULD TELL MYSELF OVER AND OVER, "I CARE FOR KAORU-SAMA MORE THAN ANYONE ELSE.
I LOVE KAORU-SAMA SO MUCH...!"
AND JUST BY REMEMBERING MY LOVE FOR KAORU-SAMA...
...I WOULD BE HAPPY AGAIN.

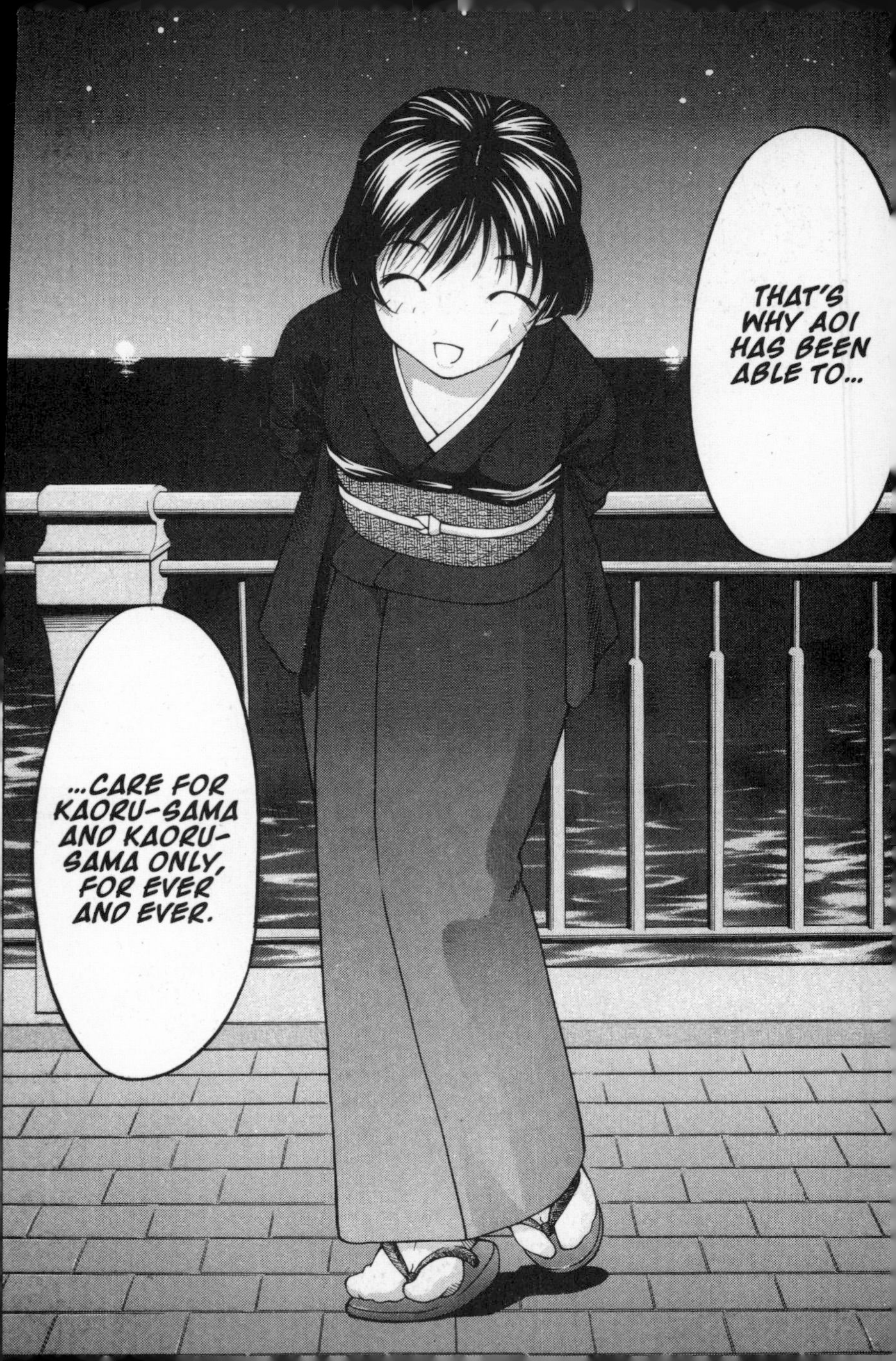
THAT'S WHY AOI HAS BEEN ABLE TO...
...CARE FOR KAORU-SAMA AND KAORU-SAMA ONLY, FOR EVER AND EVER.

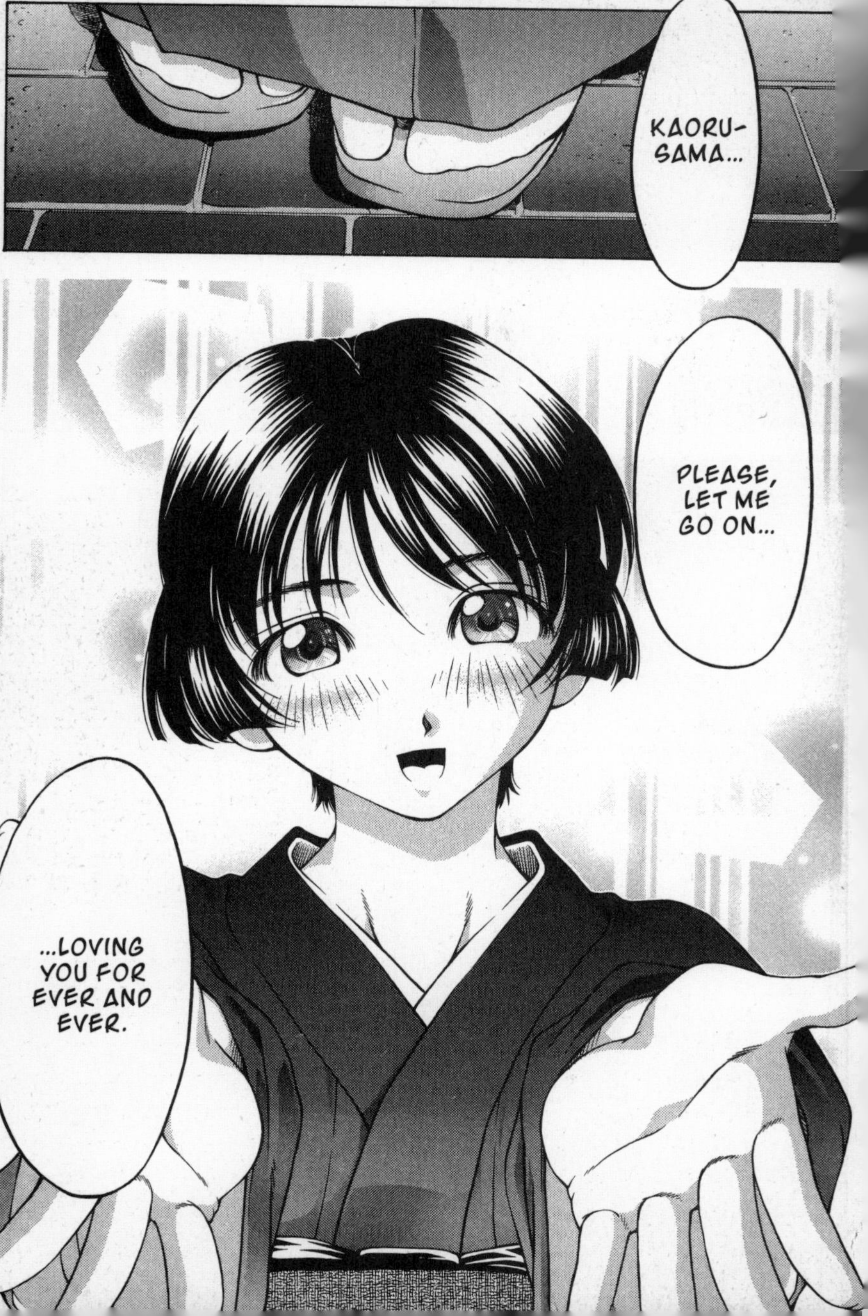
KAORU-SAMA...
PLEASE, LET ME GO ON...
...LOVING YOU FOR EVER AND EVER.

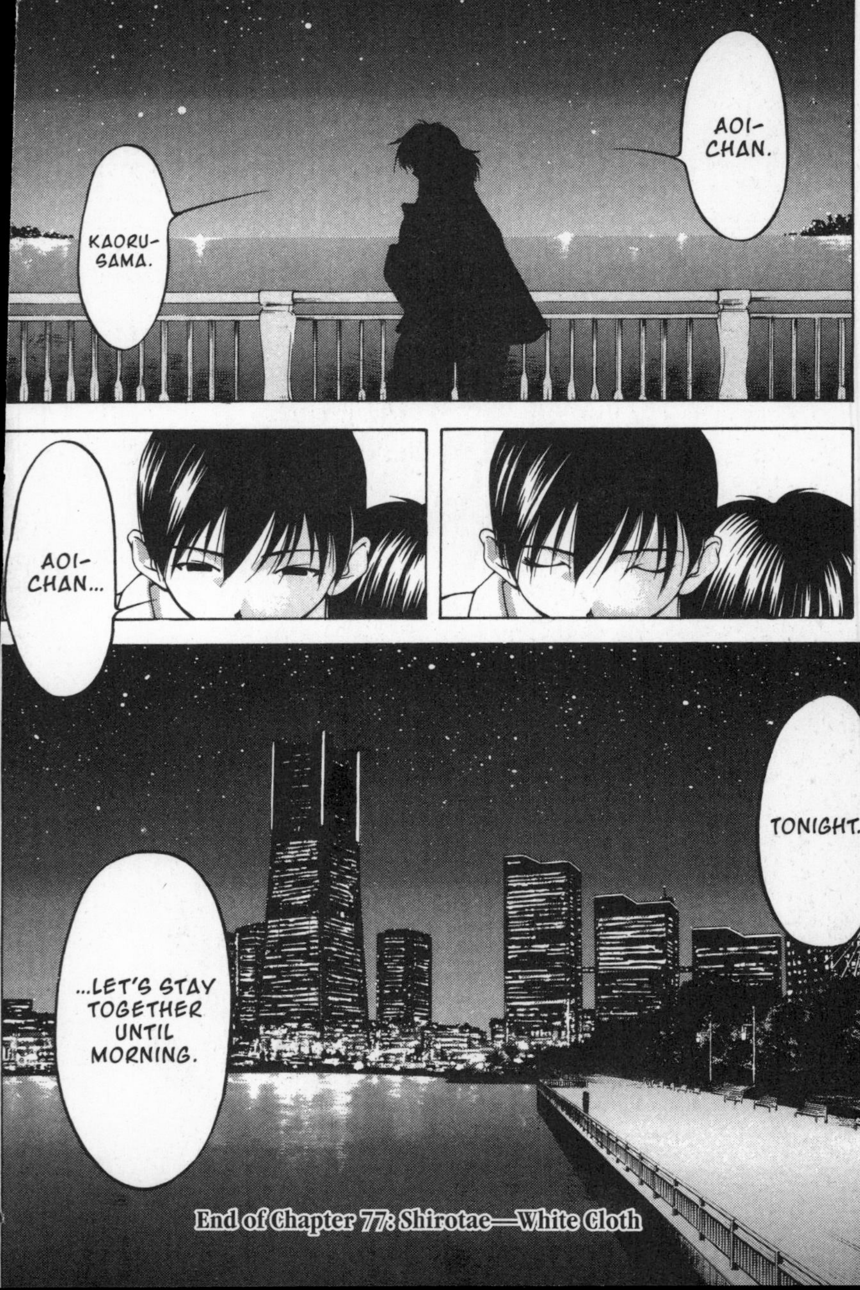
AOI-CHAN.
KAORU-SAMA.
AOI-CHAN...
TONIGHT...
...LET'S STAY TOGETHER UNTIL MORNING.
End of Chapter 77: Shirotae—White Cloth

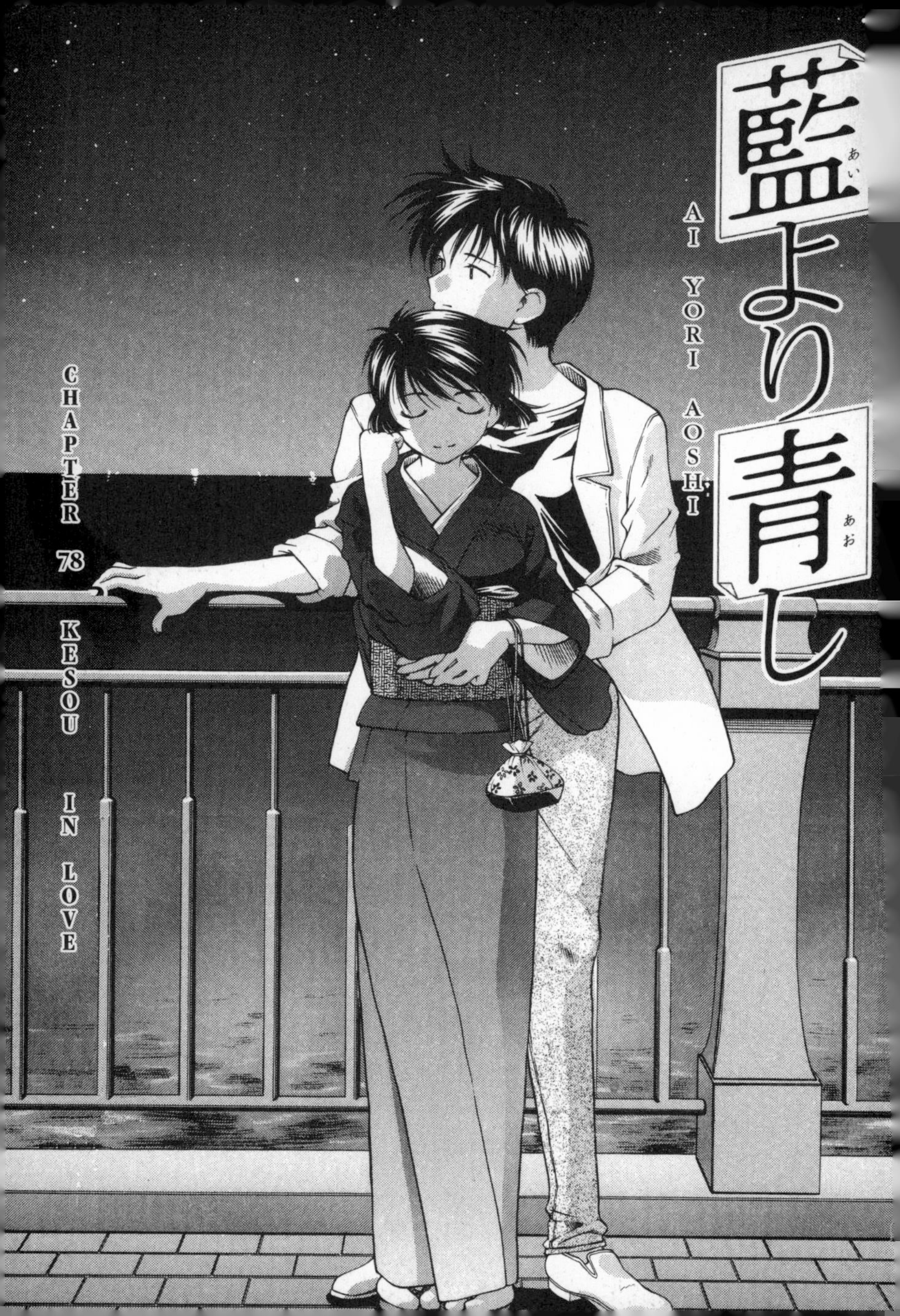

藍(あい)より青(あお)し
AI YORI AOSHI
CHAPTER 78 KESOU IN LOVE

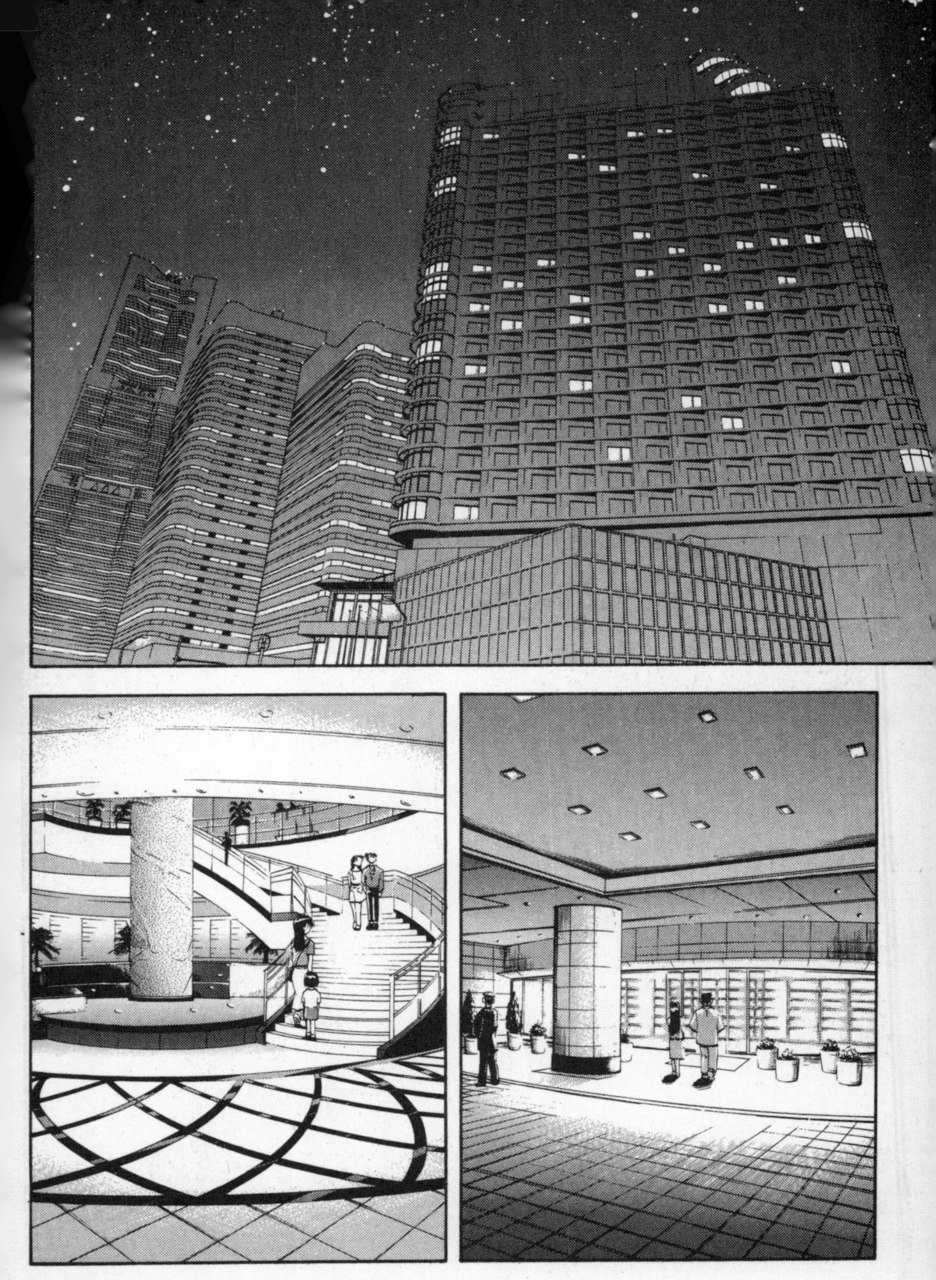

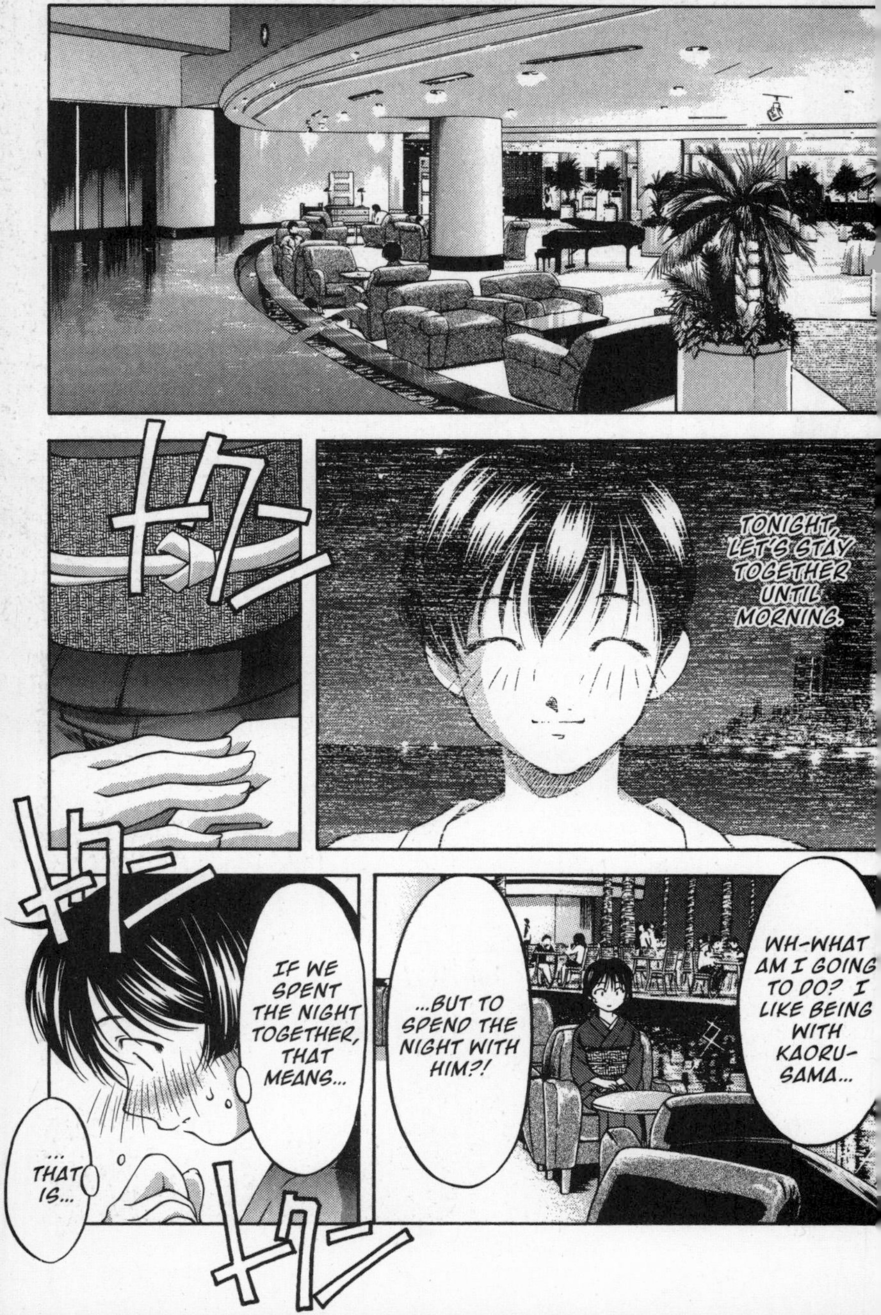
TONIGHT, LET'S STAY TOGETHER UNTIL MORNING.
WH-WHAT AM I GOING TO DO? I LIKE BEING WITH KAORU-SAMA...
...BUT TO SPEND THE NIGHT WITH HIM?!
IF WE SPENT THE NIGHT TOGETHER, THAT MEANS...
...THAT IS...

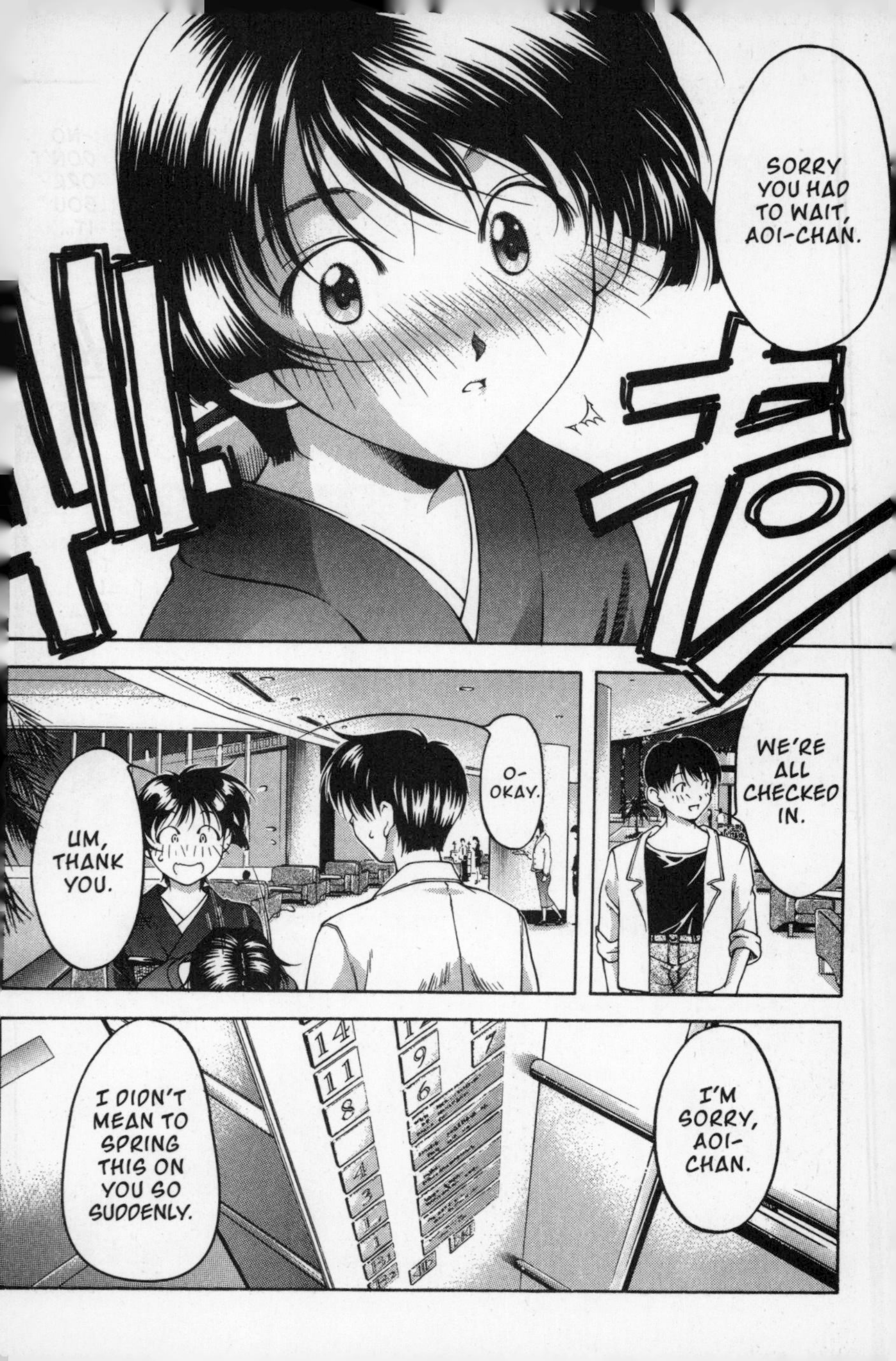
SORRY YOU HAD TO WAIT, AOI-CHAN.
WE'RE ALL CHECKED IN.
O-OKAY.
UM, THANK YOU.
I'M SORRY, AOI-CHAN.
I DIDN'T MEAN TO SPRING THIS ON YOU SO SUDDENLY.

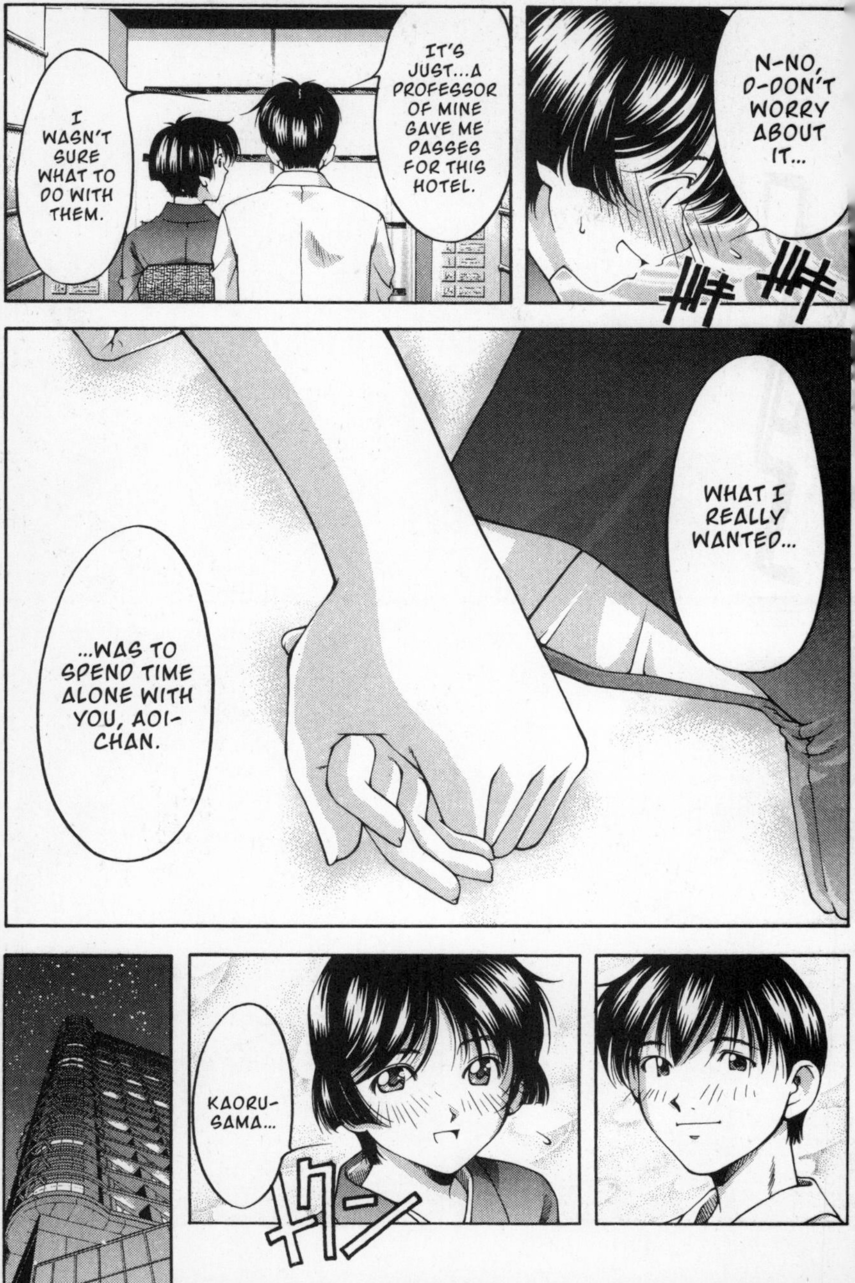
N-NO, D-DON'T WORRY ABOUT IT...
IT'S JUST...A PROFESSOR OF MINE GAVE ME PASSES FOR THIS HOTEL.
I WASN'T SURE WHAT TO DO WITH THEM.
WHAT I REALLY WANTED...
...WAS TO SPEND TIME ALONE WITH YOU, AOI-CHAN.
KAORU-SAMA...

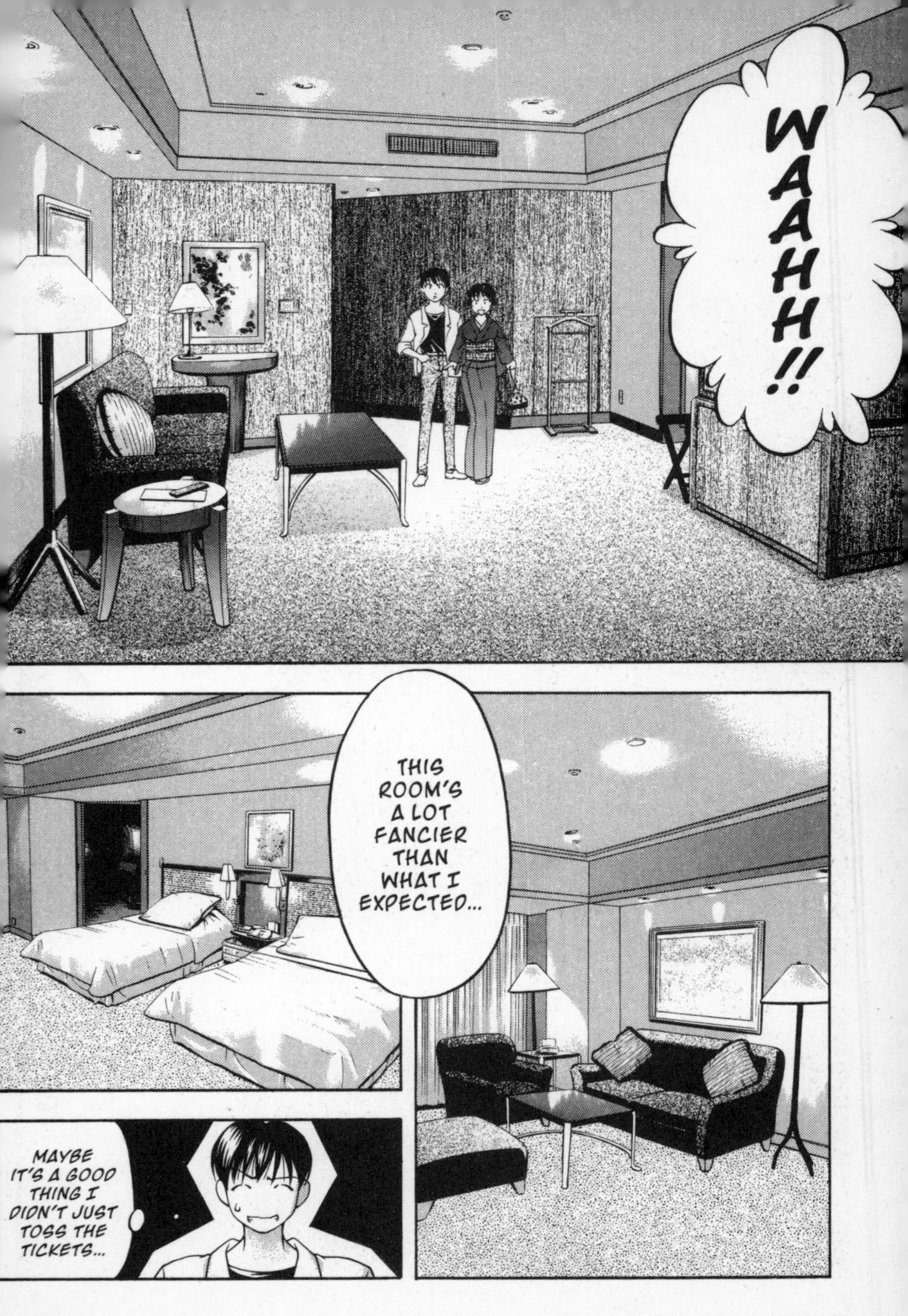
WAAHH!!
THIS ROOM'S A LOT FANCIER THAN WHAT I EXPECTED...
MAYBE IT'S A GOOD THING I DIDN'T JUST TOSS THE TICKETS...

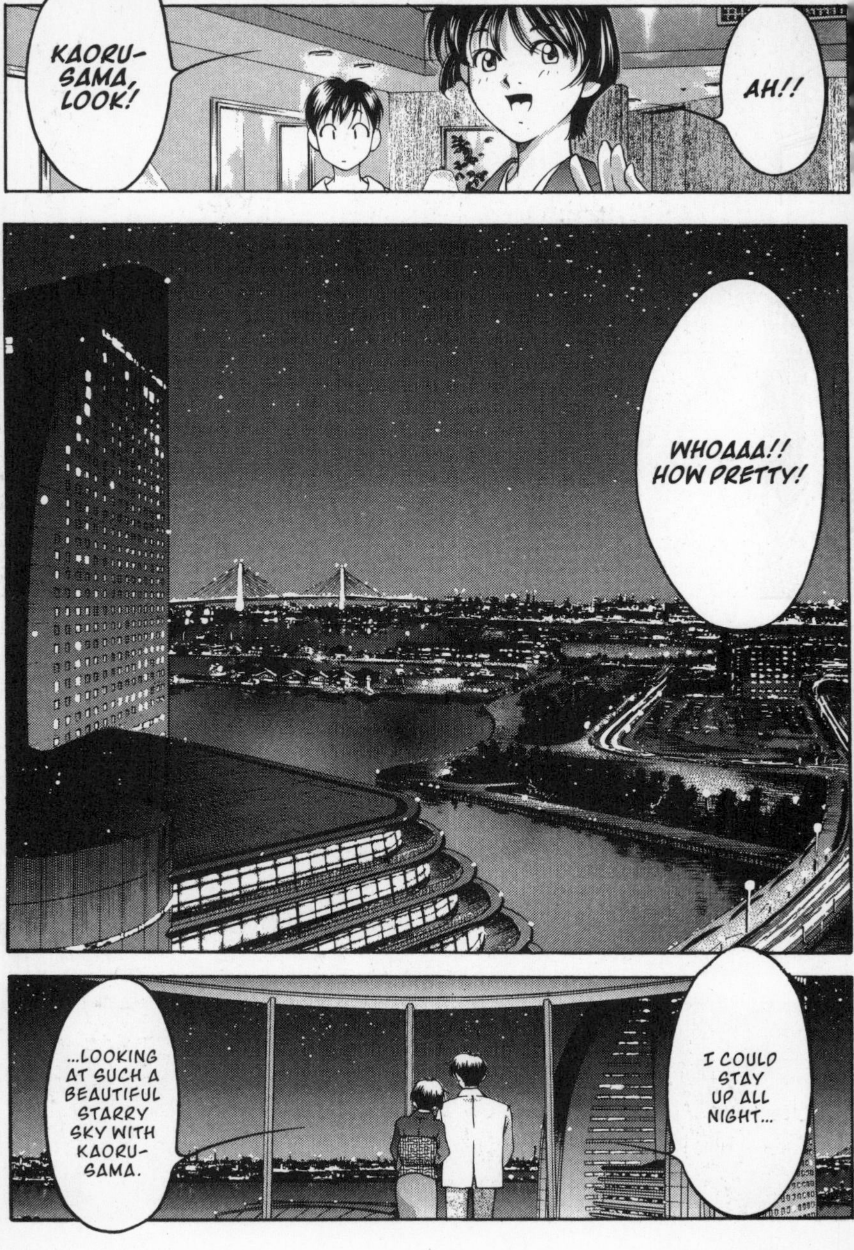
AH!!
KAORU-SAMA, LOOK!
WHOAAA!! HOW PRETTY!
I COULD STAY UP ALL NIGHT...
...LOOKING AT SUCH A BEAUTIFUL STARRY SKY WITH KAORU-SAMA.

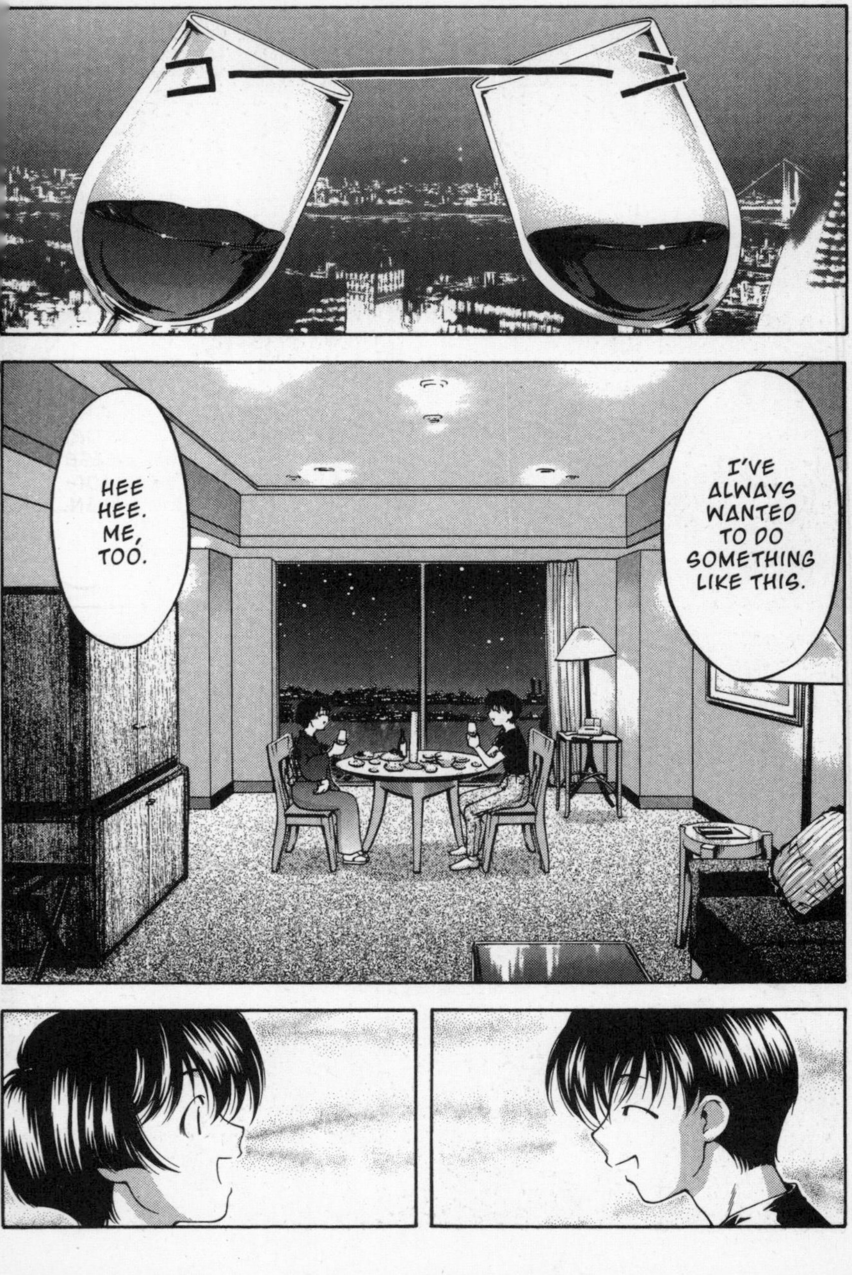
I'VE ALWAYS WANTED TO DO SOMETHING LIKE THIS.
HEE HEE. ME, TOO.

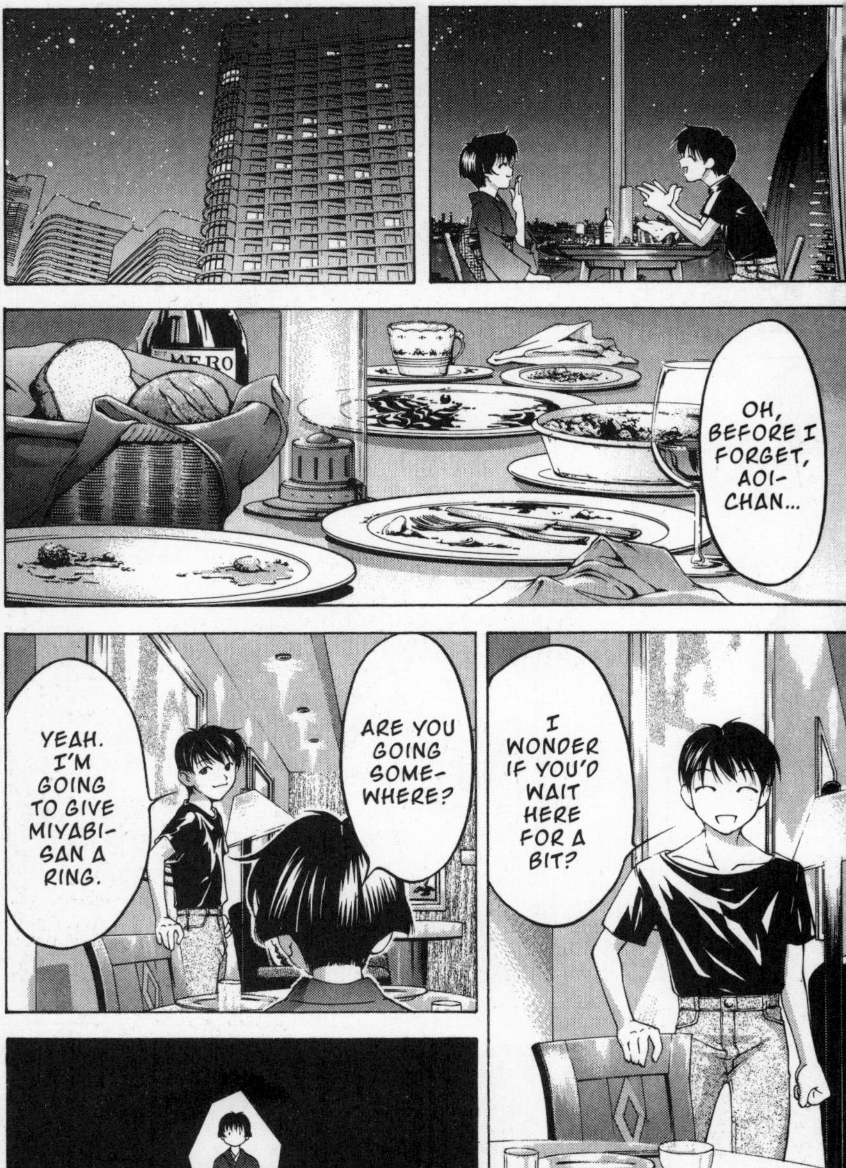
OH, BEFORE I FORGET, AOI-CHAN...
I WONDER IF YOU'D WAIT HERE FOR A BIT?
ARE YOU GOING SOME-WHERE?
YEAH. I'M GOING TO GIVE MIYABI-SAN A RING.

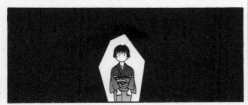

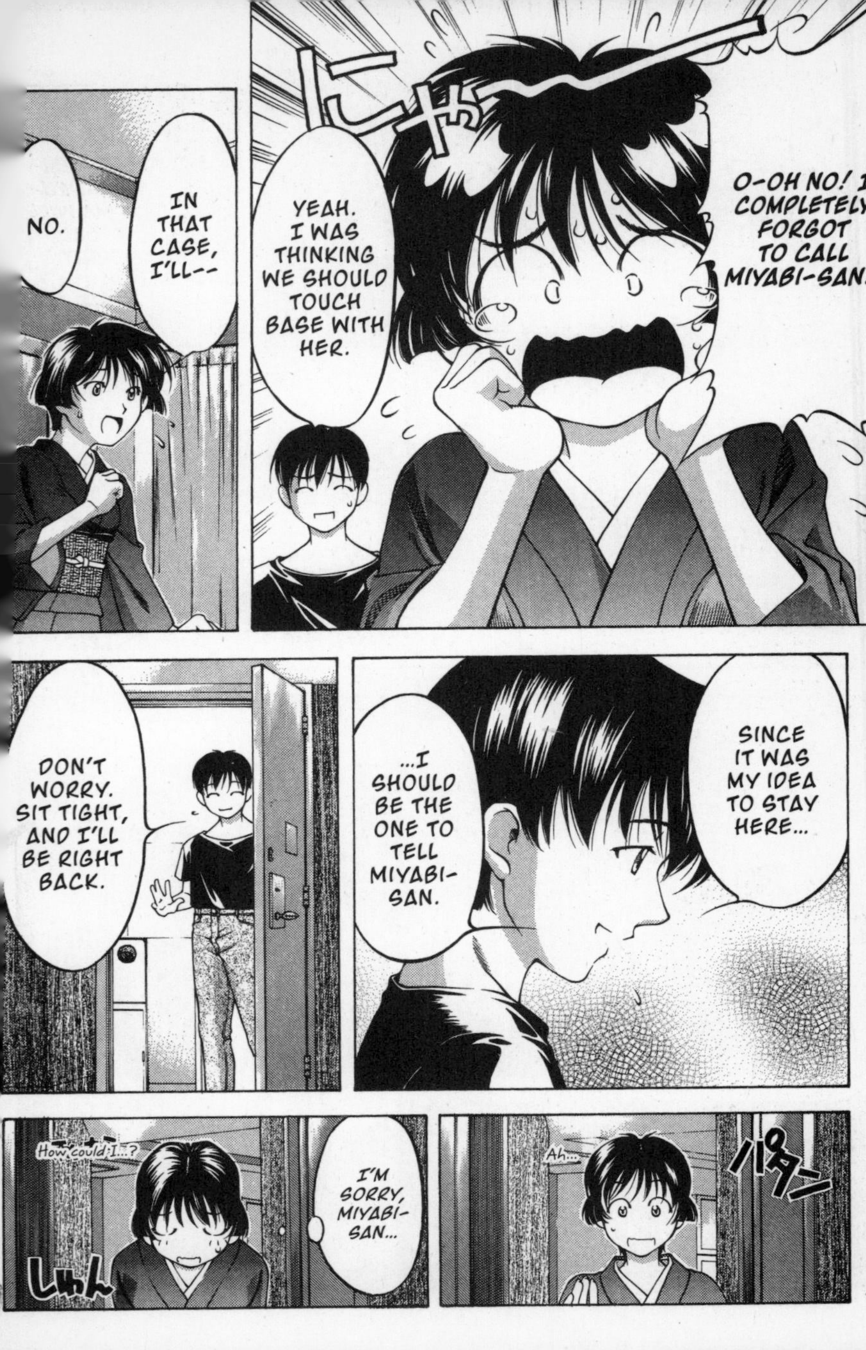
O-OH NO! I COMPLETELY FORGOT TO CALL MIYABI-SAN...
YEAH. I WAS THINKING WE SHOULD TOUCH BASE WITH HER.
IN THAT CASE, I'LL--
NO.
SINCE IT WAS MY IDEA TO STAY HERE...
...I SHOULD BE THE ONE TO TELL MIYABI-SAN.
DON'T WORRY. SIT TIGHT, AND I'LL BE RIGHT BACK.
パタン
Ah...
I'M SORRY, MIYABI-SAN...
How could I...?
しゅん

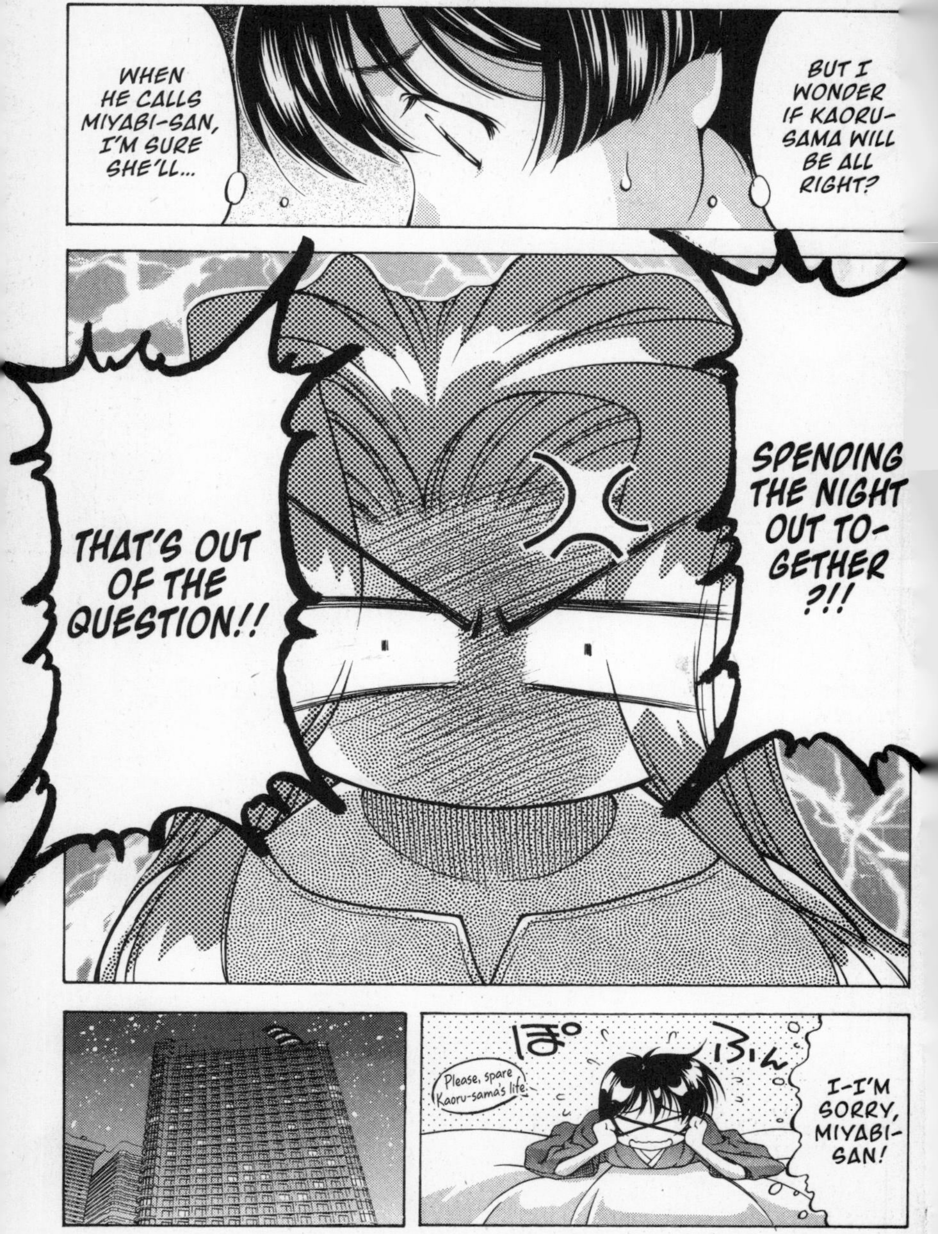
BUT I WONDER IF KAORU-SAMA WILL BE ALL RIGHT?
WHEN HE CALLS MIYABI-SAN, I'M SURE SHE'LL...
SPENDING THE NIGHT OUT TOGETHER?!!
THAT'S OUT OF THE QUESTION!!
ぽ ふん
I-I'M SORRY, MIYABI-SAN!
Please, spare Kaoru-sama's life.

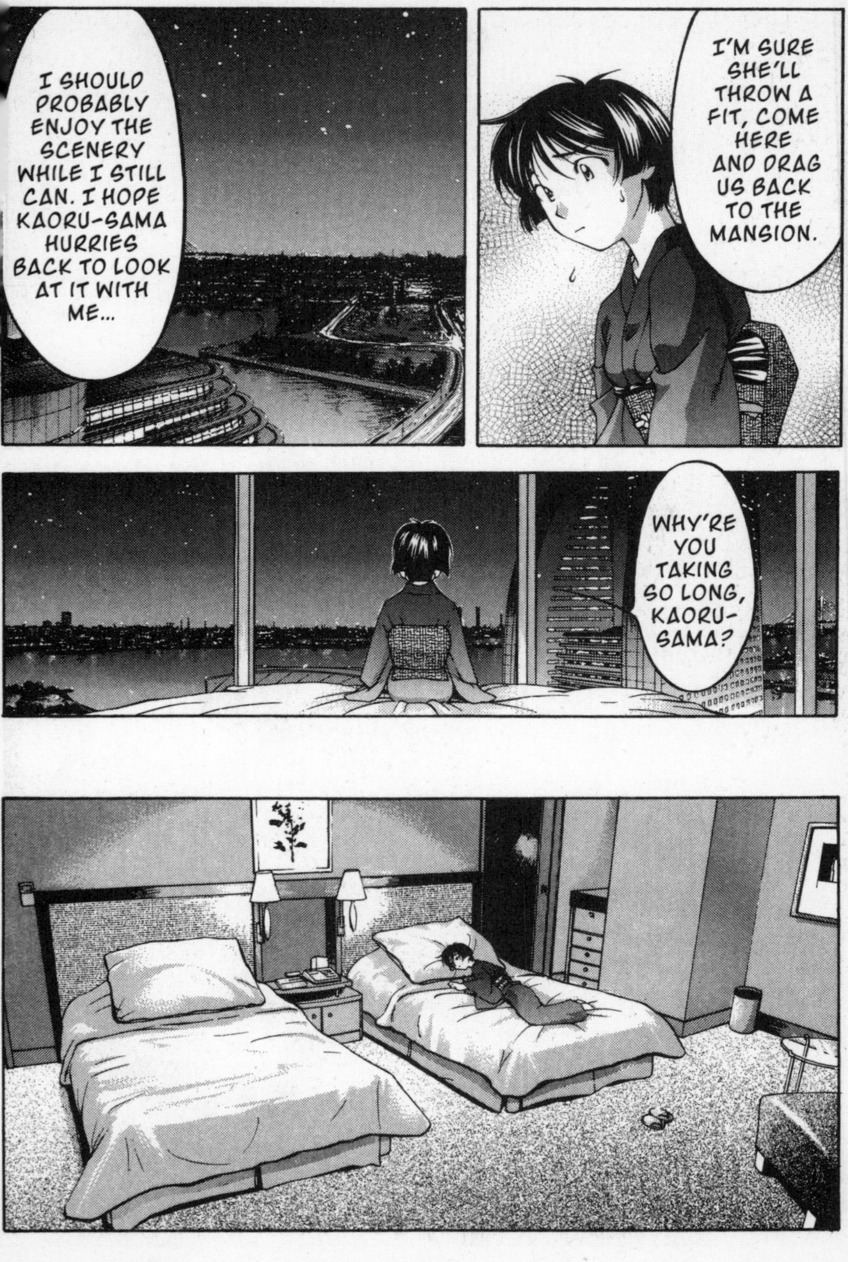
I'M SURE SHE'LL THROW A FIT, COME HERE AND DRAG US BACK TO THE MANSION.
I SHOULD PROBABLY ENJOY THE SCENERY WHILE I STILL CAN. I HOPE KAORU-SAMA HURRIES BACK TO LOOK AT IT WITH ME...
WHY'RE YOU TAKING SO LONG, KAORU-SAMA?

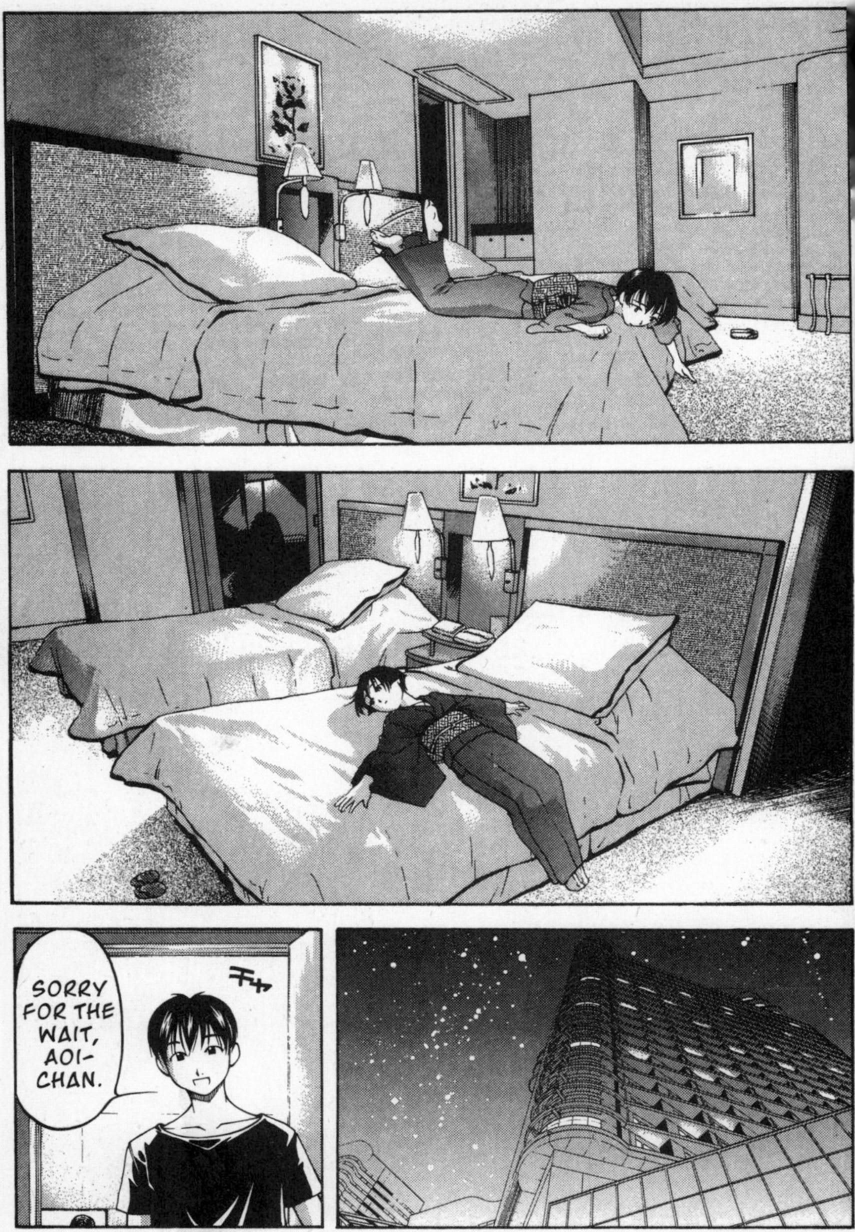
チャ
SORRY FOR THE WAIT, AOI-CHAN.

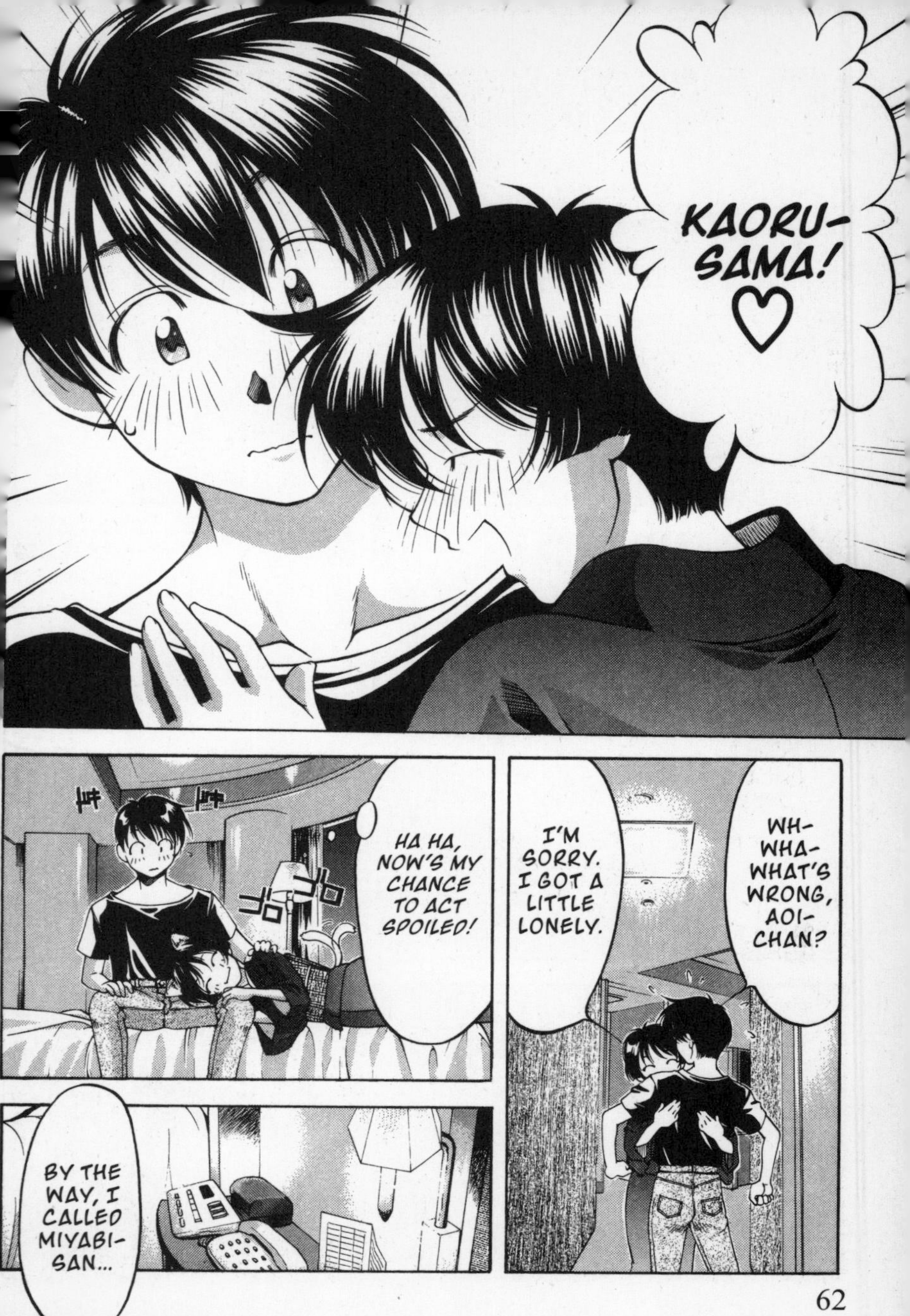
KAORU-SAMA! ♡
WH-WHA-WHAT'S WRONG, AOI-CHAN?
I'M SORRY. I GOT A LITTLE LONELY.
HA HA, NOW'S MY CHANCE TO ACT SPOILED!
BY THE WAY, I CALLED MIYABI-SAN...

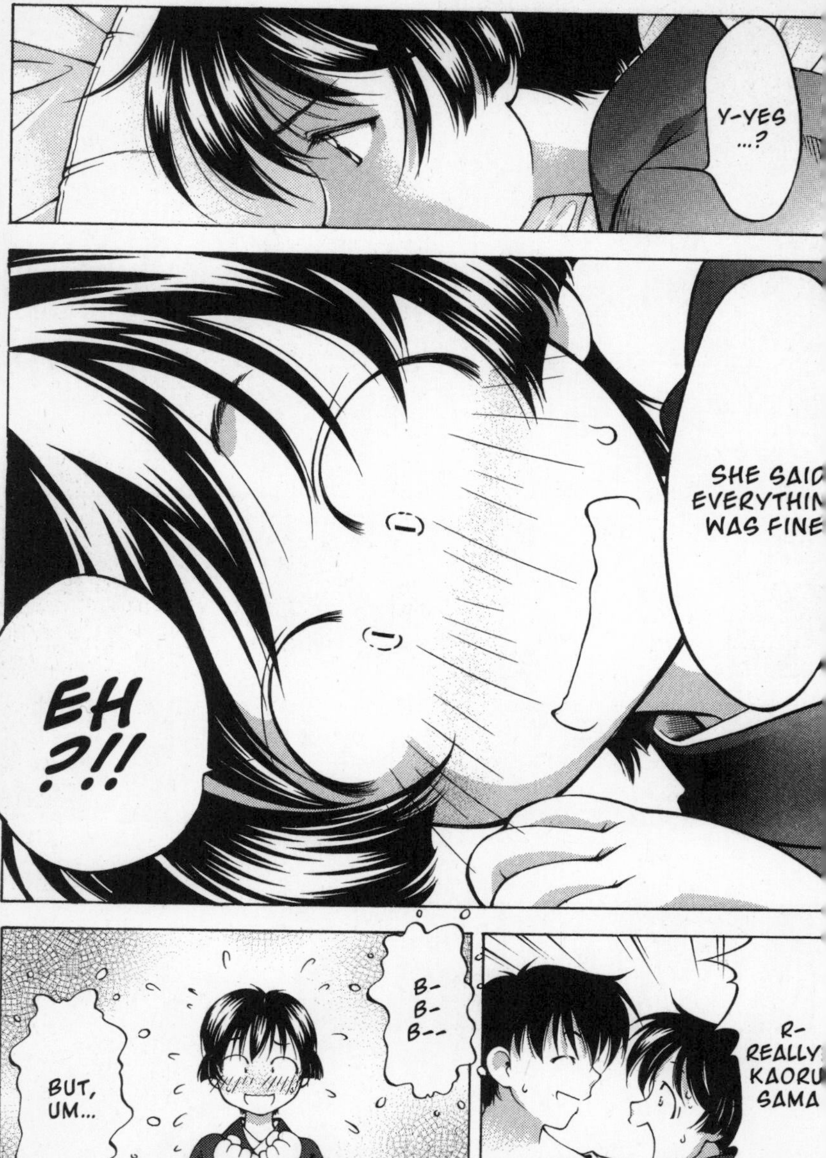
Y-YES ...?
SHE SAID EVERYTHIN WAS FINE
EH ?!!
R- REALLY KAORU SAMA
B- B- B--
BUT, UM...

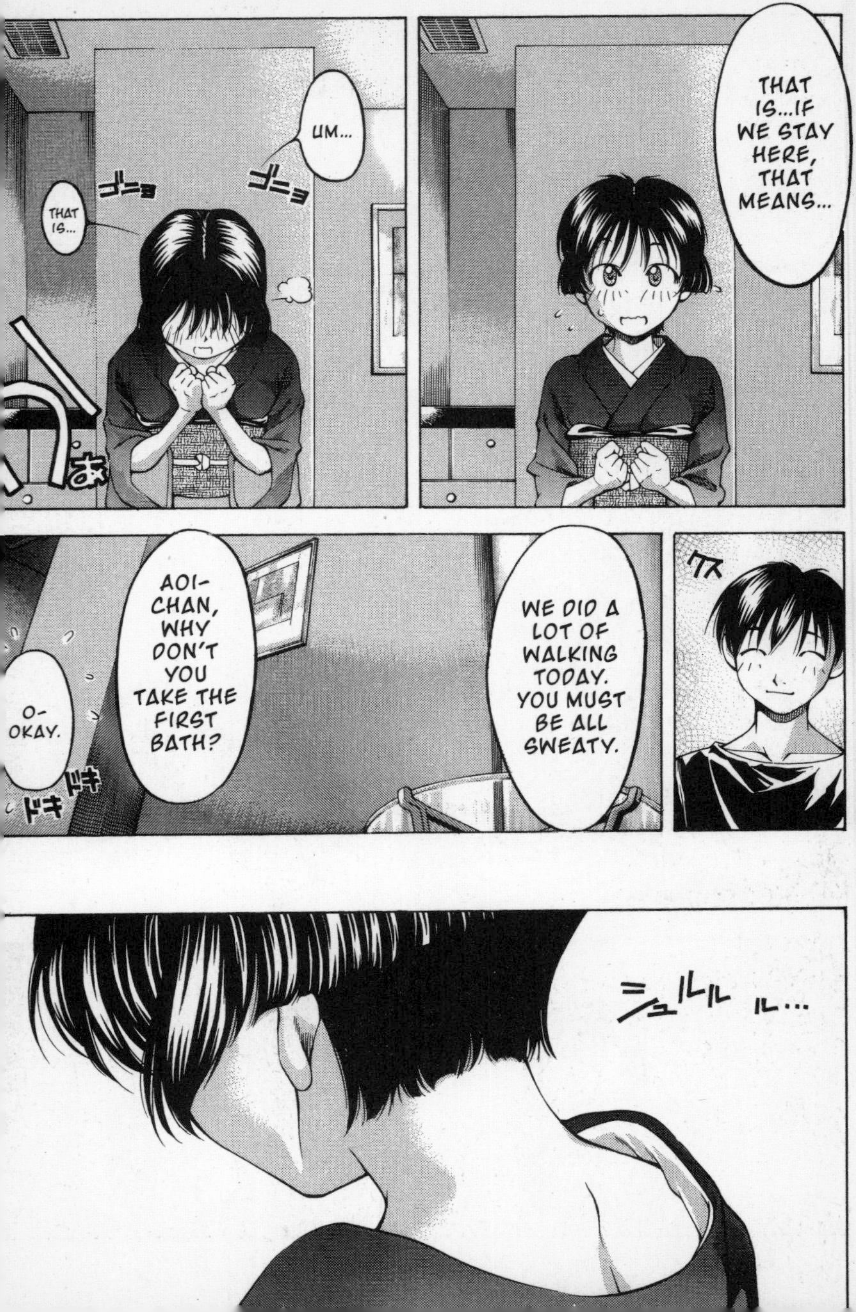
THAT IS...IF WE STAY HERE, THAT MEANS...
UM...
ゴニョ
ゴニョ
THAT IS...
あ
クス
WE DID A LOT OF WALKING TODAY. YOU MUST BE ALL SWEATY.
AOI-CHAN, WHY DON'T YOU TAKE THE FIRST BATH?
O-OKAY.
ドキ
ドキ
シュルルル ル…

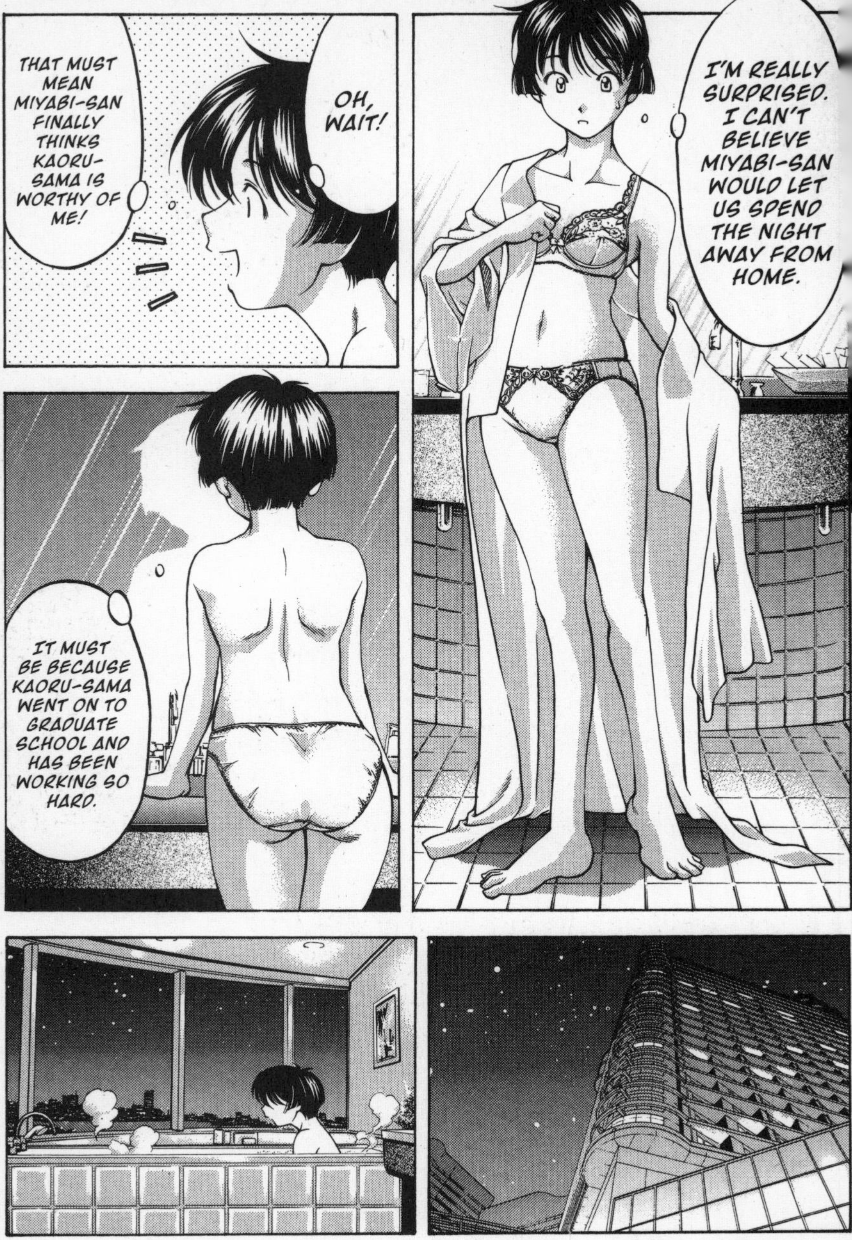
I'M REALLY SURPRISED. I CAN'T BELIEVE MIYABI-SAN WOULD LET US SPEND THE NIGHT AWAY FROM HOME.
OH, WAIT!
THAT MUST MEAN MIYABI-SAN FINALLY THINKS KAORU-SAMA IS WORTHY OF ME!
IT MUST BE BECAUSE KAORU-SAMA WENT ON TO GRADUATE SCHOOL AND HAS BEEN WORKING SO HARD.

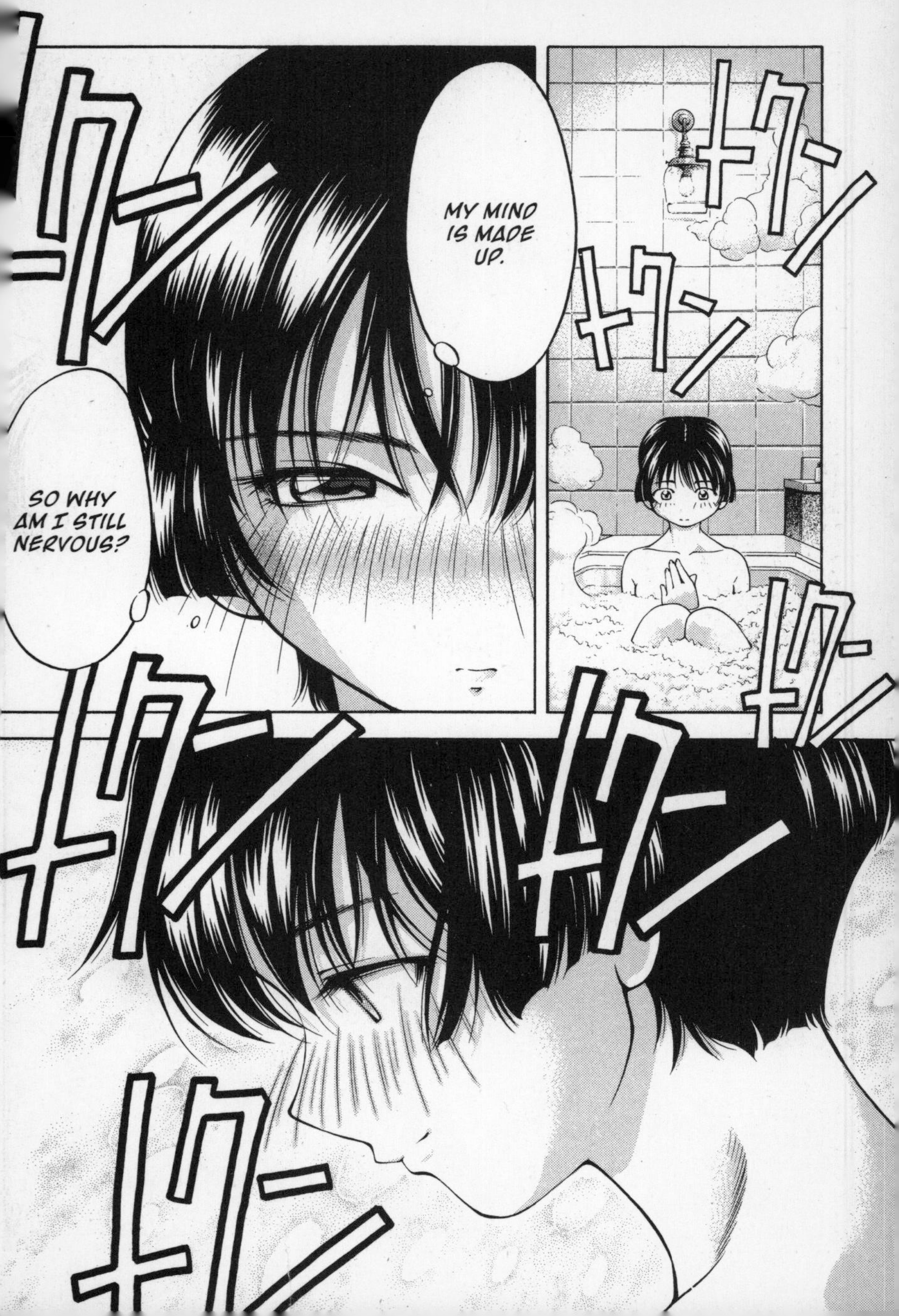
MY MIND IS MADE UP.
SO WHY AM I STILL NERVOUS?

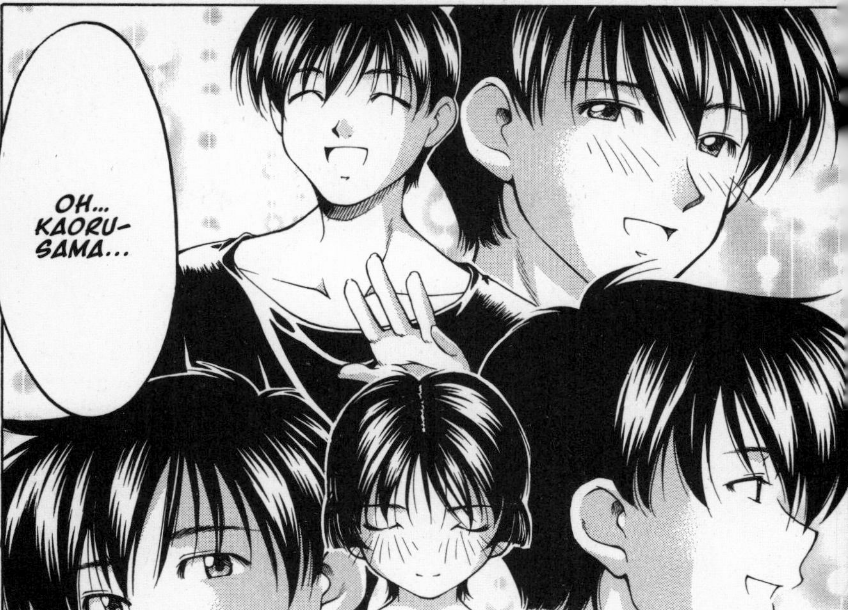
OH... KAORU-SAMA...
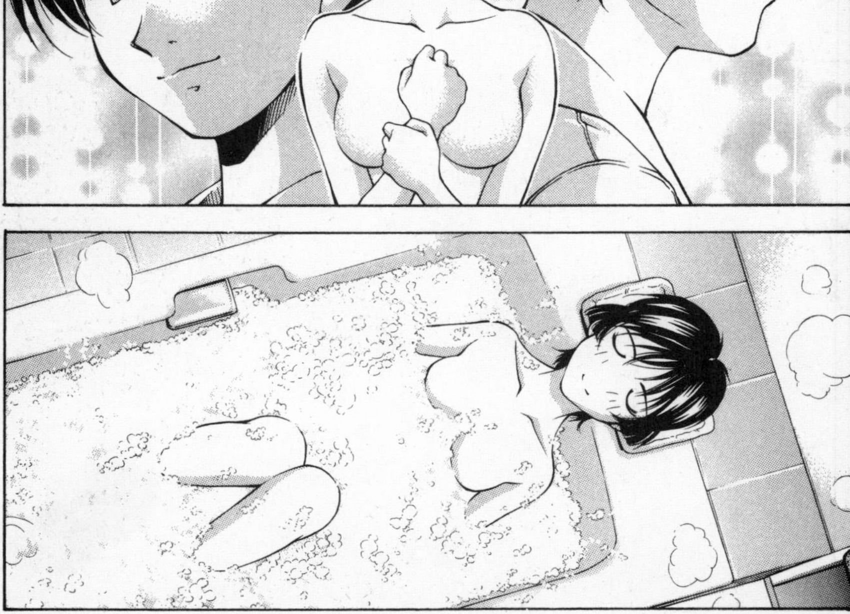

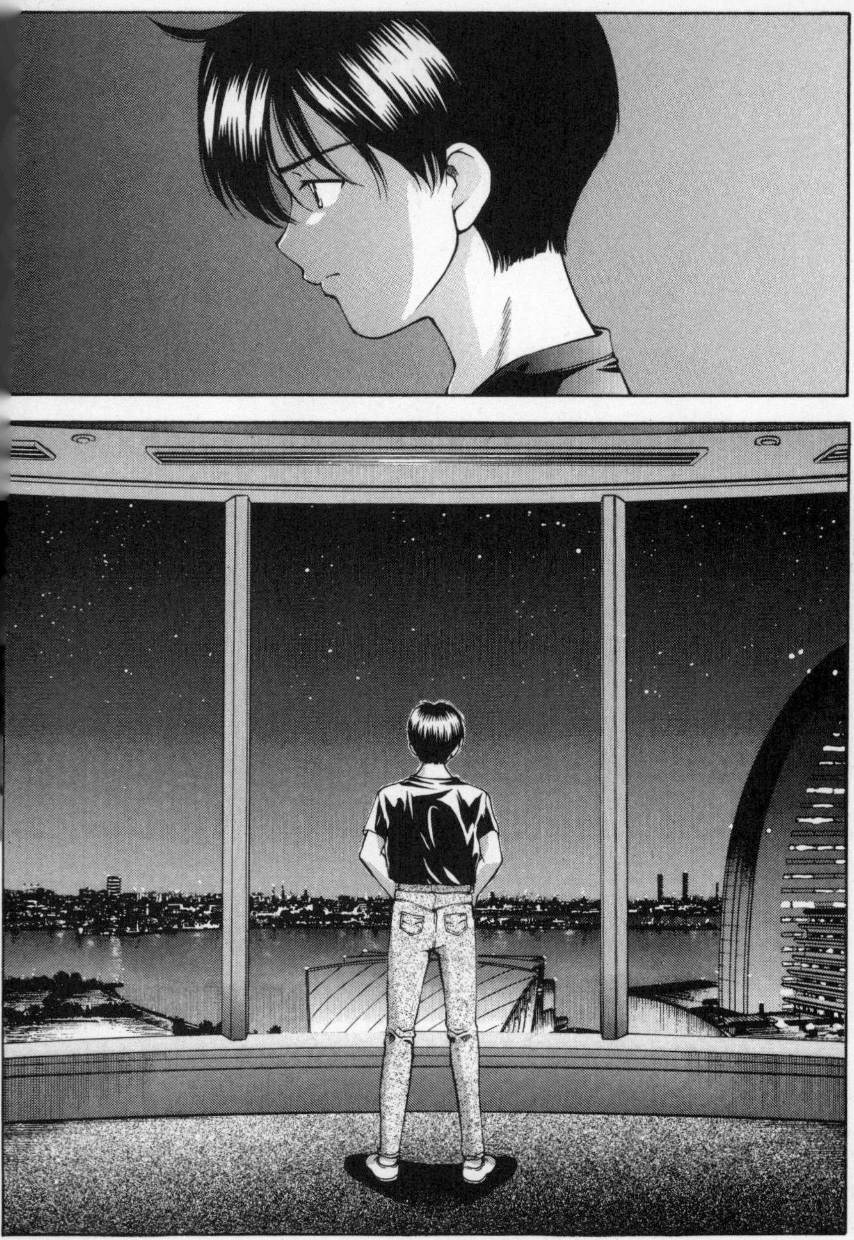

End of Chapter 78: Kesou—In Love

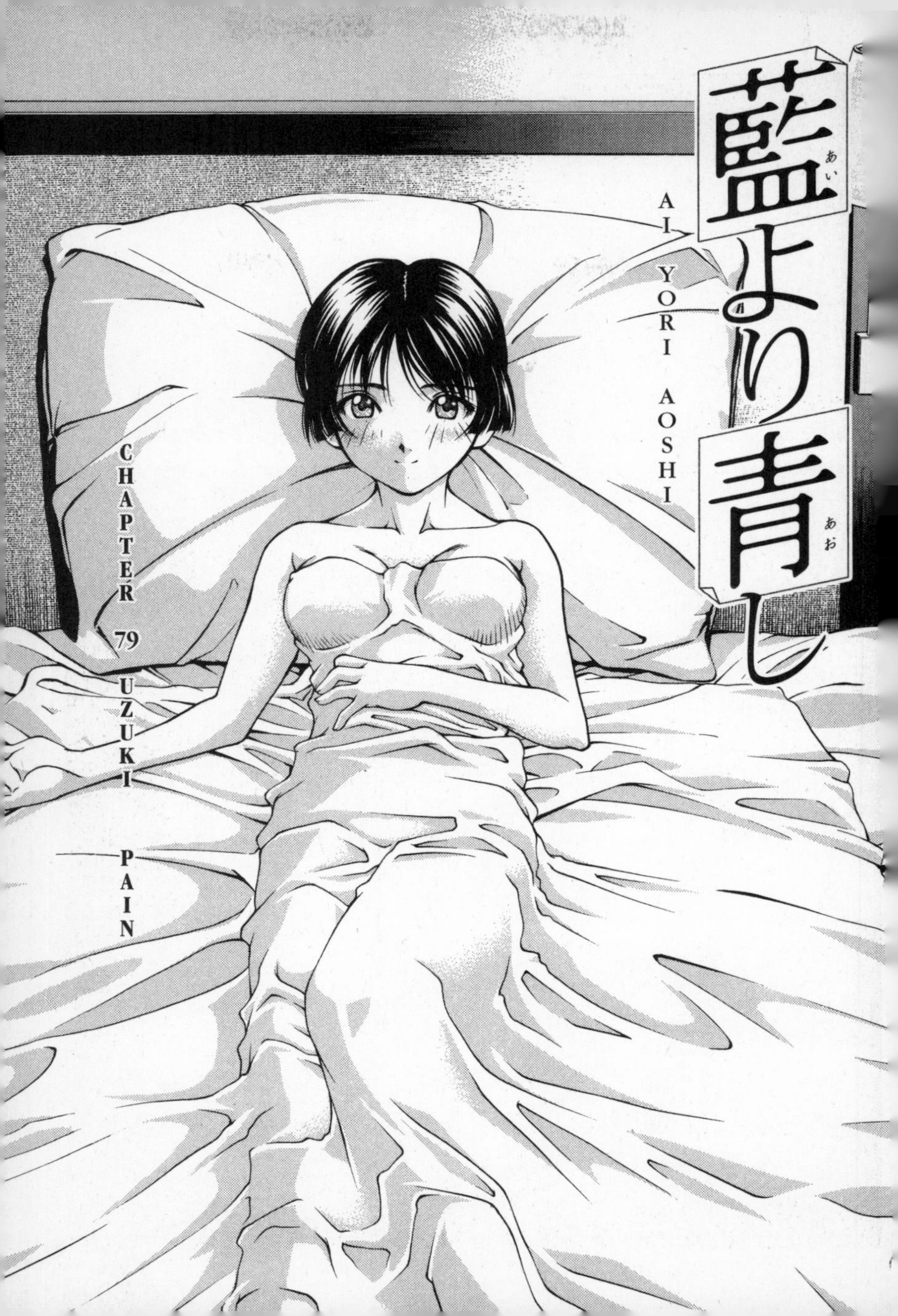
藍より青し
あい
あお
AI YORI AOSHI
CHAPTER 79
UZUKI PAIN

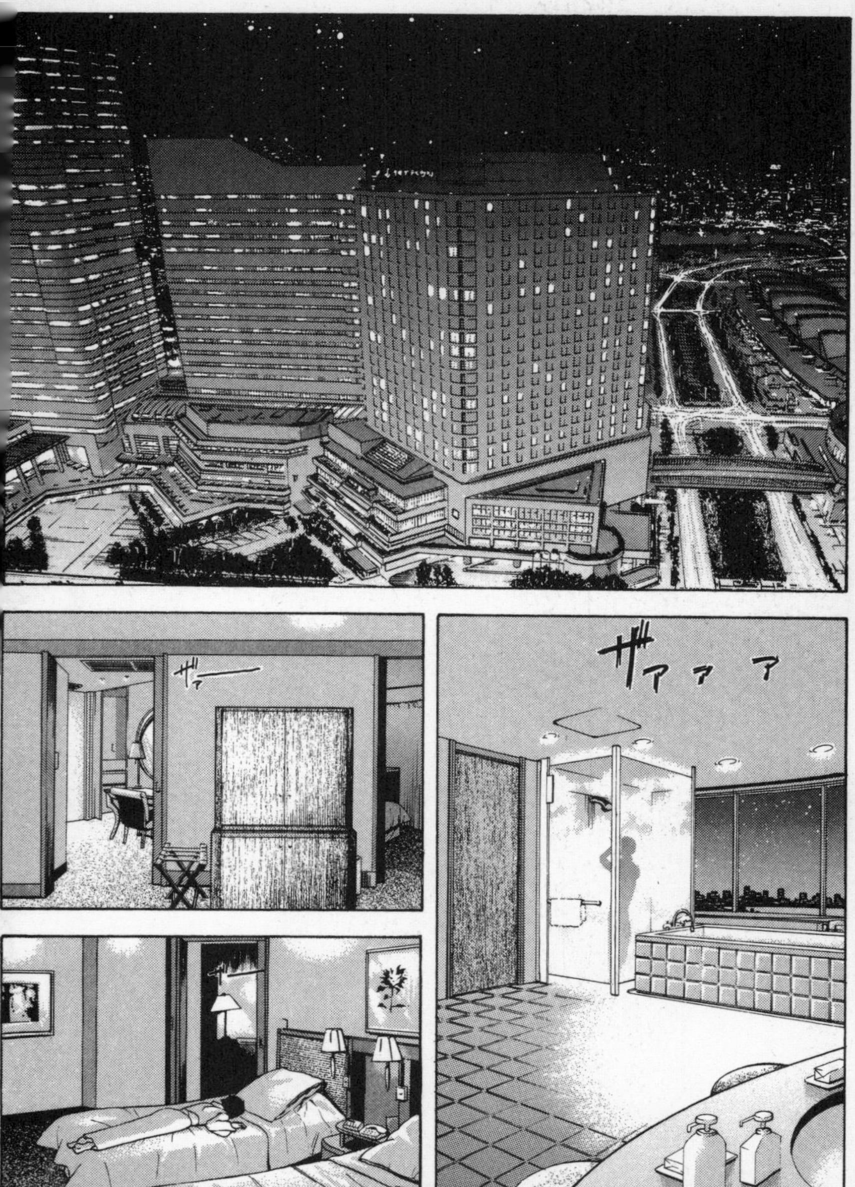
ザァァァ
ザァー

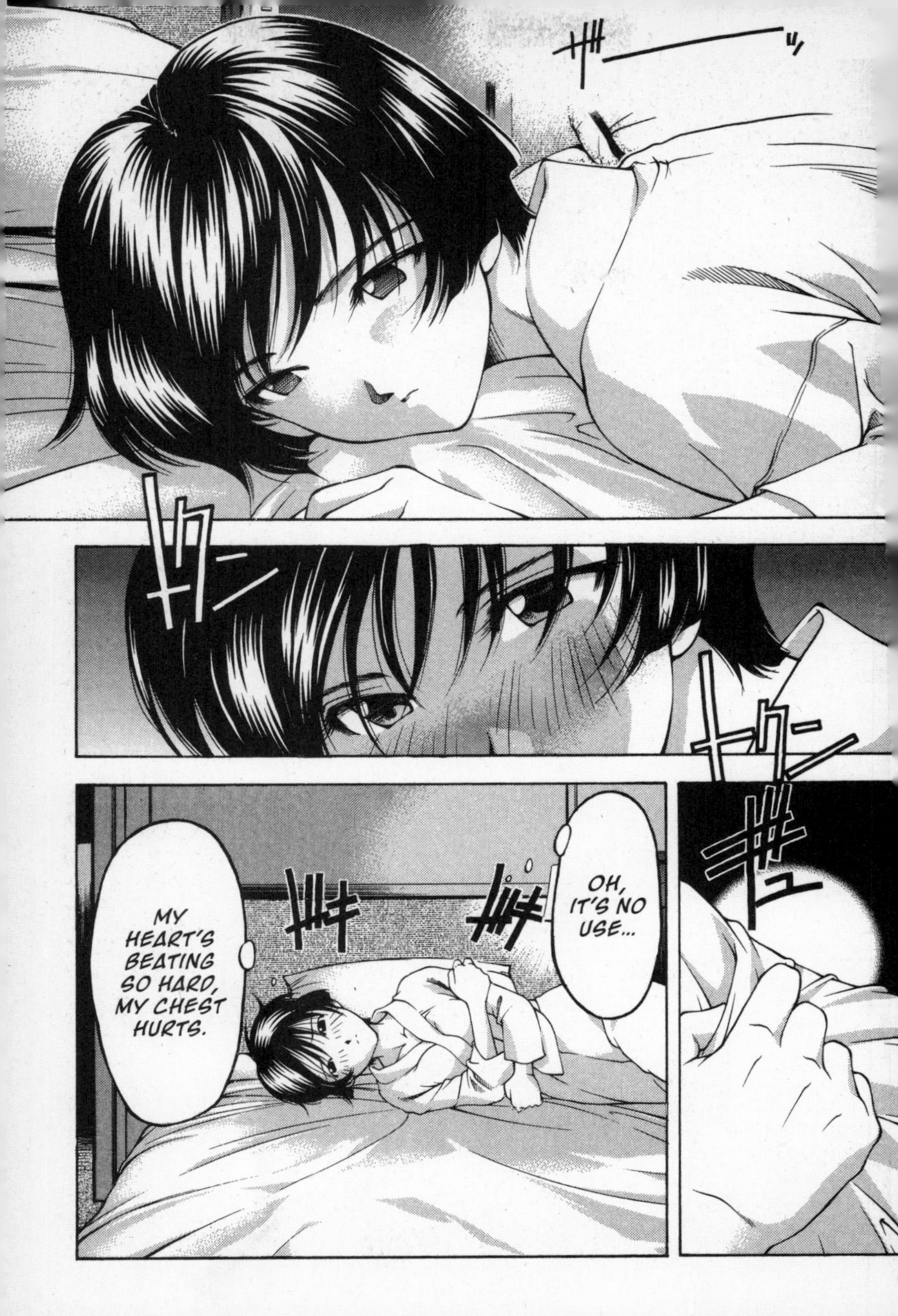
OH, IT'S NO USE...
MY HEART'S BEATING SO HARD, MY CHEST HURTS.

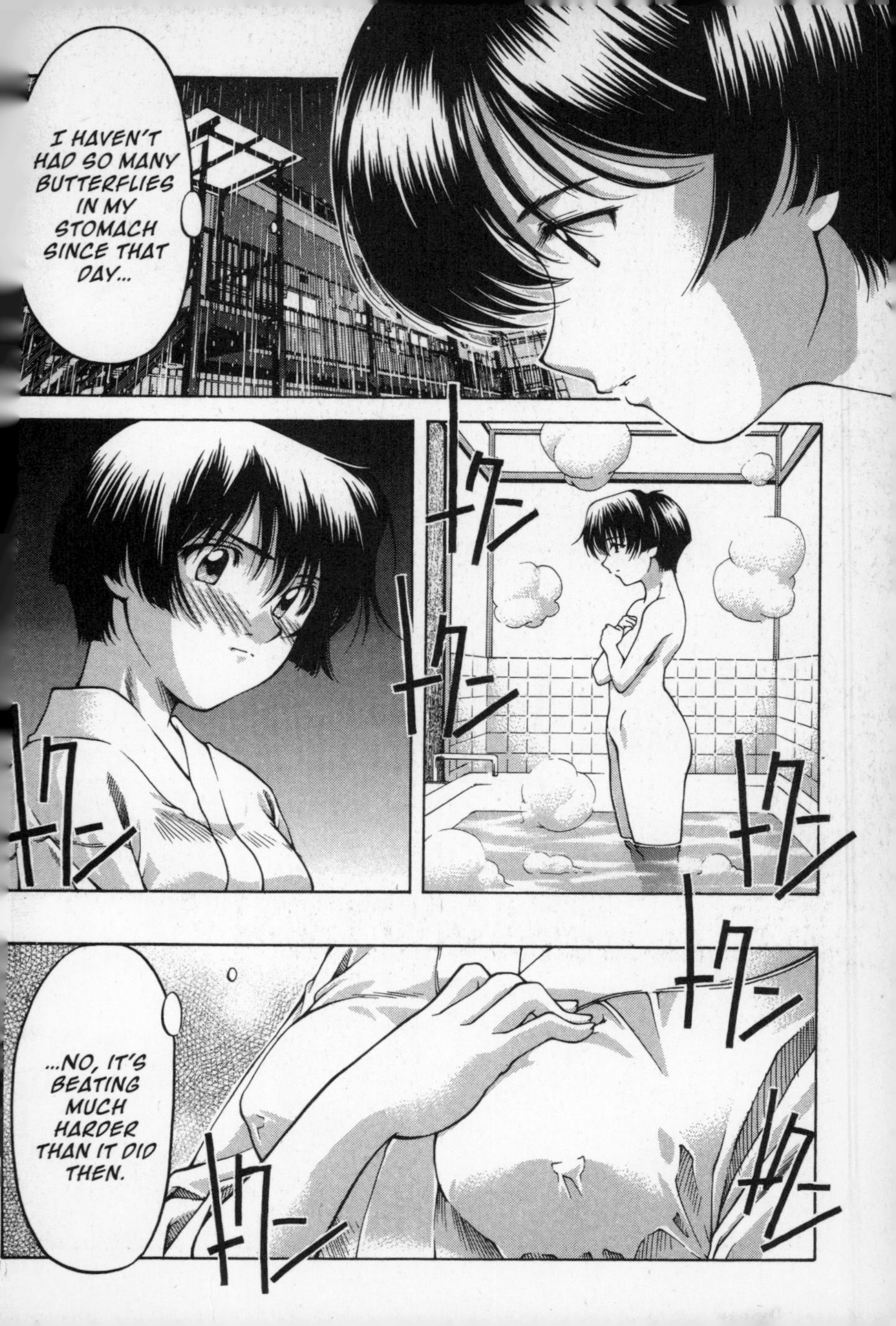
I HAVEN'T HAD SO MANY BUTTERFLIES IN MY STOMACH SINCE THAT DAY...
ドクン
ドクン
ドクン
ドクン
ドクン
...NO, IT'S BEATING MUCH HARDER THAN IT DID THEN.
ドクン
ドクン

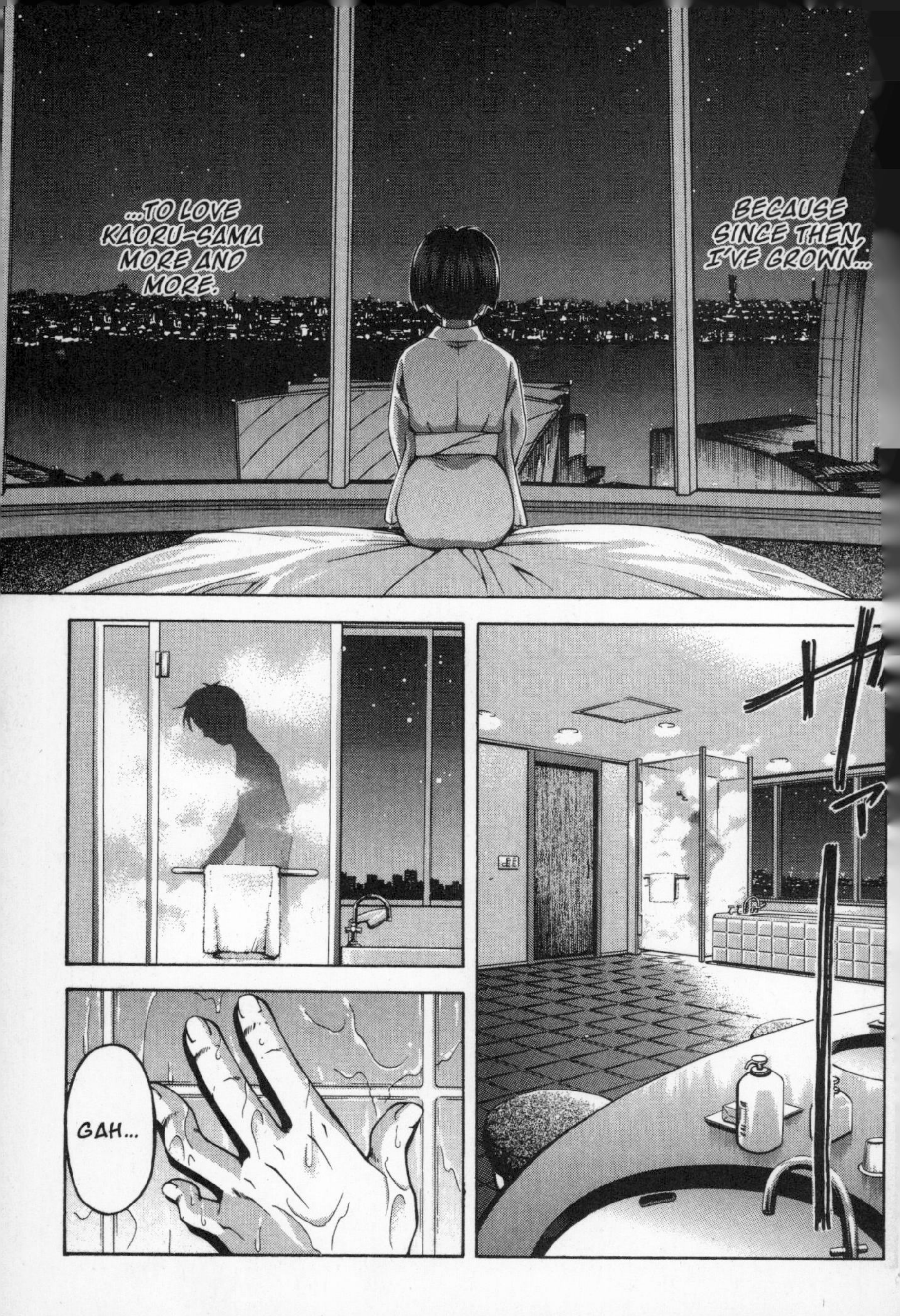
BECAUSE SINCE THEN, I'VE GROWN...
...TO LOVE KAORU-SAMA MORE AND MORE.
GAH...

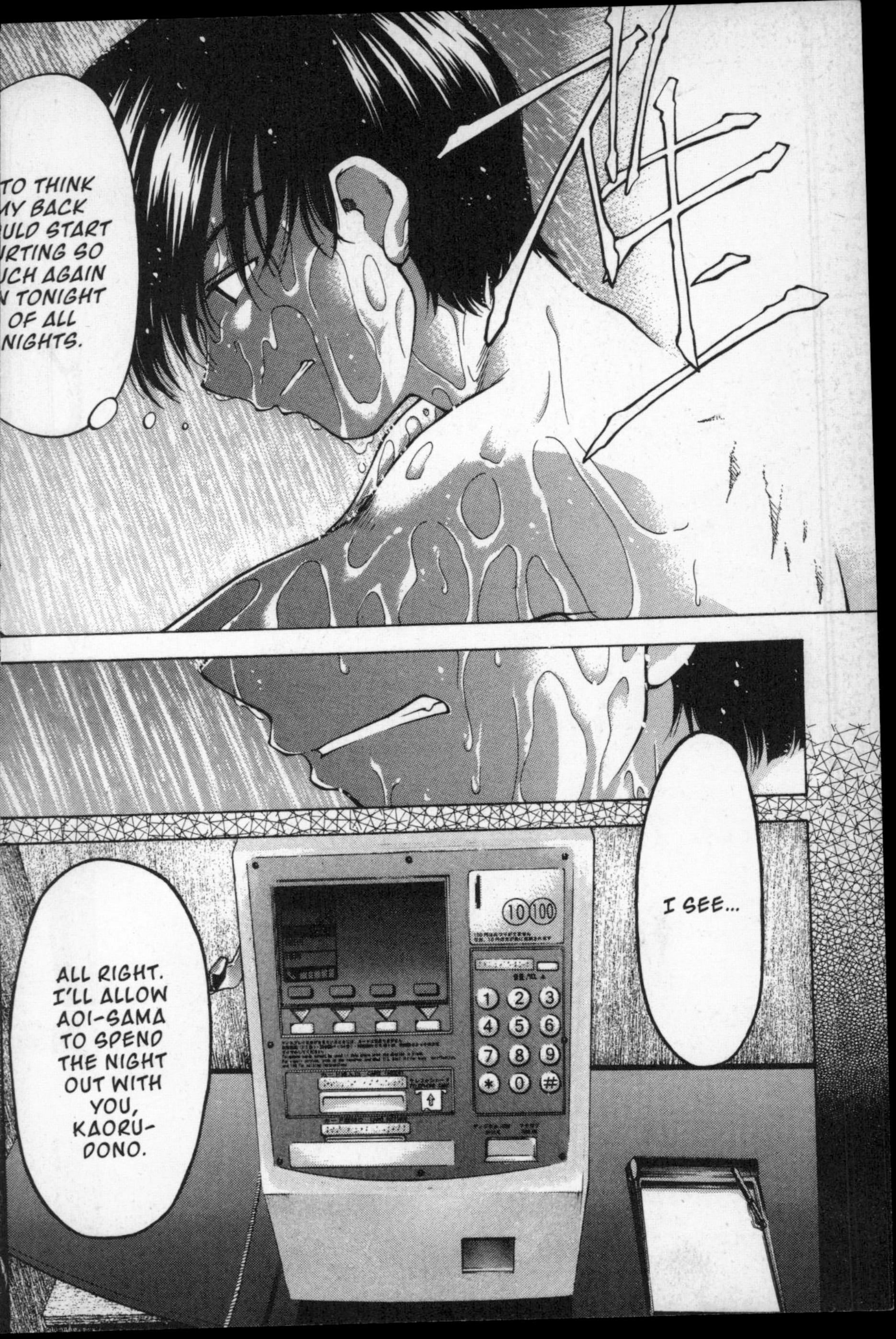
TO THINK MY BACK ULD START URTING SO UCH AGAIN N TONIGHT OF ALL NIGHTS.
I SEE...
ALL RIGHT. I'LL ALLOW AOI-SAMA TO SPEND THE NIGHT OUT WITH YOU, KAORU-DONO.

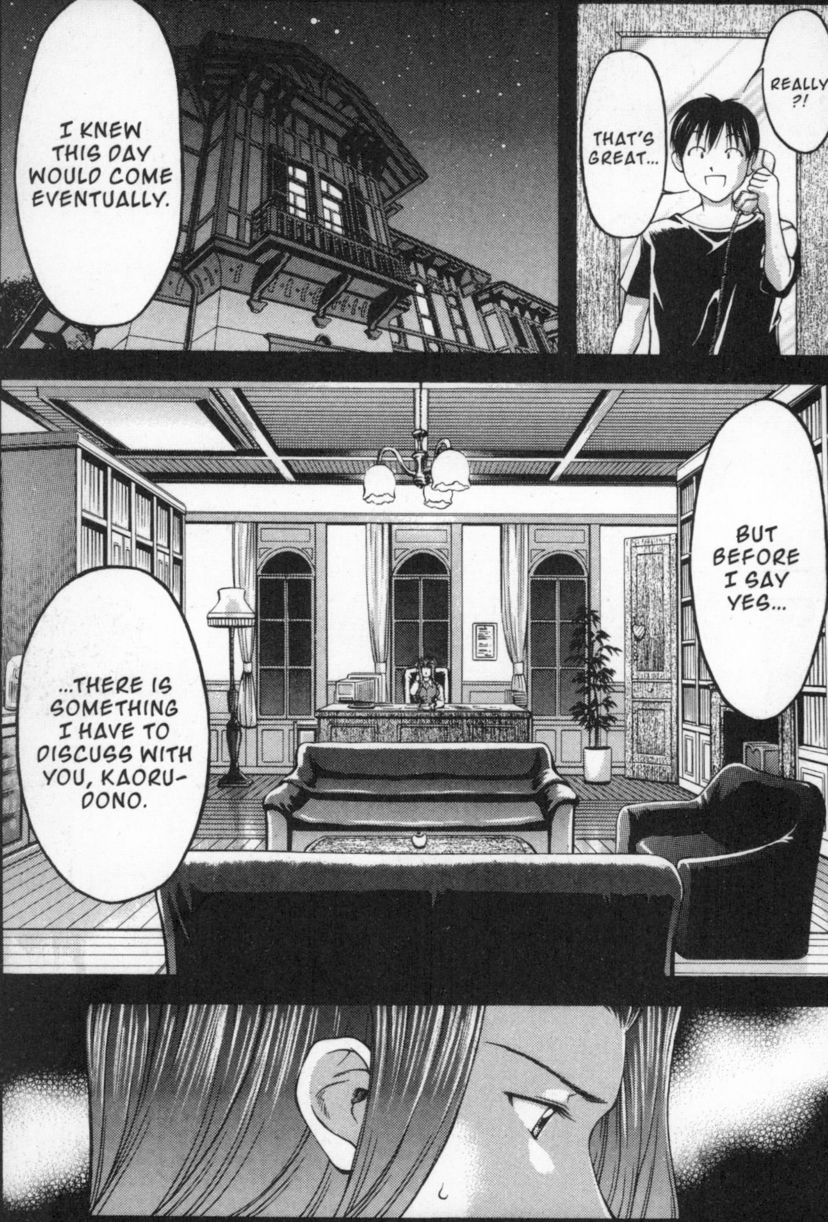
REALLY ?!
THAT'S GREAT...
I KNEW THIS DAY WOULD COME EVENTUALLY.
BUT BEFORE I SAY YES...
...THERE IS SOMETHING I HAVE TO DISCUSS WITH YOU, KAORU-DONO.

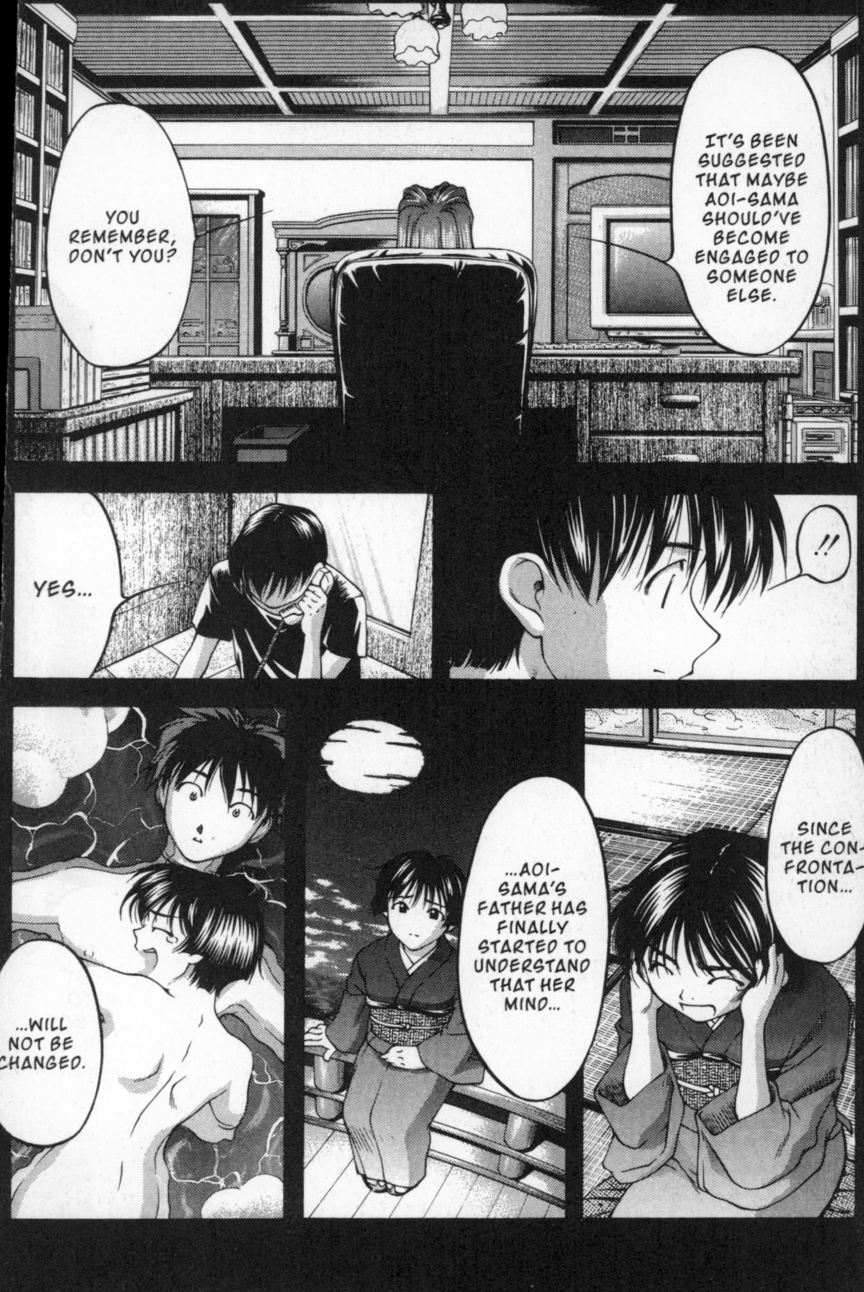
IT'S BEEN SUGGESTED THAT MAYBE AOI-SAMA SHOULD'VE BECOME ENGAGED TO SOMEONE ELSE.
YOU REMEMBER, DON'T YOU?
!!
YES...
SINCE THE CON-FRONTA-TION...
...AOI-SAMA'S FATHER HAS FINALLY STARTED TO UNDERSTAND THAT HER MIND...
...WILL NOT BE CHANGED.

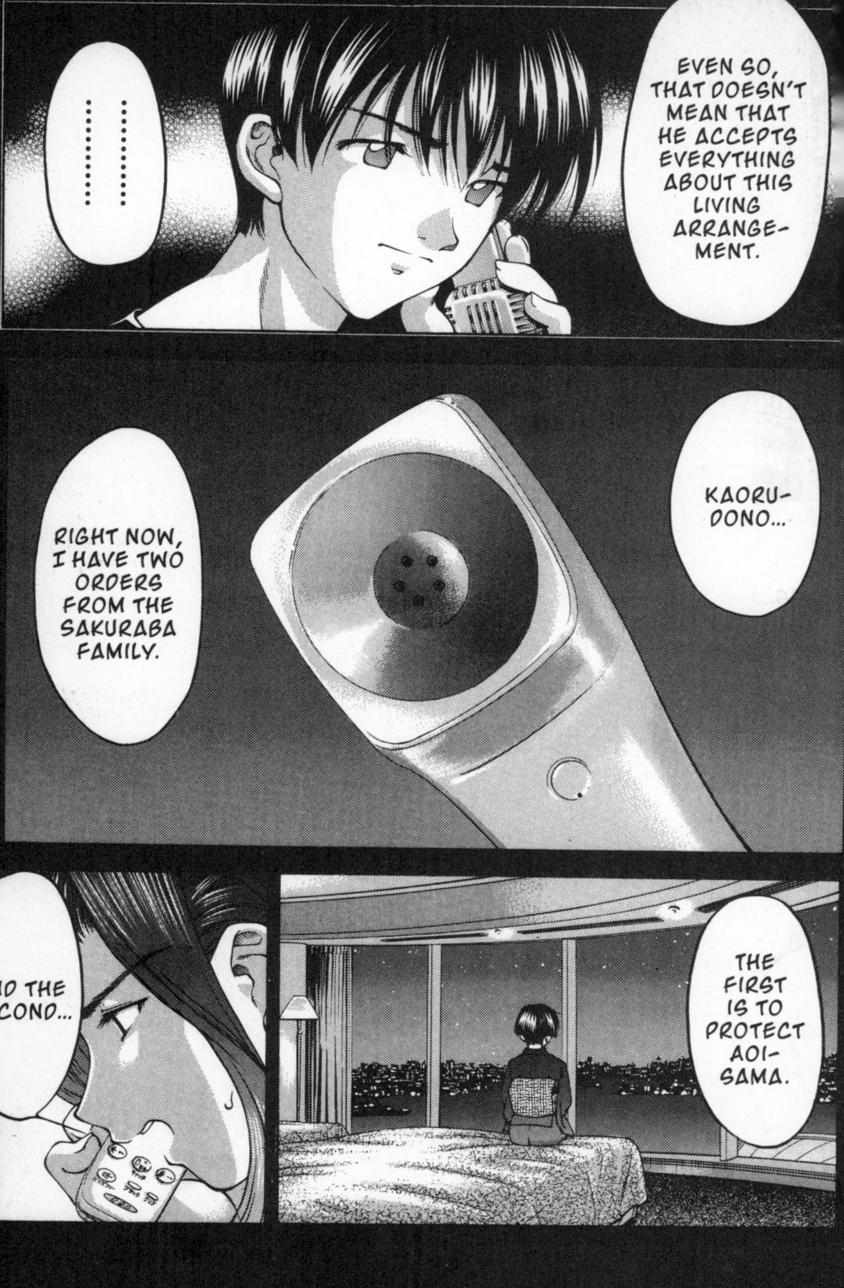
EVEN SO, THAT DOESN'T MEAN THAT HE ACCEPTS EVERYTHING ABOUT THIS LIVING ARRANGE-MENT.
……
KAORU-DONO...
RIGHT NOW, I HAVE TWO ORDERS FROM THE SAKURABA FAMILY.
THE FIRST IS TO PROTECT AOI-SAMA.
AND THE SECOND...

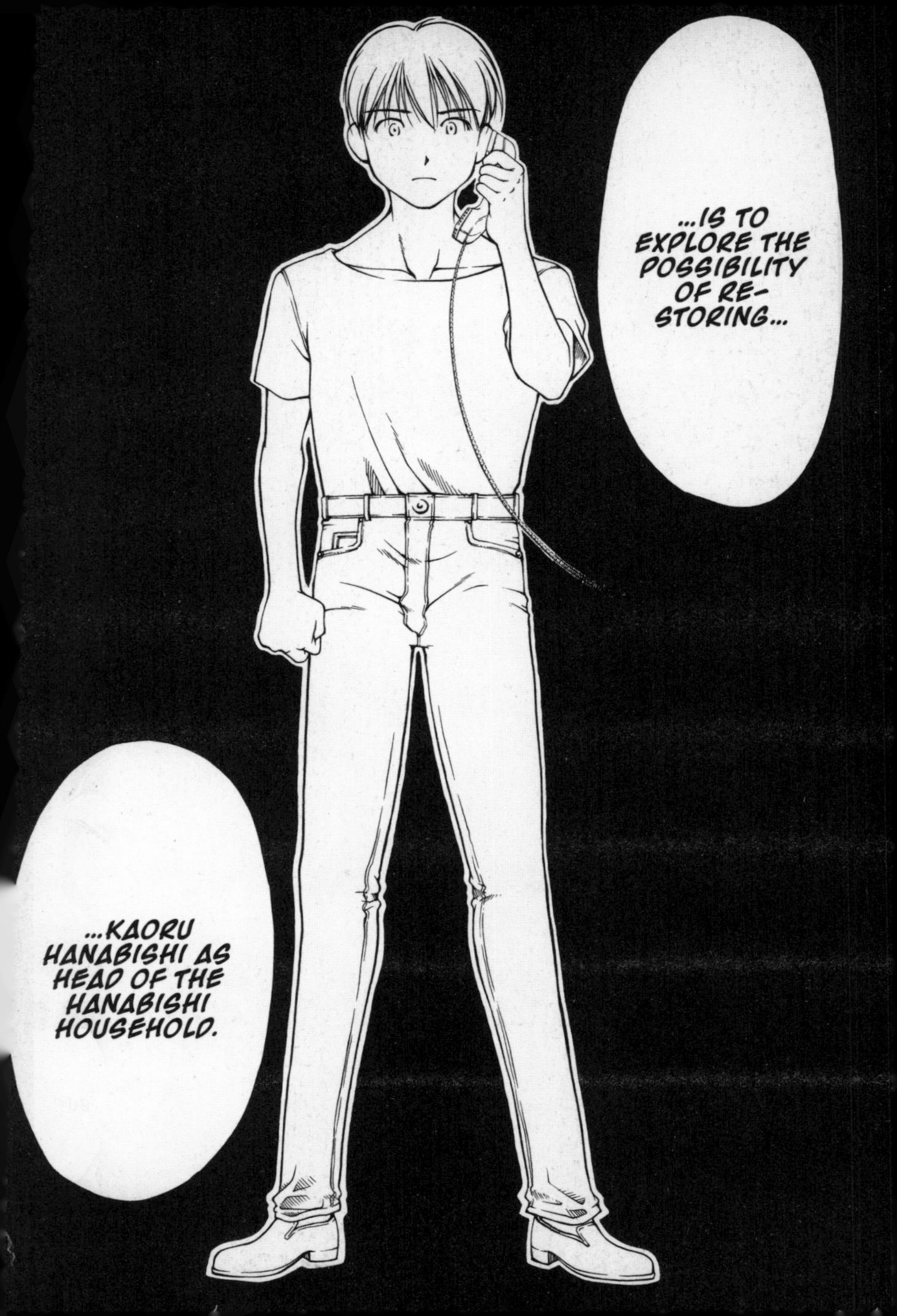
...IS TO EXPLORE THE POSSIBILITY OF RE-STORING...
...KAORU HANABISHI AS HEAD OF THE HANABISHI HOUSEHOLD.

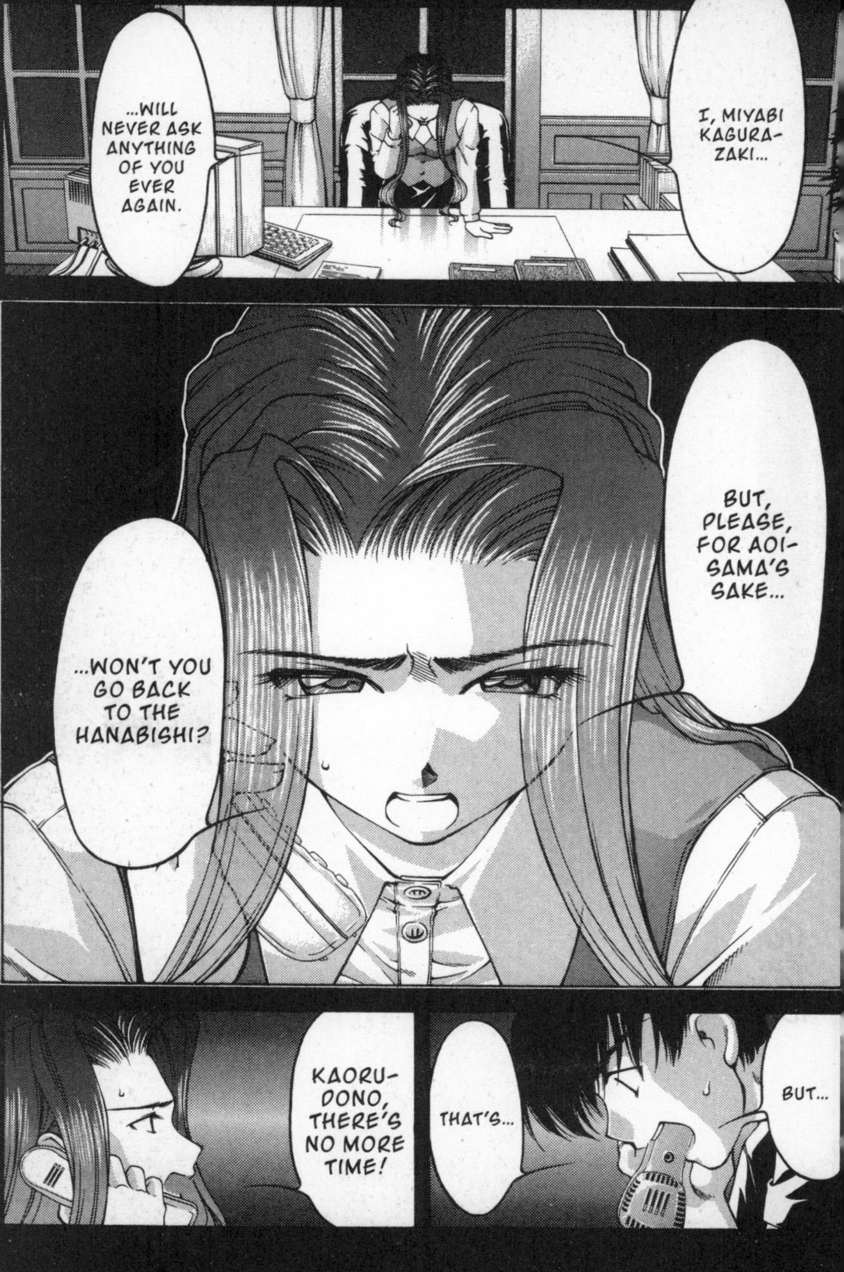
I, MIYABI KAGURA-ZAKI...
...WILL NEVER ASK ANYTHING OF YOU EVER AGAIN.
BUT, PLEASE, FOR AOI-SAMA'S SAKE...
...WON'T YOU GO BACK TO THE HANABISHI?
BUT...
THAT'S...
KAORU-DONO, THERE'S NO MORE TIME!

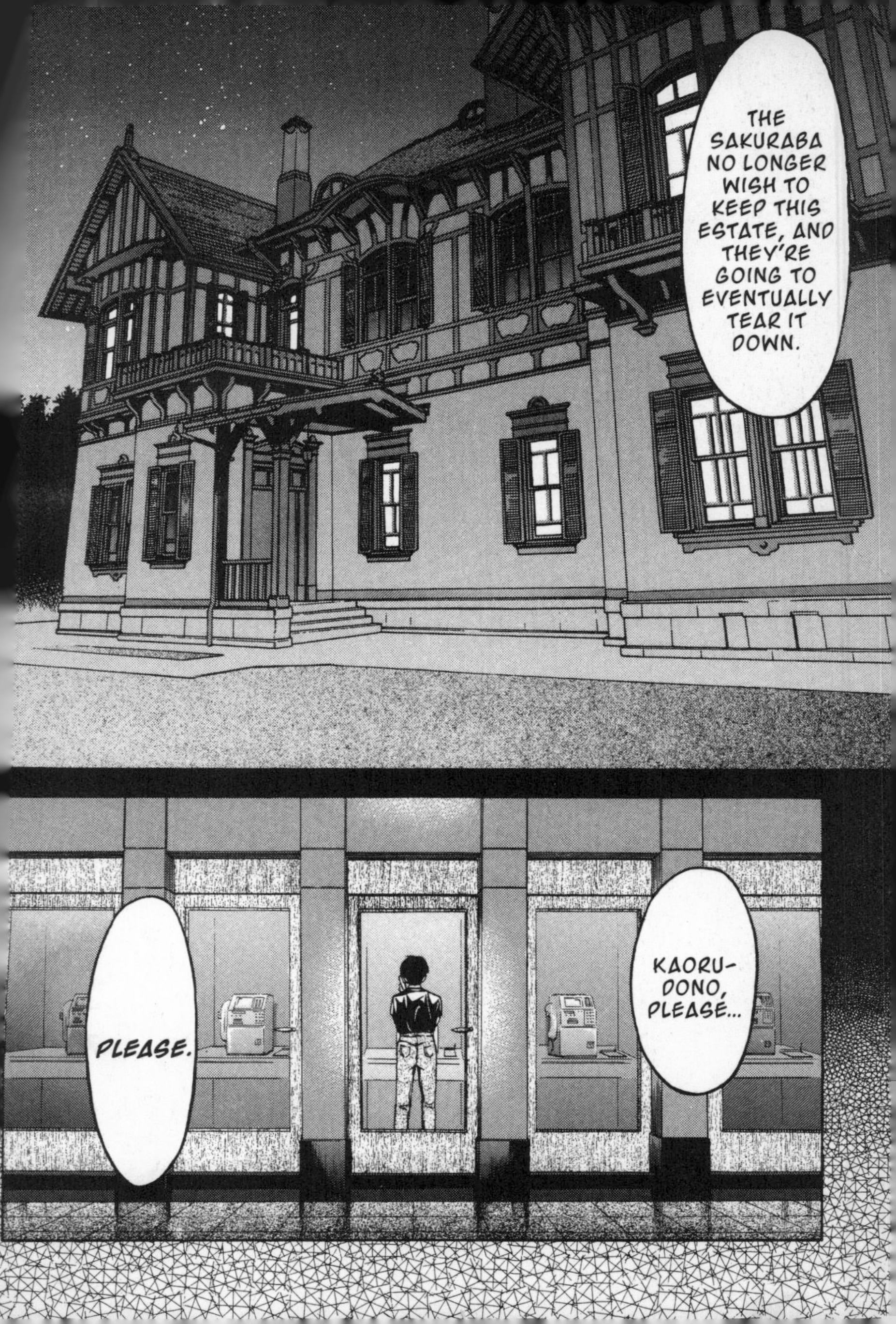
THE SAKURABA NO LONGER WISH TO KEEP THIS ESTATE, AND THEY'RE GOING TO EVENTUALLY TEAR IT DOWN.
KAORU-DONO, PLEASE...
PLEASE.

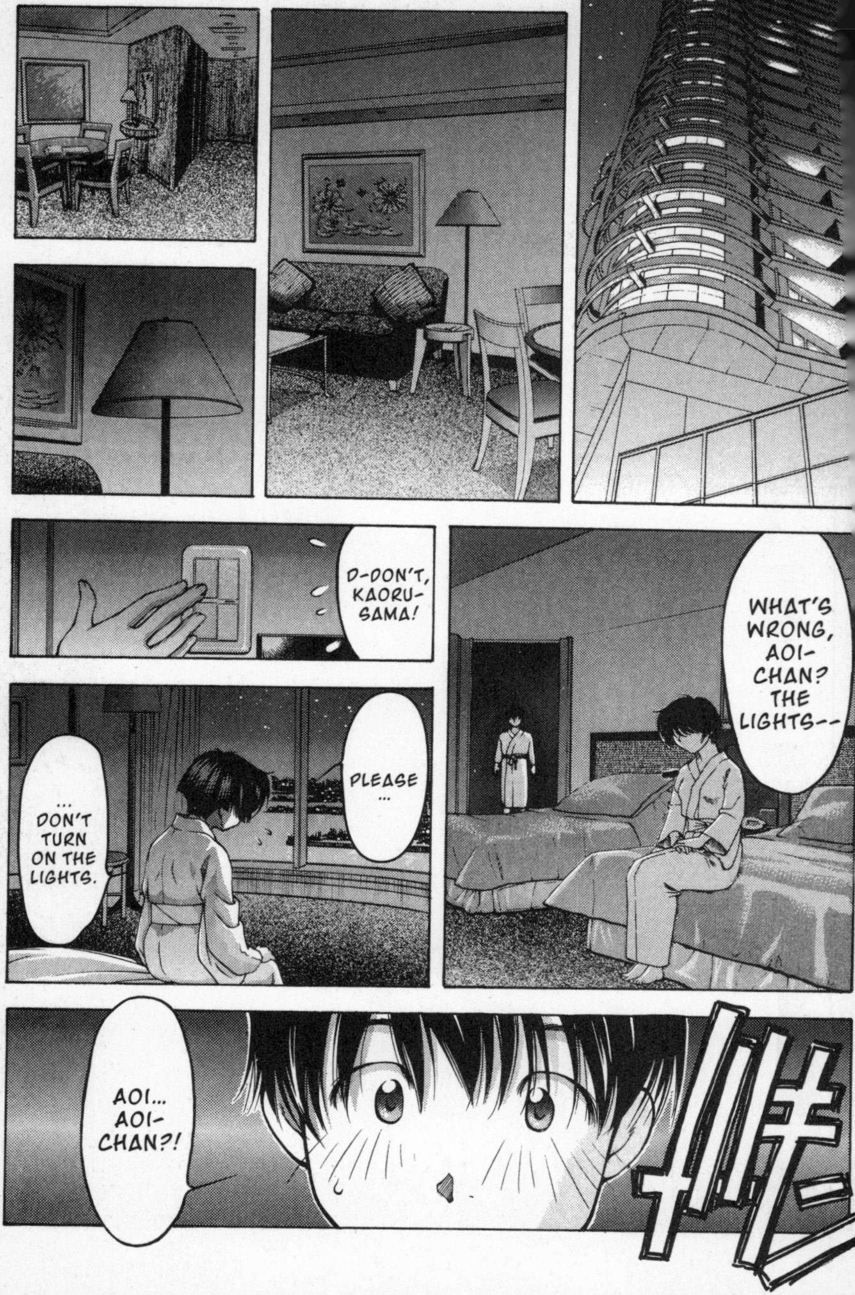
WHAT'S WRONG, AOI-CHAN? THE LIGHTS--
D-DON'T, KAORU-SAMA!
PLEASE ...
... DON'T TURN ON THE LIGHTS.
AOI... AOI-CHAN?!

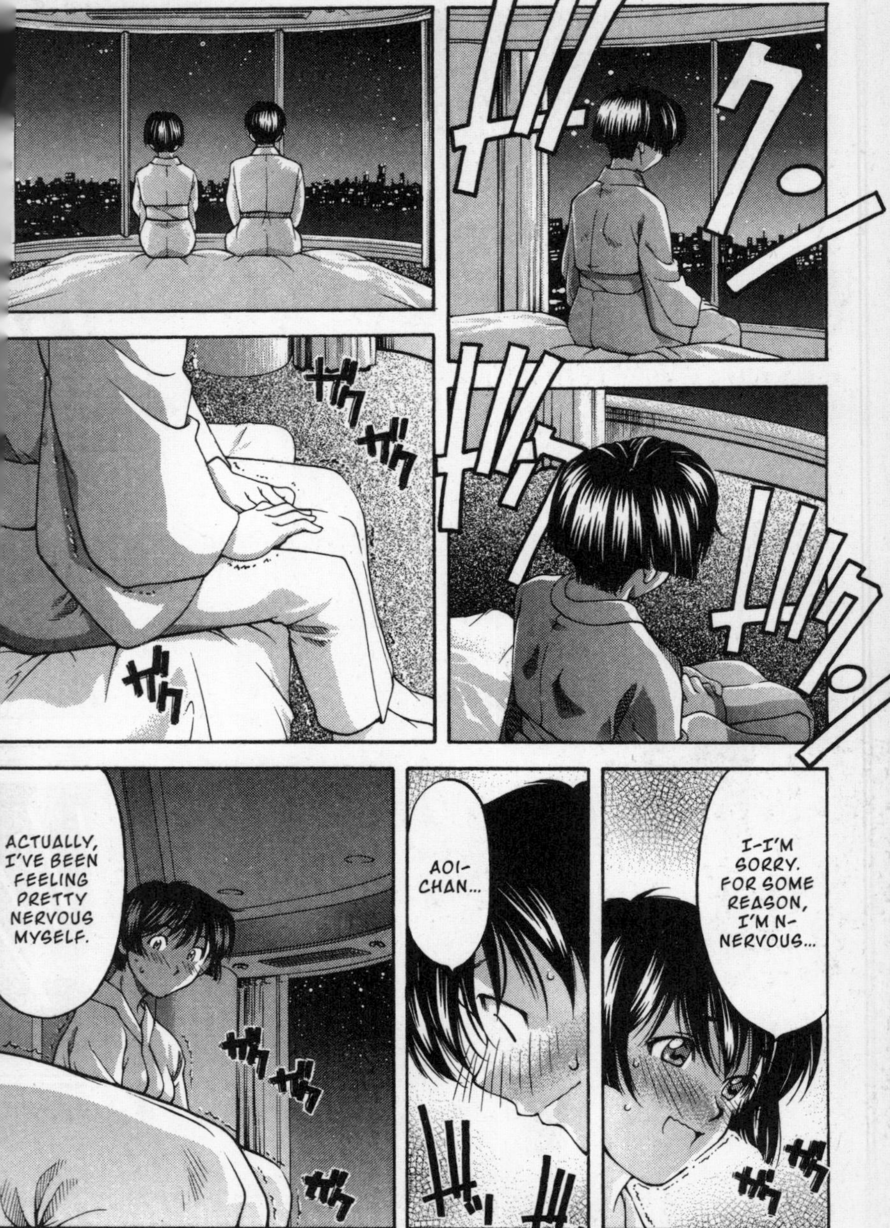
I-I'M SORRY. FOR SOME REASON, I'M N-NERVOUS...
AOI-CHAN...
ACTUALLY, I'VE BEEN FEELING PRETTY NERVOUS MYSELF.

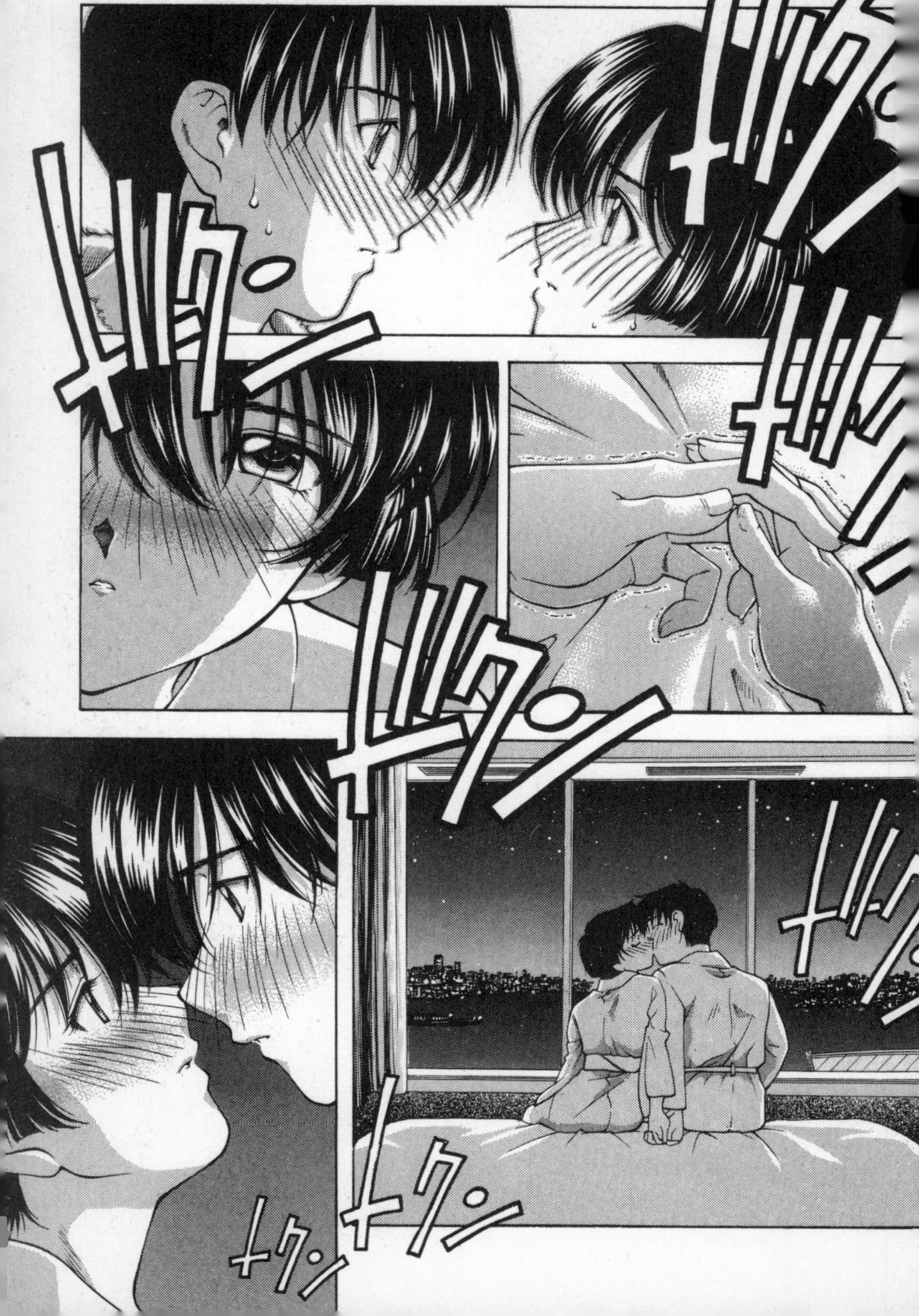
ドクン
ドクン
ドクン
ドクン
ドクン
ドクン
ドクン

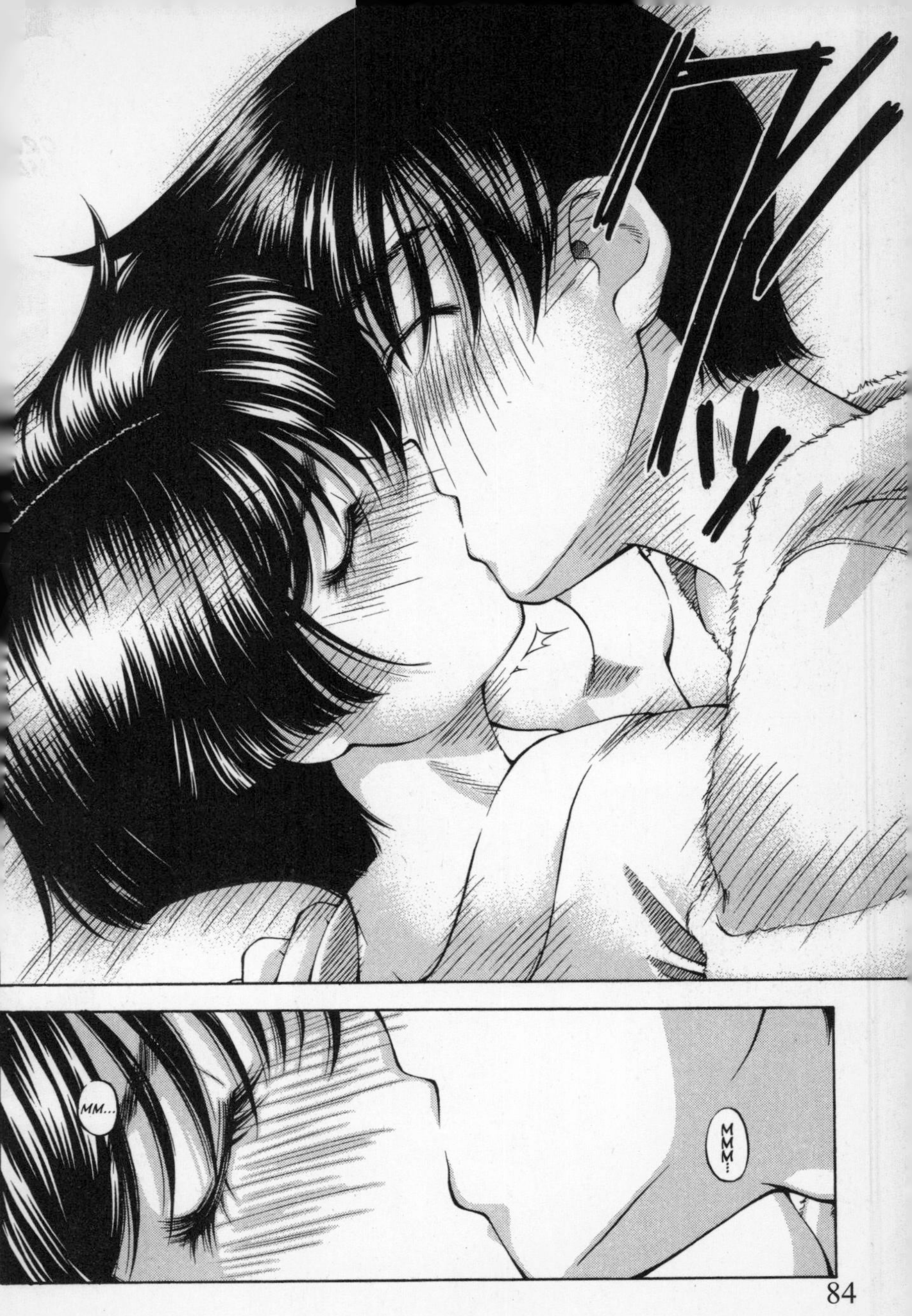
MMM...
MM...

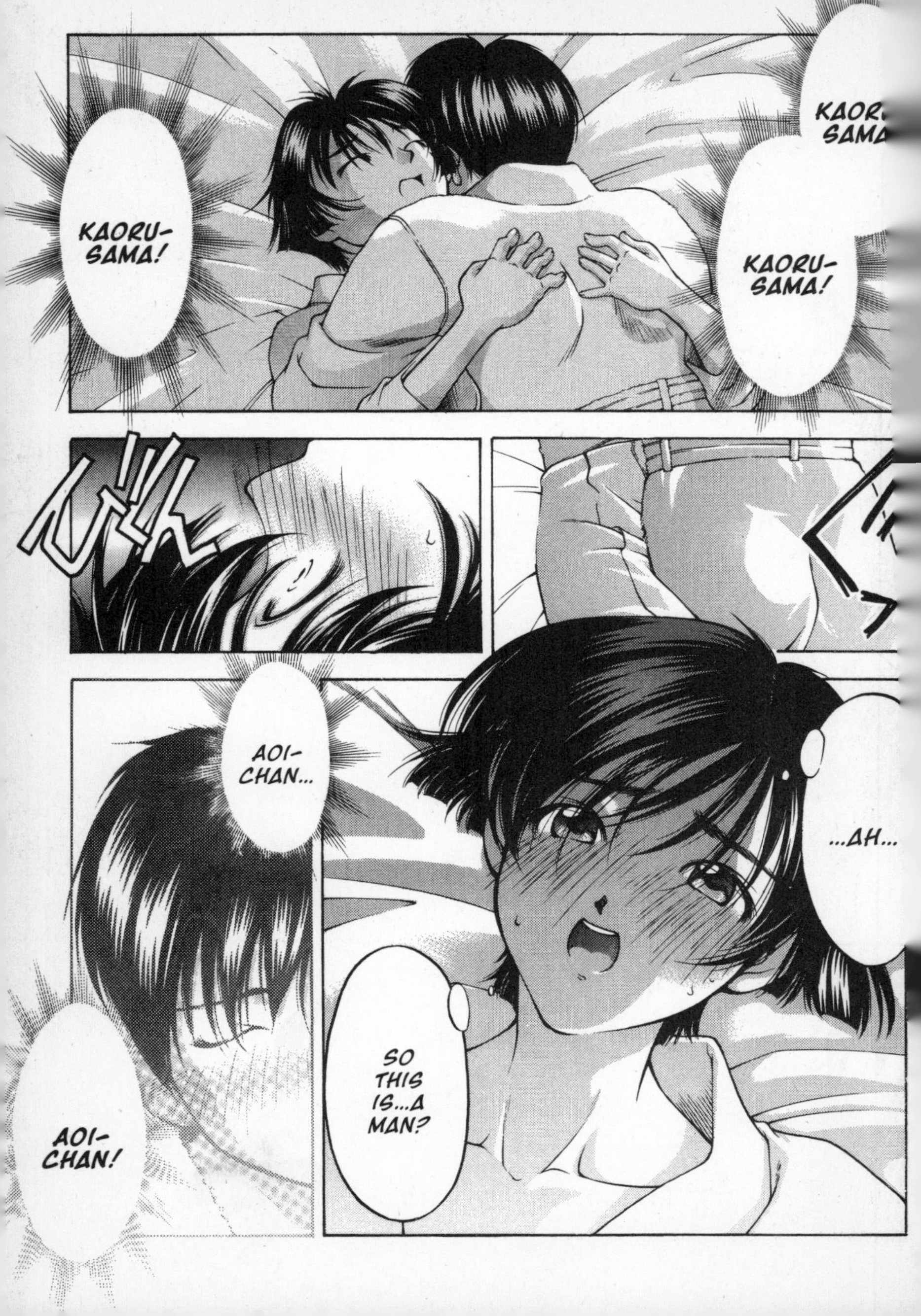
KAORU-SAMA
KAORU-SAMA!
KAORU-SAMA!
...AH...
SO THIS IS...A MAN?
AOI-CHAN...
AOI-CHAN!

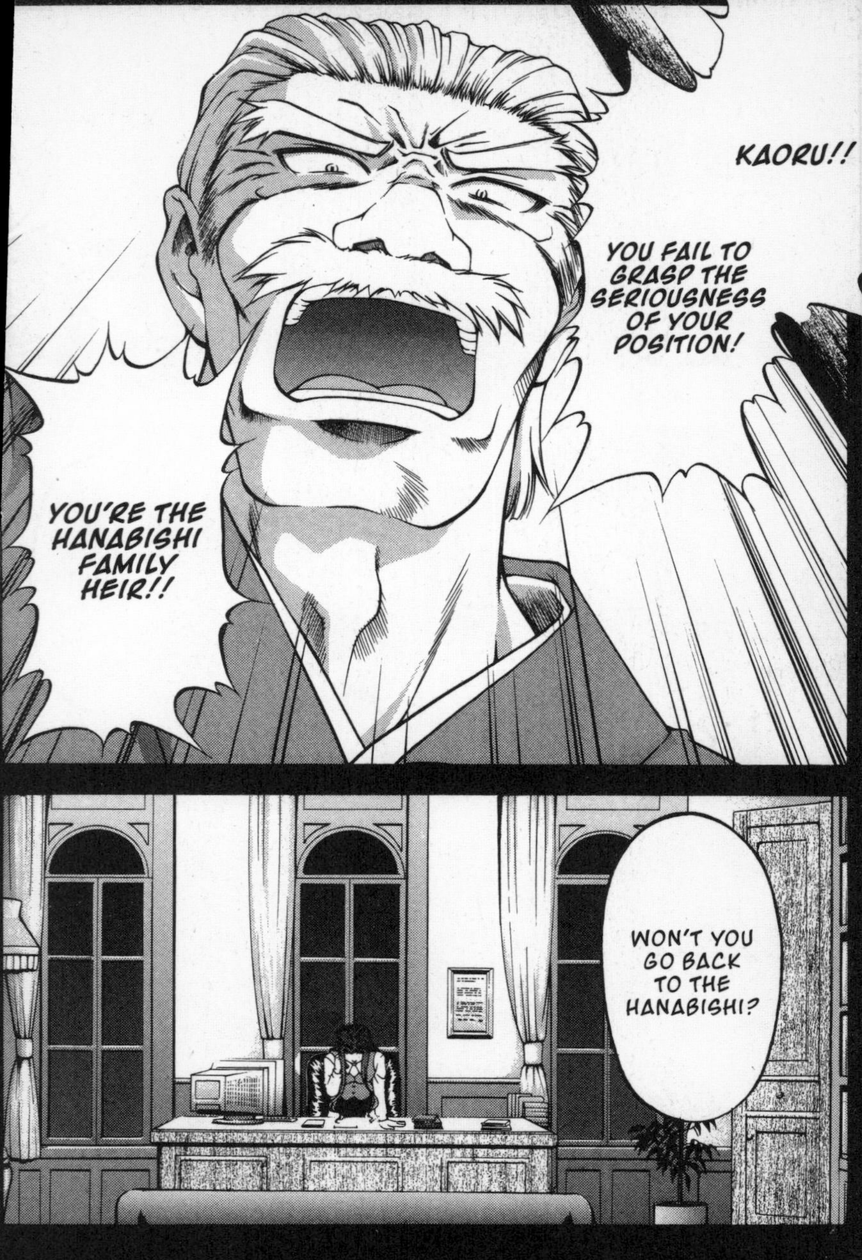
KAORU!!
YOU FAIL TO GRASP THE SERIOUSNESS OF YOUR POSITION!
YOU'RE THE HANABISHI FAMILY HEIR!!
WON'T YOU GO BACK TO THE HANABISHI?

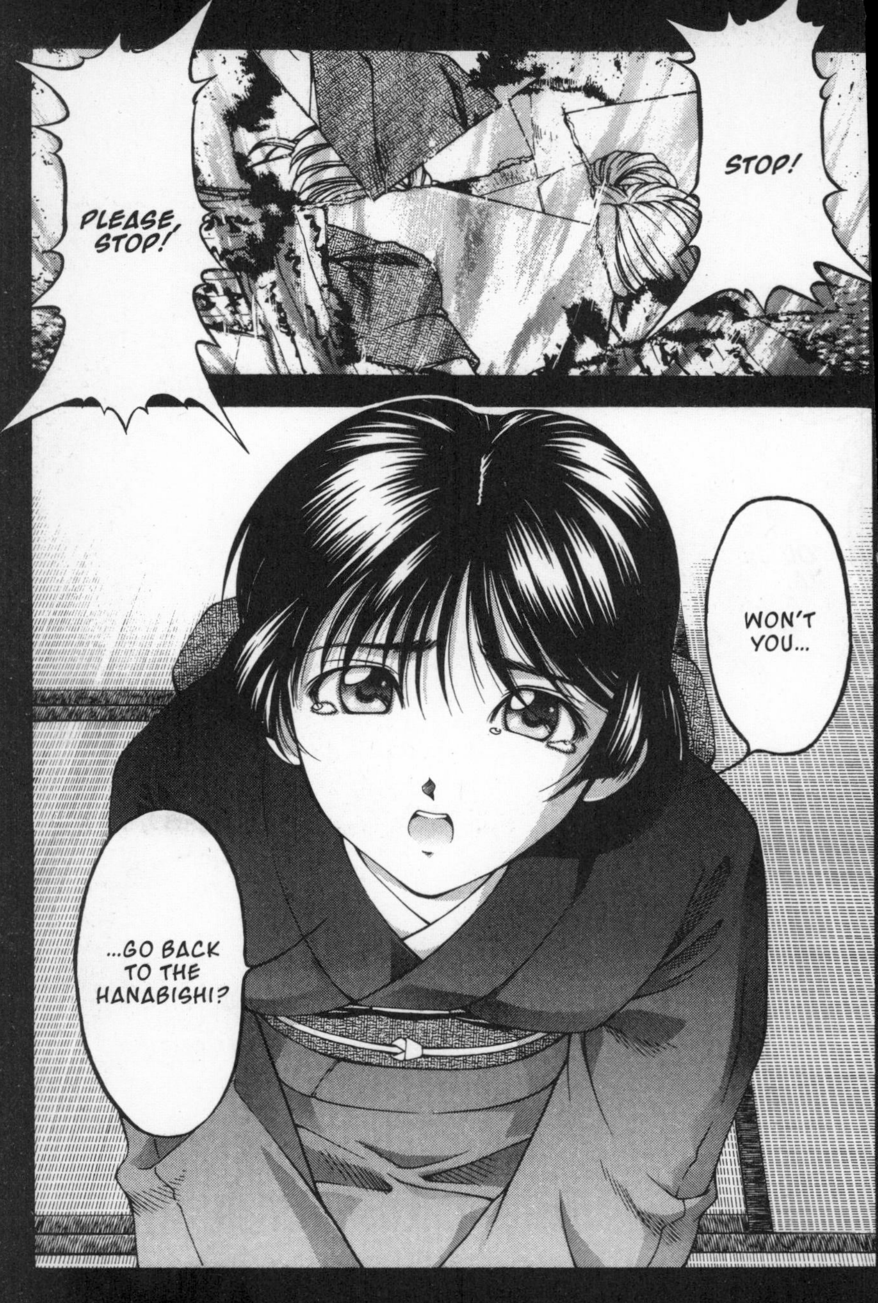
STOP!
PLEASE, STOP!
WON'T YOU...
...GO BACK TO THE HANABISHI?

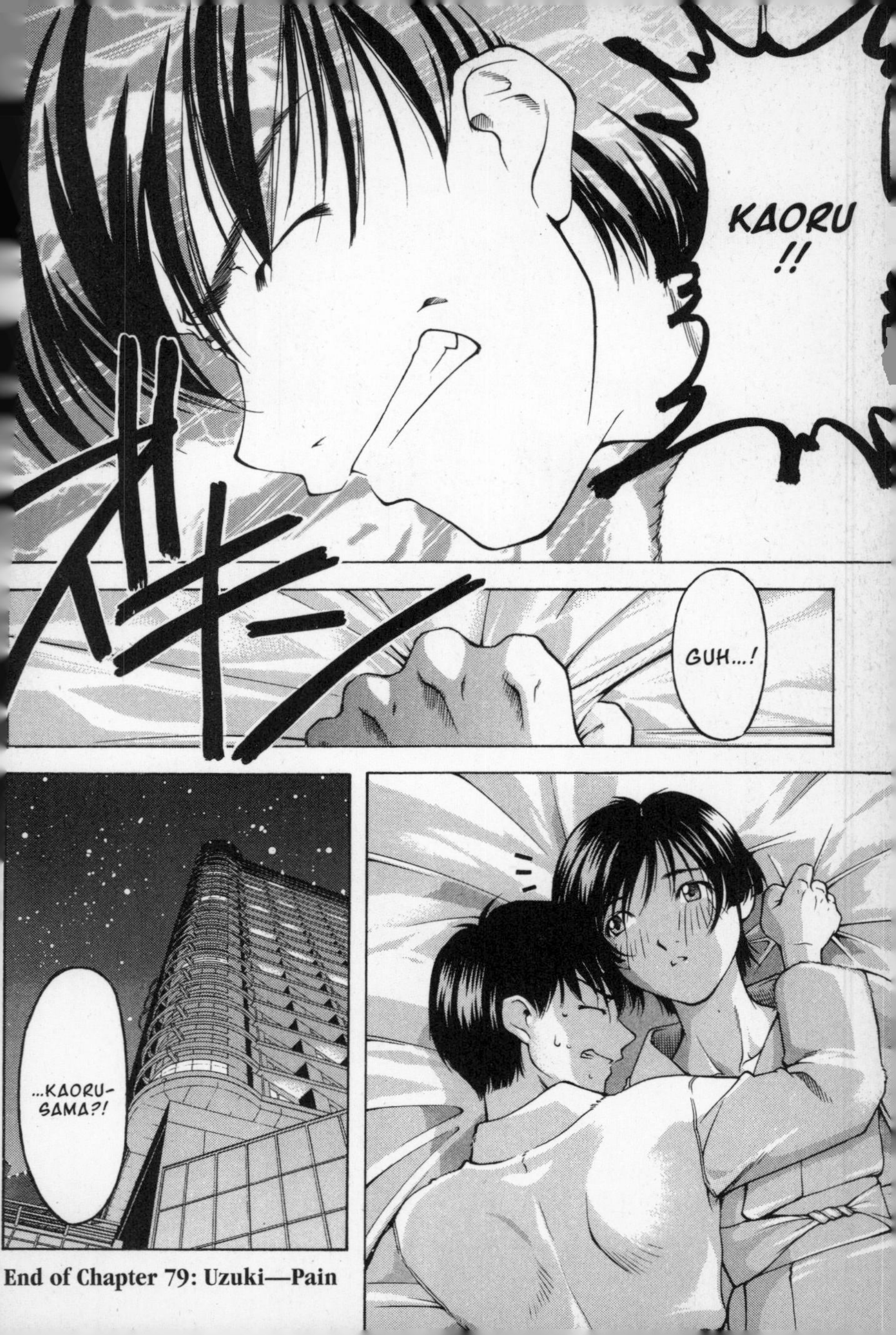
KAORU !!
ズキーン
GUH...!
...KAORU-SAMA?!

End of Chapter 79: Uzuki—Pain

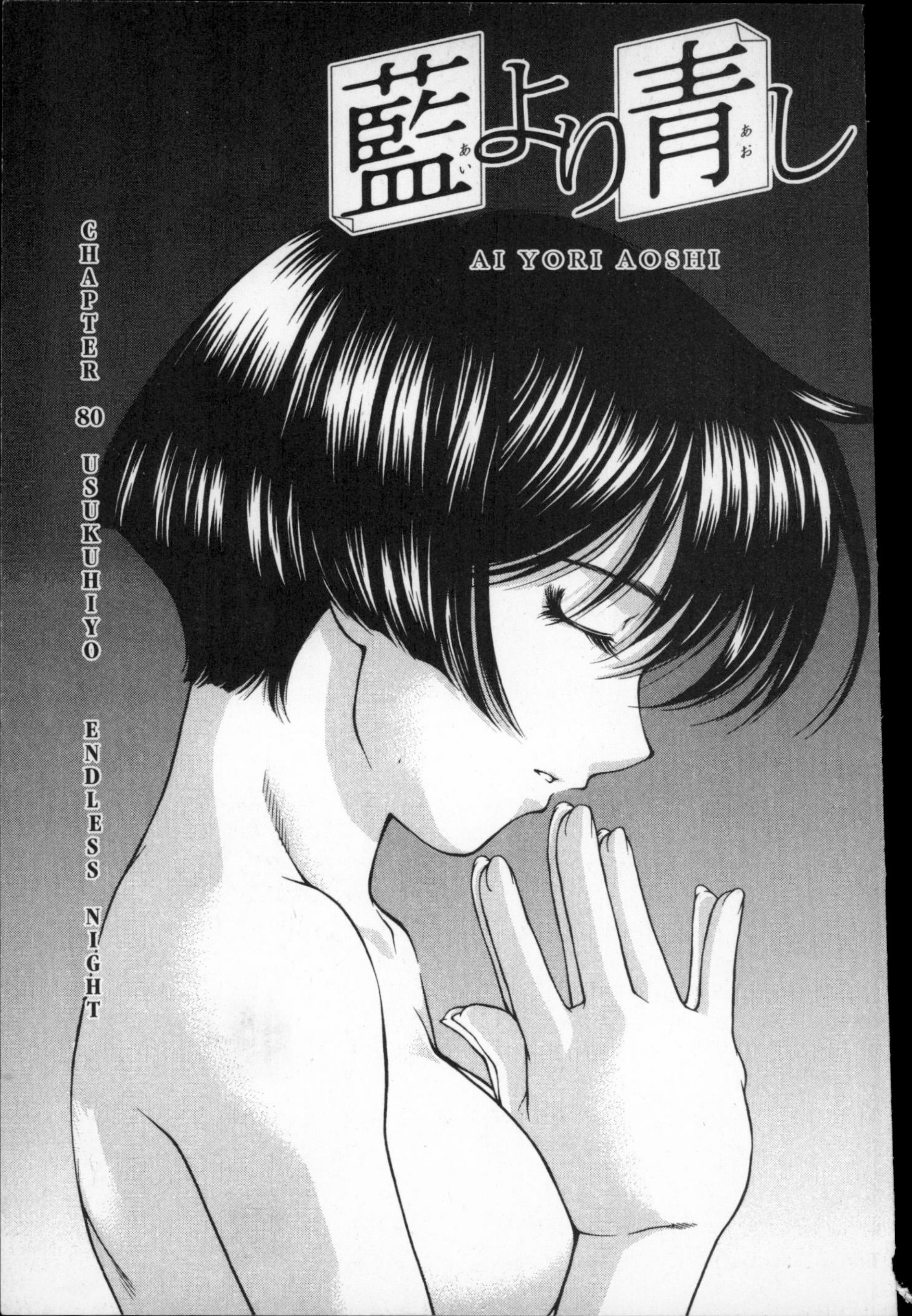
藍より青し
あい
あお
AI YORI AOSHI
CHAPTER 80 USUKUHIYO ENDLESS NIGHT

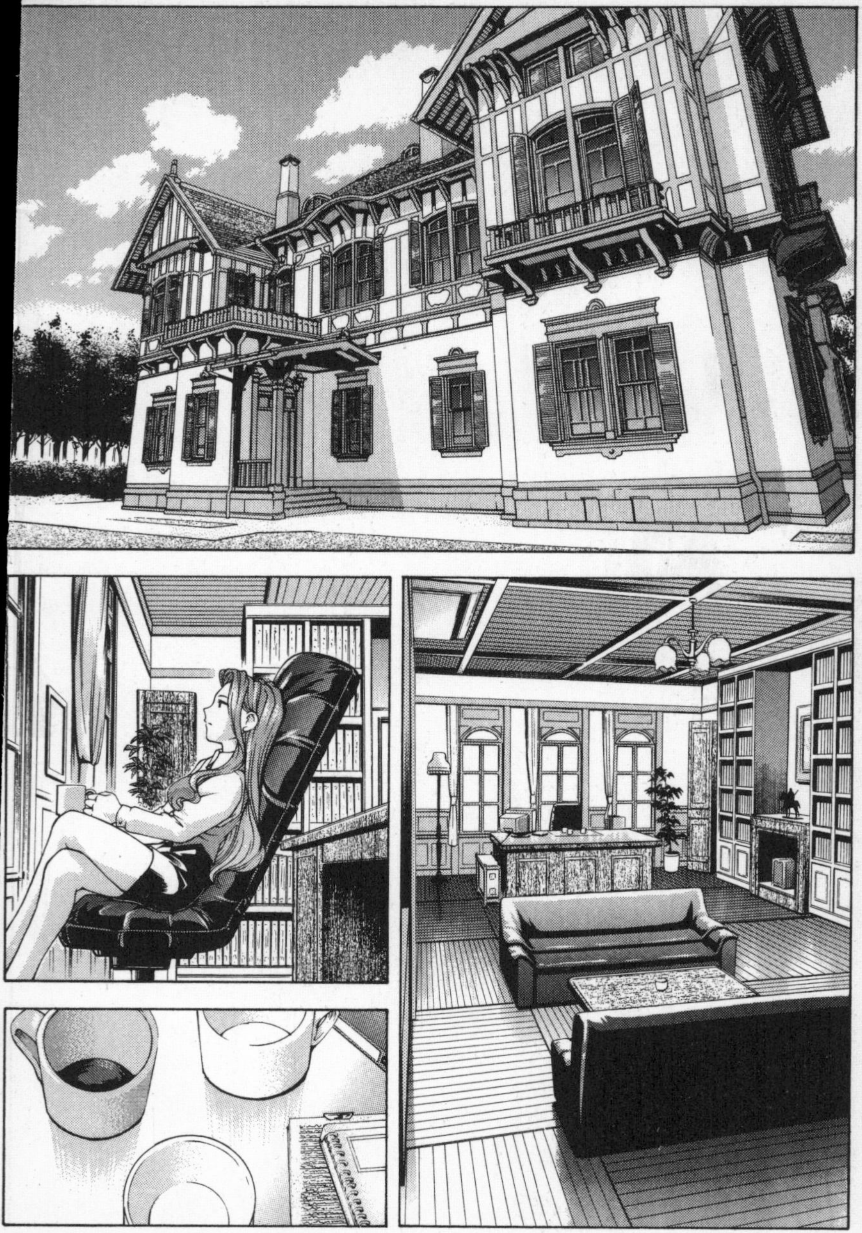

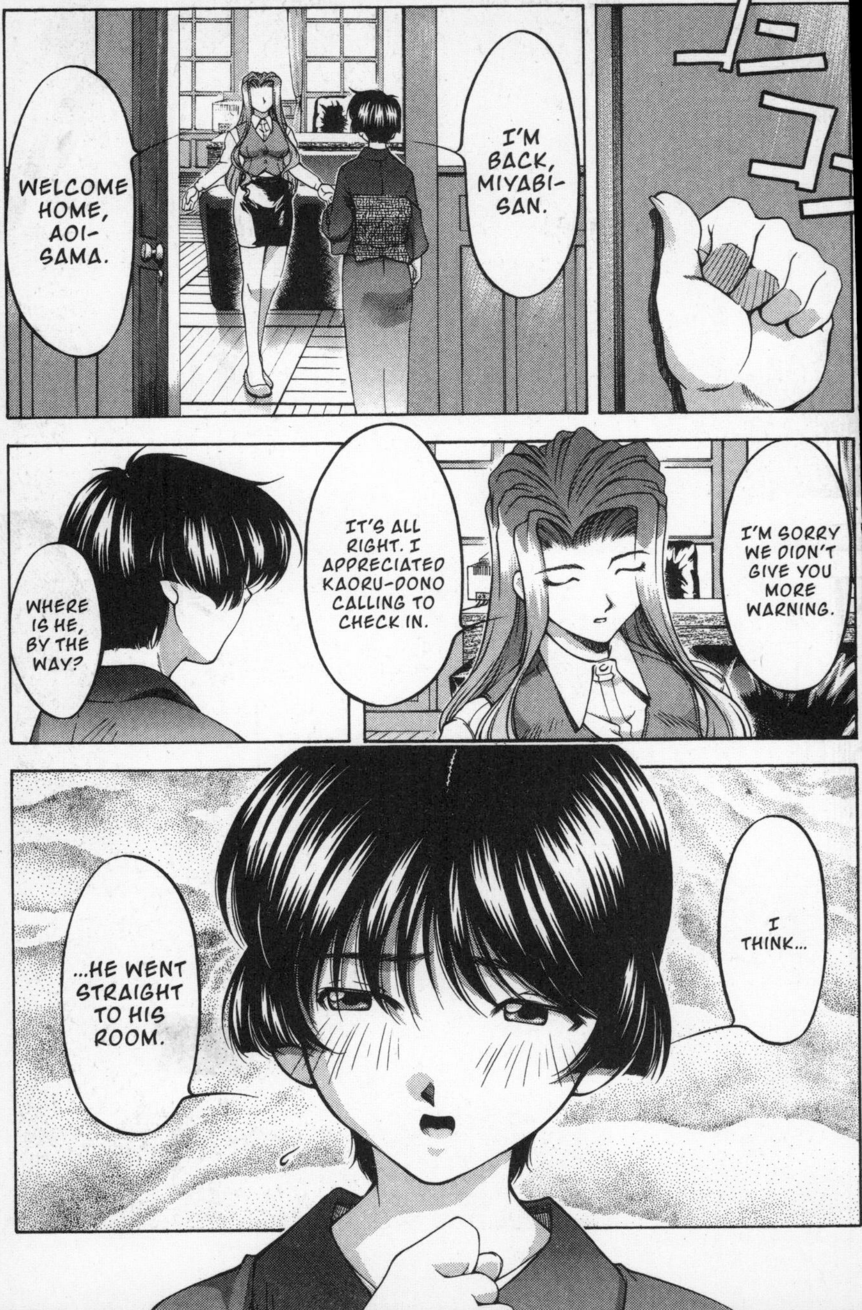
I'M BACK, MIYABI-SAN.
WELCOME HOME, AOI-SAMA.
I'M SORRY WE DIDN'T GIVE YOU MORE WARNING.
IT'S ALL RIGHT. I APPRECIATED KAORU-DONO CALLING TO CHECK IN.
WHERE IS HE, BY THE WAY?
I THINK...
...HE WENT STRAIGHT TO HIS ROOM.

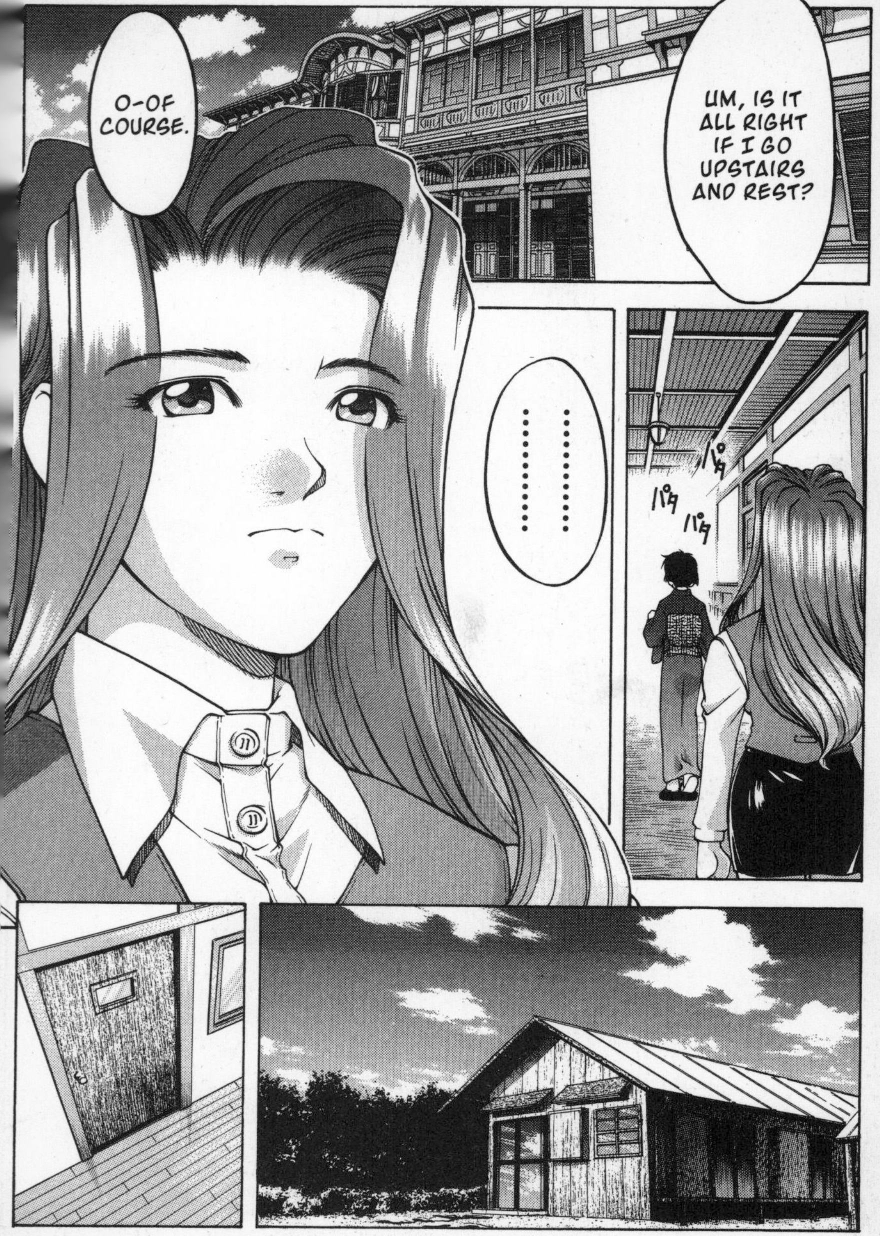
UM, IS IT ALL RIGHT IF I GO UPSTAIRS AND REST?
O-OF COURSE.
パタ
パタ
パタ
……

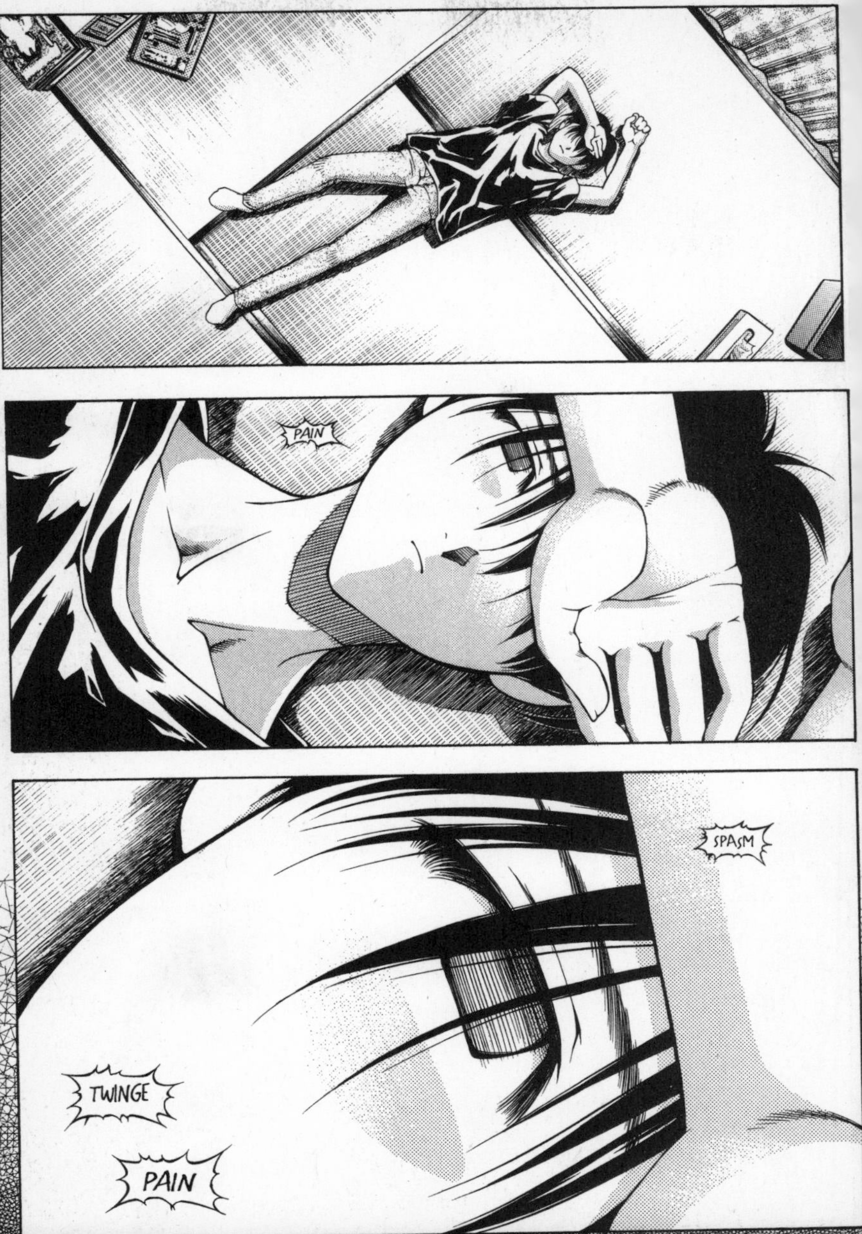
PAIN
SPASM
TWINGE
PAIN

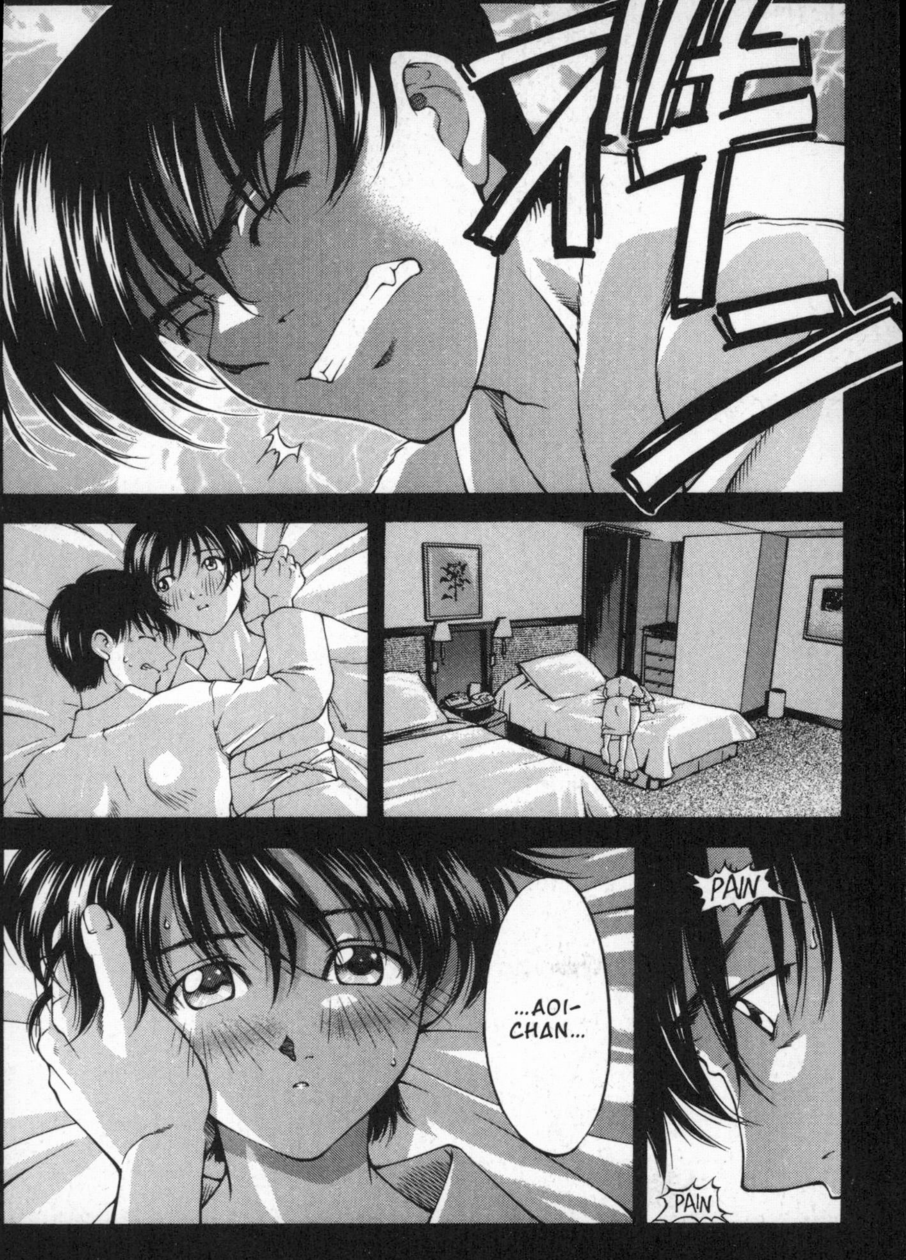
PAIN
PAIN
...AOI-CHAN...

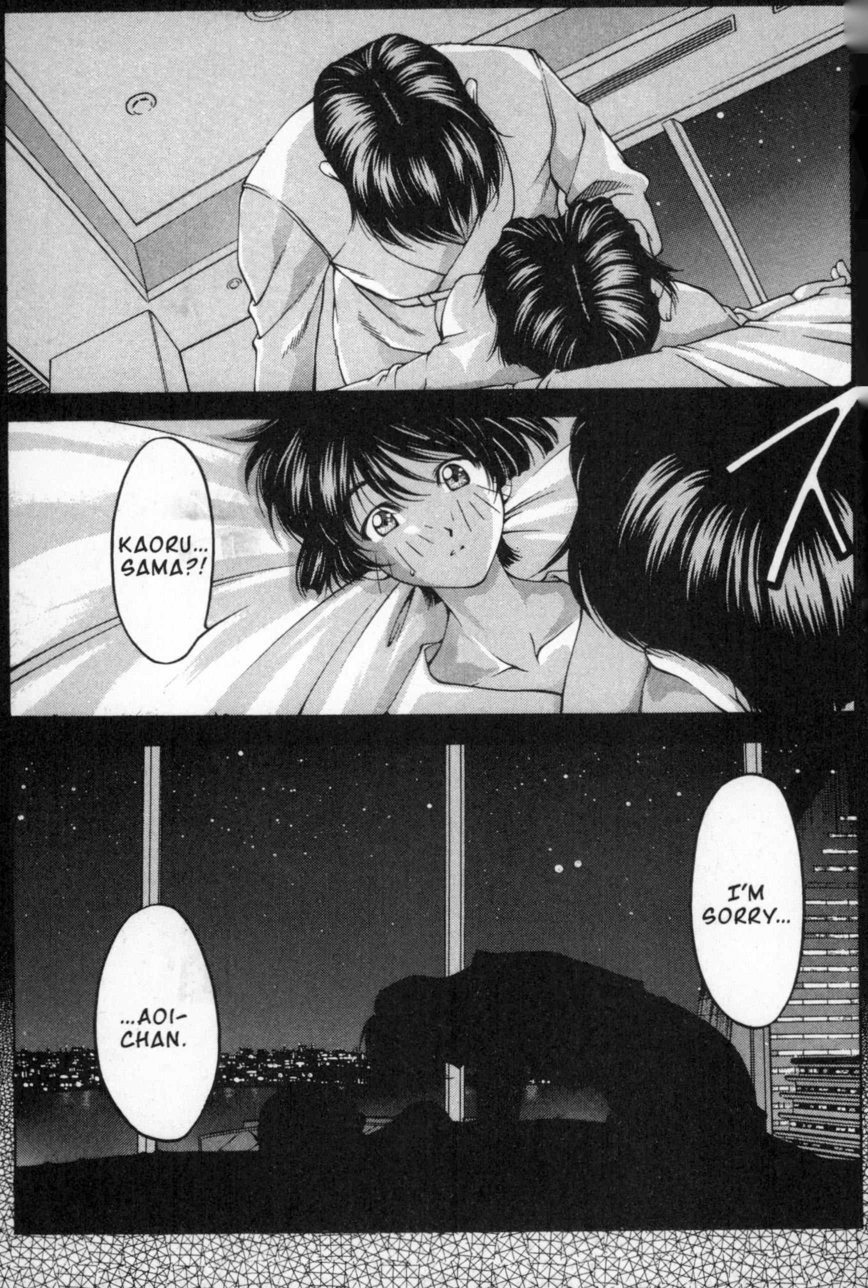
KAORU... SAMA?!
I'M SORRY...
...AOI-CHAN.

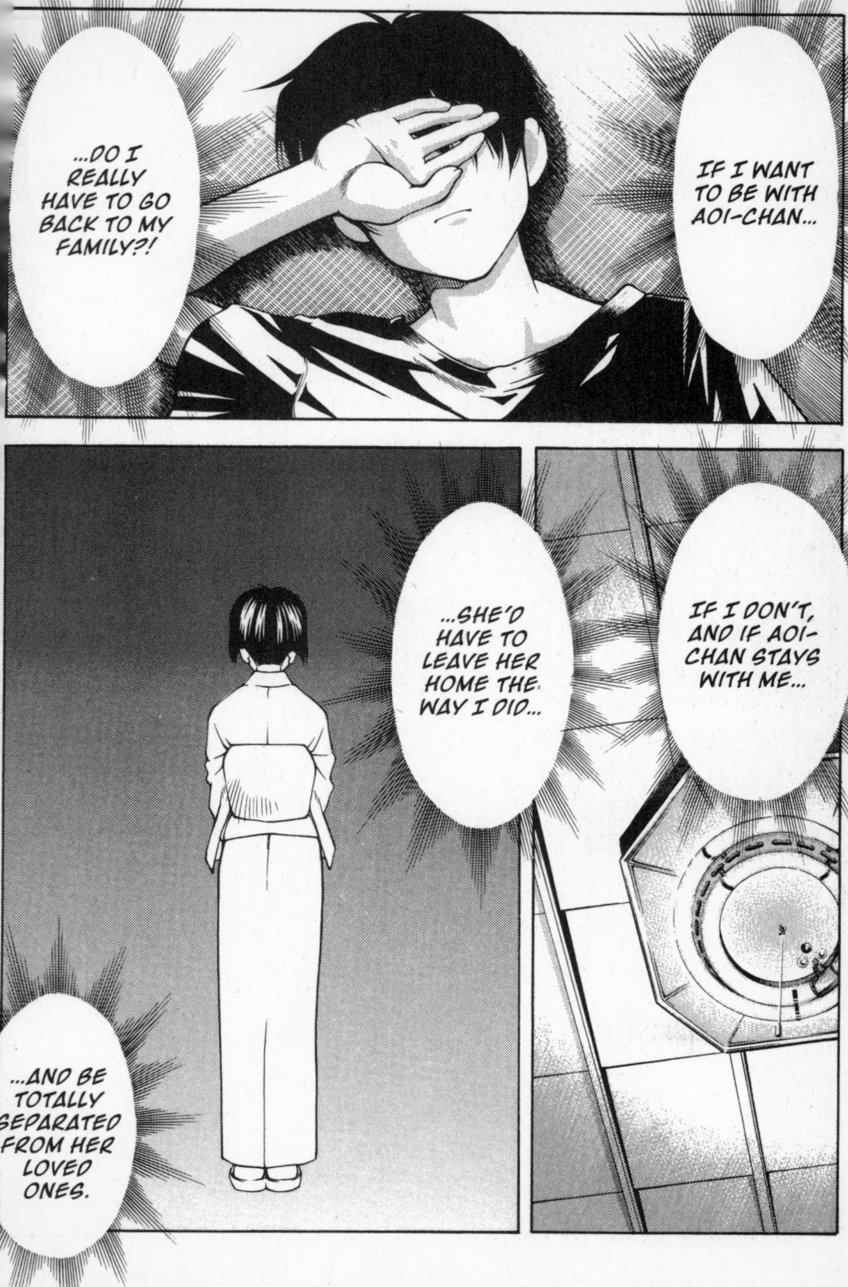
IF I WANT TO BE WITH AOI-CHAN...
...DO I REALLY HAVE TO GO BACK TO MY FAMILY?!
IF I DON'T, AND IF AOI-CHAN STAYS WITH ME...
...SHE'D HAVE TO LEAVE HER HOME THE WAY I DID...
...AND BE TOTALLY SEPARATED FROM HER LOVED ONES.

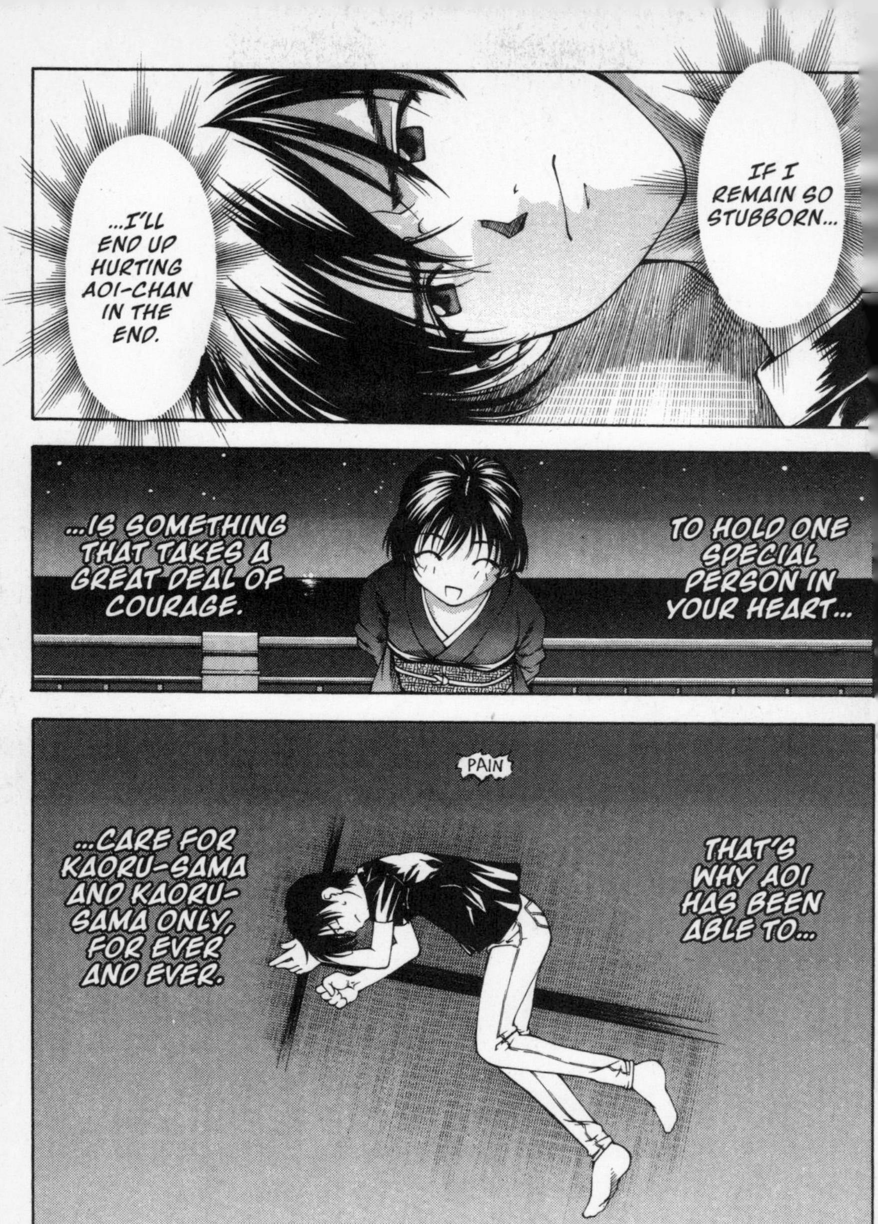
IF I REMAIN SO STUBBORN...
...I'LL END UP HURTING AOI-CHAN IN THE END.
TO HOLD ONE SPECIAL PERSON IN YOUR HEART...
...IS SOMETHING THAT TAKES A GREAT DEAL OF COURAGE.
PAIN
THAT'S WHY AOI HAS BEEN ABLE TO...
...CARE FOR KAORU-SAMA AND KAORU-SAMA ONLY, FOR EVER AND EVER.

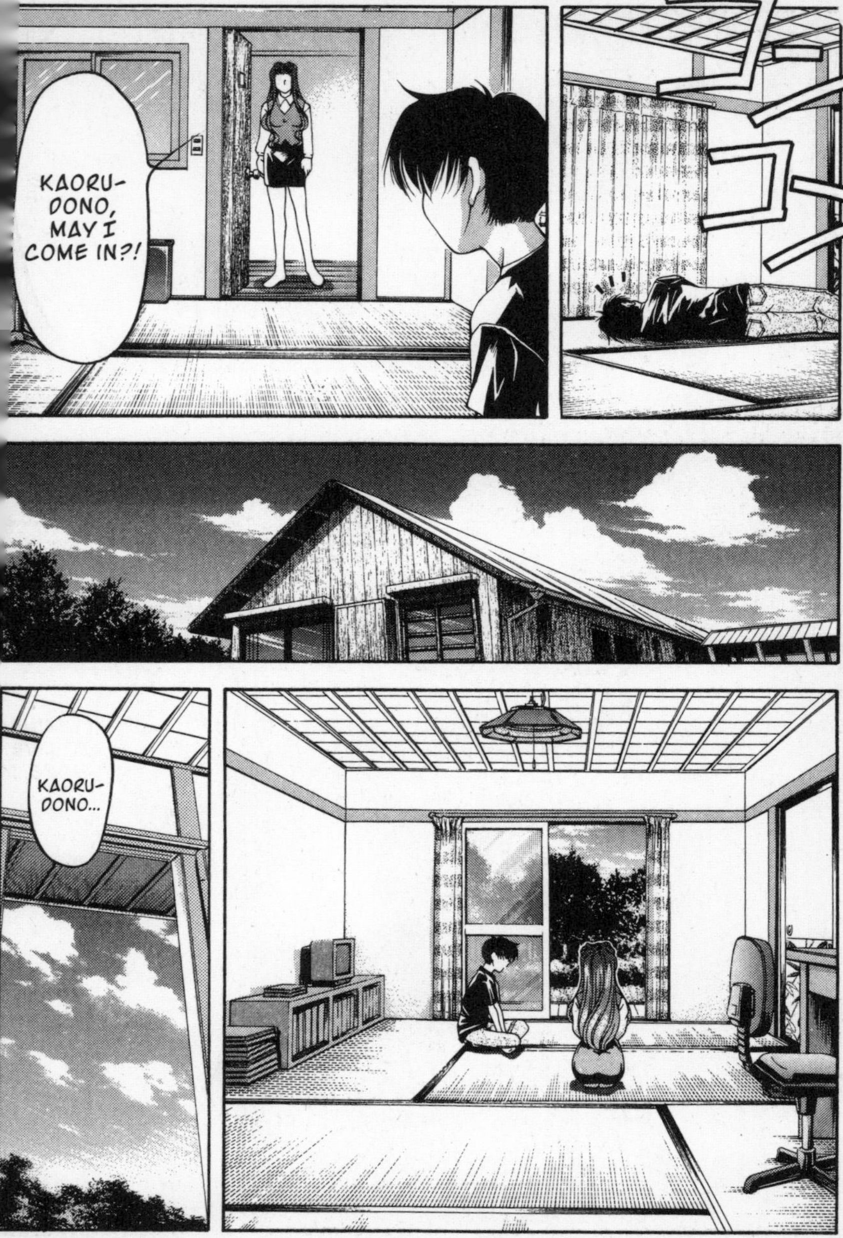
KAORU-DONO, MAY I COME IN?!
KAORU-DONO...

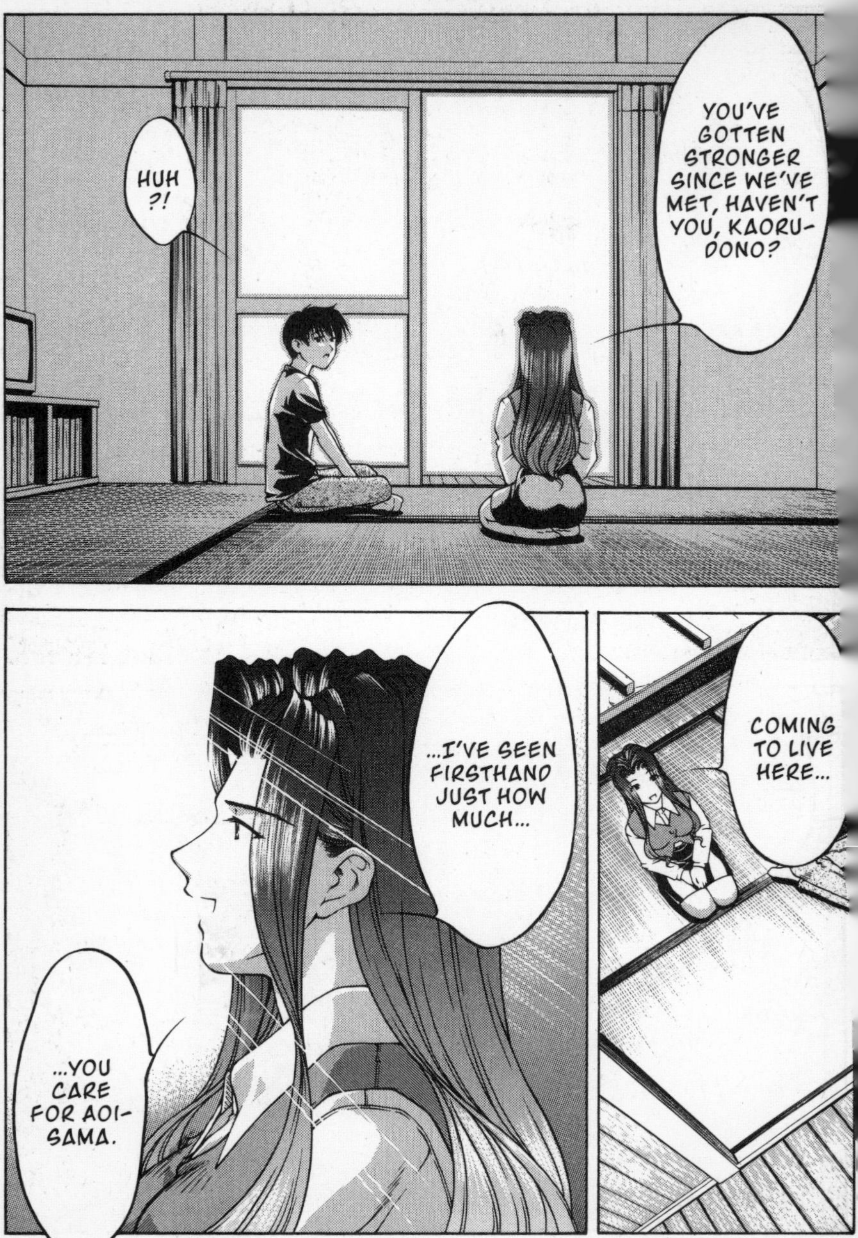
YOU'VE GOTTEN STRONGER SINCE WE'VE MET, HAVEN'T YOU, KAORU-DONO?
HUH?!
COMING TO LIVE HERE...
...I'VE SEEN FIRSTHAND JUST HOW MUCH...
...YOU CARE FOR AOI-SAMA.

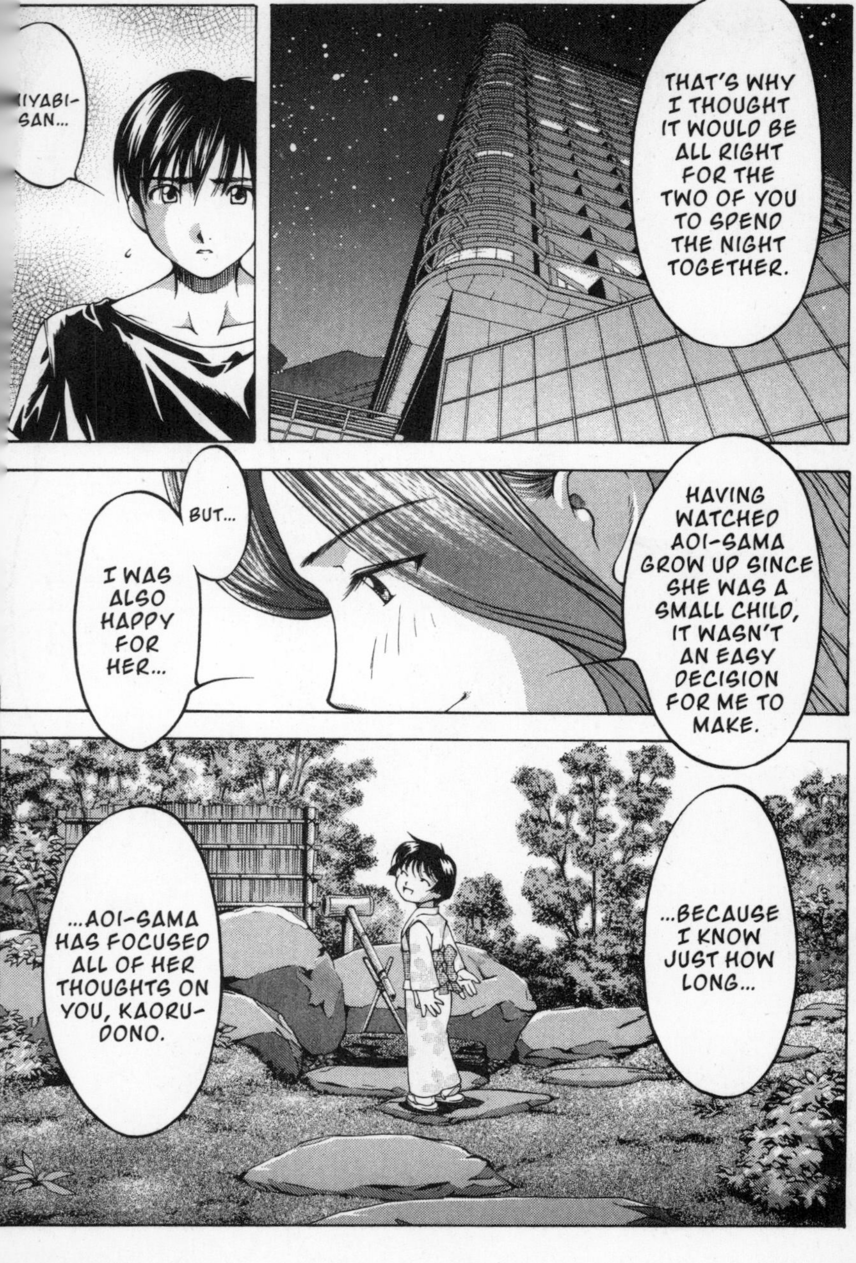
THAT'S WHY I THOUGHT IT WOULD BE ALL RIGHT FOR THE TWO OF YOU TO SPEND THE NIGHT TOGETHER.
IYABI-SAN...
HAVING WATCHED AOI-SAMA GROW UP SINCE SHE WAS A SMALL CHILD, IT WASN'T AN EASY DECISION FOR ME TO MAKE.
BUT...
I WAS ALSO HAPPY FOR HER...
...BECAUSE I KNOW JUST HOW LONG...
...AOI-SAMA HAS FOCUSED ALL OF HER THOUGHTS ON YOU, KAORU-DONO.

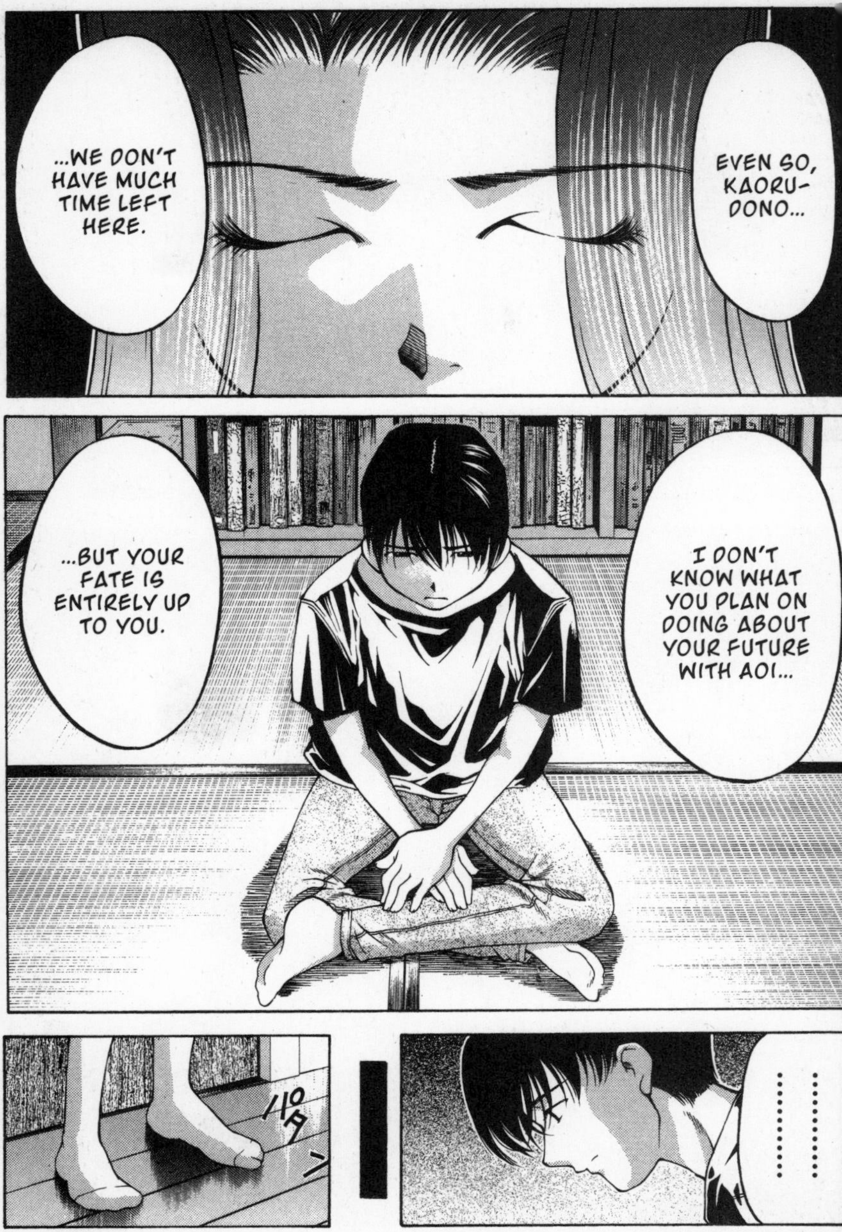
EVEN SO, KAORU-DONO...
...WE DON'T HAVE MUCH TIME LEFT HERE.
I DON'T KNOW WHAT YOU PLAN ON DOING ABOUT YOUR FUTURE WITH AOI...
...BUT YOUR FATE IS ENTIRELY UP TO YOU.
......
パタ

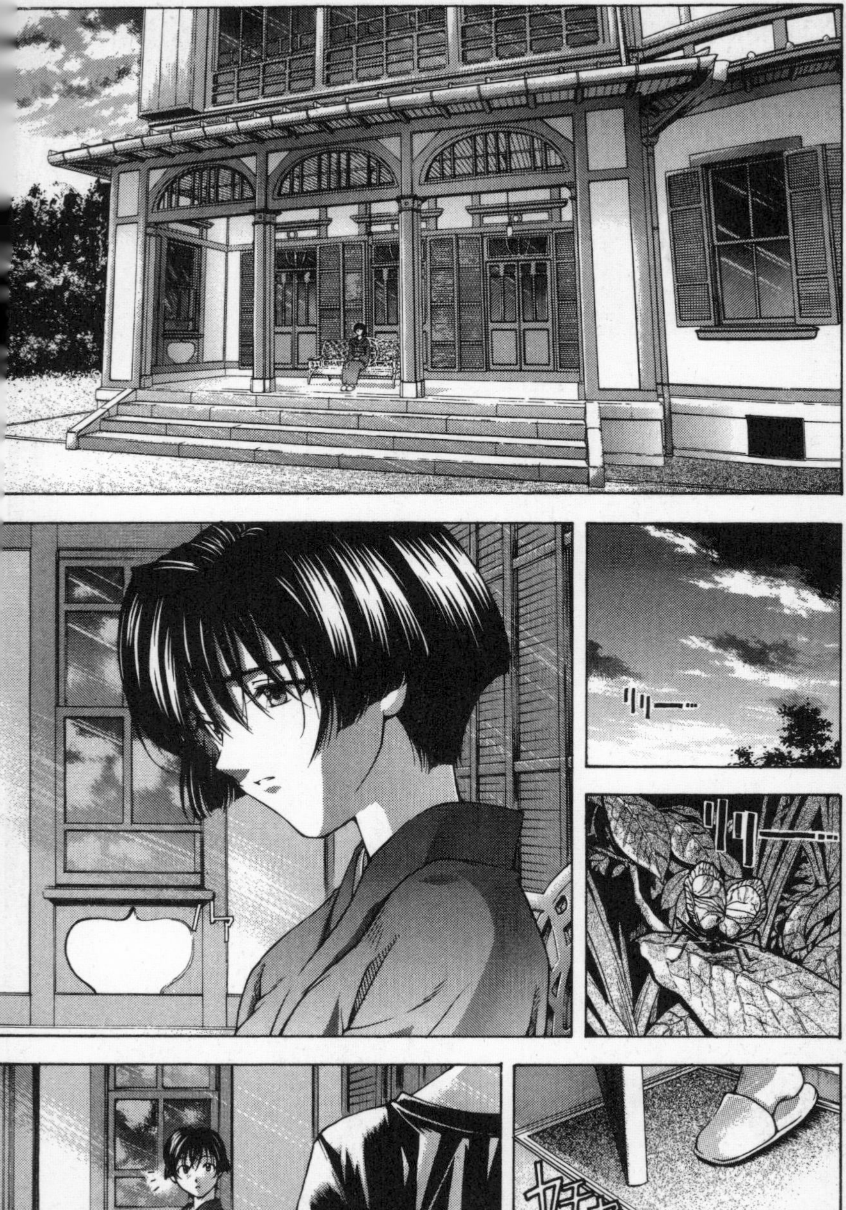
リリー…
リリー…
カチャ

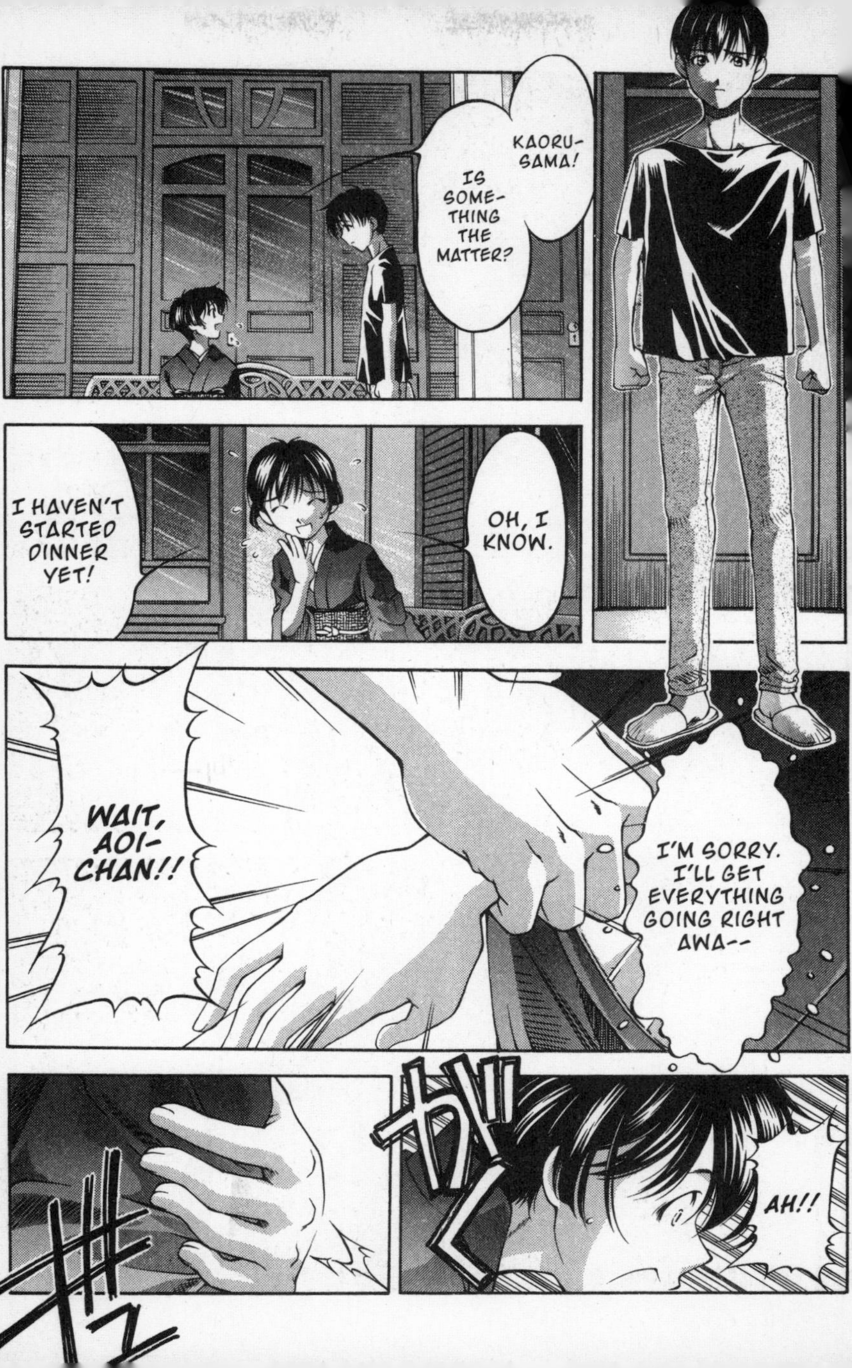
KAORU-SAMA!
IS SOME-THING THE MATTER?
OH, I KNOW.
I HAVEN'T STARTED DINNER YET!
I'M SORRY. I'LL GET EVERYTHING GOING RIGHT AWA--
WAIT, AOI-CHAN!!
AH!!

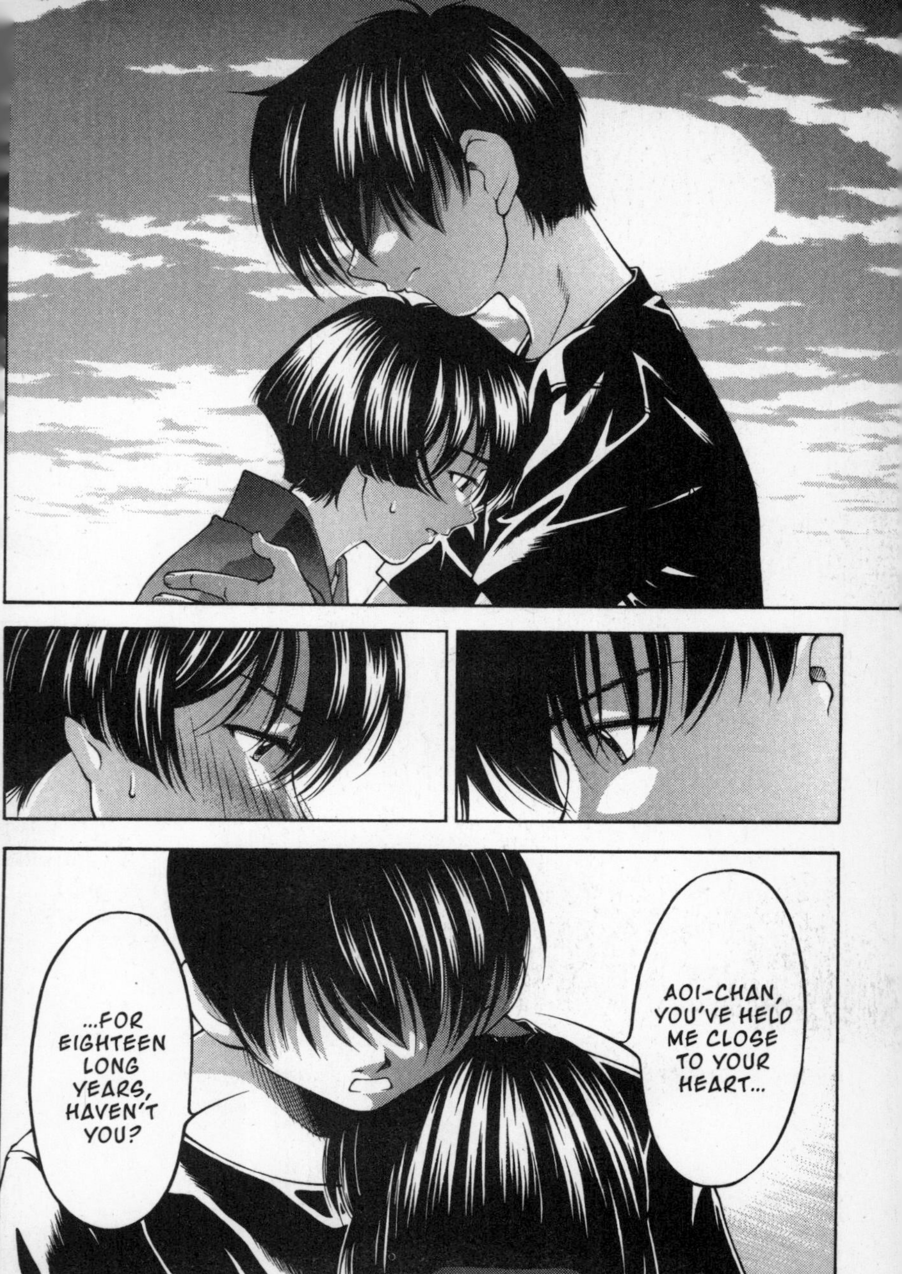
AOI-CHAN, YOU'VE HELD ME CLOSE TO YOUR HEART...
...FOR EIGHTEEN LONG YEARS, HAVEN'T YOU?

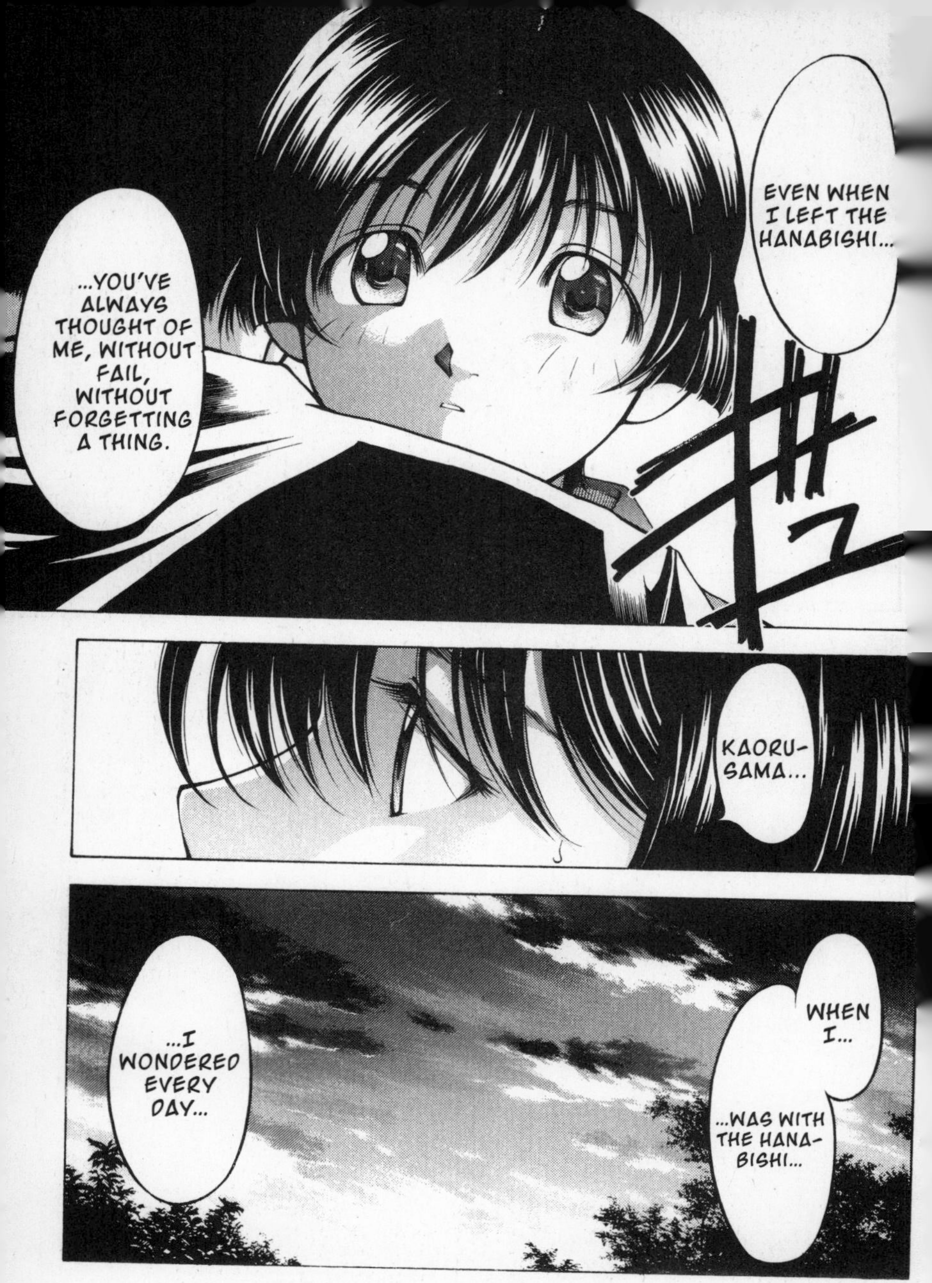
EVEN WHEN I LEFT THE HANABISHI...
...YOU'VE ALWAYS THOUGHT OF ME, WITHOUT FAIL, WITHOUT FORGETTING A THING.
KAORU-SAMA...
WHEN I...
...WAS WITH THE HANA-BISHI...
...I WONDERED EVERY DAY...

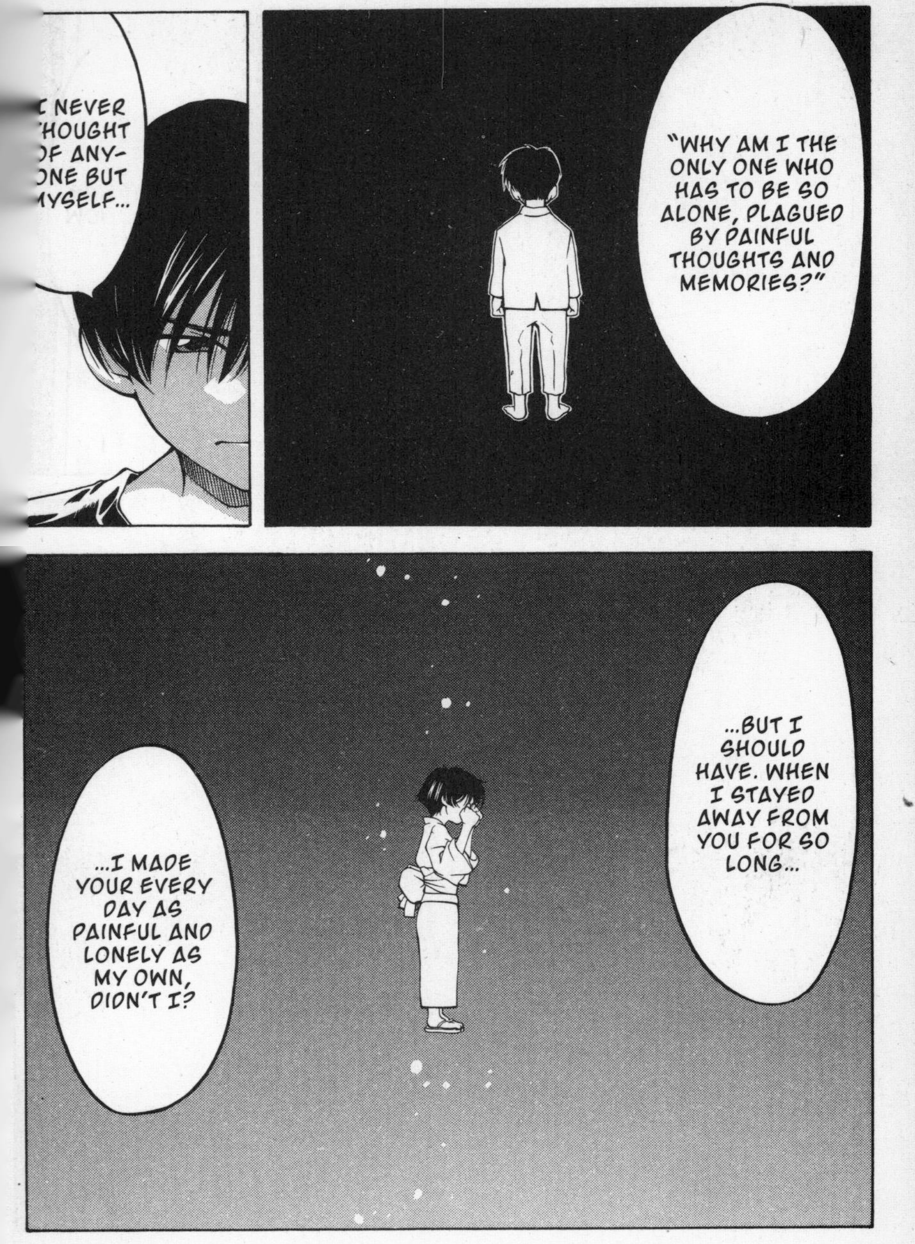
"WHY AM I THE ONLY ONE WHO HAS TO BE SO ALONE, PLAGUED BY PAINFUL THOUGHTS AND MEMORIES?"
I NEVER THOUGHT OF ANY-ONE BUT MYSELF...
...BUT I SHOULD HAVE. WHEN I STAYED AWAY FROM YOU FOR SO LONG...
...I MADE YOUR EVERY DAY AS PAINFUL AND LONELY AS MY OWN, DIDN'T I?

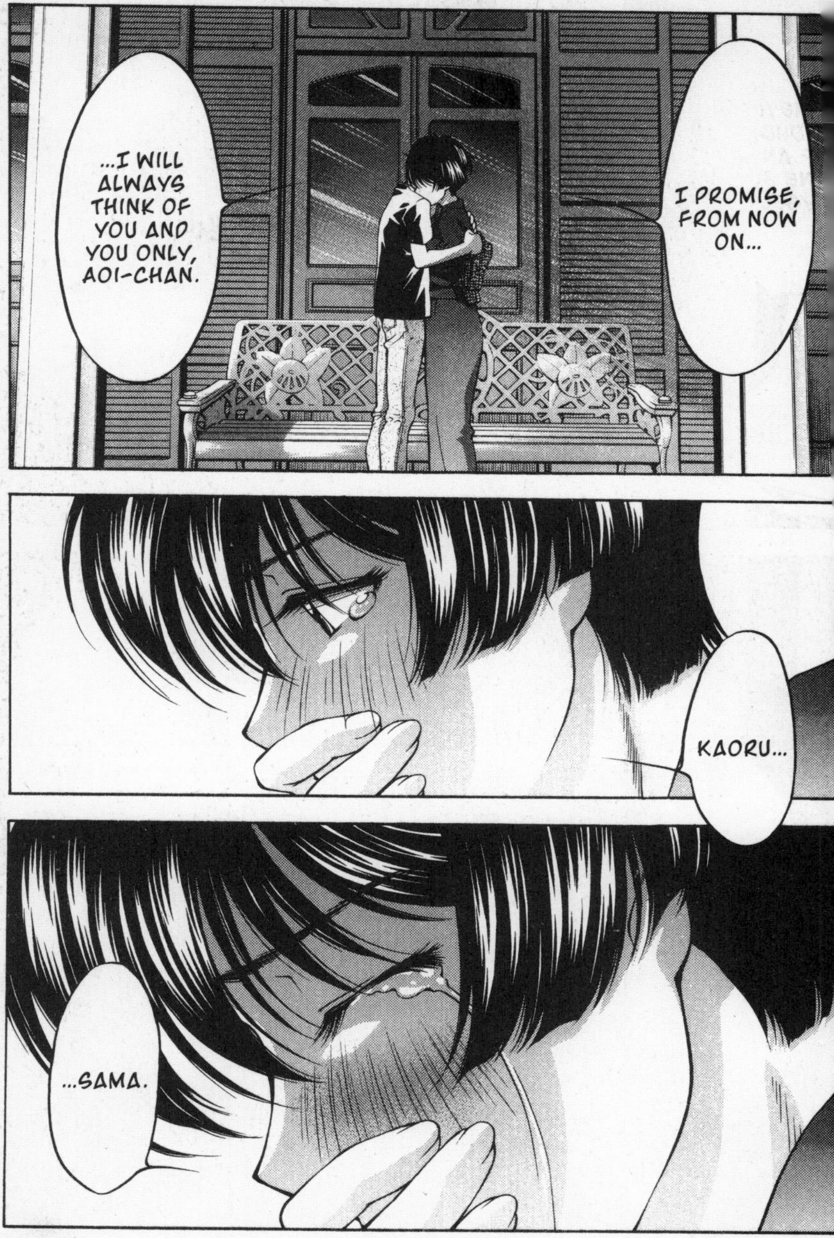
I PROMISE, FROM NOW ON...
...I WILL ALWAYS THINK OF YOU AND YOU ONLY, AOI-CHAN.
KAORU...
...SAMA.

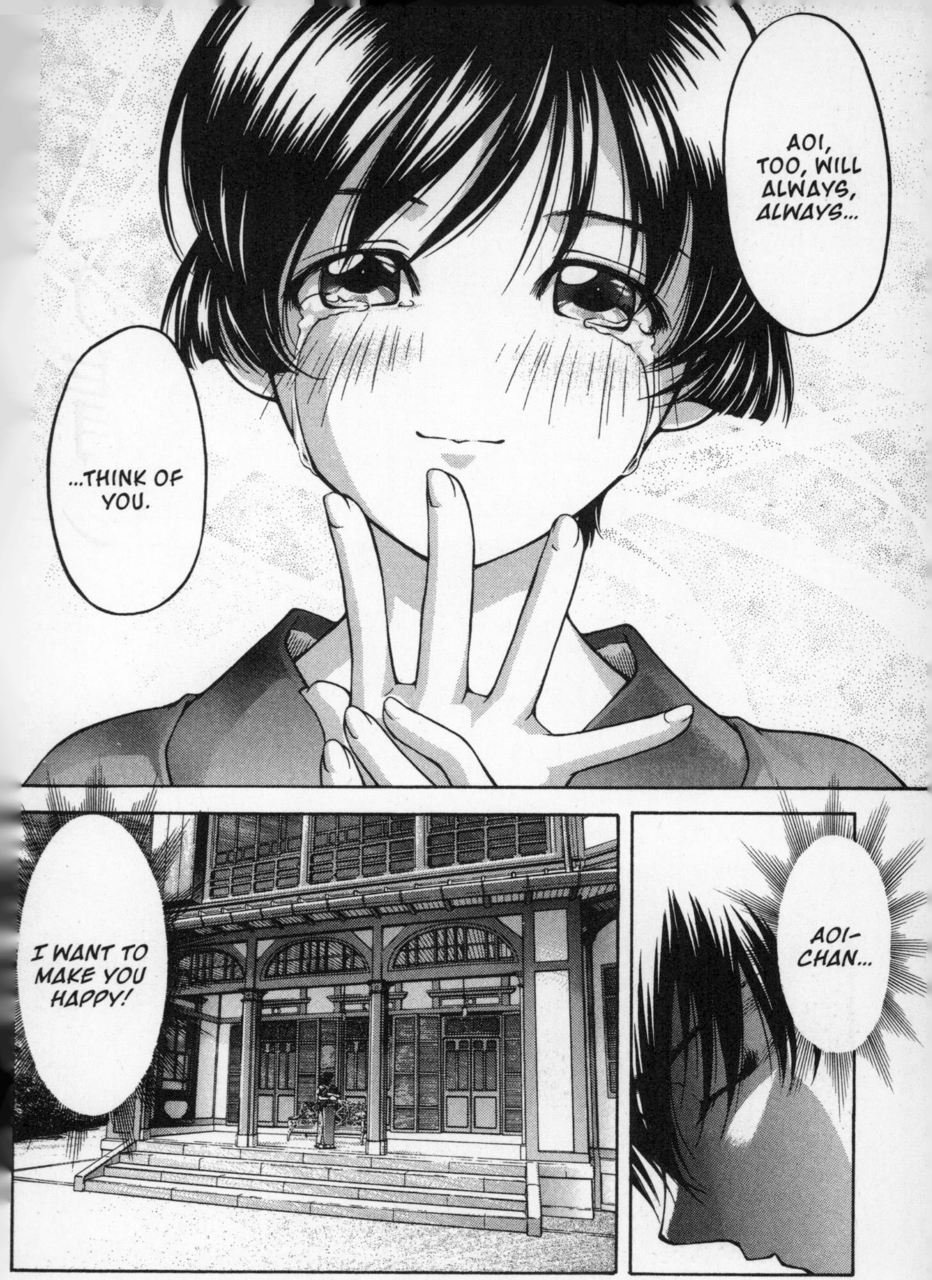
AOI, TOO, WILL ALWAYS, ALWAYS...
...THINK OF YOU.
AOI-CHAN...
I WANT TO MAKE YOU HAPPY!

End of Chapter 80: Tsukuhiyo—Endless Night

藍(あい)より青(あお)し

AI YORI AOSHI

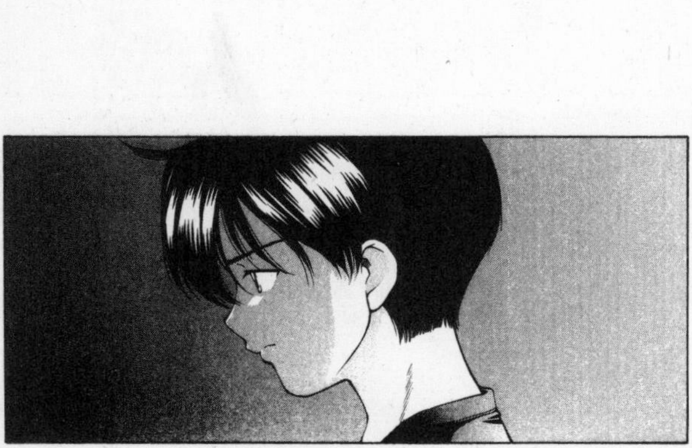

Ai-Ao Theatre, part 21:

Sadness

...Ai-Ao anime!

sigh

I wanted to see more...

藍（あい）より青（あお）し

AI YORI AOSHI

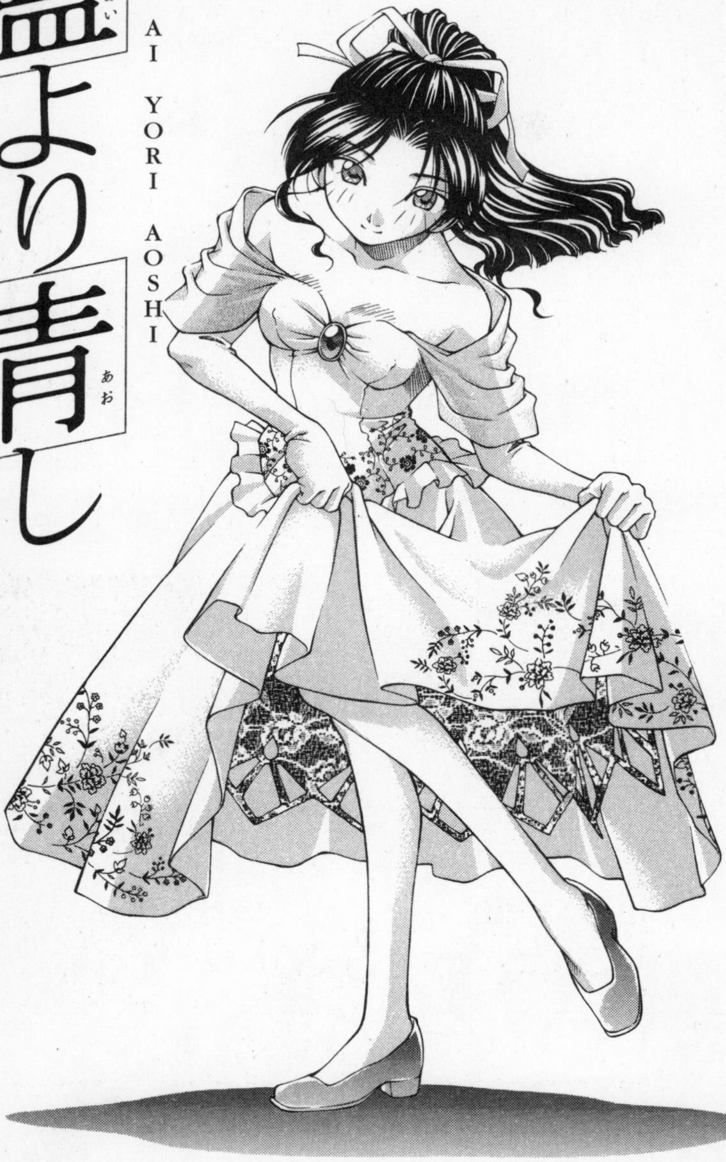

CHAPTER 81

UKIFUNE BOAT

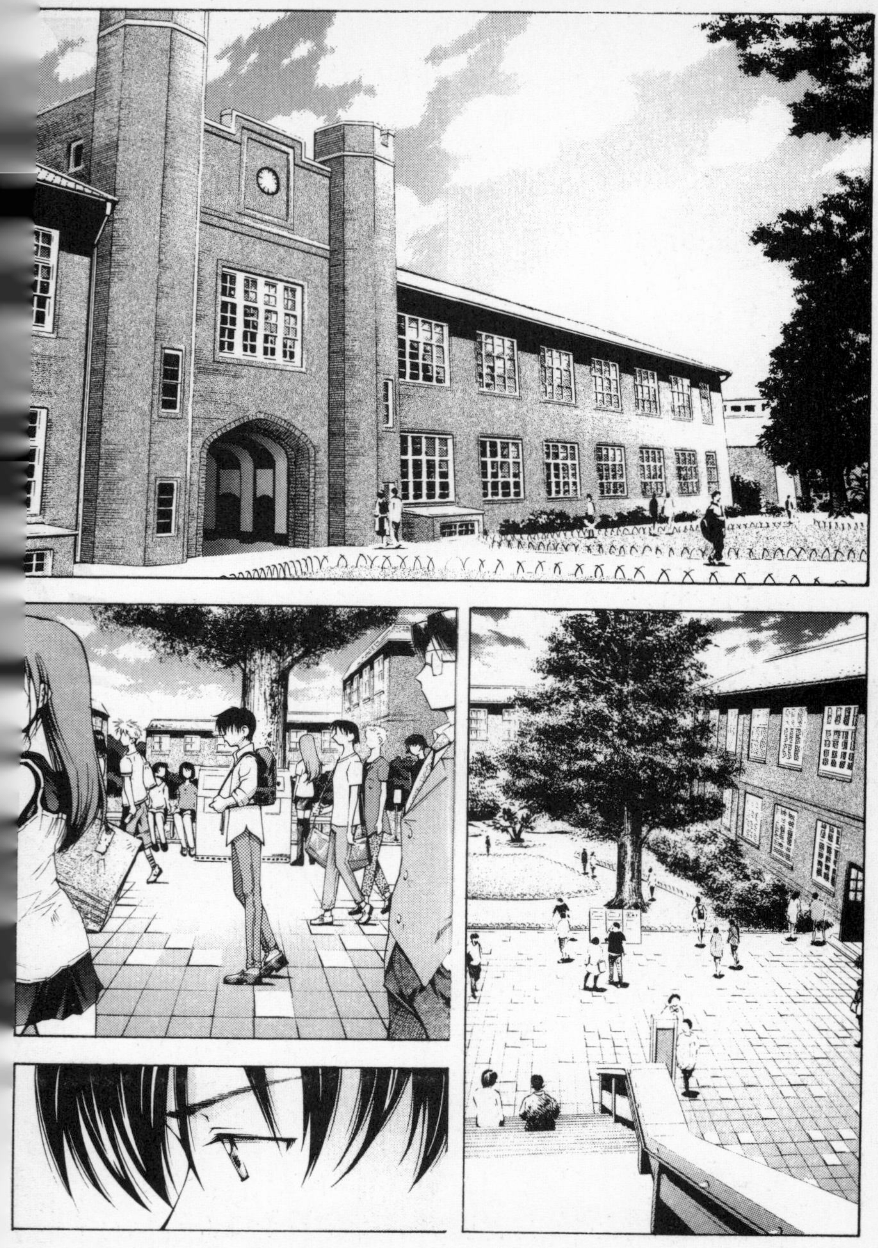

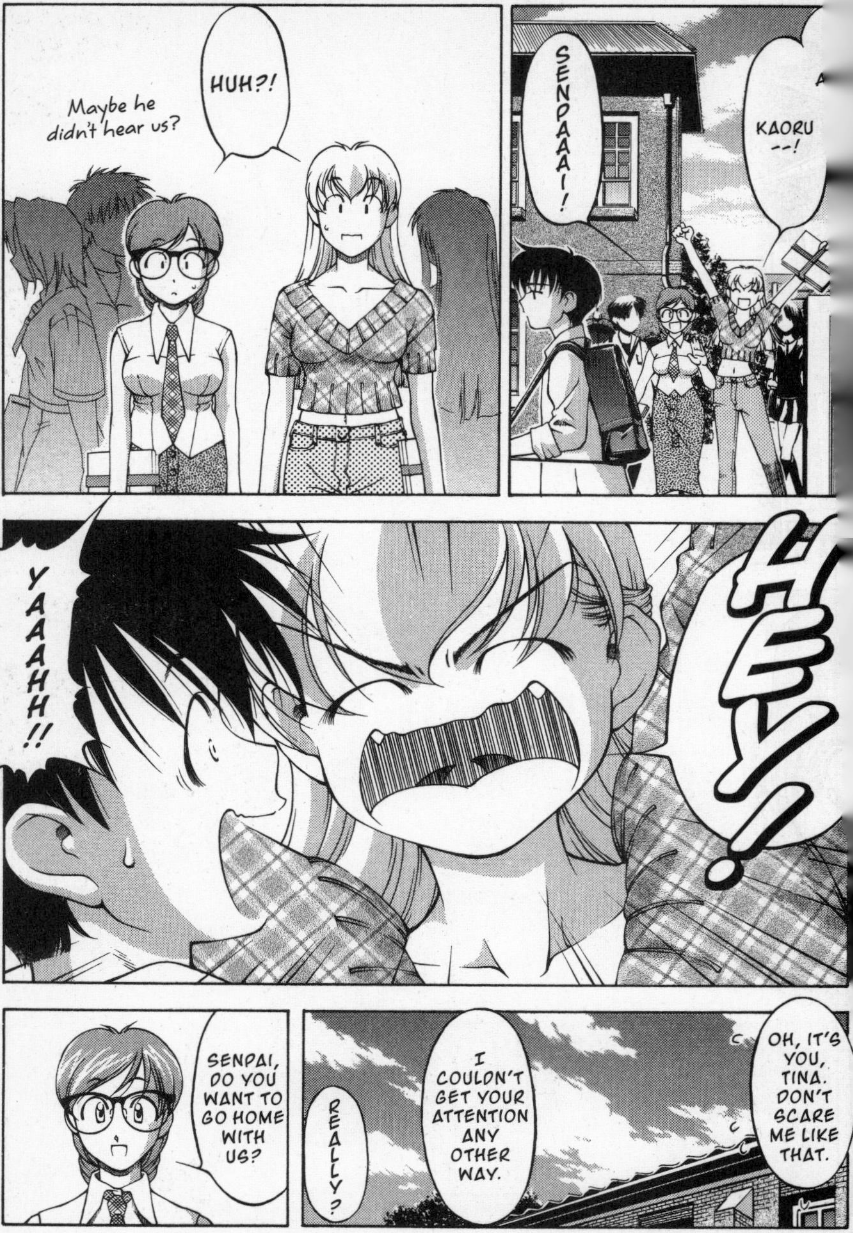
KAORU --!
SENPAAAI!
HUH?!
Maybe he didn't hear us?
HEY!!
YAAAAHH!!
OH, IT'S YOU, TINA. DON'T SCARE ME LIKE THAT.
I COULDN'T GET YOUR ATTENTION ANY OTHER WAY.
REALLY?
SENPAI, DO YOU WANT TO GO HOME WITH US?

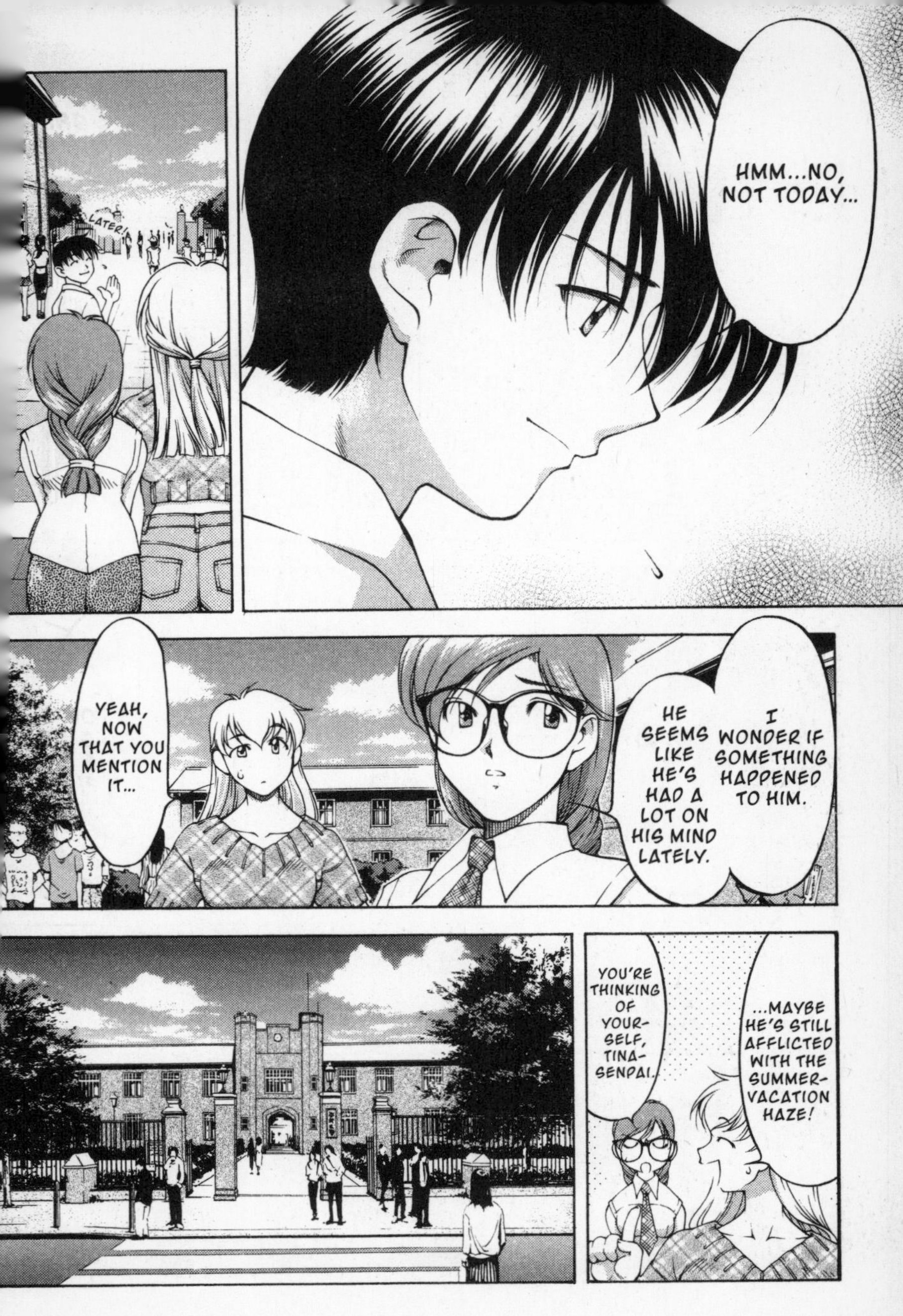
HMM...NO, NOT TODAY...
LATER!
I WONDER IF SOMETHING HAPPENED TO HIM.
HE SEEMS LIKE HE'S HAD A LOT ON HIS MIND LATELY.
YEAH, NOW THAT YOU MENTION IT...
...MAYBE HE'S STILL AFFLICTED WITH THE SUMMER-VACATION HAZE!
YOU'RE THINKING OF YOURSELF, TINA-SENPAI.

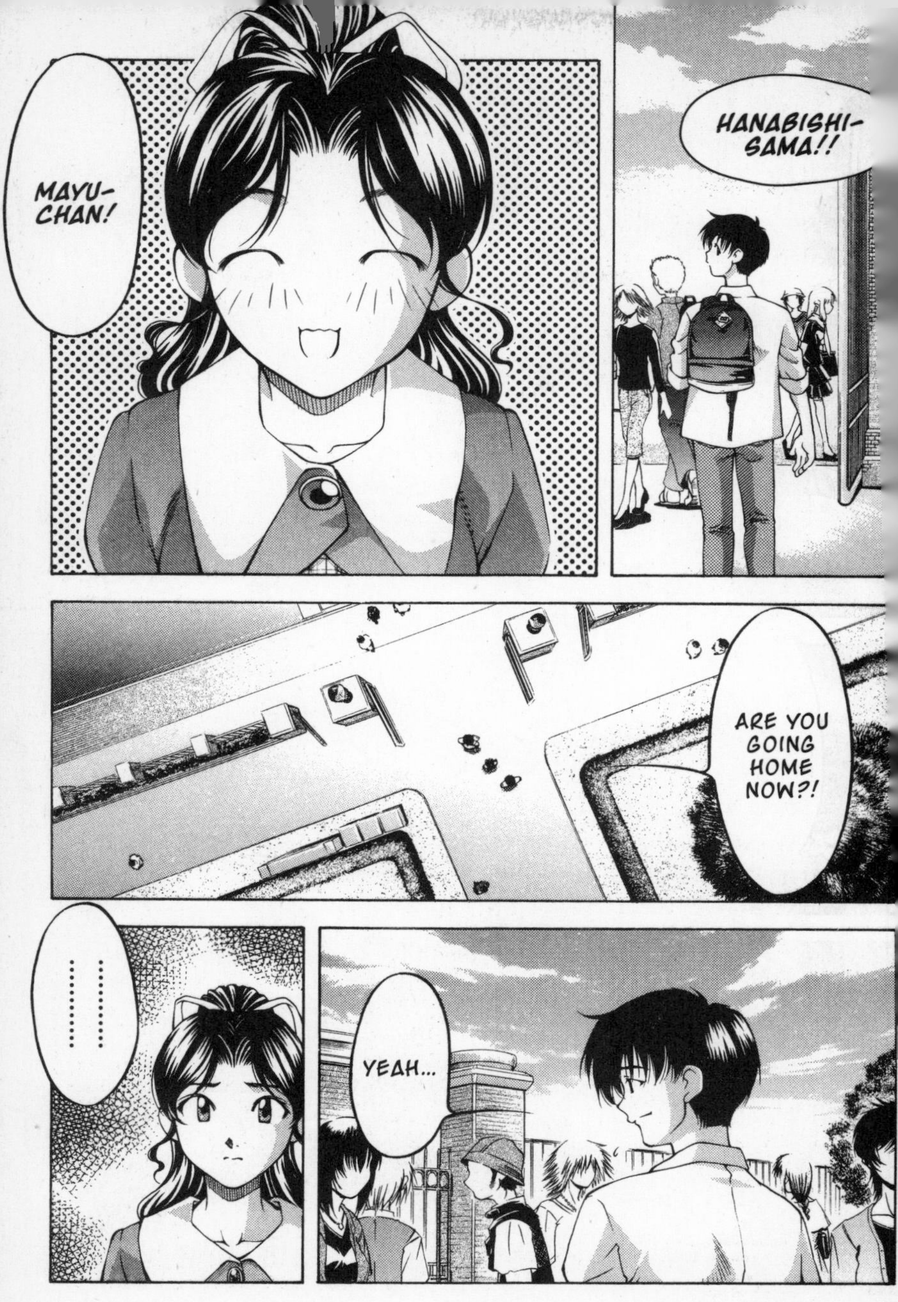
HANABISHI-SAMA!!
MAYU-CHAN!
ARE YOU GOING HOME NOW?!
YEAH...
......

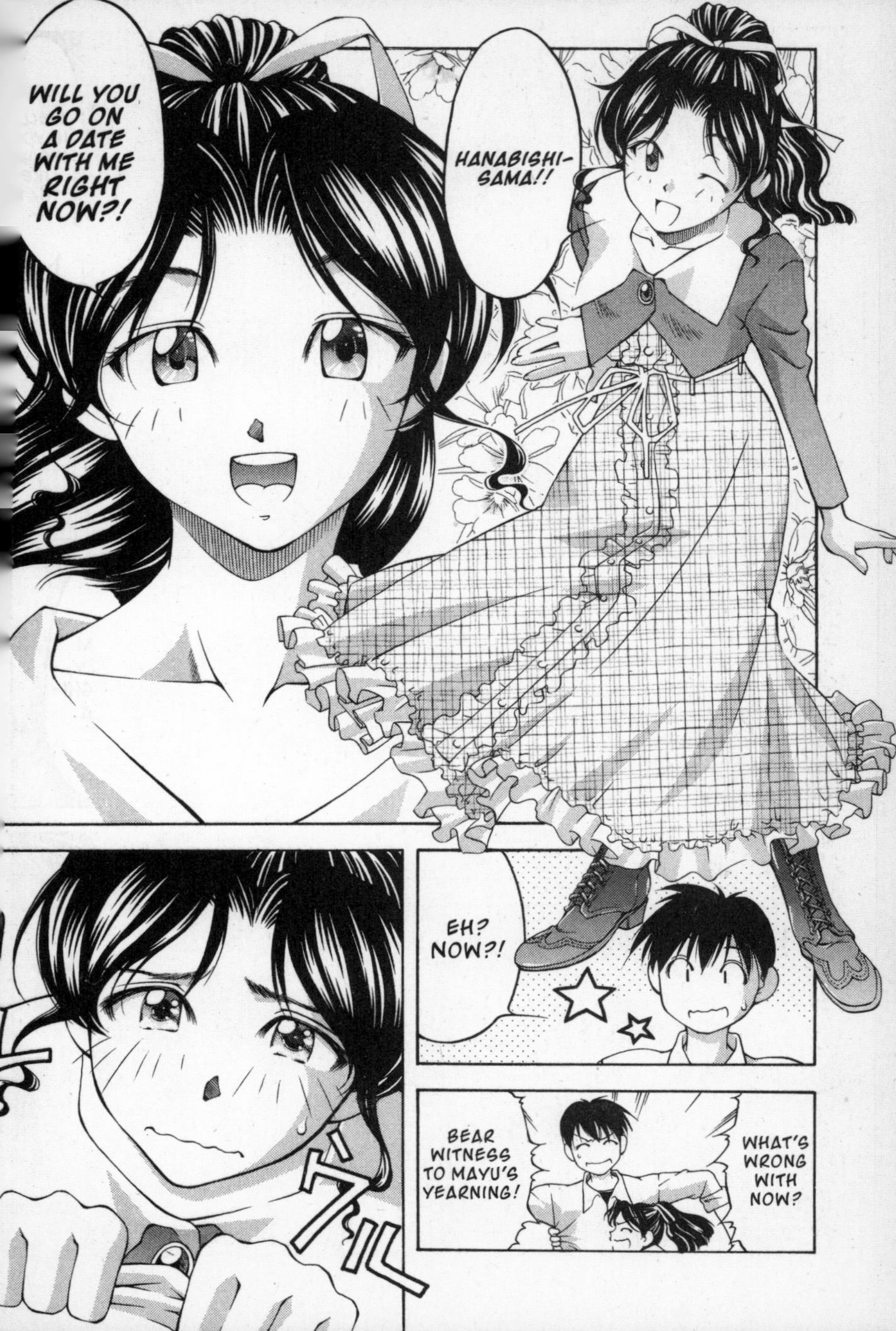
HANABISHI-SAMA!!
WILL YOU GO ON A DATE WITH ME RIGHT NOW?!
EH? NOW?!
WHAT'S WRONG WITH NOW?
BEAR WITNESS TO MAYU'S YEARNING!

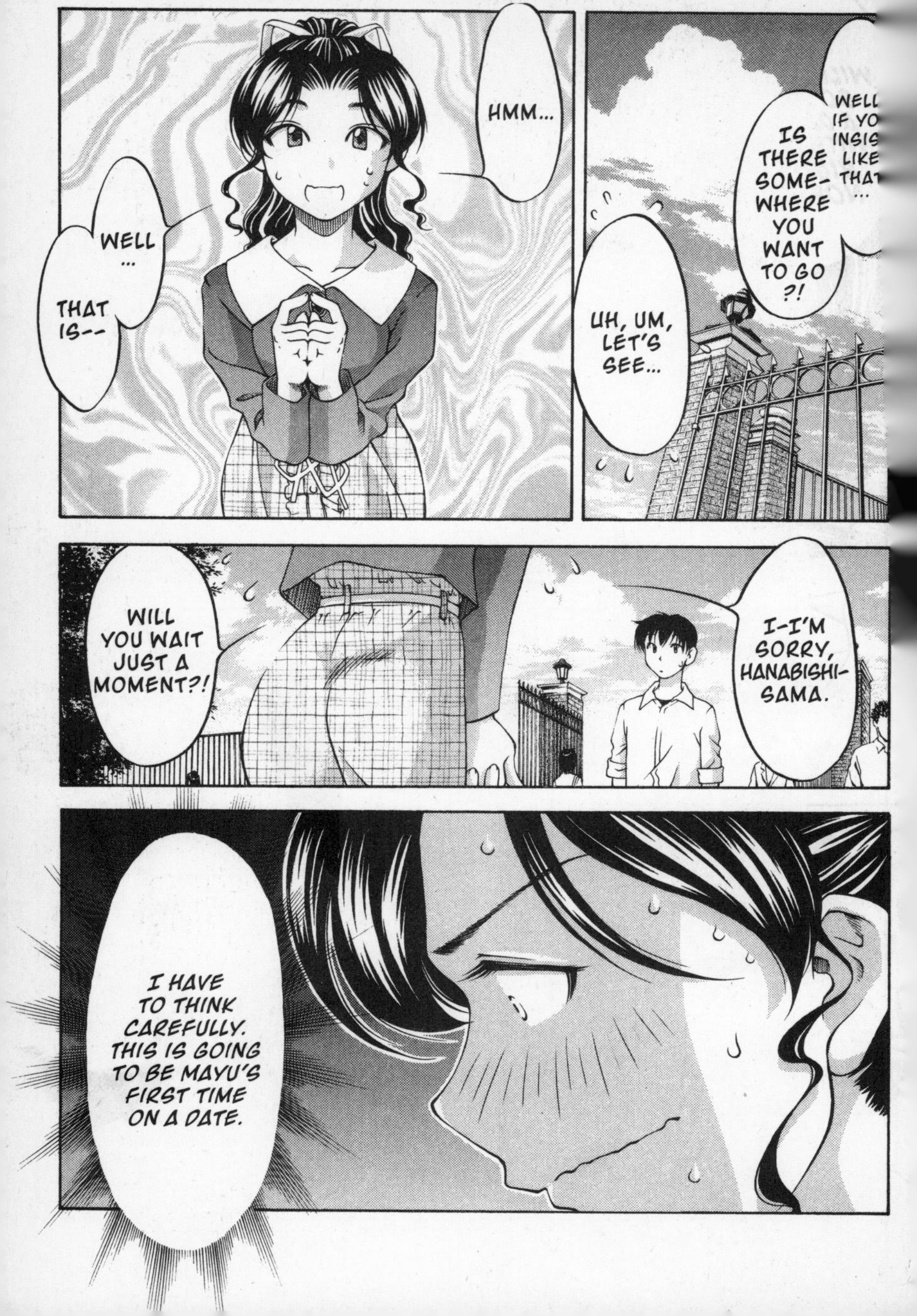
WELL IF YO INSIS LIKE THA ...
IS THERE SOME-WHERE YOU WANT TO GO ?!
UH, UM, LET'S SEE...
HMM...
WELL ... THAT IS--
I-I'M SORRY, HANABISHI-SAMA.
WILL YOU WAIT JUST A MOMENT?!
I HAVE TO THINK CAREFULLY. THIS IS GOING TO BE MAYU'S FIRST TIME ON A DATE.

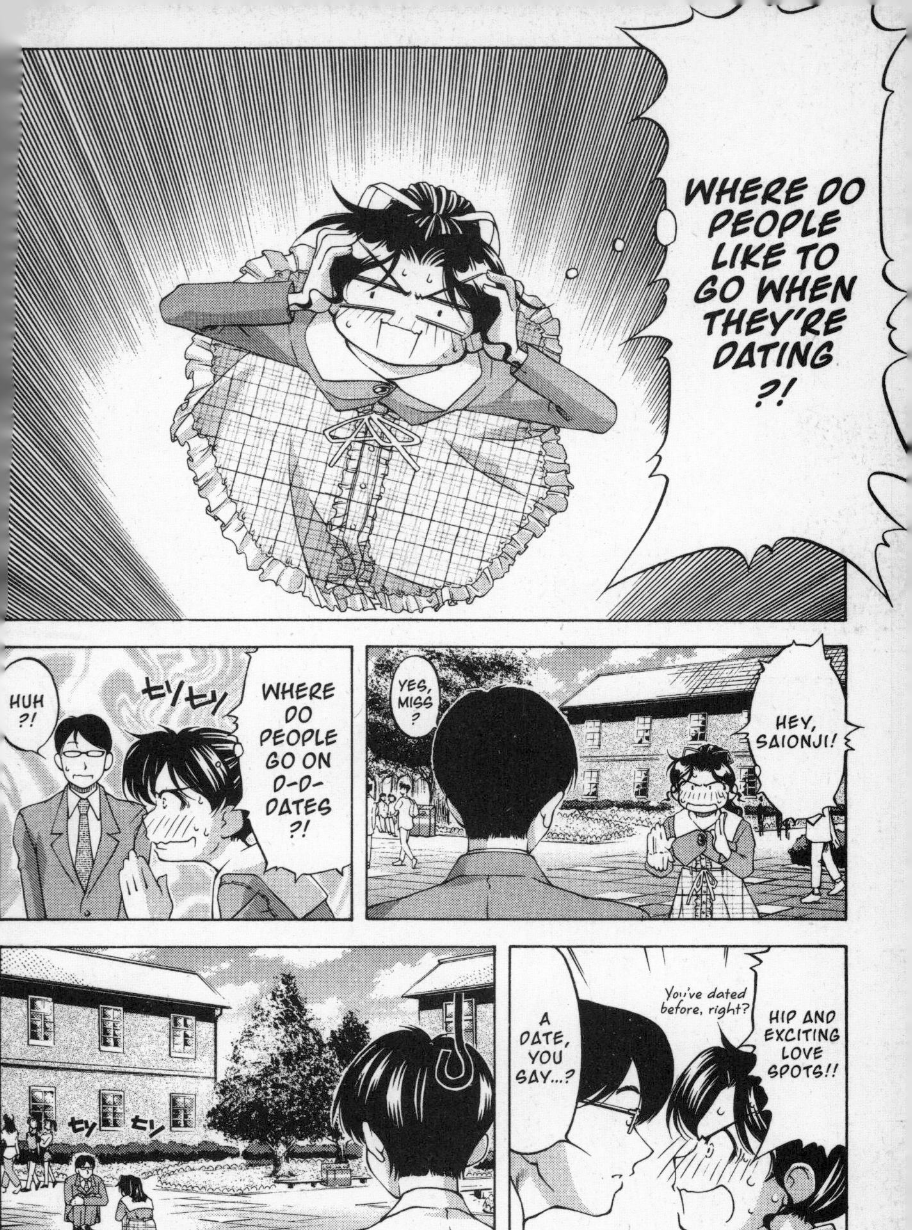
WHERE DO PEOPLE LIKE TO GO WHEN THEY'RE DATING ?!
HEY, SAIONJI!
YES, MISS ?
WHERE DO PEOPLE GO ON D-D-DATES ?!
ヒソヒソ
HUH ?!
HIP AND EXCITING LOVE SPOTS!!
You've dated before, right?
A DATE, YOU SAY...?
ヒソ ヒソ

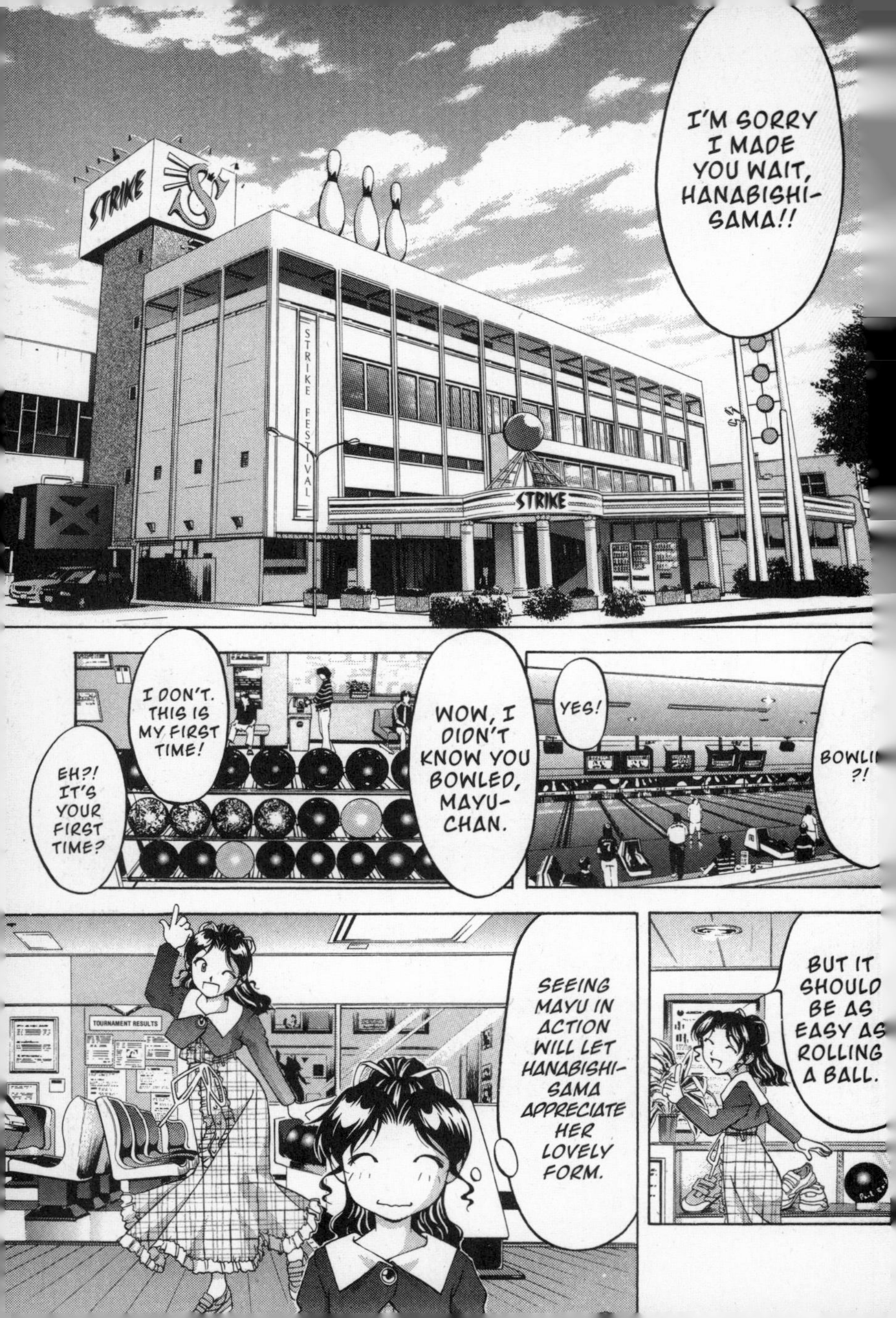
STRIKE
STRIKE FESTIVAL
STRIKE
I'M SORRY I MADE YOU WAIT, HANABISHI-SAMA!!
BOWLI ?!
YES!
WOW, I DIDN'T KNOW YOU BOWLED, MAYU-CHAN.
I DON'T. THIS IS MY FIRST TIME!
EH?! IT'S YOUR FIRST TIME?
BUT IT SHOULD BE AS EASY AS ROLLING A BALL.
TOURNAMENT RESULTS
SEEING MAYU IN ACTION WILL LET HANABISHI-SAMA APPRECIATE HER LOVELY FORM.

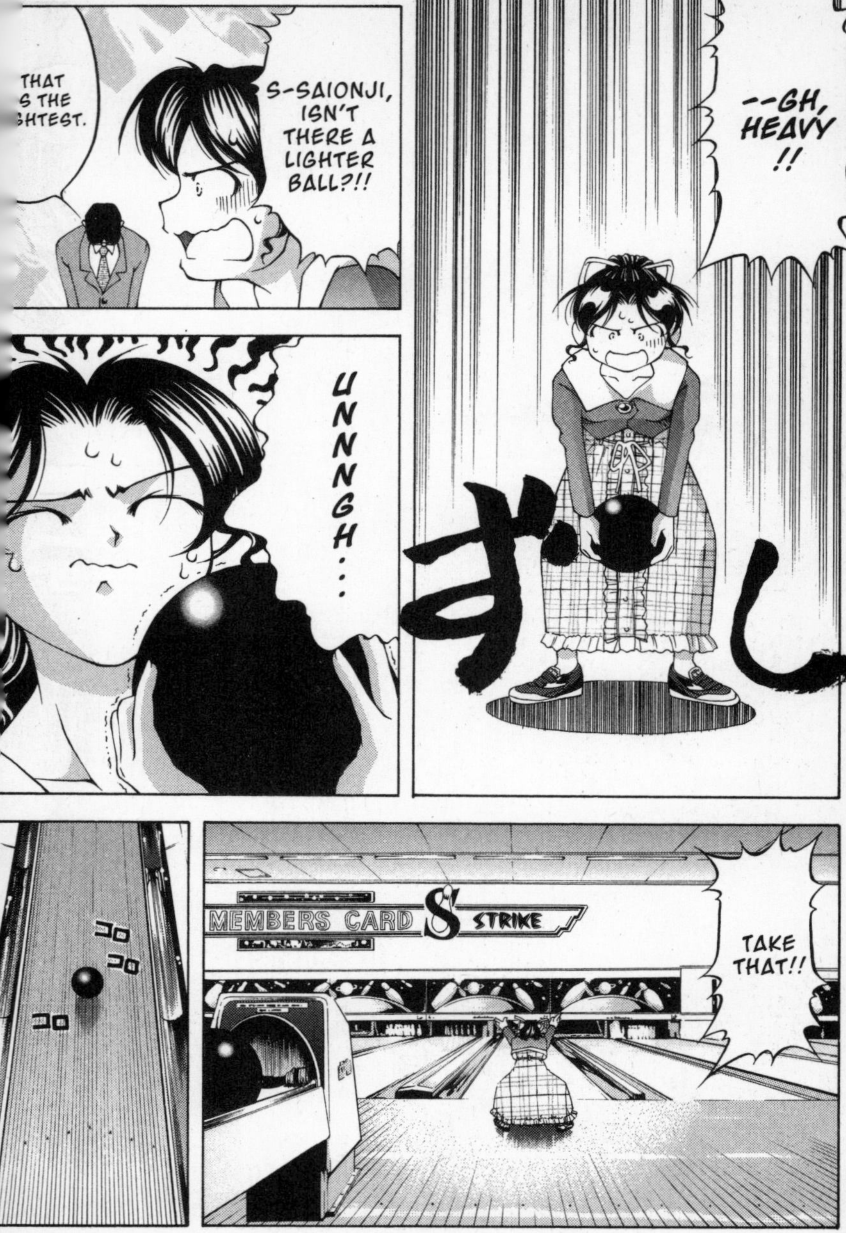
--GH, HEAVY !!
ずし
S-SAIONJI, ISN'T THERE A LIGHTER BALL?!!
THAT S THE GHTEST.
UNNNGH...
TAKE THAT!!
MEMBERS CARD
STRIKE
コロ
コロ
コロ

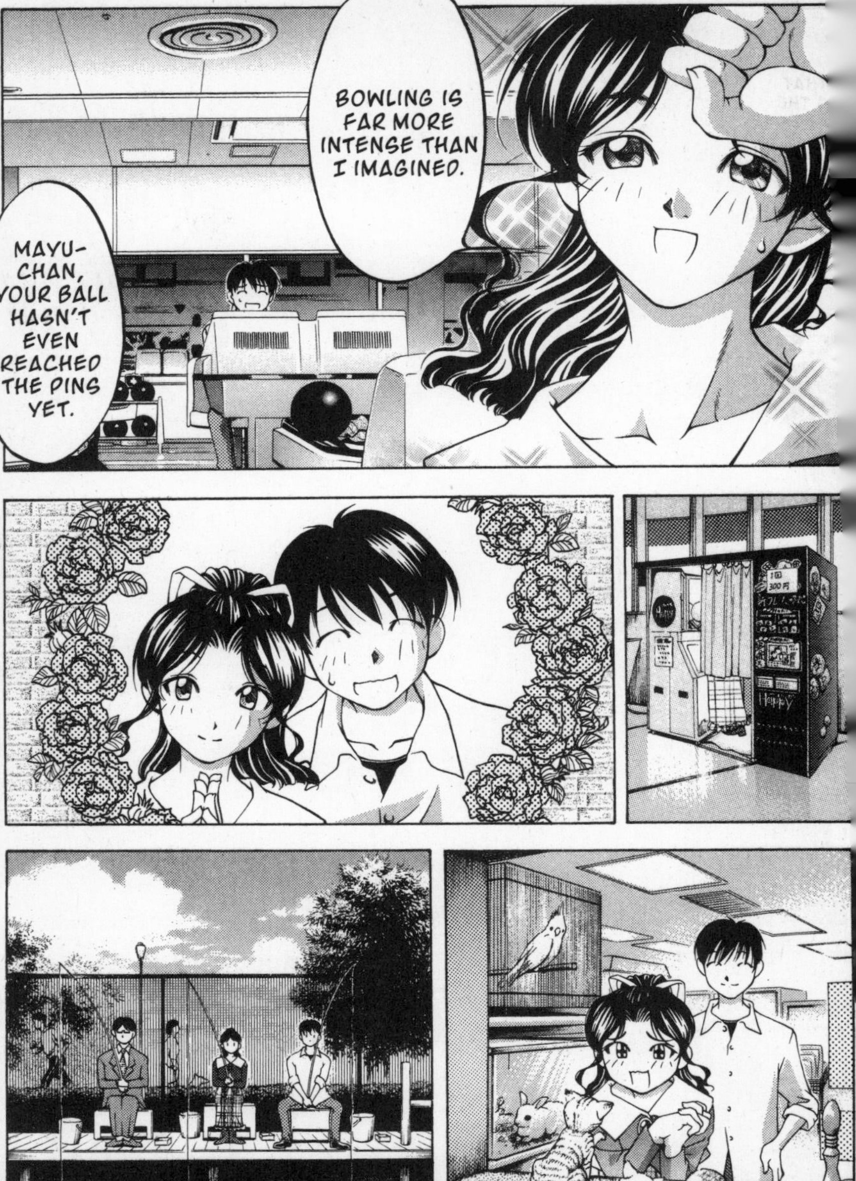
BOWLING IS FAR MORE INTENSE THAN I IMAGINED.
MAYU-CHAN, YOUR BALL HASN'T EVEN REACHED THE PINS YET.
1回 300円
Happy

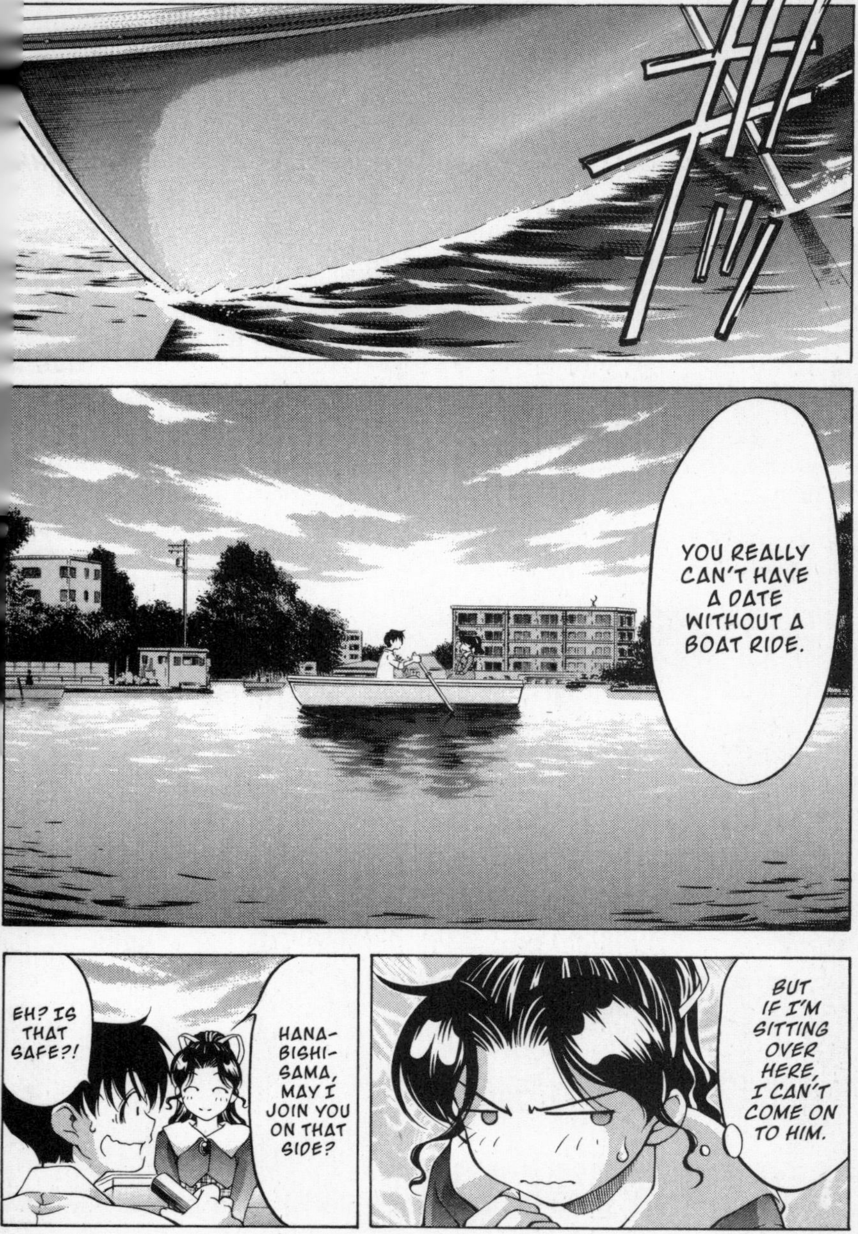
YOU REALLY CAN'T HAVE A DATE WITHOUT A BOAT RIDE.
BUT IF I'M SITTING OVER HERE, I CAN'T COME ON TO HIM.
HANA-BISHI-SAMA, MAY I JOIN YOU ON THAT SIDE?
EH? IS THAT SAFE?!

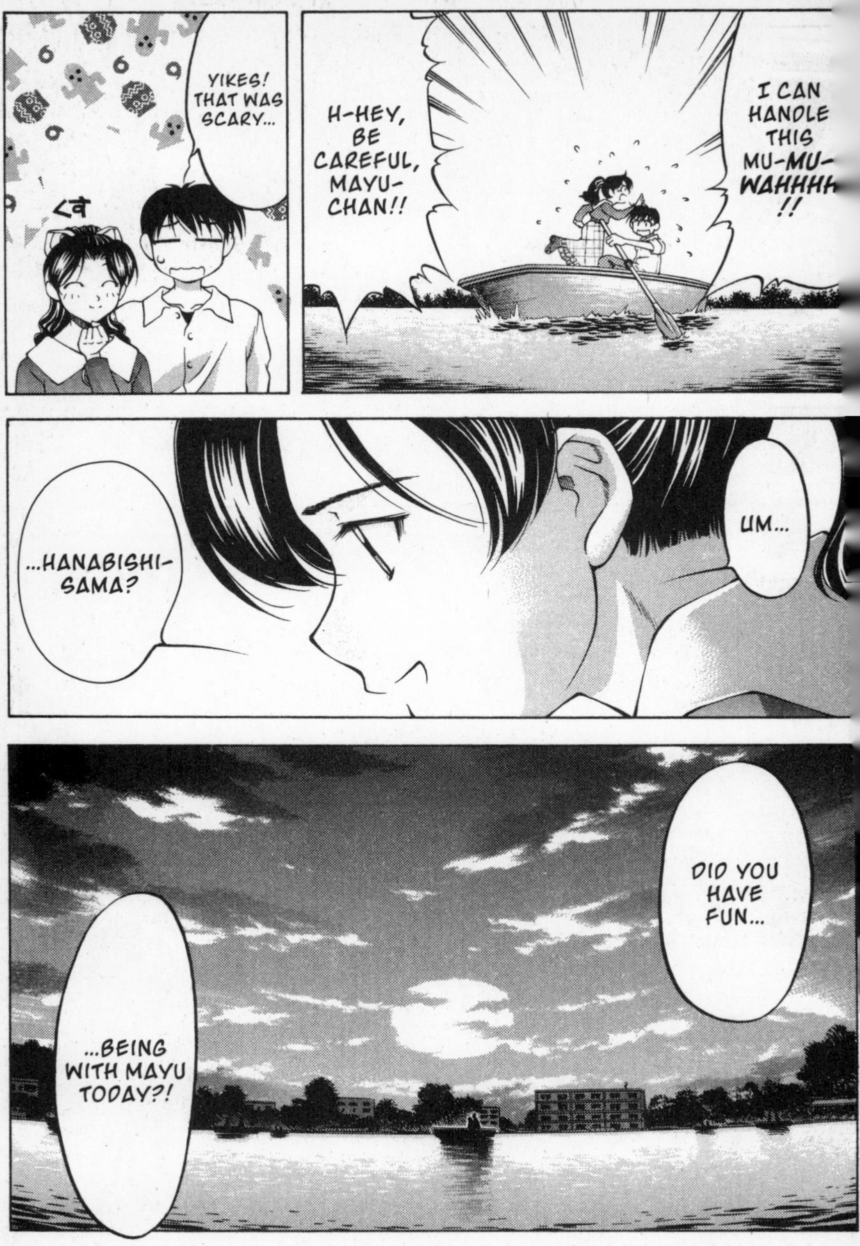
I CAN HANDLE THIS MU-MU-WAHHHH !!
H-HEY, BE CAREFUL, MAYU-CHAN!!
YIKES! THAT WAS SCARY...
くす
UM...
...HANABISHI-SAMA?
DID YOU HAVE FUN...
...BEING WITH MAYU TODAY?!

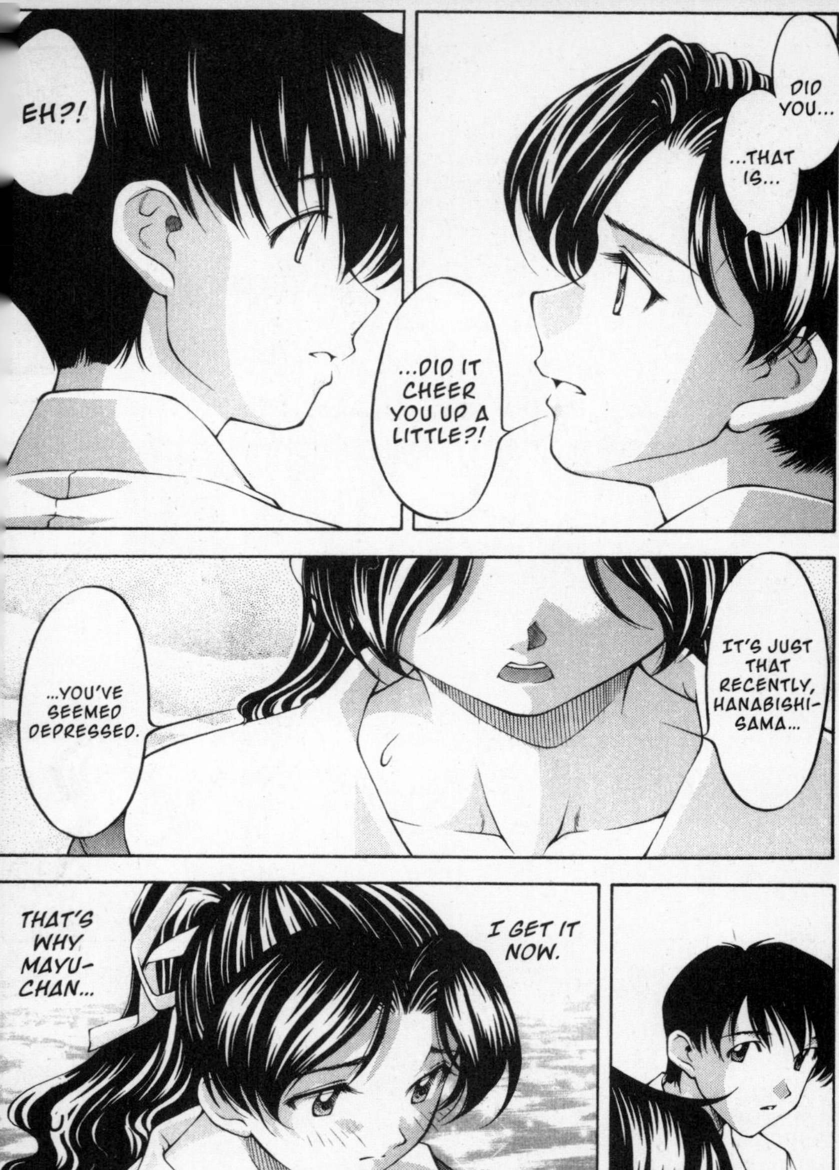
DID YOU...
...THAT IS...
...DID IT CHEER YOU UP A LITTLE?!
EH?!
IT'S JUST THAT RECENTLY, HANABISHI-SAMA...
...YOU'VE SEEMED DEPRESSED.
I GET IT NOW.
THAT'S WHY MAYU-CHAN...

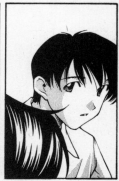

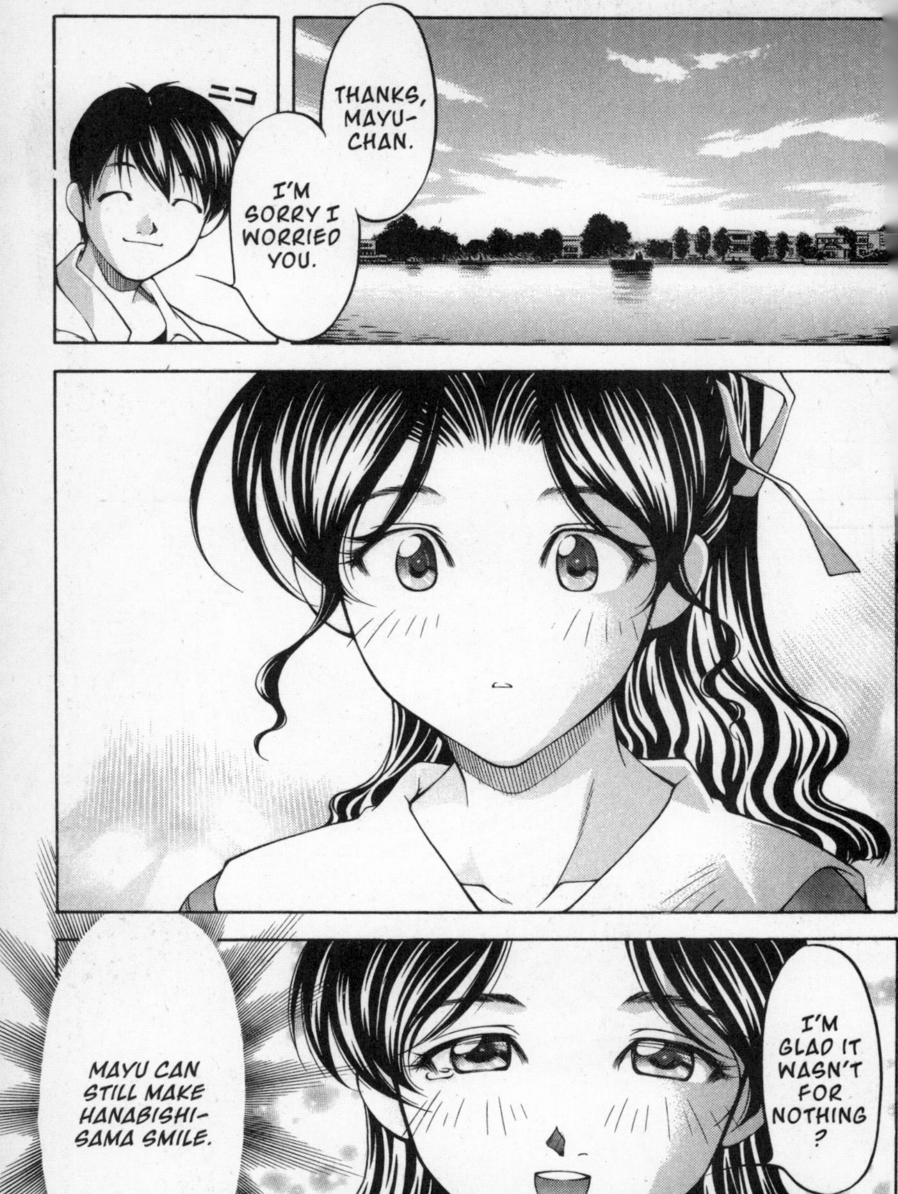
THANKS, MAYU-CHAN.
I'M SORRY I WORRIED YOU.
ニコ
I'M GLAD IT WASN'T FOR NOTHING?
MAYU CAN STILL MAKE HANABISHI-SAMA SMILE.

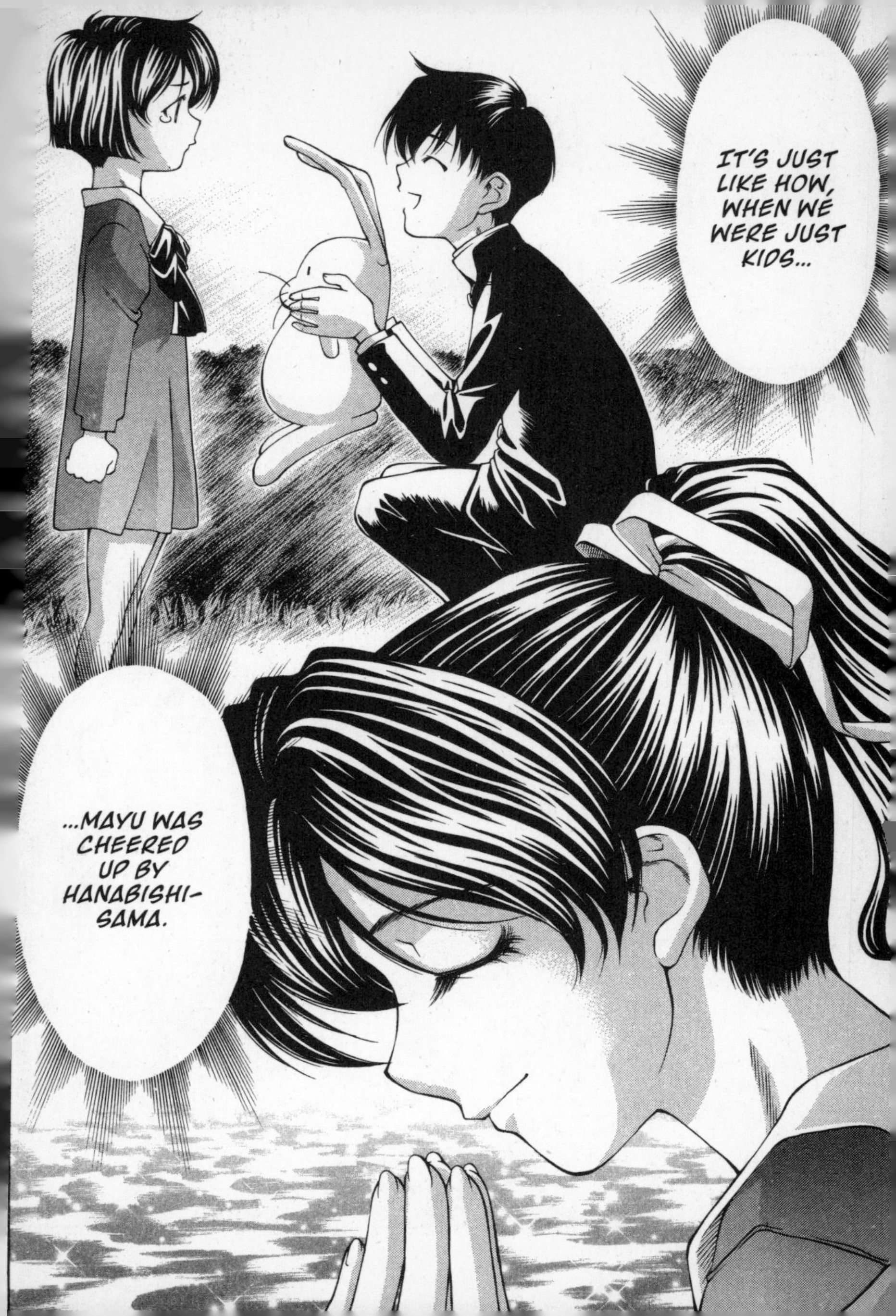
IT'S JUST LIKE HOW, WHEN WE WERE JUST KIDS...
...MAYU WAS CHEERED UP BY HANABISHI-SAMA.

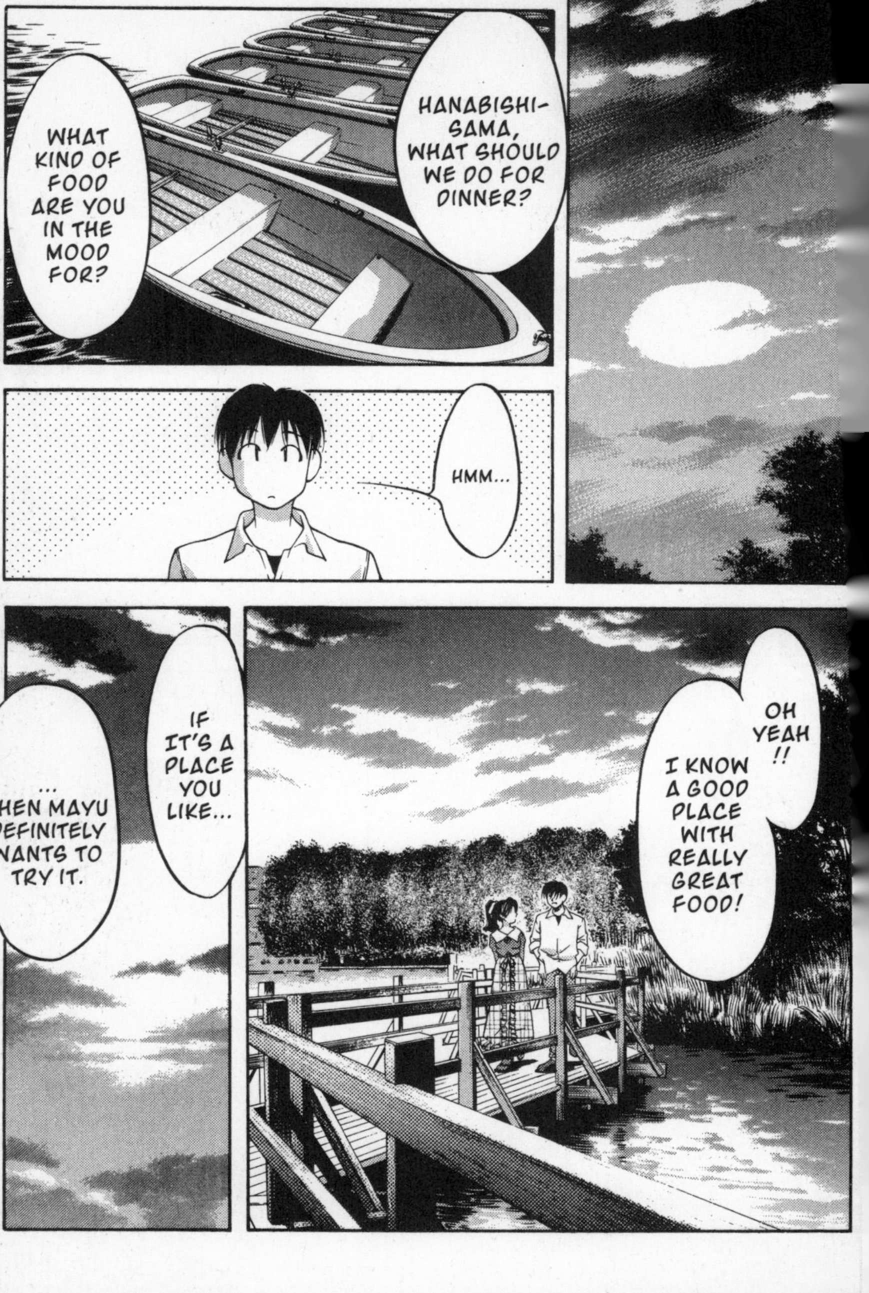
HANABISHI-SAMA, WHAT SHOULD WE DO FOR DINNER?
WHAT KIND OF FOOD ARE YOU IN THE MOOD FOR?
HMM...
OH YEAH !!
I KNOW A GOOD PLACE WITH REALLY GREAT FOOD!
IF IT'S A PLACE YOU LIKE...
... THEN MAYU DEFINITELY WANTS TO TRY IT.

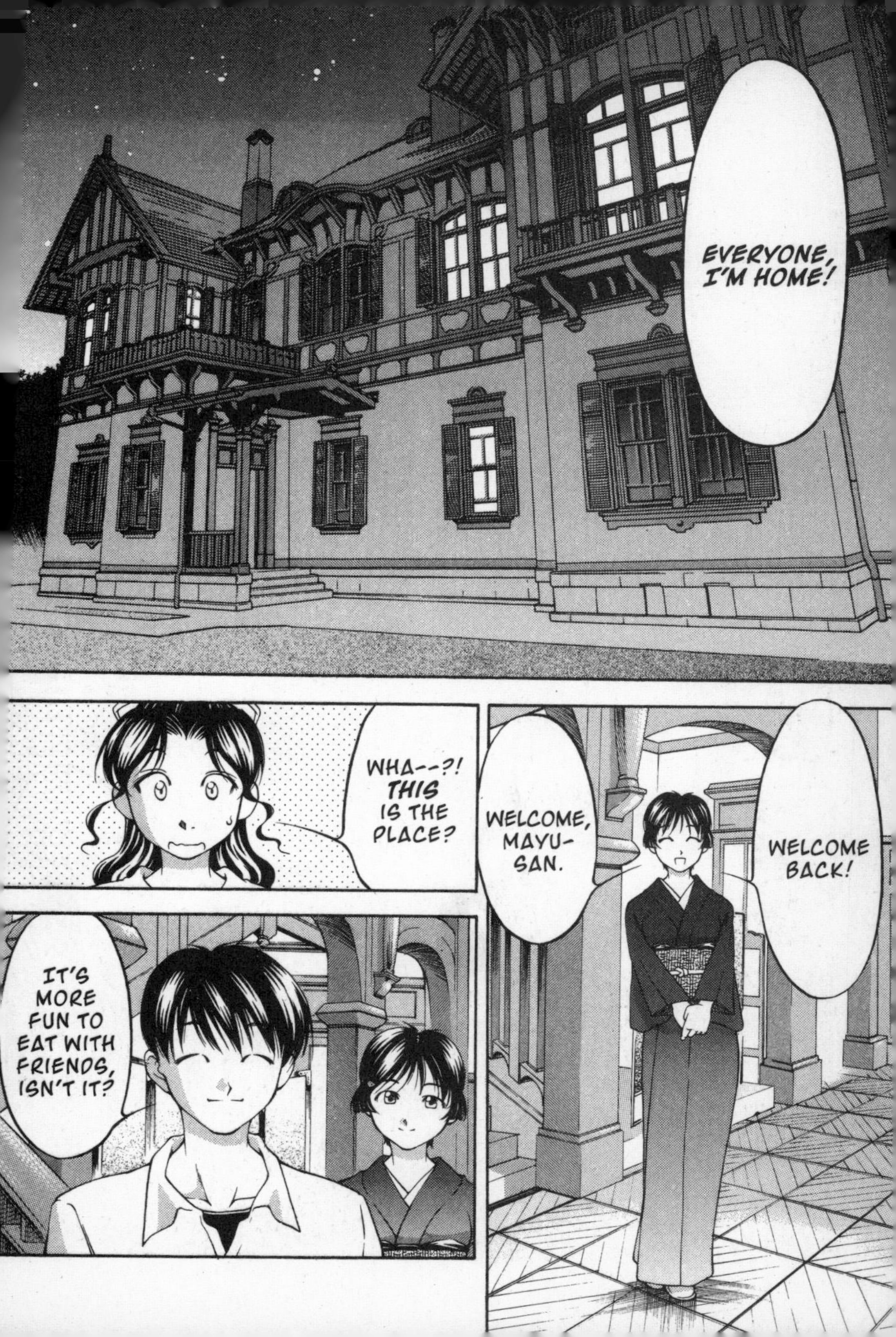
EVERYONE, I'M HOME!
WELCOME BACK!
WELCOME, MAYU-SAN.
WHA--?! THIS IS THE PLACE?
IT'S MORE FUN TO EAT WITH FRIENDS, ISN'T IT?

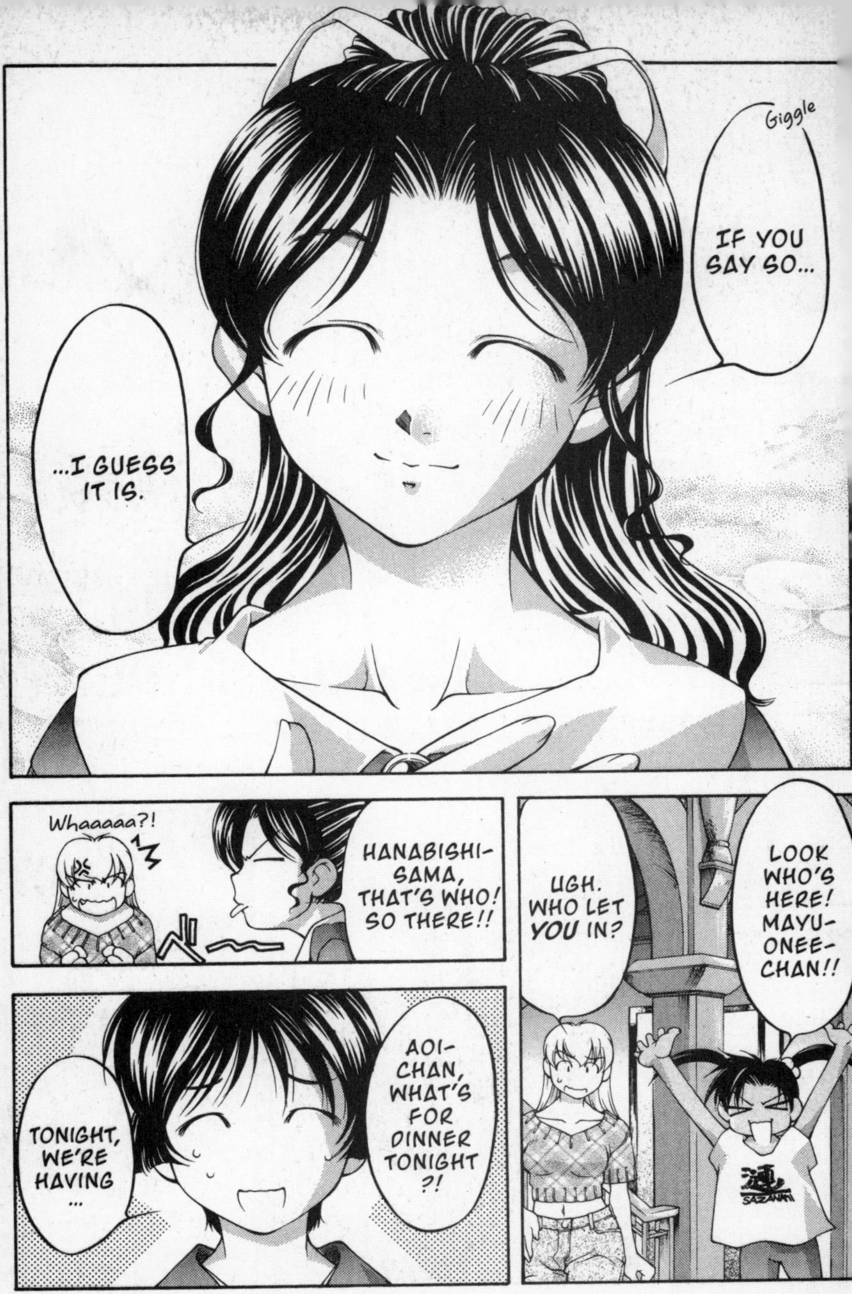
Giggle
IF YOU SAY SO...
...I GUESS IT IS.
LOOK WHO'S HERE! MAYU-ONEE-CHAN!!
UGH. WHO LET YOU IN?
HANABISHI-SAMA, THAT'S WHO! SO THERE!!
Whaaaaa?!
AOI-CHAN, WHAT'S FOR DINNER TONIGHT?!
TONIGHT, WE'RE HAVING ...
SAZANAMI

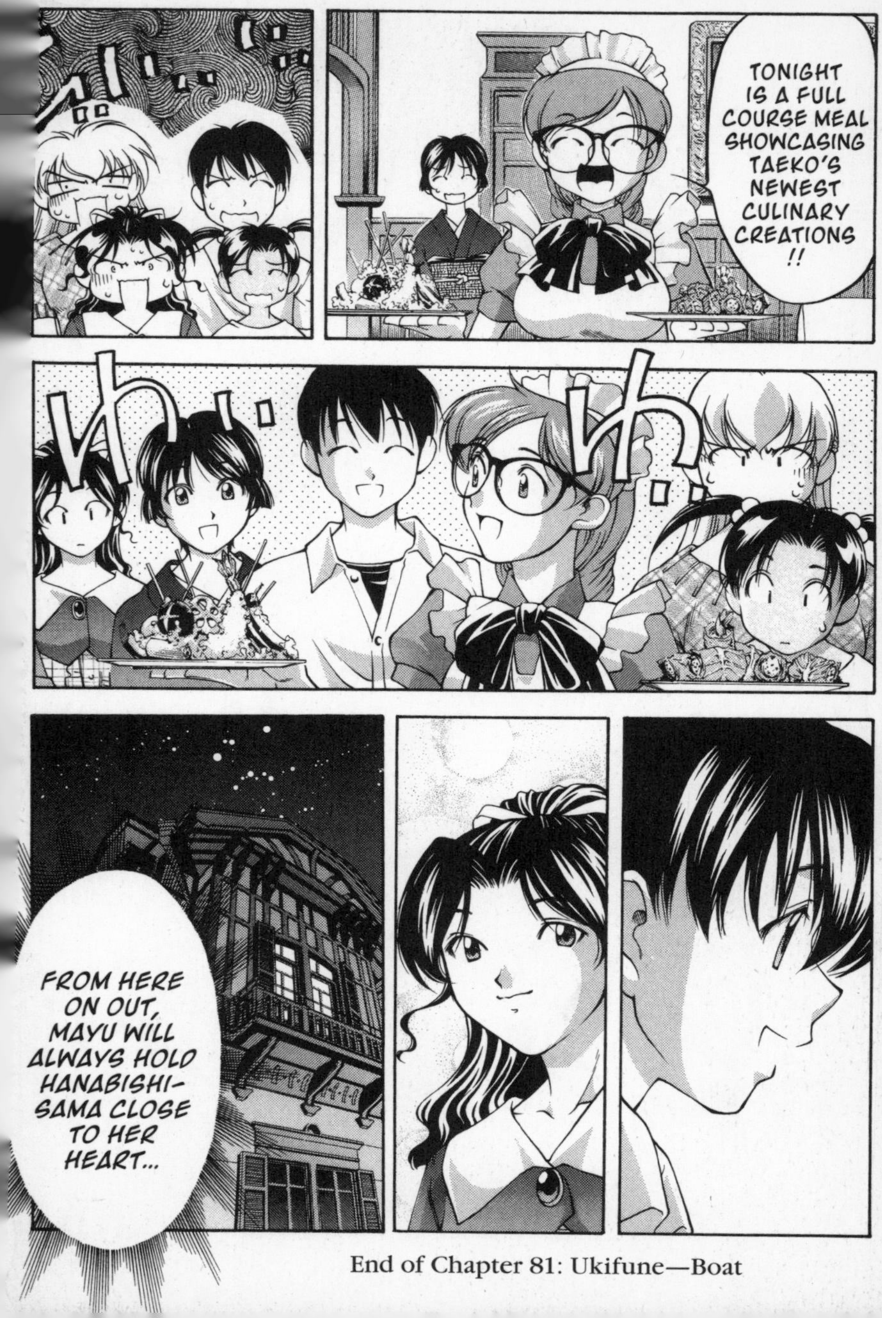
TONIGHT IS A FULL COURSE MEAL SHOWCASING TAEKO'S NEWEST CULINARY CREATIONS !!
FROM HERE ON OUT, MAYU WILL ALWAYS HOLD HANABISHI-SAMA CLOSE TO HER HEART...

End of Chapter 81: Ukifune—Boat

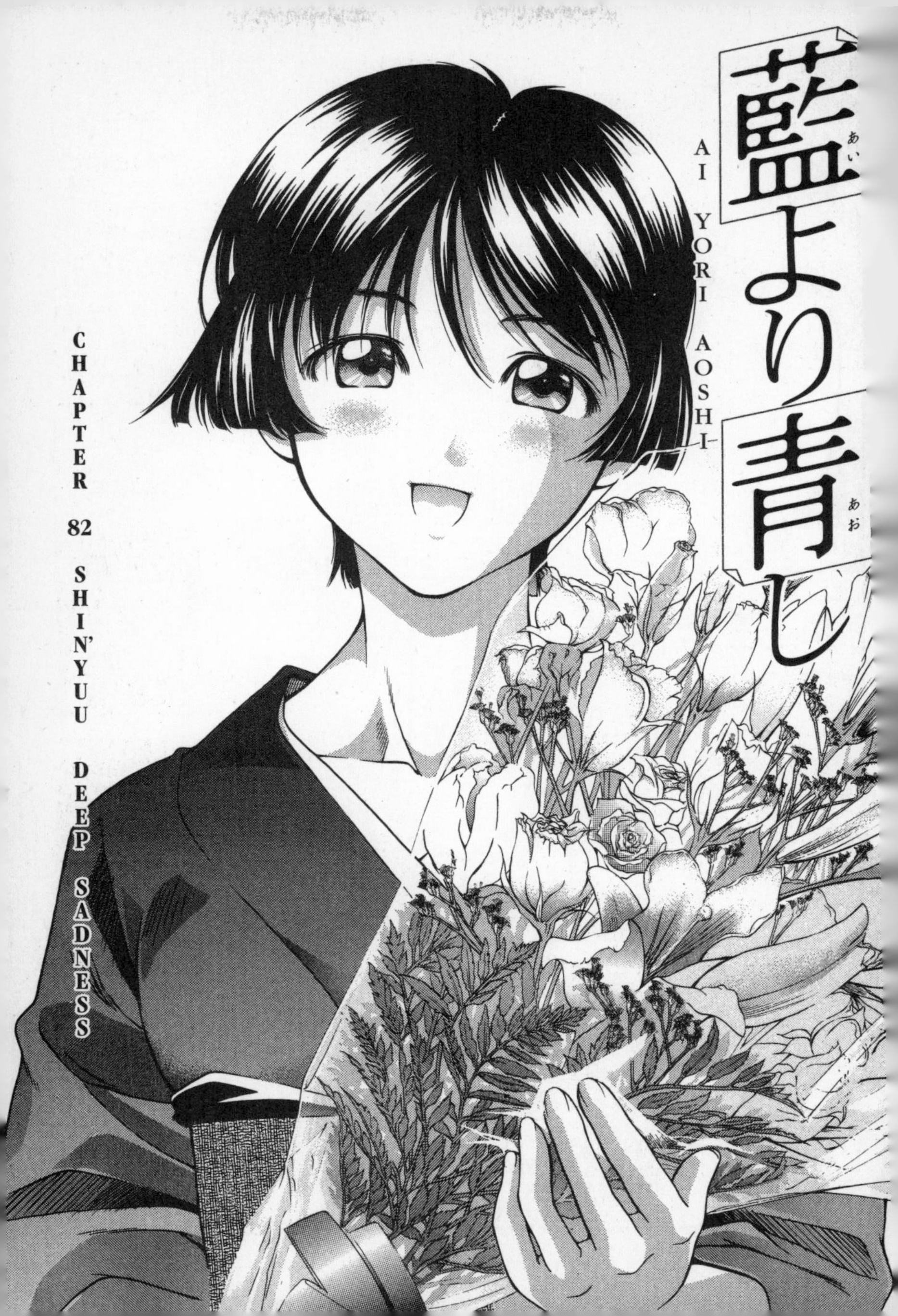
藍より青し
あい
あお
AI YORI AOSHI
CHAPTER 82
SHIN'YUU
DEEP SADNESS

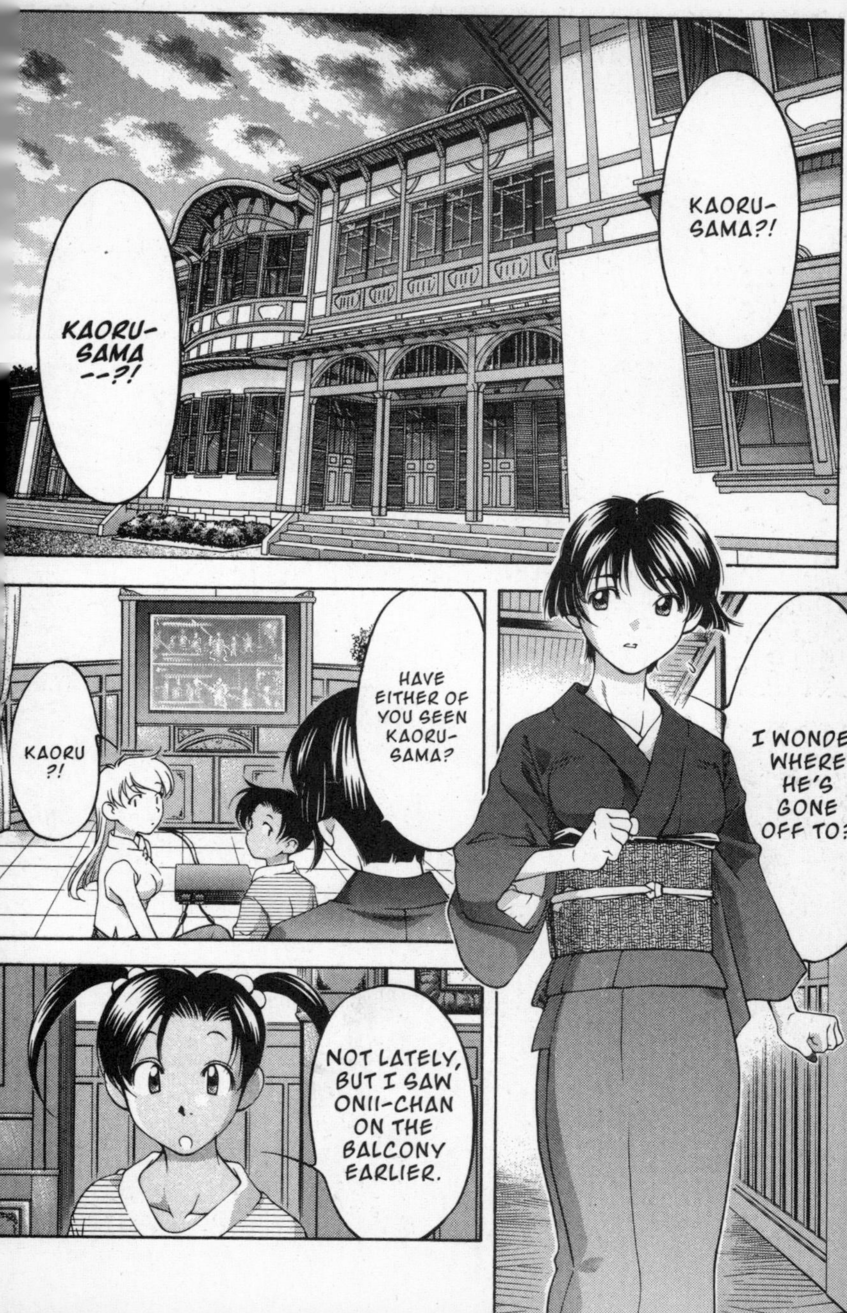
KAORU-SAMA?!
KAORU-SAMA--?!
I WONDER WHERE HE'S GONE OFF TO?
HAVE EITHER OF YOU SEEN KAORU-SAMA?
KAORU ?!
NOT LATELY, BUT I SAW ONII-CHAN ON THE BALCONY EARLIER.

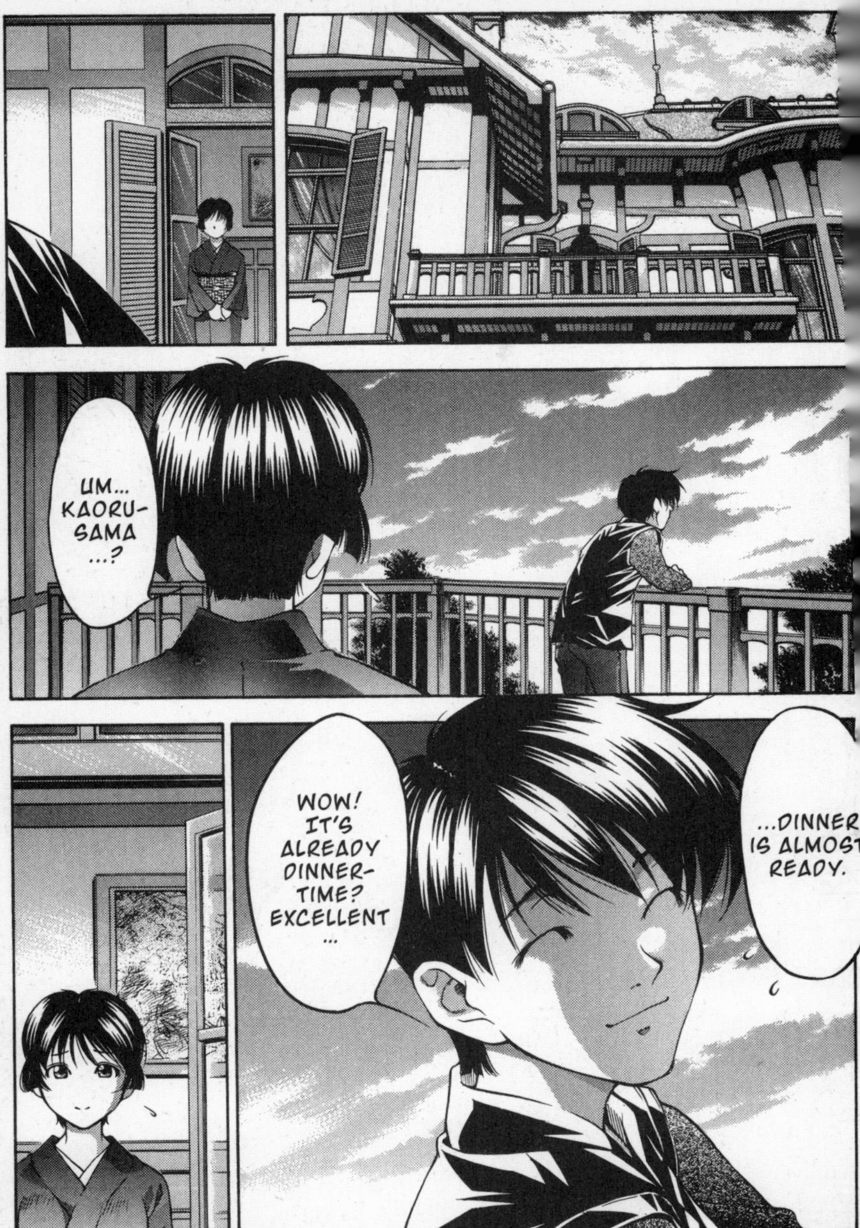
UM... KAORU-SAMA ...?
...DINNER IS ALMOST READY.
WOW! IT'S ALREADY DINNER-TIME? EXCELLENT ...

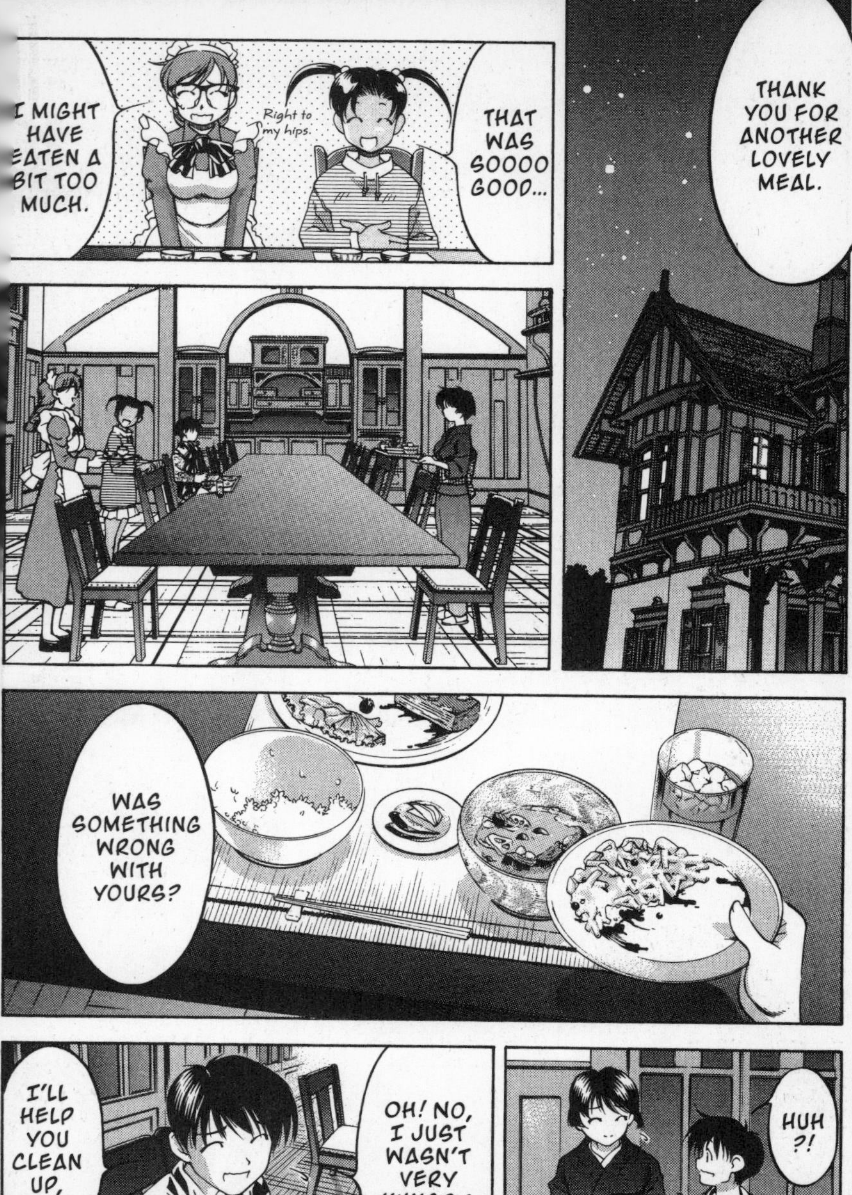
THANK YOU FOR ANOTHER LOVELY MEAL.
THAT WAS SOOOO GOOD...
Right to my hips.
I MIGHT HAVE EATEN A BIT TOO MUCH.
WAS SOMETHING WRONG WITH YOURS?
HUH?!
OH! NO, I JUST WASN'T VERY HUNGRY.
I'LL HELP YOU CLEAN UP, THOUGH.

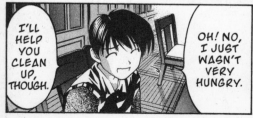

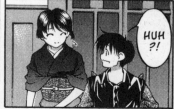

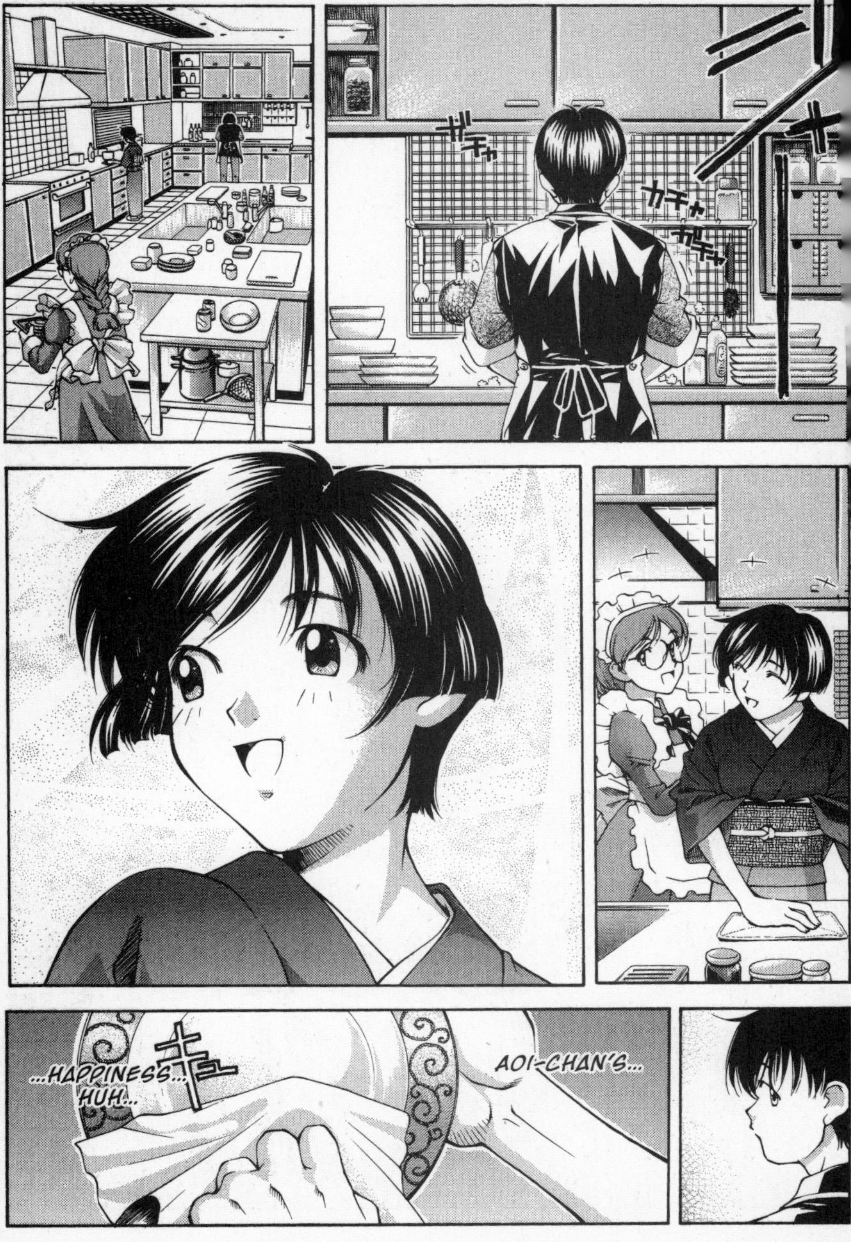
カチャ
ガチャ
ガチャ
AOI-CHAN'S...
キュ
...HAPPINESS... HUH...

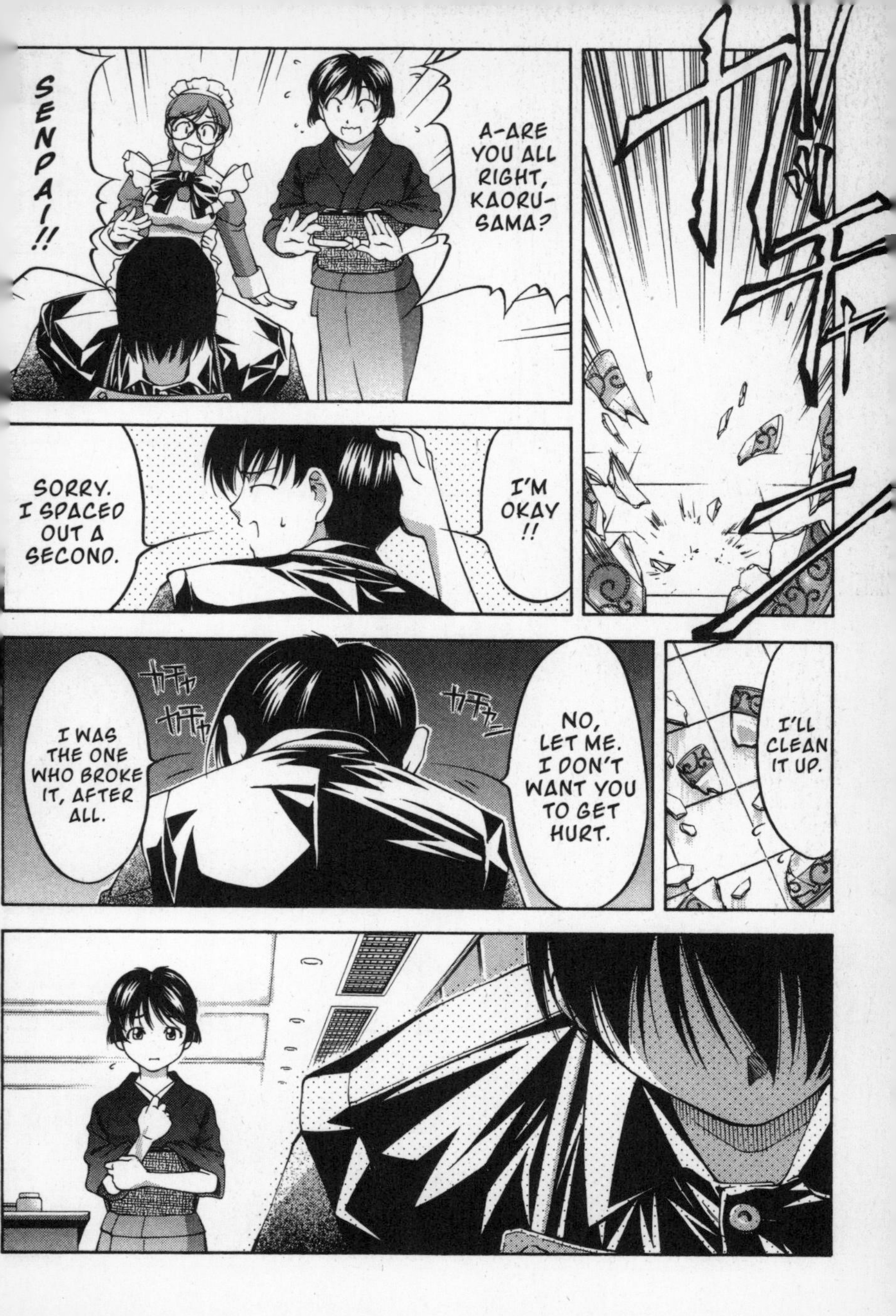
A-ARE YOU ALL RIGHT, KAORU-SAMA?
SENPAI!!
I'M OKAY!!
SORRY. I SPACED OUT A SECOND.
I'LL CLEAN IT UP.
NO, LET ME. I DON'T WANT YOU TO GET HURT.
カチャン
カチャ
カチャ
I WAS THE ONE WHO BROKE IT, AFTER ALL.

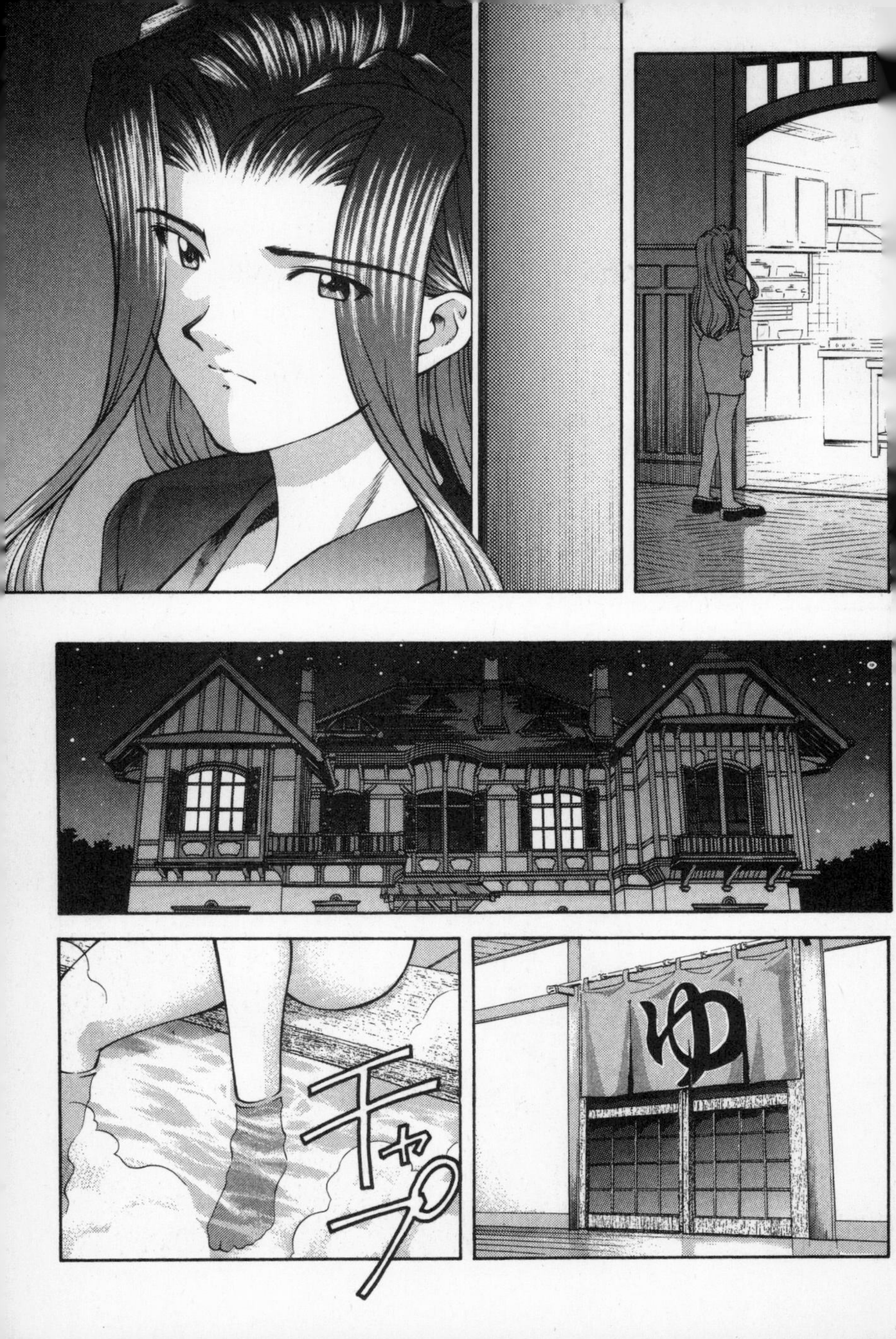
ゆ
チャプ

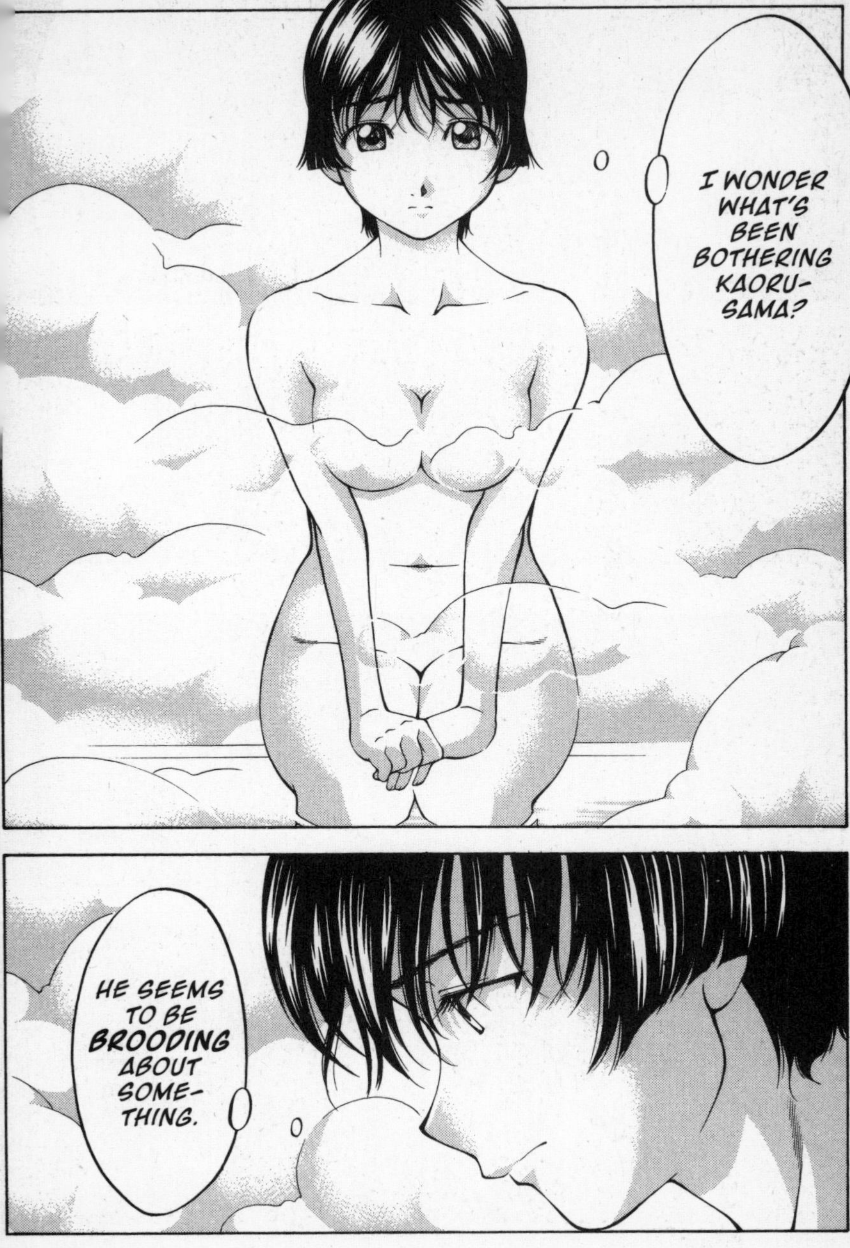
I WONDER WHAT'S BEEN BOTHERING KAORU-SAMA?
HE SEEMS TO BE BROODING ABOUT SOME-THING.

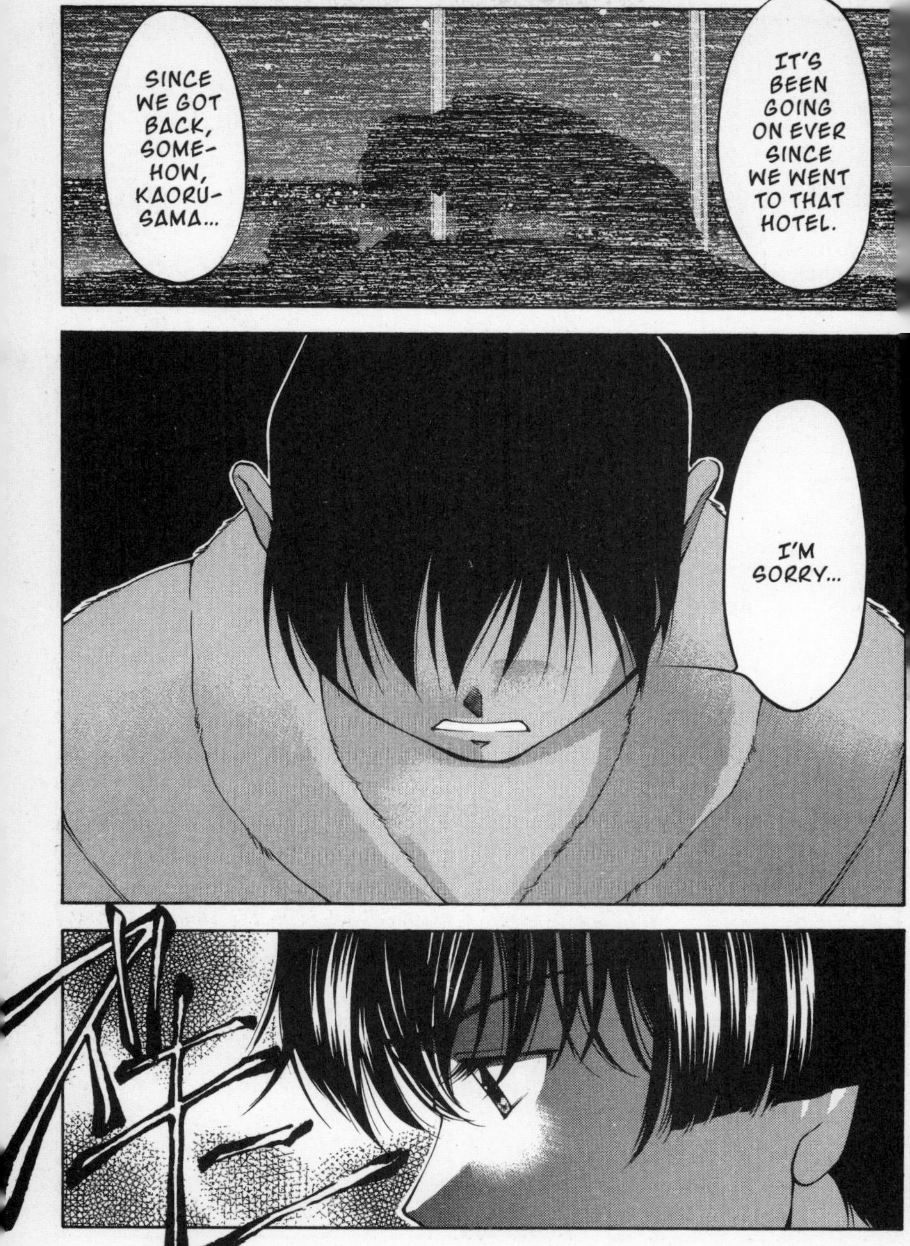
IT'S BEEN GOING ON EVER SINCE WE WENT TO THAT HOTEL.
SINCE WE GOT BACK, SOMEHOW, KAORU-SAMA...
I'M SORRY...

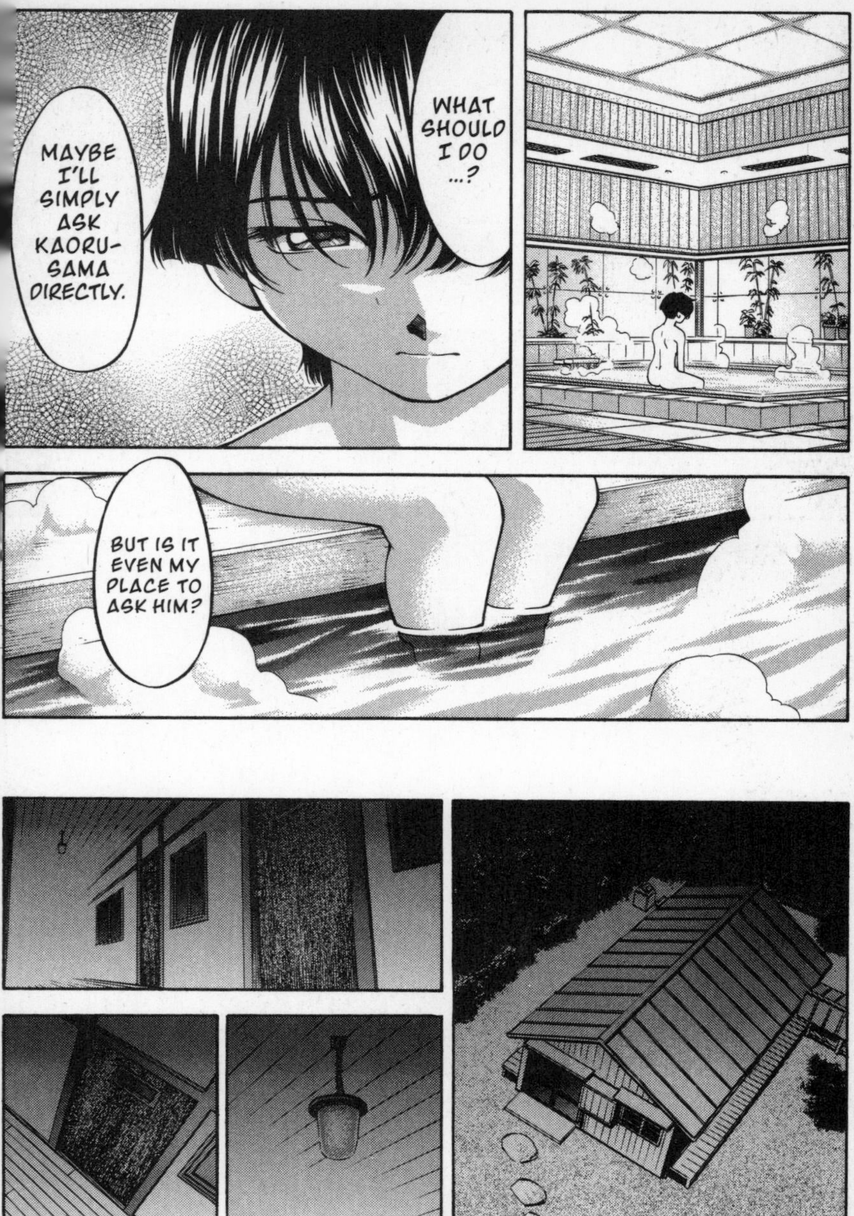
WHAT SHOULD I DO ...?
MAYBE I'LL SIMPLY ASK KAORU-SAMA DIRECTLY.
BUT IS IT EVEN MY PLACE TO ASK HIM?

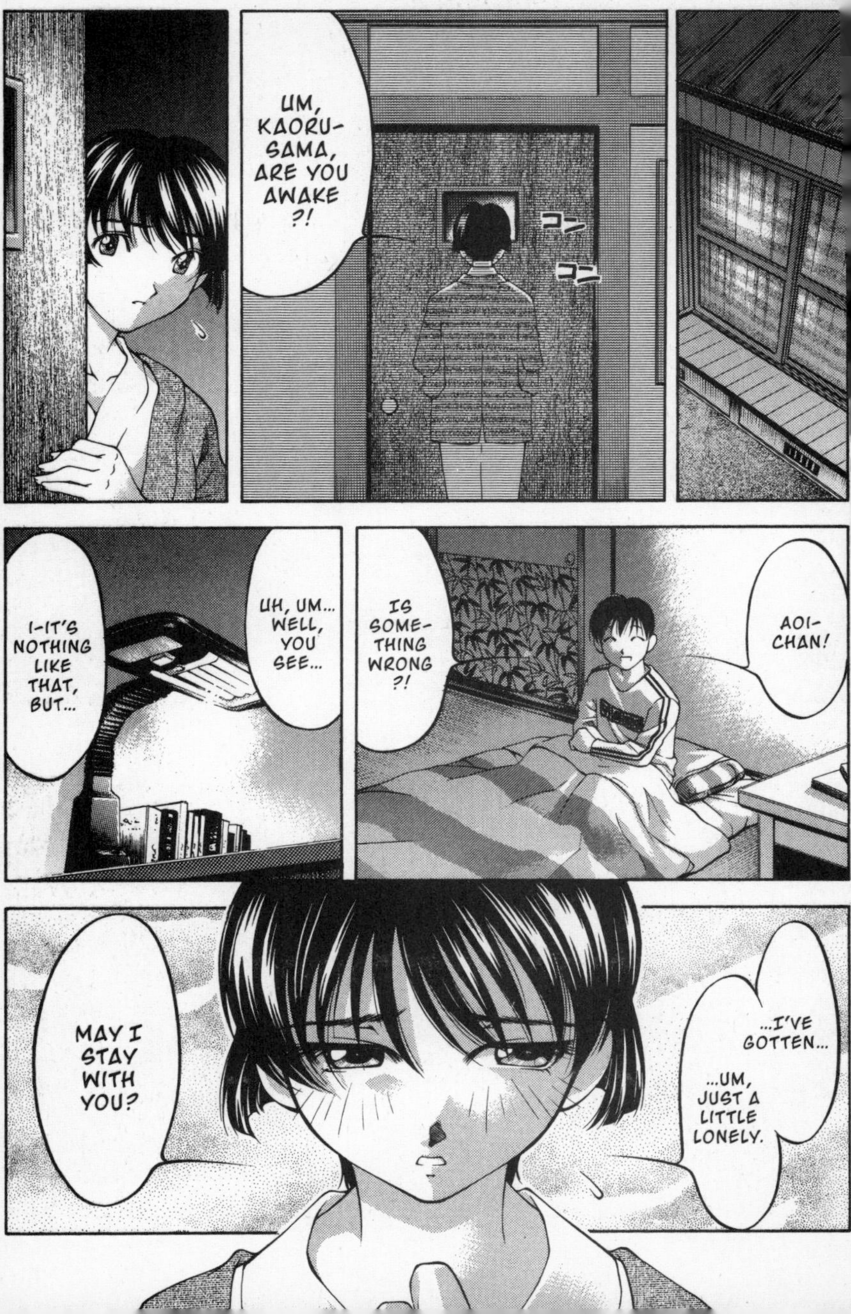
UM, KAORU-SAMA, ARE YOU AWAKE ?!
コン
コン
AOI-CHAN!
IS SOME-THING WRONG ?!
UH, UM... WELL, YOU SEE...
I-IT'S NOTHING LIKE THAT, BUT...
...I'VE GOTTEN...
...UM, JUST A LITTLE LONELY.
MAY I STAY WITH YOU?

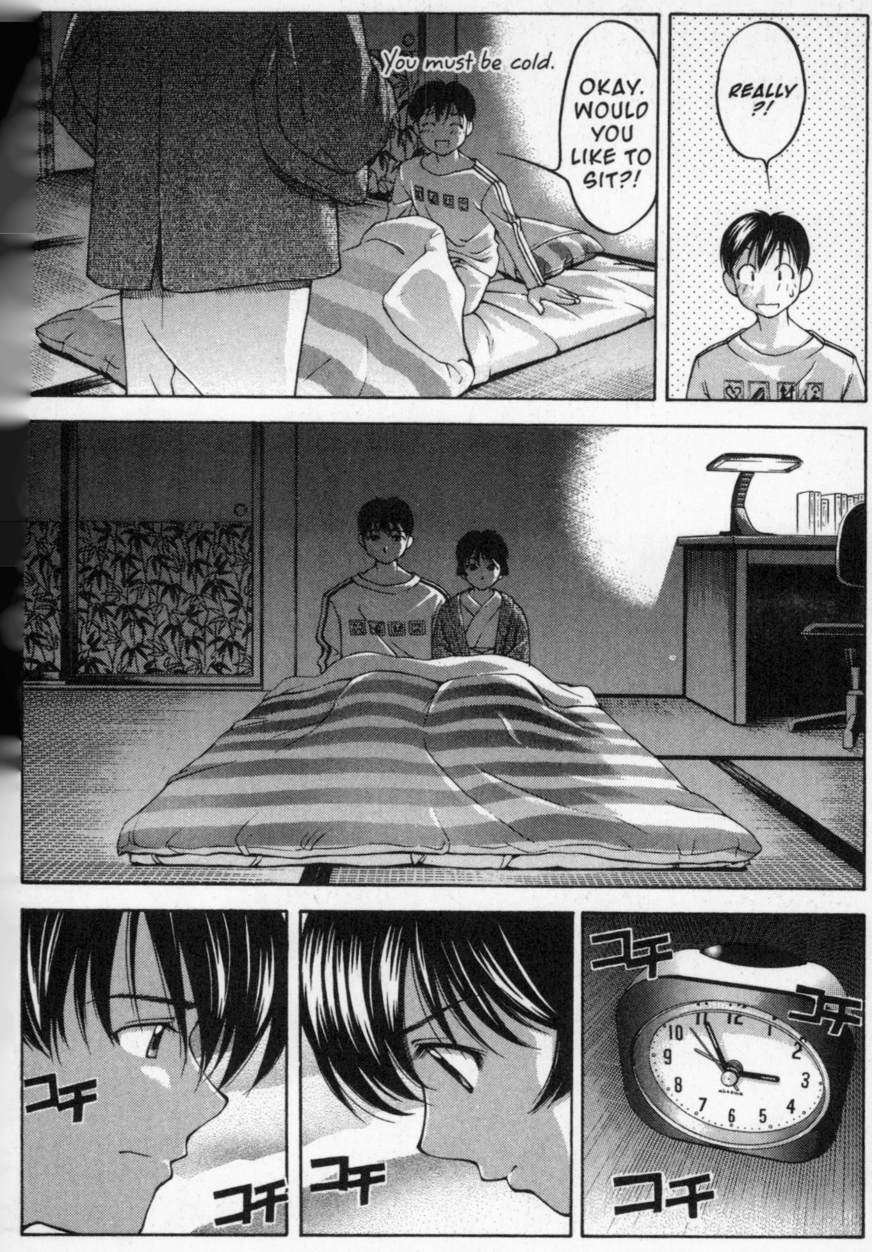
REALLY ?!
OKAY. WOULD YOU LIKE TO SIT?!
You must be cold.
コチ
コチ
コチ
コチ
コチ
コチ

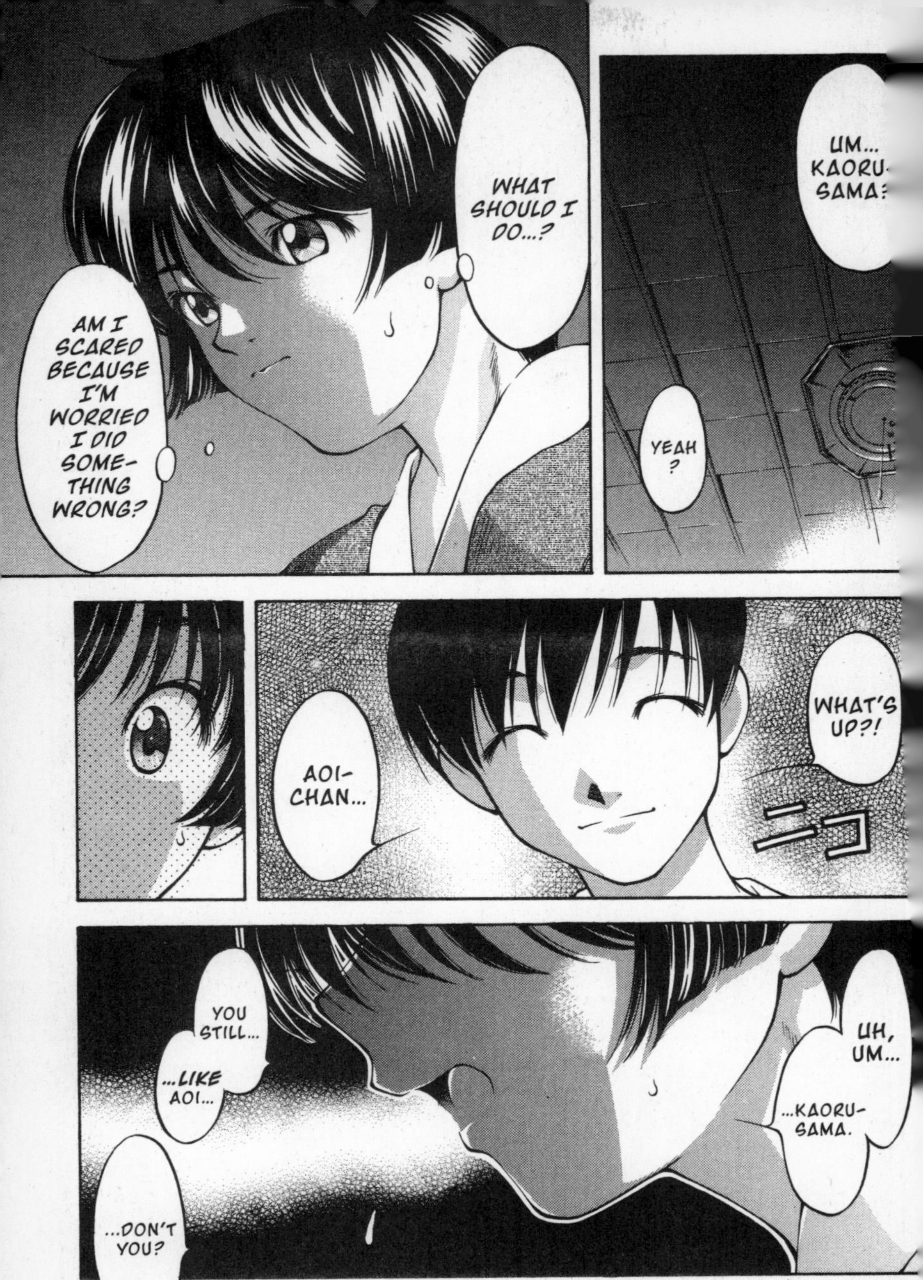
UM... KAORU-SAMA?
YEAH?
WHAT SHOULD I DO...?
AM I SCARED BECAUSE I'M WORRIED I DID SOME-THING WRONG?
WHAT'S UP?!
ニコ
AOI-CHAN...
UH, UM...
...KAORU-SAMA.
YOU STILL...
...LIKE AOI...
...DON'T YOU?

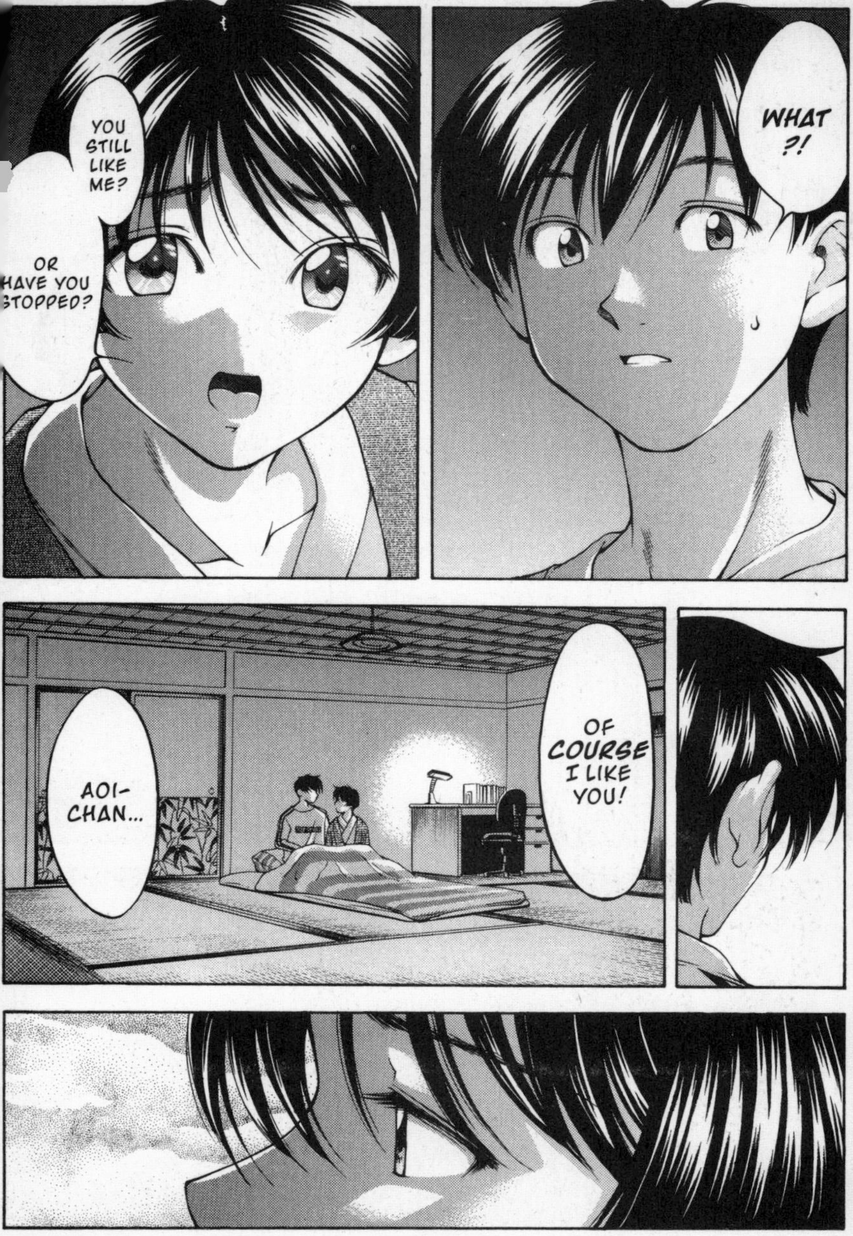
WHAT ?!
YOU STILL LIKE ME?
OR HAVE YOU STOPPED?
OF COURSE I LIKE YOU!
AOI-CHAN...

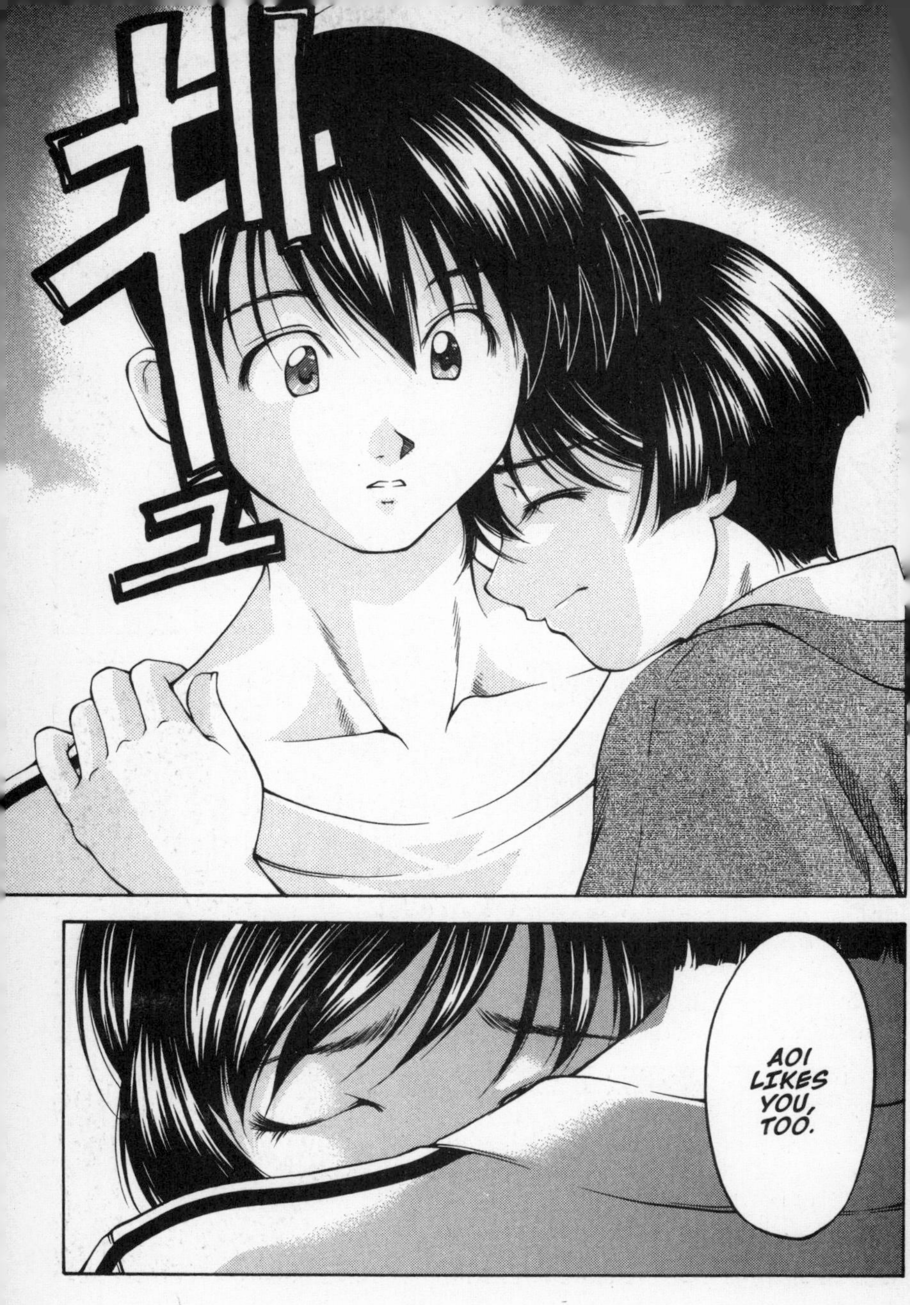

ギュ
AOI LIKES YOU, TOO.

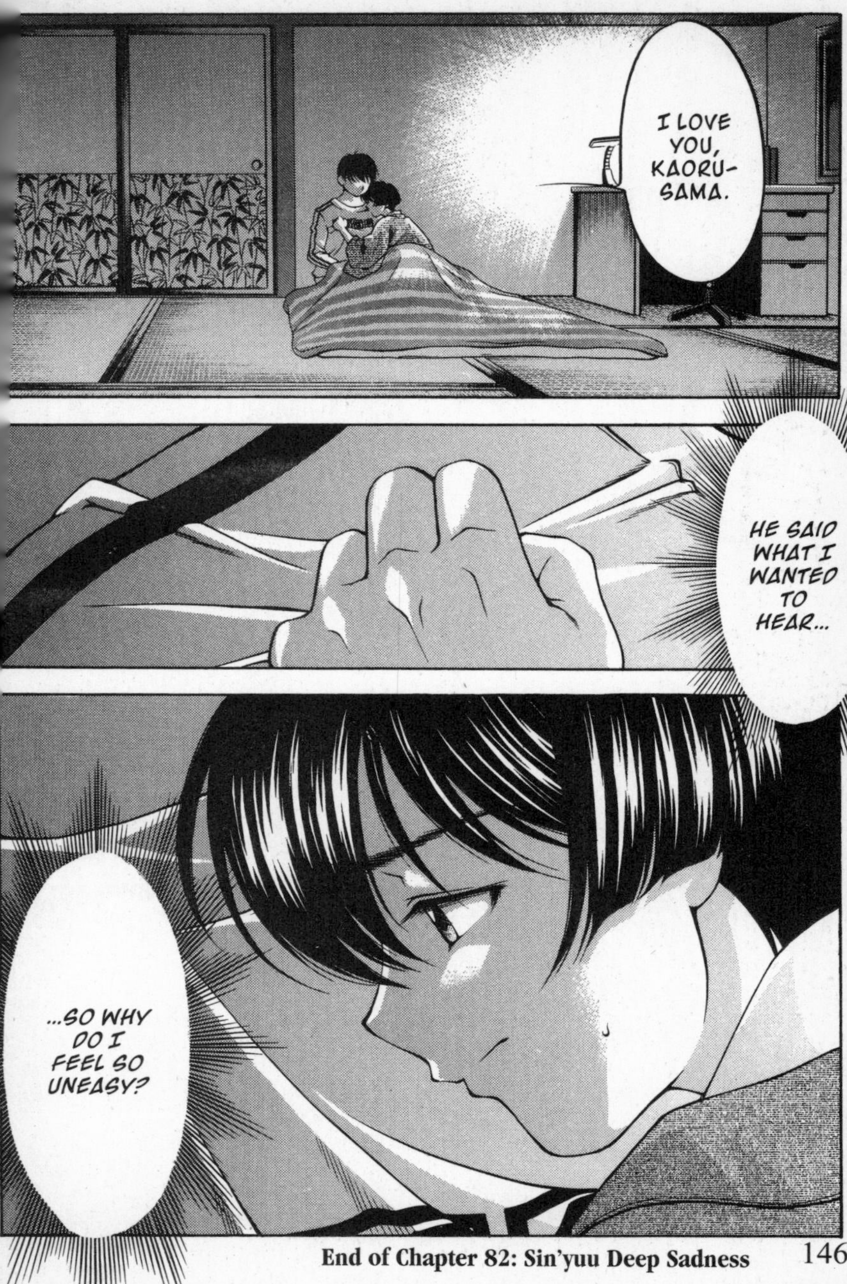
I LOVE YOU, KAORU-SAMA.
HE SAID WHAT I WANTED TO HEAR...
...SO WHY DO I FEEL SO UNEASY?

End of Chapter 82: Sin'yuu Deep Sadness

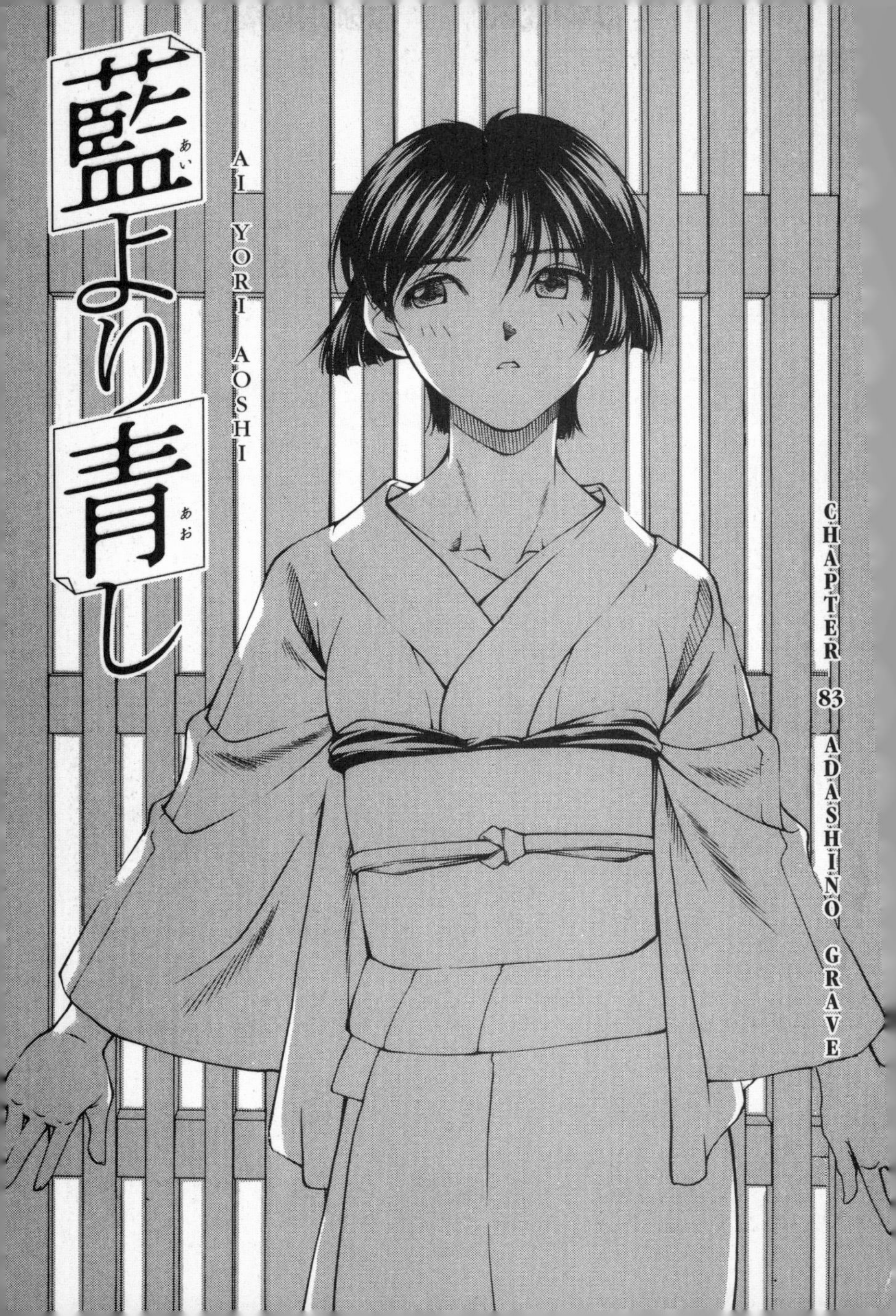
藍(あい)より青(あお)し
AI YORI AOSHI
CHAPTER 83
ADASHINO GRAVE

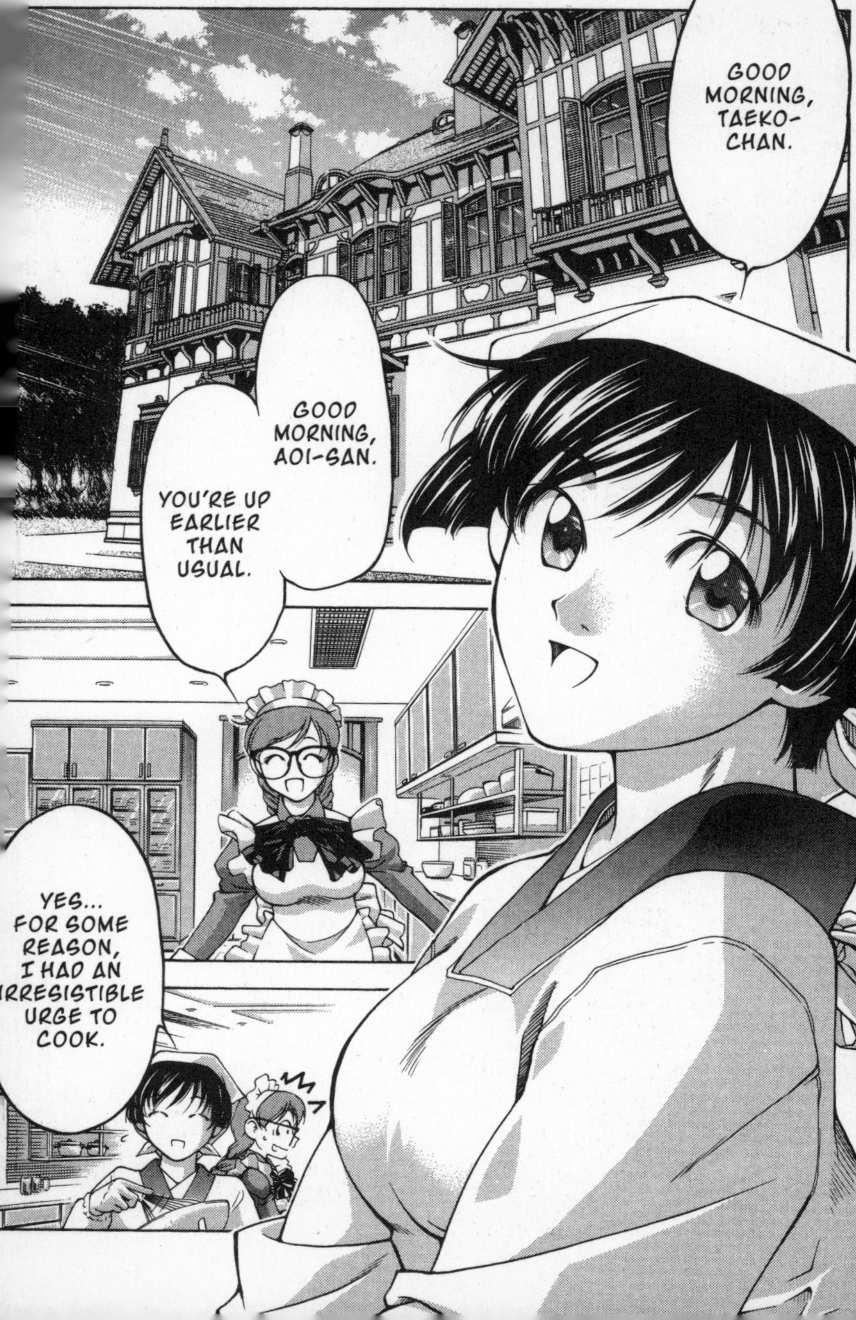
GOOD MORNING, TAEKO-CHAN.
GOOD MORNING, AOI-SAN.
YOU'RE UP EARLIER THAN USUAL.
YES... FOR SOME REASON, I HAD AN IRRESISTIBLE URGE TO COOK.

OH, WOW! DID YOU MAKE ALL OF THIS FOOD THIS MORNING, AOI-SAN?

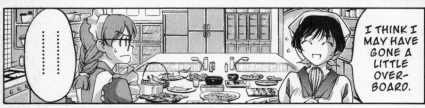

······

······

I THINK I MAY HAVE GONE A LITTLE OVER-BOARD.

GOOD MORNING, MIYABI-SAN.

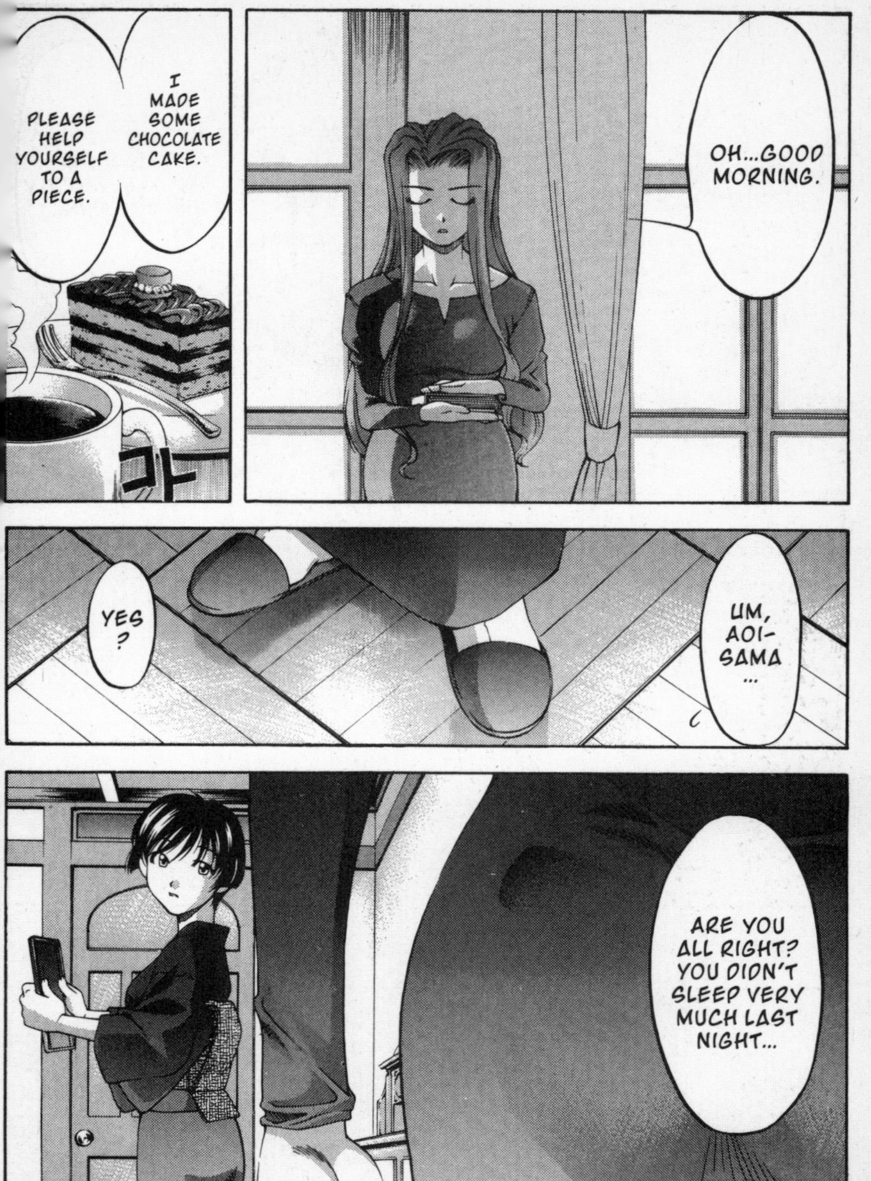
OH...GOOD MORNING.
I MADE SOME CHOCOLATE CAKE.
PLEASE HELP YOURSELF TO A PIECE.
コト
UM, AOI-SAMA...
YES?
ARE YOU ALL RIGHT? YOU DIDN'T SLEEP VERY MUCH LAST NIGHT...

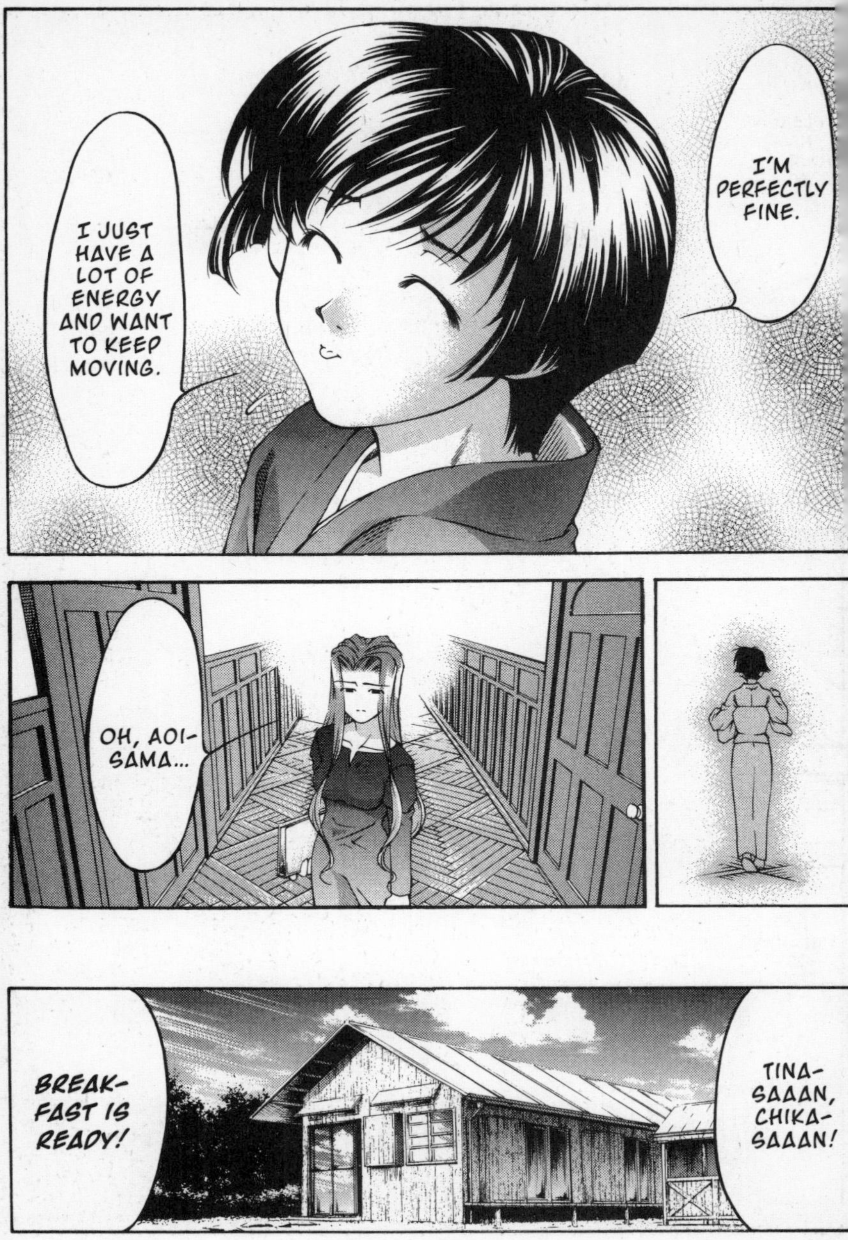
I'M PERFECTLY FINE.
I JUST HAVE A LOT OF ENERGY AND WANT TO KEEP MOVING.
OH, AOI-SAMA...
TINA-SAAAN, CHIKA-SAAAN!
BREAK-FAST IS READY!

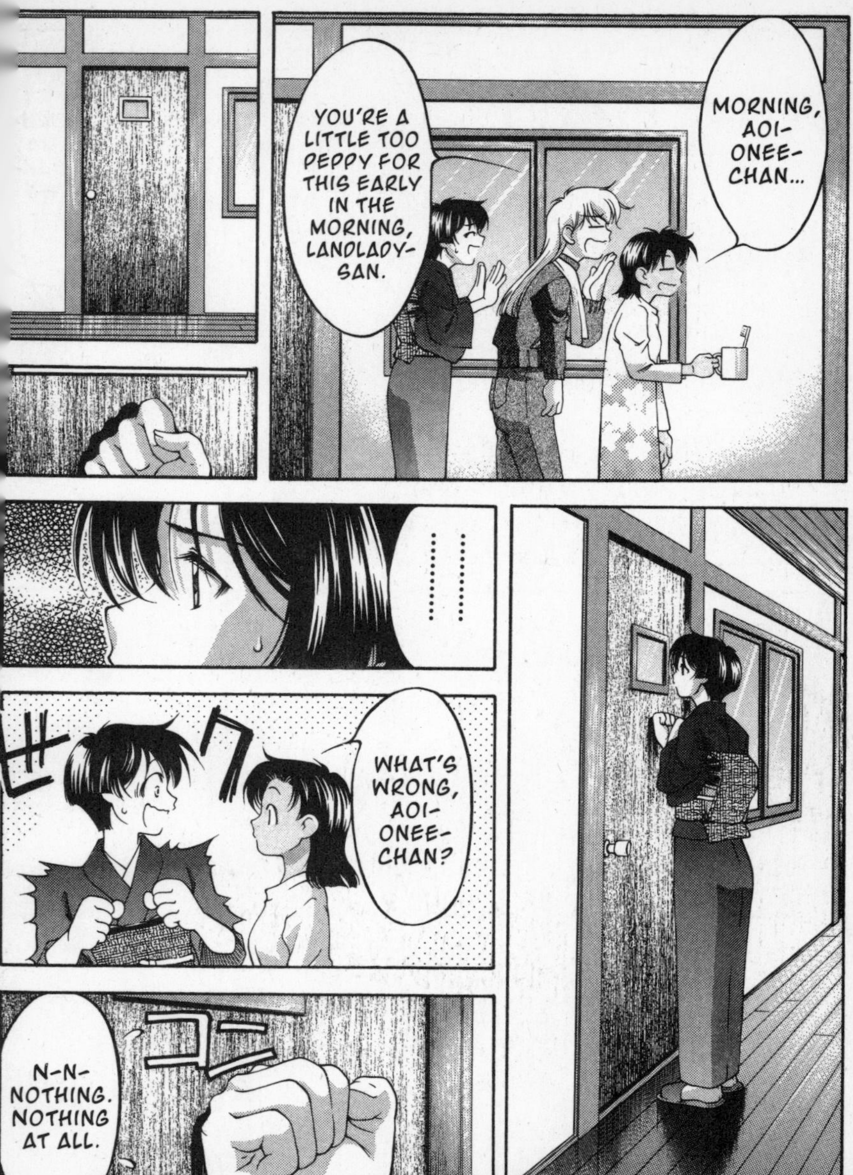
MORNING, AOI-ONEE-CHAN...
YOU'RE A LITTLE TOO PEPPY FOR THIS EARLY IN THE MORNING, LANDLADY-SAN.
......
WHAT'S WRONG, AOI-ONEE-CHAN?
N-N-NOTHING. NOTHING AT ALL.

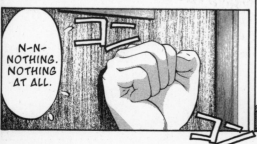

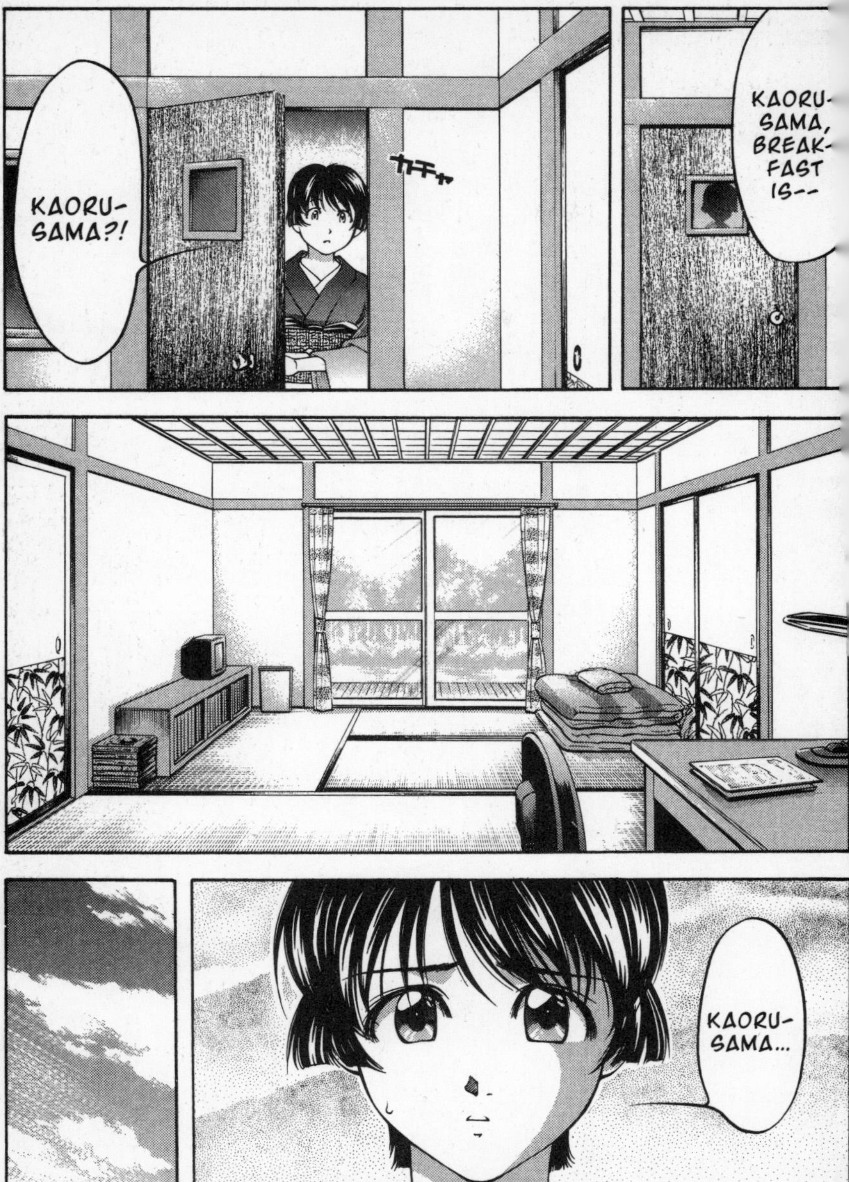
KAORU-SAMA, BREAK-FAST IS--
KAORU-SAMA?!
カチャ
KAORU-SAMA...

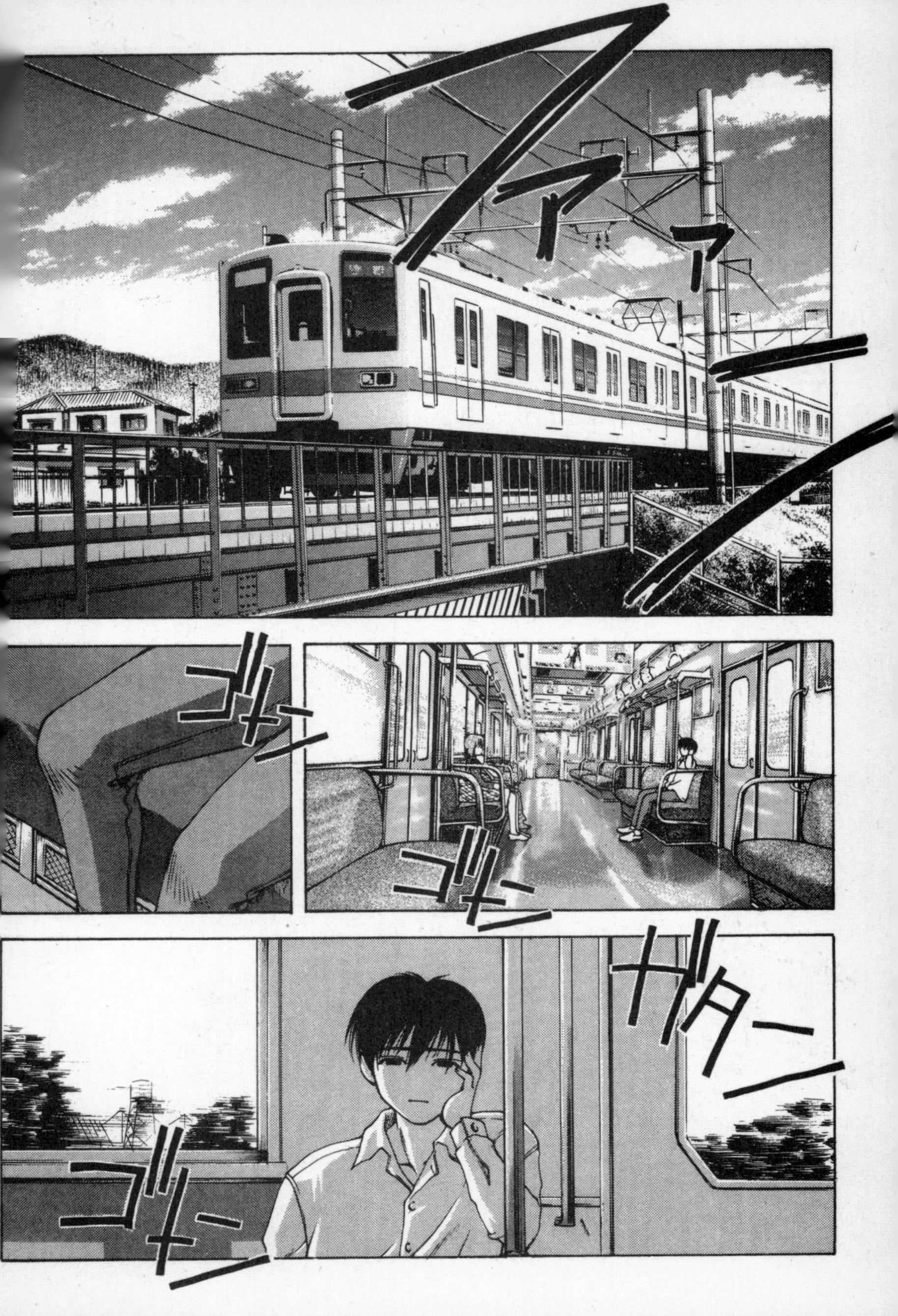
アァァーン
ゴトン
ゴトン
ガターー
ゴトーン

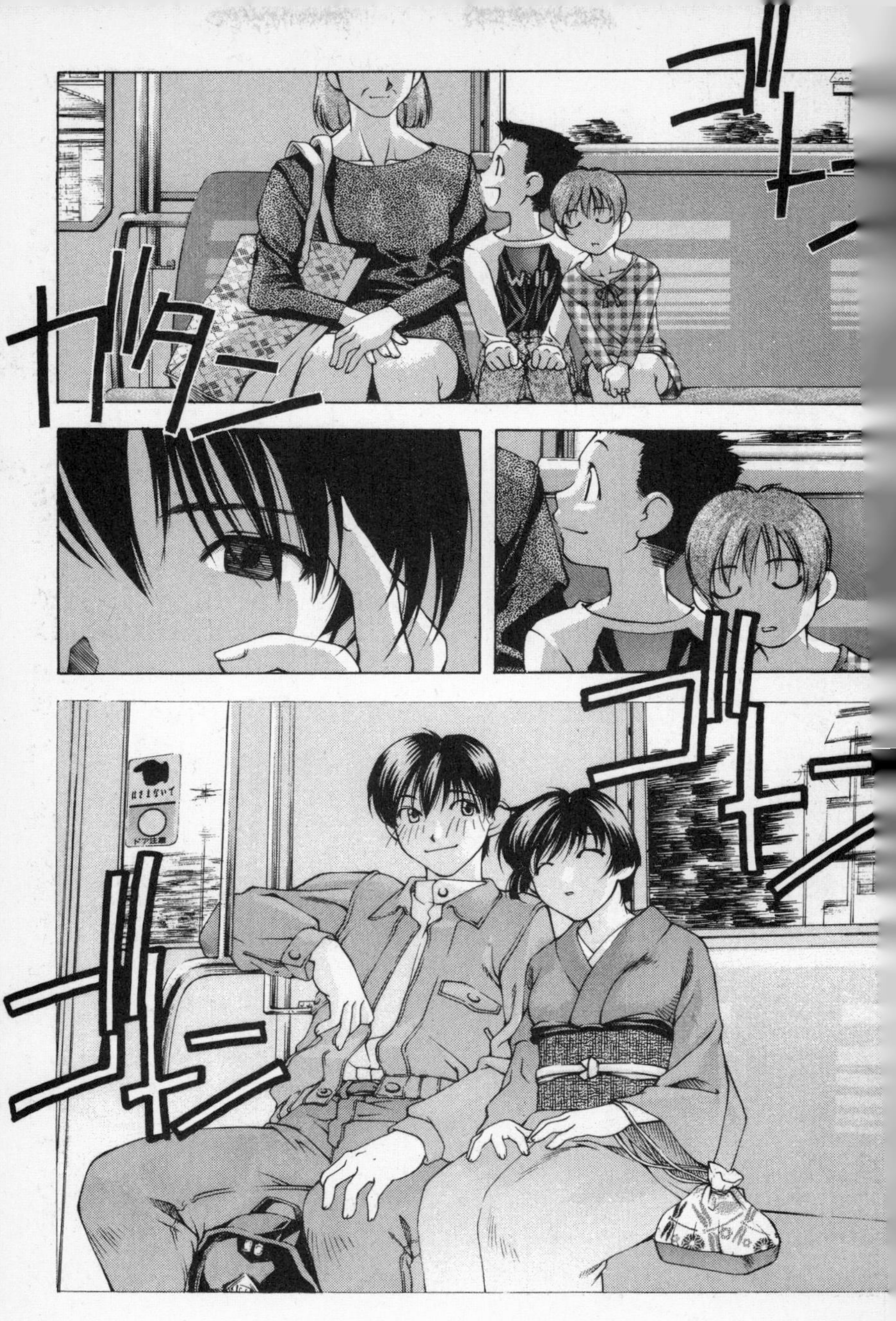

ゴトーン
ガターン
ゴトーン
ゴトーン

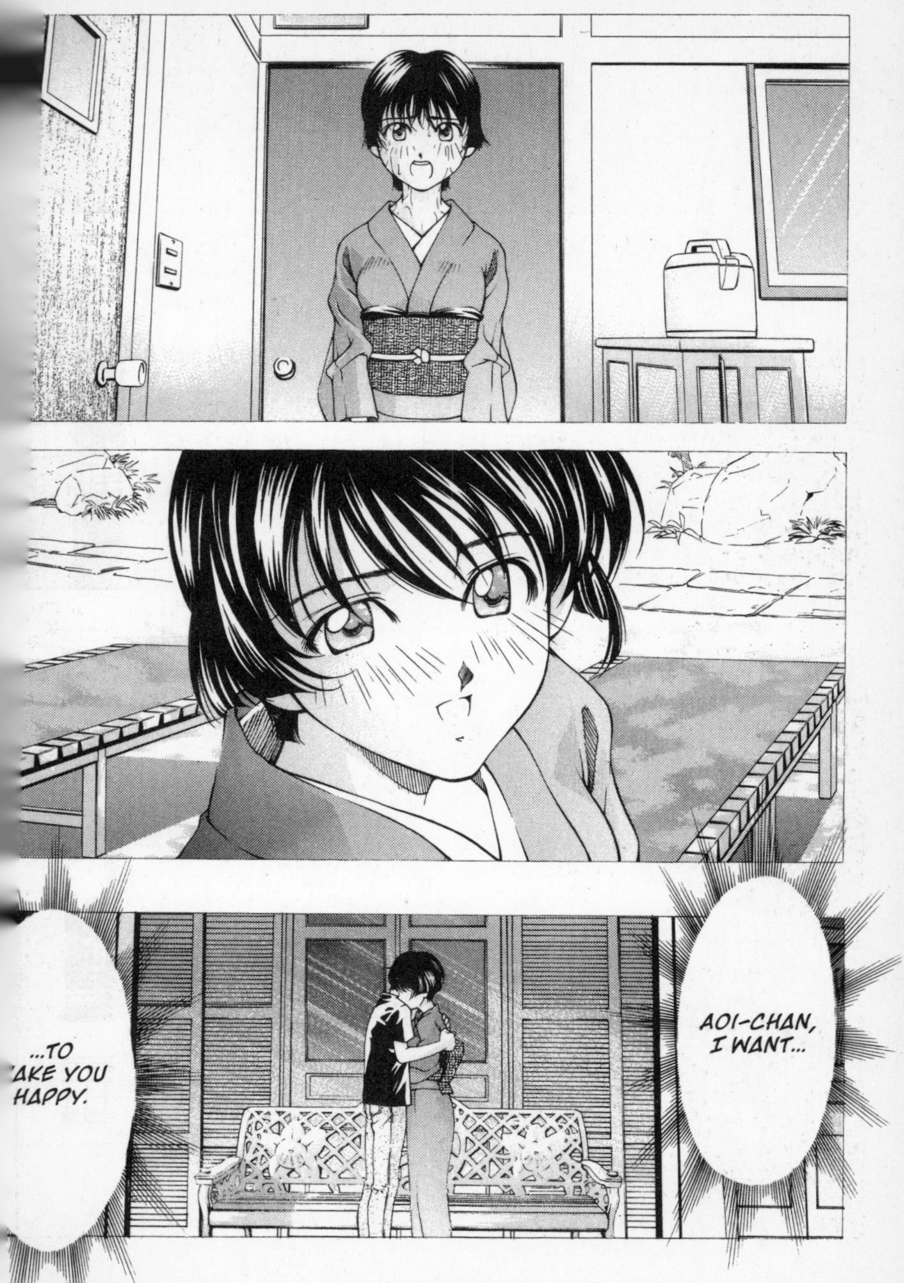
AOI-CHAN, I WANT...
...TO AKE YOU HAPPY.

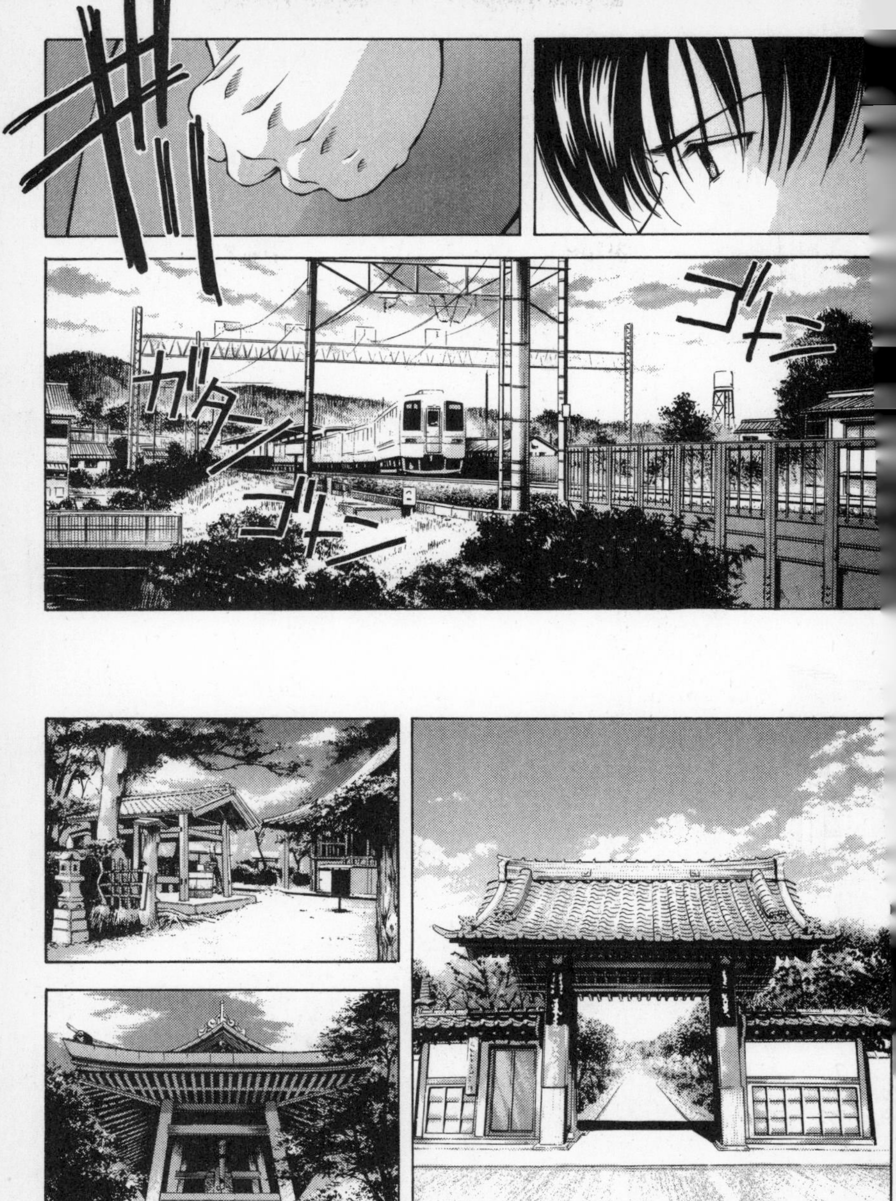
ギリ
ゴトン
ガタン
ゴトン

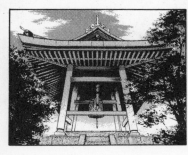

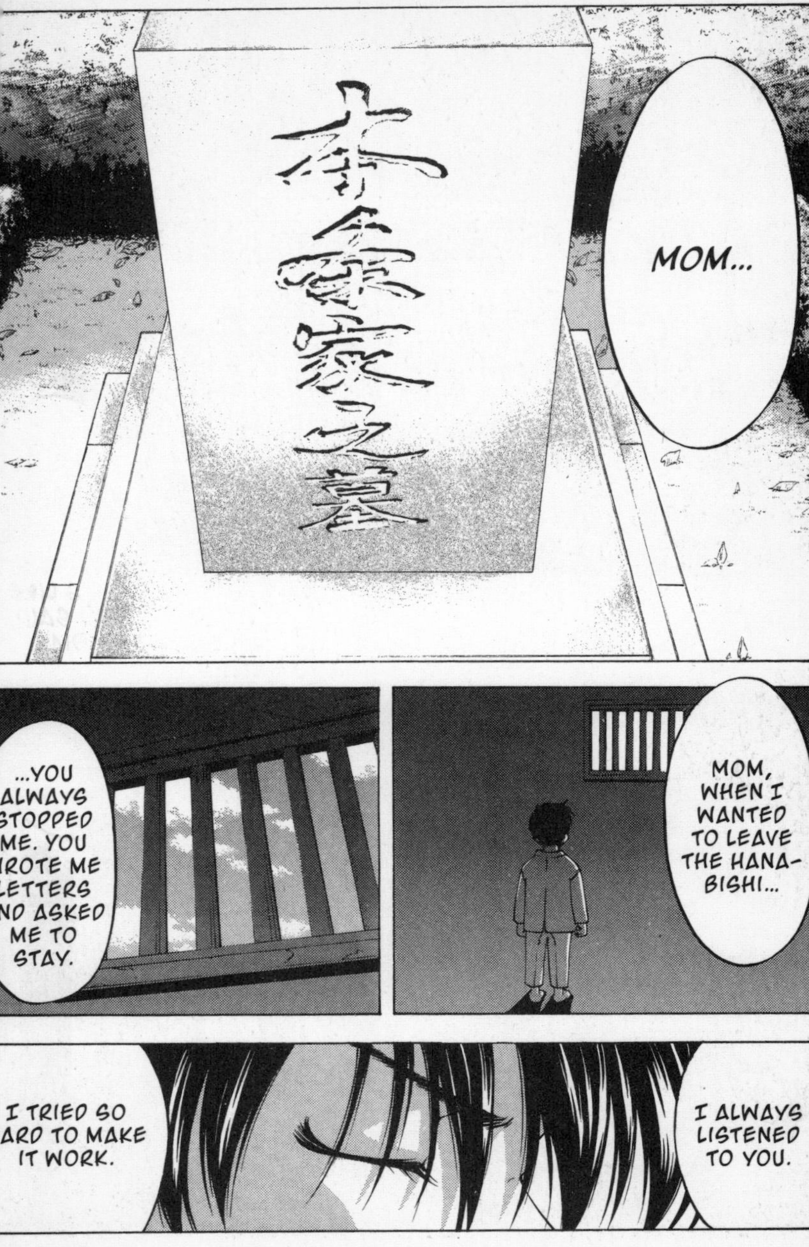
MOM...
MOM, WHEN I WANTED TO LEAVE THE HANA-BISHI...
...YOU ALWAYS STOPPED ME. YOU WROTE ME LETTERS AND ASKED ME TO STAY.
I ALWAYS LISTENED TO YOU.
I TRIED SO HARD TO MAKE IT WORK.

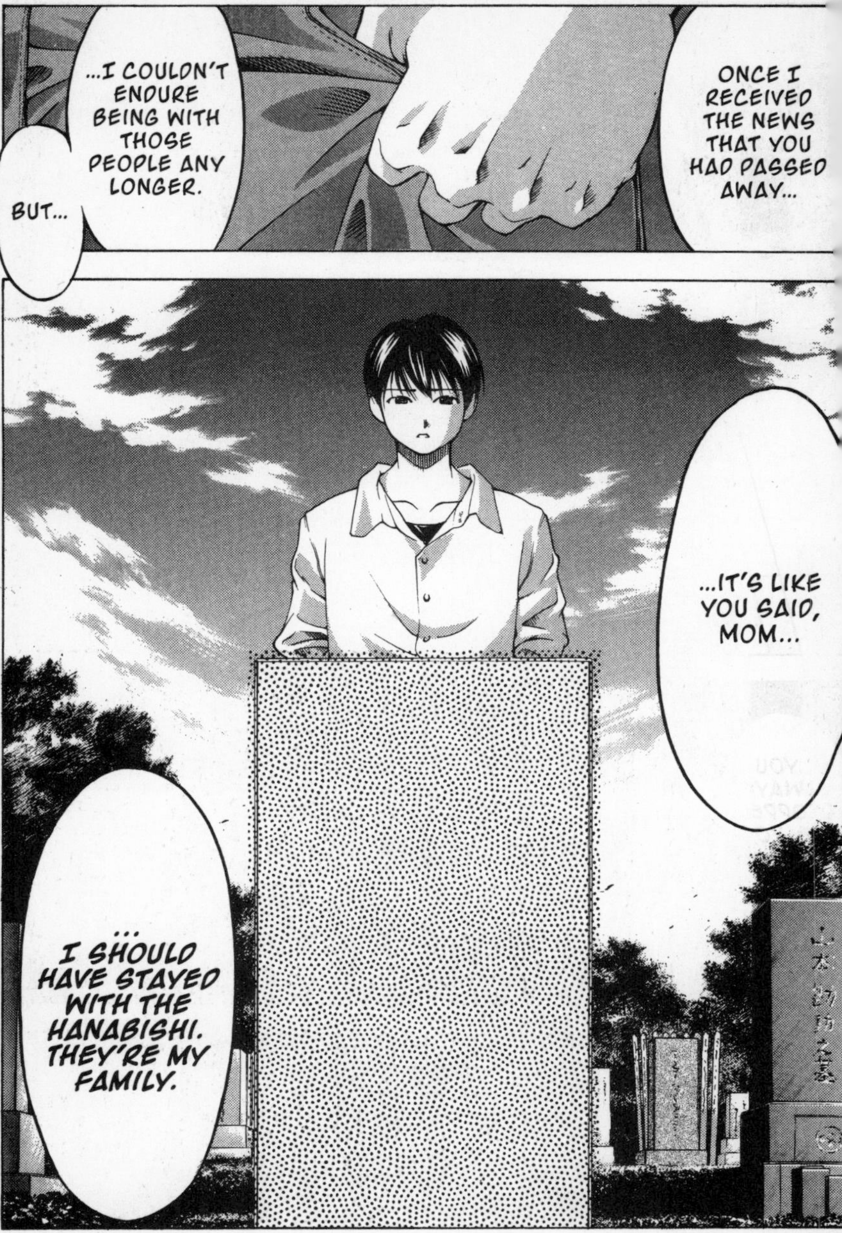
ONCE I RECEIVED THE NEWS THAT YOU HAD PASSED AWAY...
...I COULDN'T ENDURE BEING WITH THOSE PEOPLE ANY LONGER.
BUT...
...IT'S LIKE YOU SAID, MOM...
... I SHOULD HAVE STAYED WITH THE HANABISHI. THEY'RE MY FAMILY.

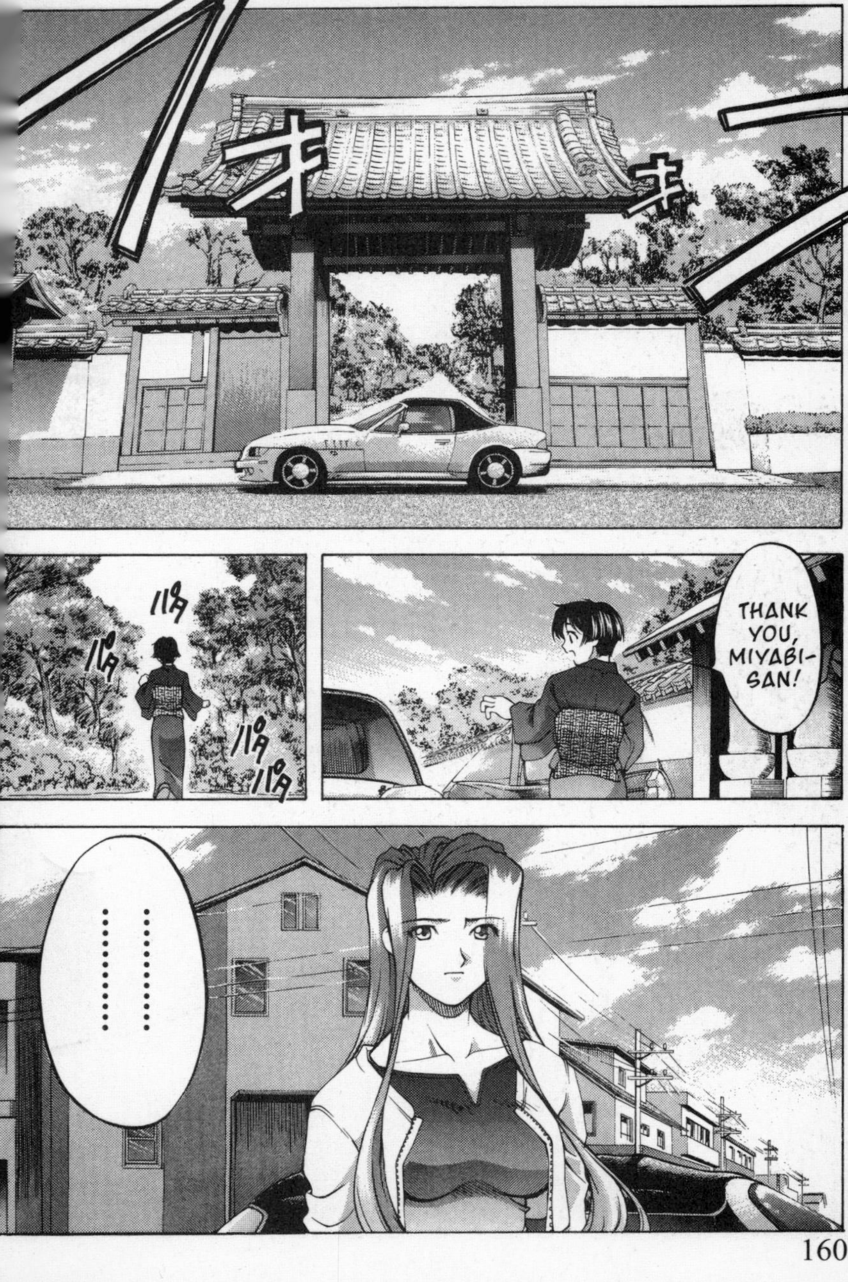
THANK YOU, MIYABI-SAN!
パタ
パタ
パタ
パタ
……
……

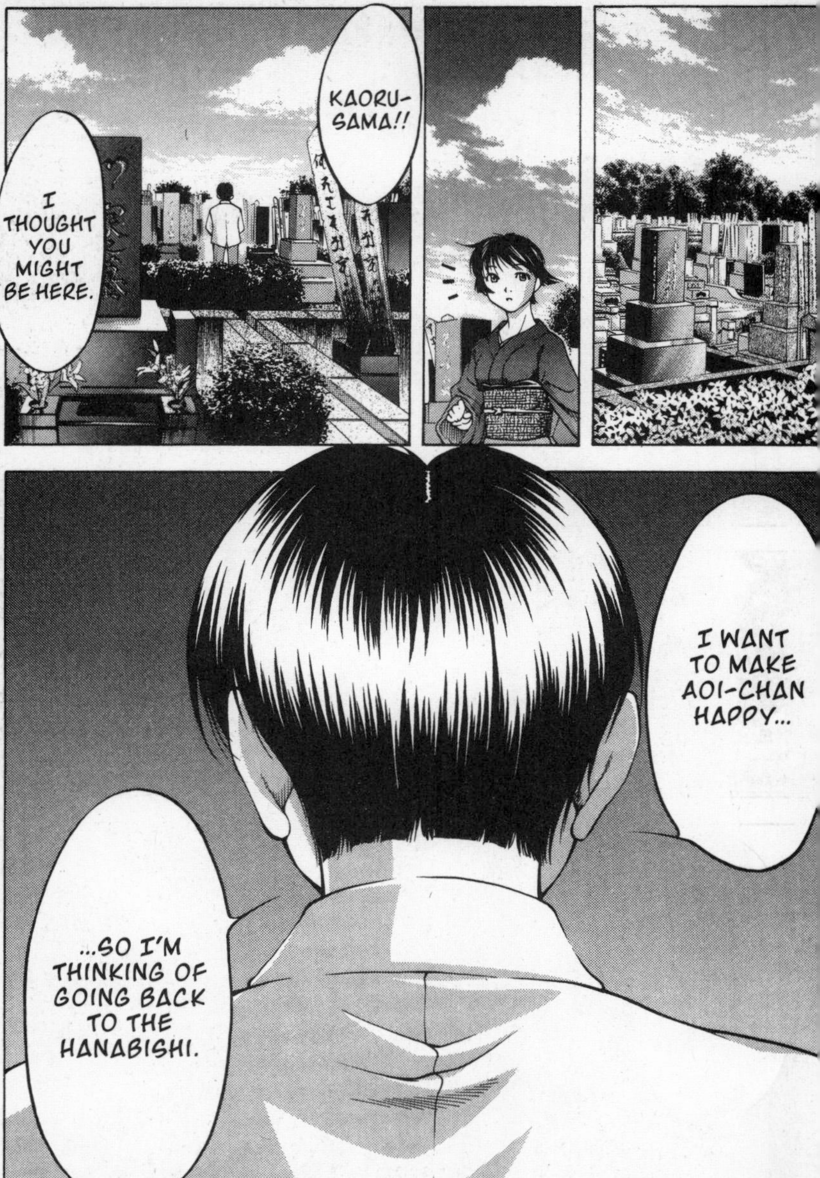
KAORU-SAMA!!
I THOUGHT YOU MIGHT BE HERE.
I WANT TO MAKE AOI-CHAN HAPPY...
...SO I'M THINKING OF GOING BACK TO THE HANABISHI.

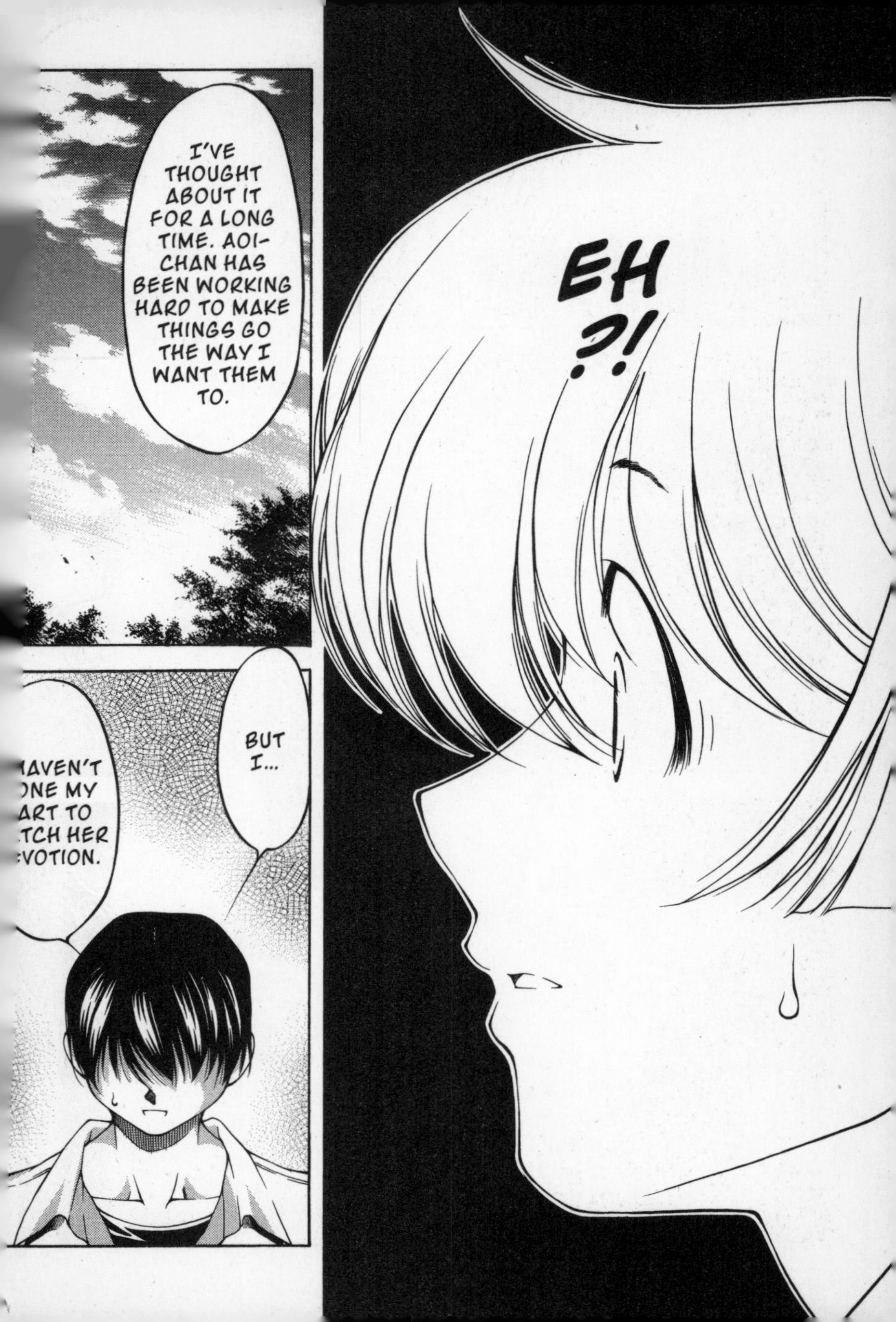
EH ?!
I'VE THOUGHT ABOUT IT FOR A LONG TIME. AOI-CHAN HAS BEEN WORKING HARD TO MAKE THINGS GO THE WAY I WANT THEM TO.
BUT I...
AVEN'T ONE MY ART TO TCH HER EVOTION.

BUT...

...AND THAT'S NOT ENOUGH FOR AOI-CHAN, NOT FOR THE HAPPINESS SHE DESERVES.

I'VE ONLY INDULGED HALF-BAKED FEELINGS...

IF AOI-CHAN IS HAPPY...

YOU CAN'T...

NO, KAORU-SAMA, NO...!

BUT...

...KAORU-SAMA!

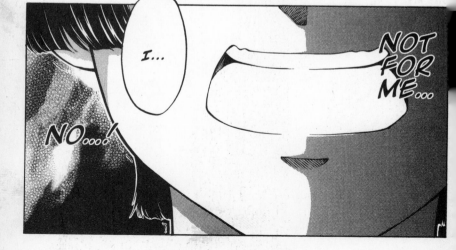

I...

NOT FOR ME...

NO....!

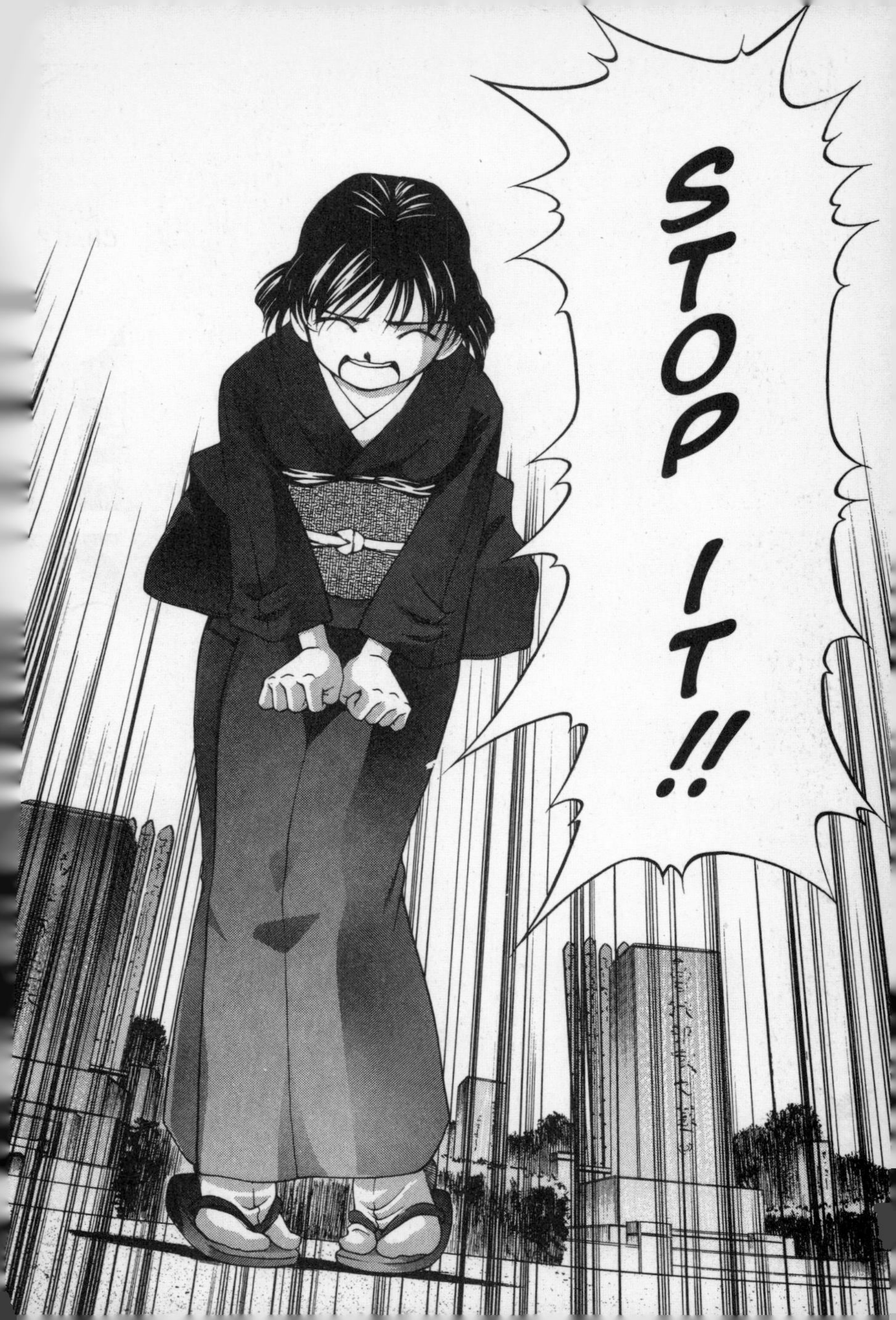
STOP IT!!

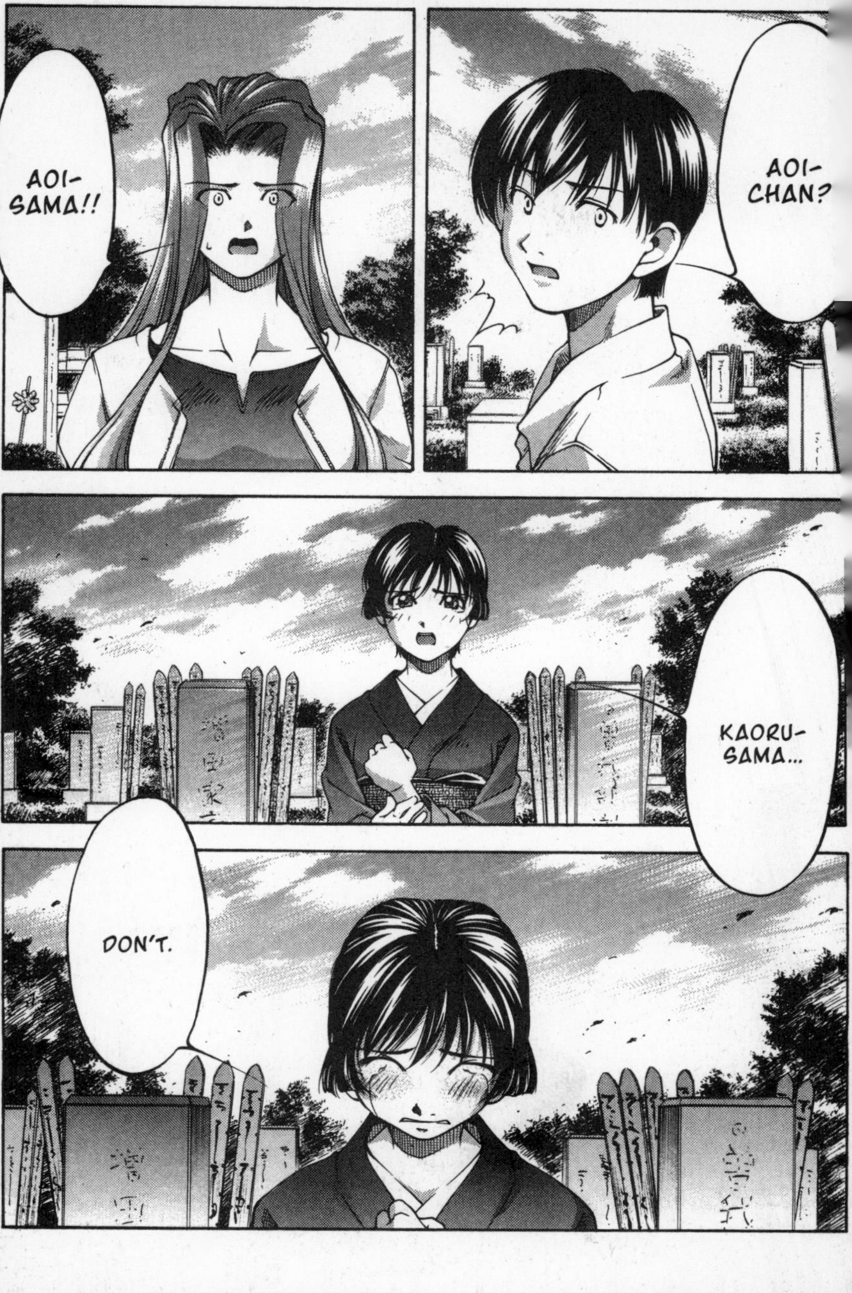
AOI-CHAN?
AOI-SAMA!!
KAORU-SAMA...
DON'T.

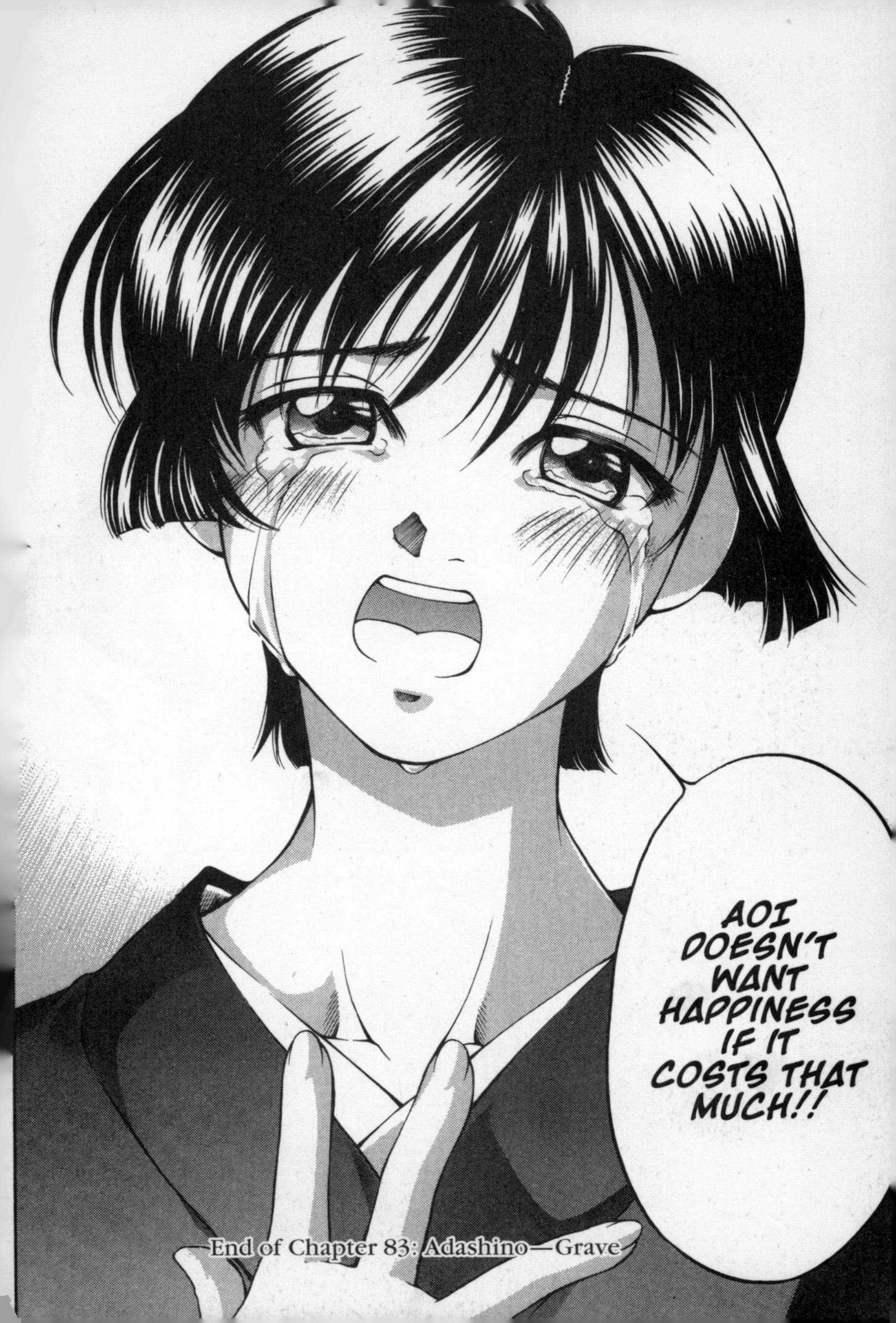
AOI DOESN'T WANT HAPPINESS IF IT COSTS THAT MUCH!!

—End of Chapter 83: Adashino—Grave—

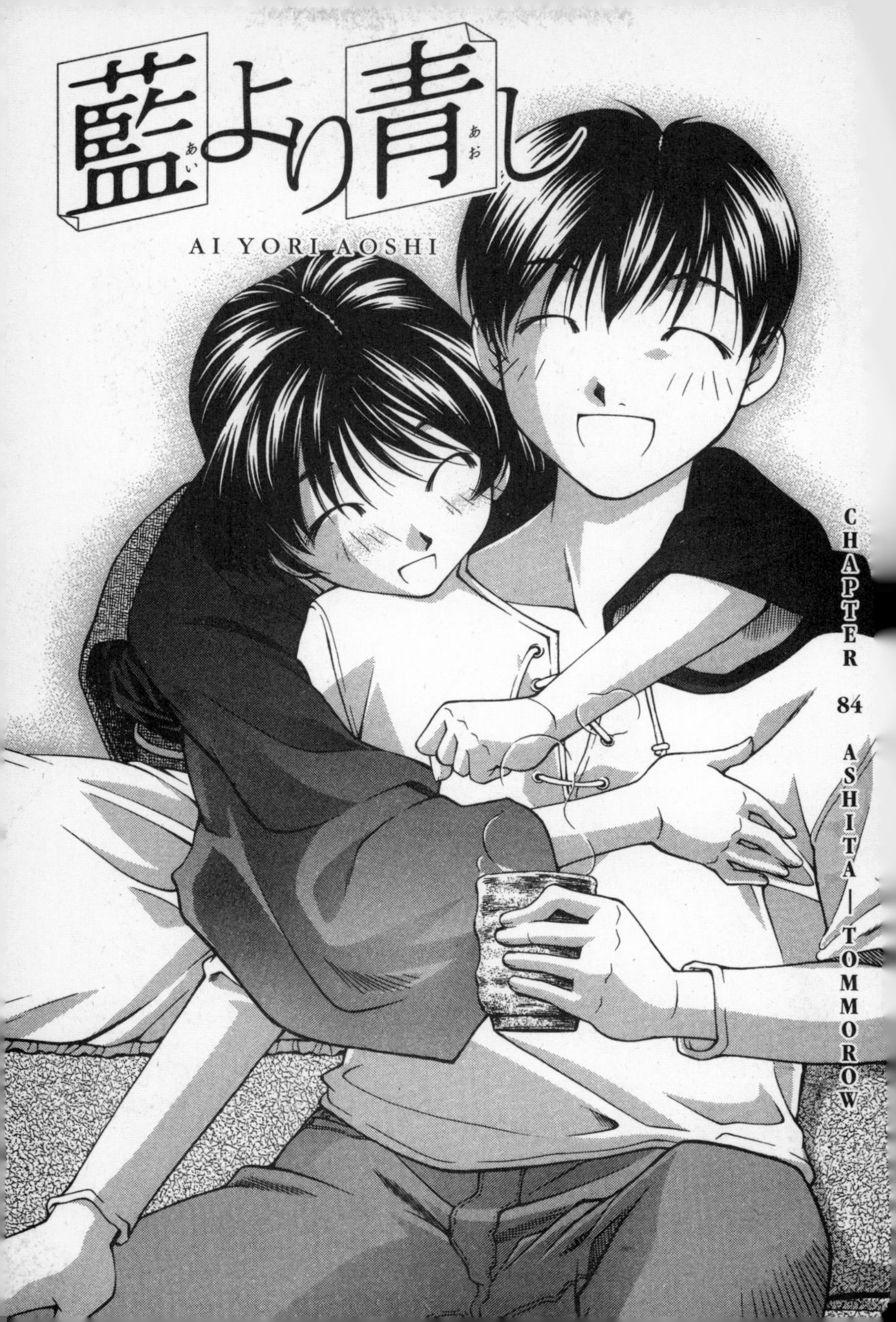
藍より青し
あい あお
AI YORI AOSHI
CHAPTER 84
ASHITA—TOMMOROW

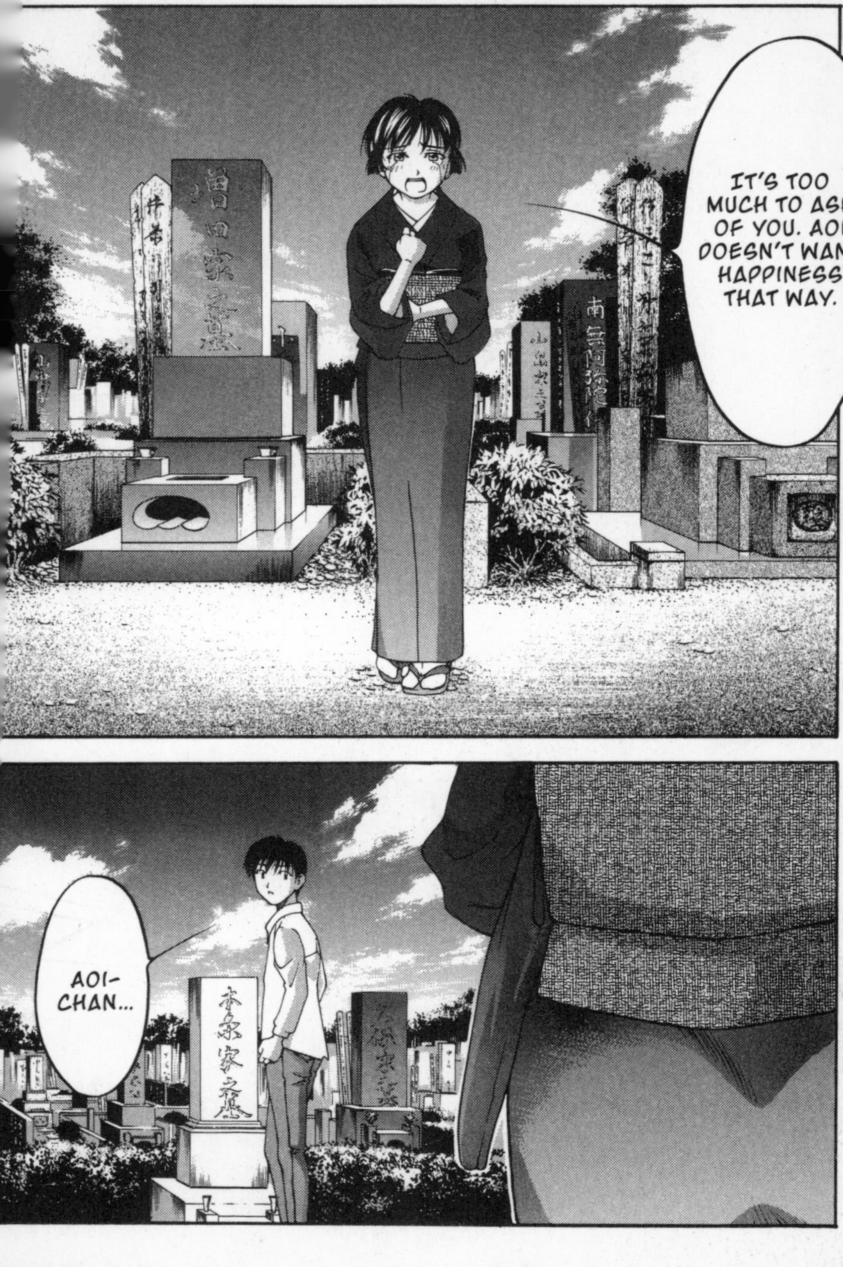
IT'S TOO MUCH TO ASK OF YOU. AOI DOESN'T WANT HAPPINESS THAT WAY.
AOI-CHAN...

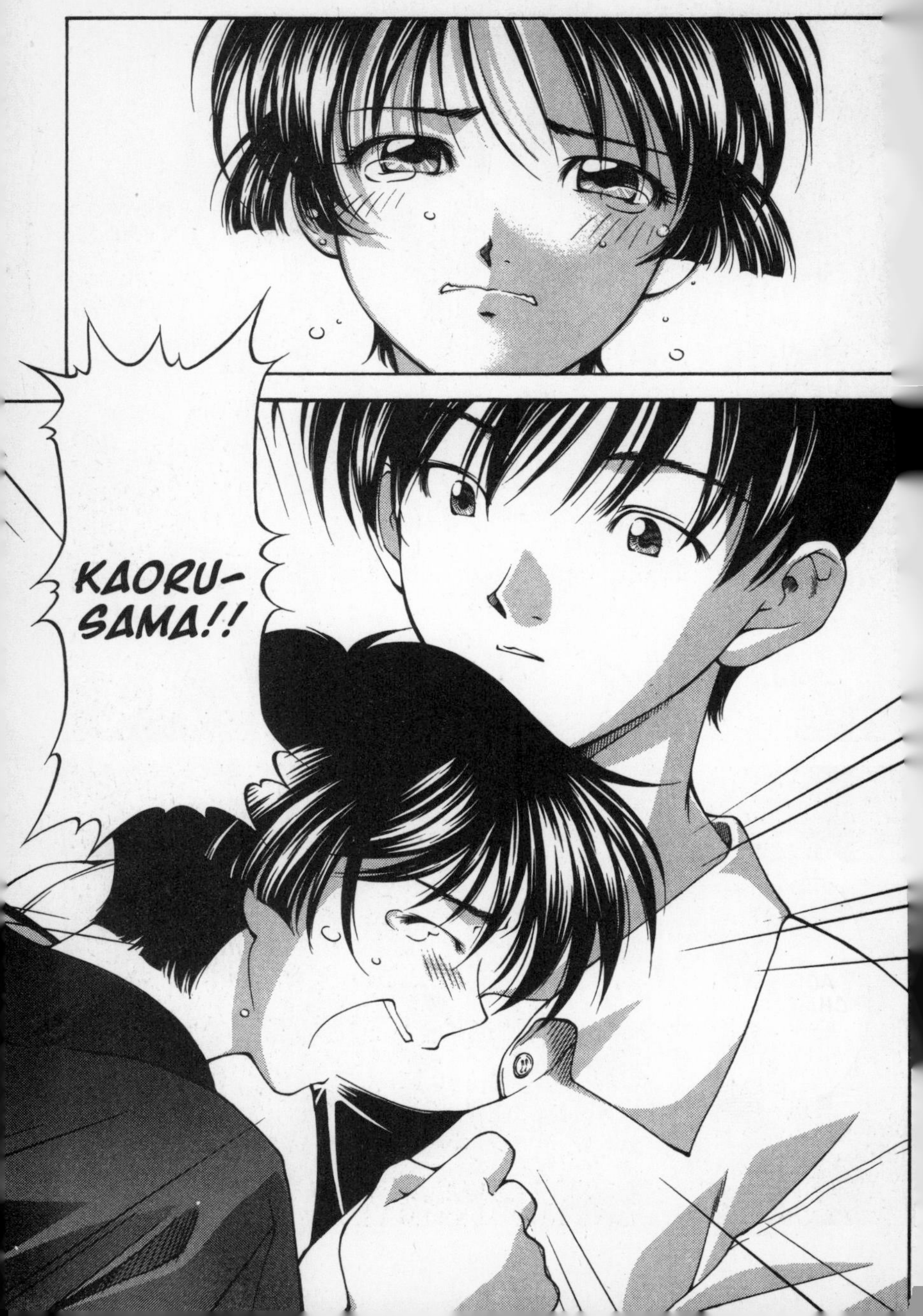
KAORU-SAMA!!

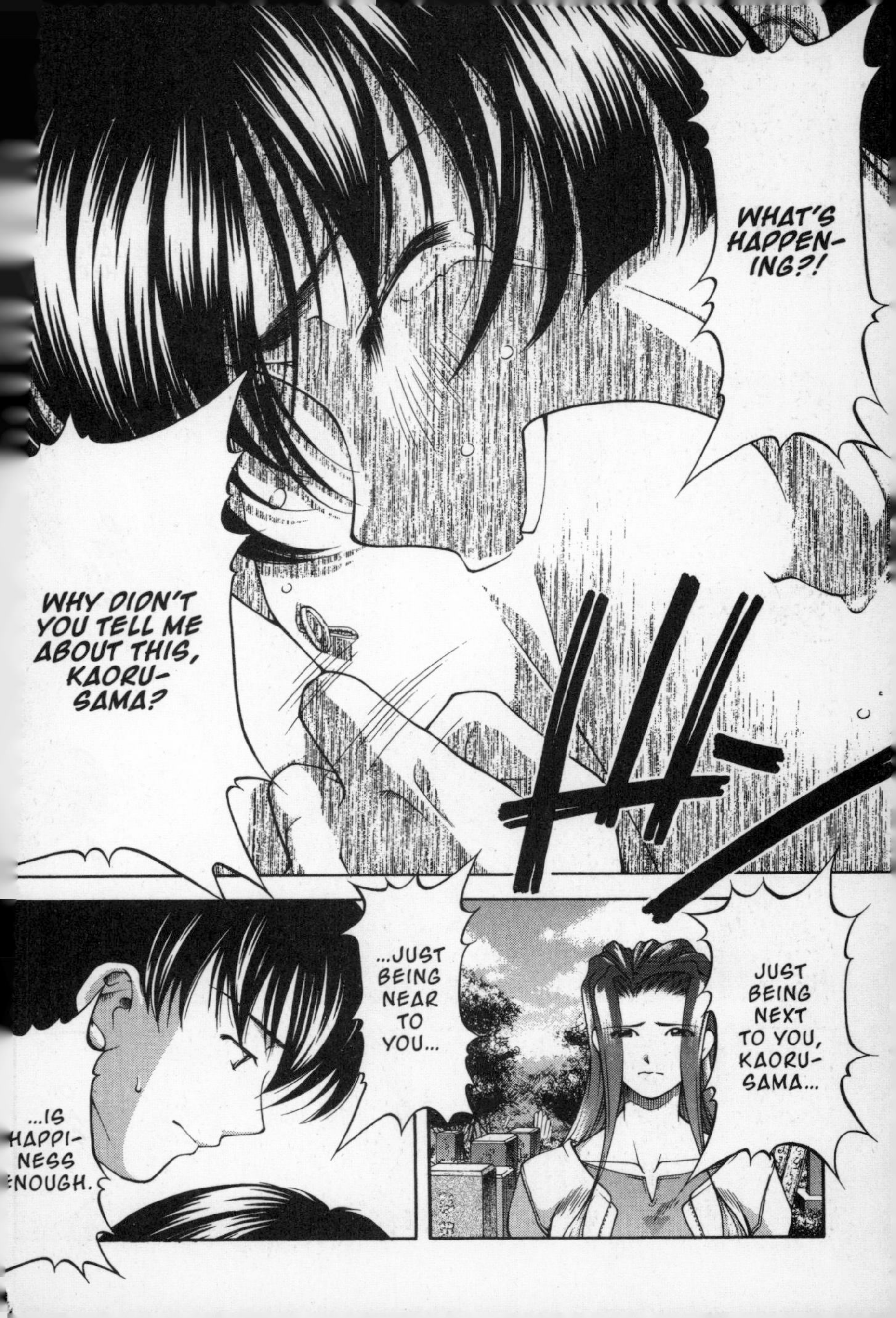
WHAT'S HAPPEN-ING?!
WHY DIDN'T YOU TELL ME ABOUT THIS, KAORU-SAMA?
JUST BEING NEXT TO YOU, KAORU-SAMA...
...JUST BEING NEAR TO YOU...
...IS HAPPI-NESS ENOUGH.

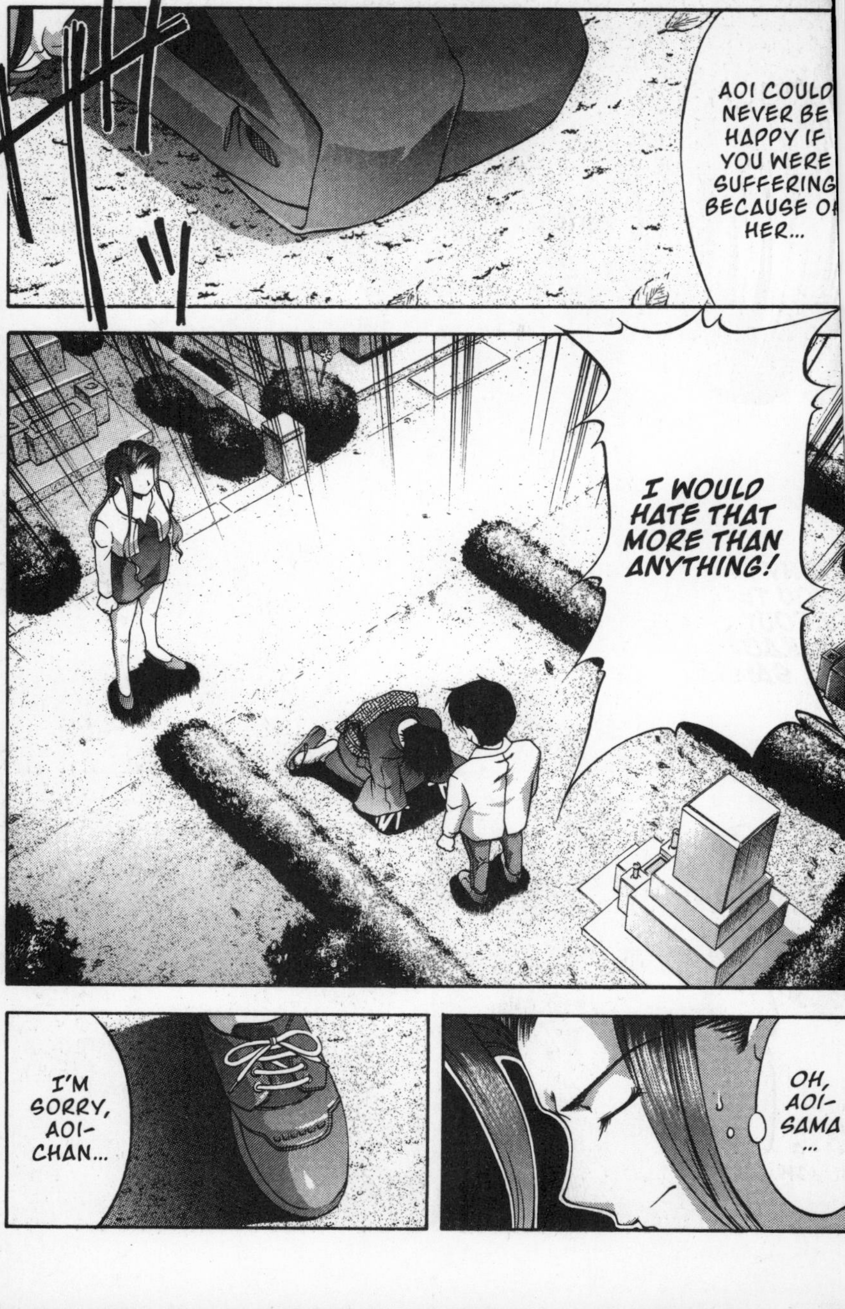
AOI COULD NEVER BE HAPPY IF YOU WERE SUFFERING BECAUSE OF HER...
I WOULD HATE THAT MORE THAN ANYTHING!
OH, AOI-SAMA ...
I'M SORRY, AOI-CHAN...

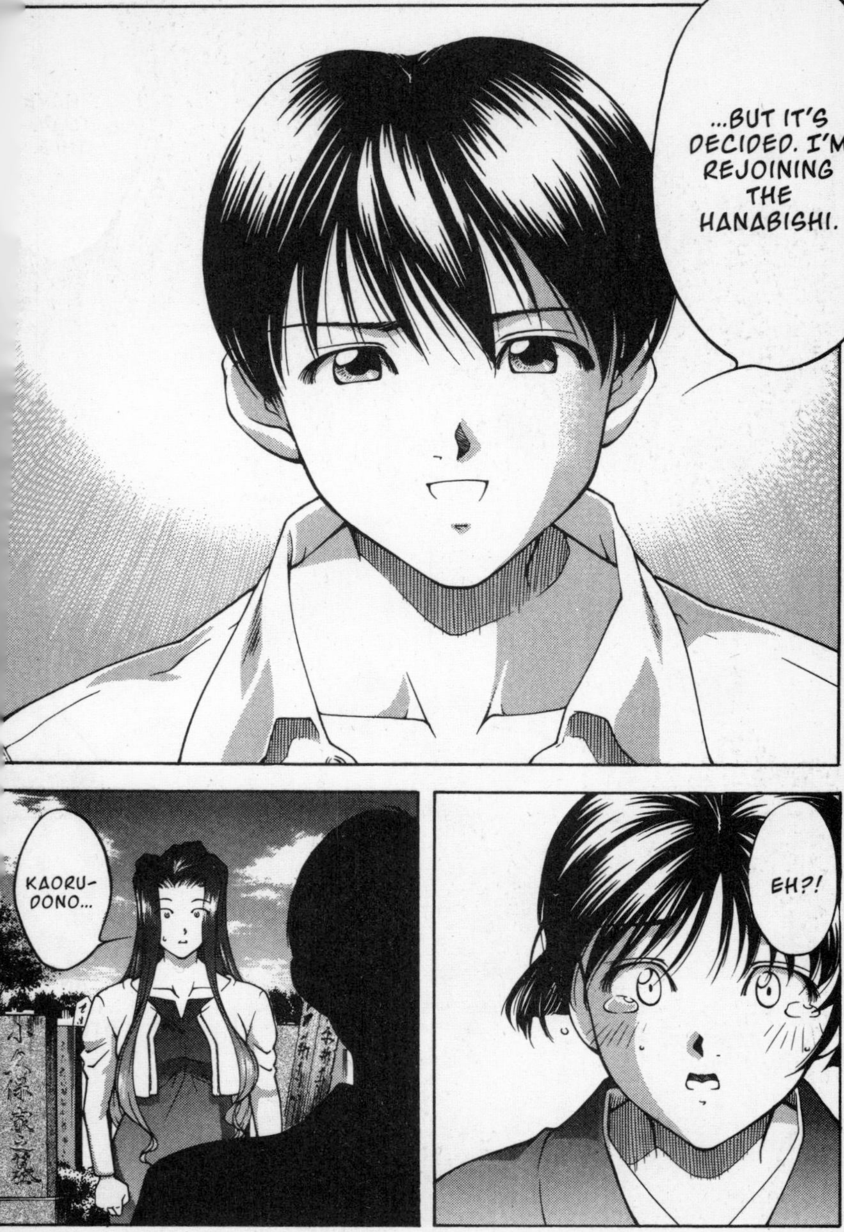
...BUT IT'S DECIDED. I'M REJOINING THE HANABISHI.
EH?!
KAORU-DONO...

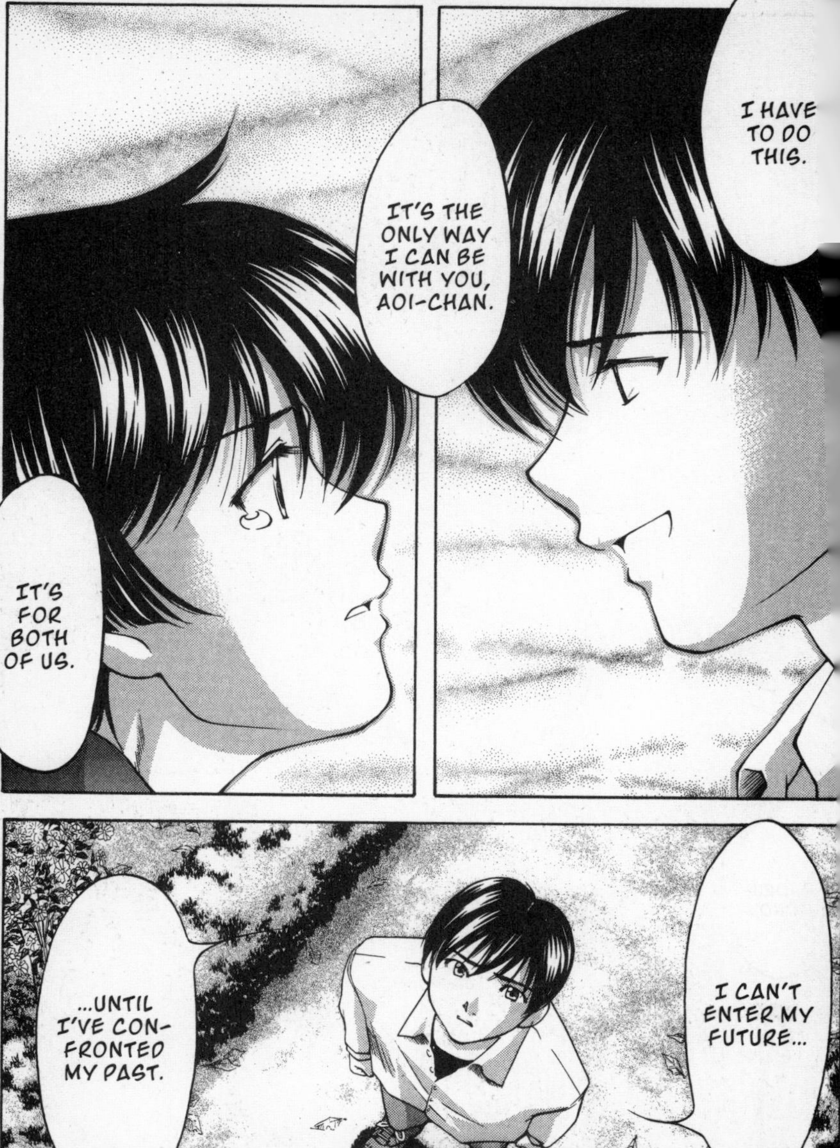
I HAVE TO DO THIS.
IT'S THE ONLY WAY I CAN BE WITH YOU, AOI-CHAN.
IT'S FOR BOTH OF US.
I CAN'T ENTER MY FUTURE...
...UNTIL I'VE CON-FRONTED MY PAST.

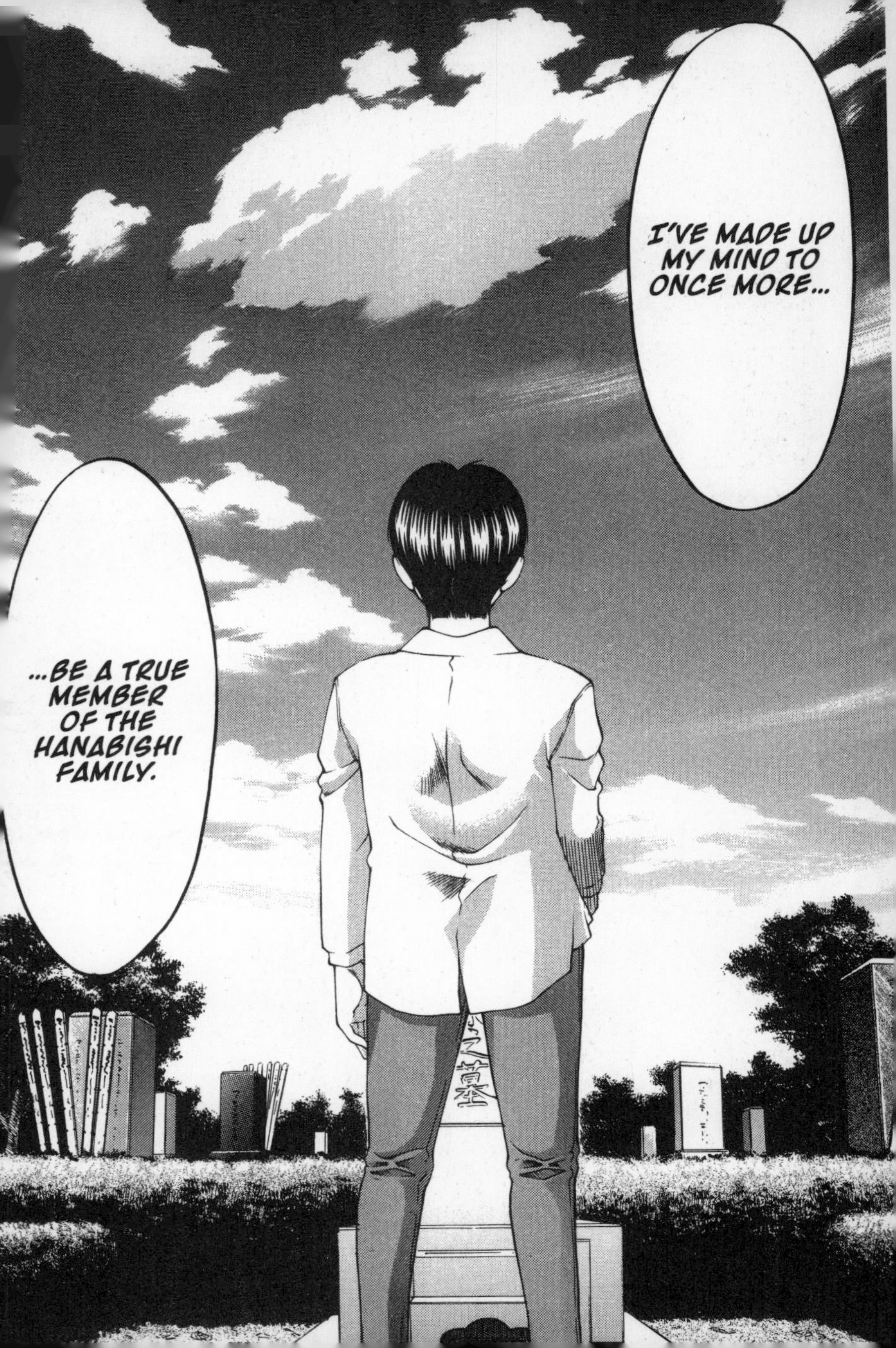
I'VE MADE UP MY MIND TO ONCE MORE...
...BE A TRUE MEMBER OF THE HANABISHI FAMILY.

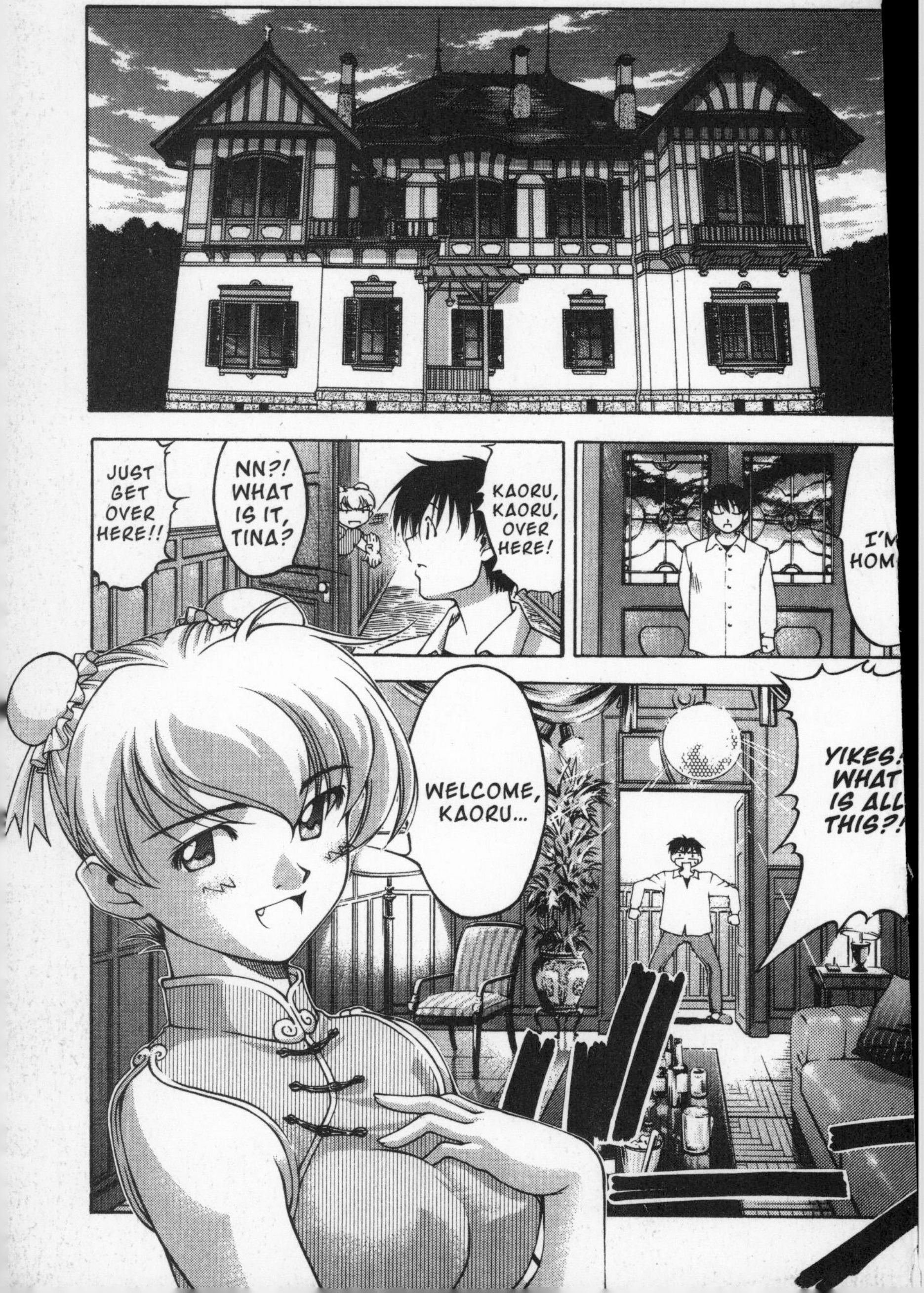
I'M HOM
KAORU, KAORU, OVER HERE!
NN?! WHAT IS IT, TINA?
JUST GET OVER HERE!!
YIKES! WHAT IS ALL THIS?!
WELCOME, KAORU...

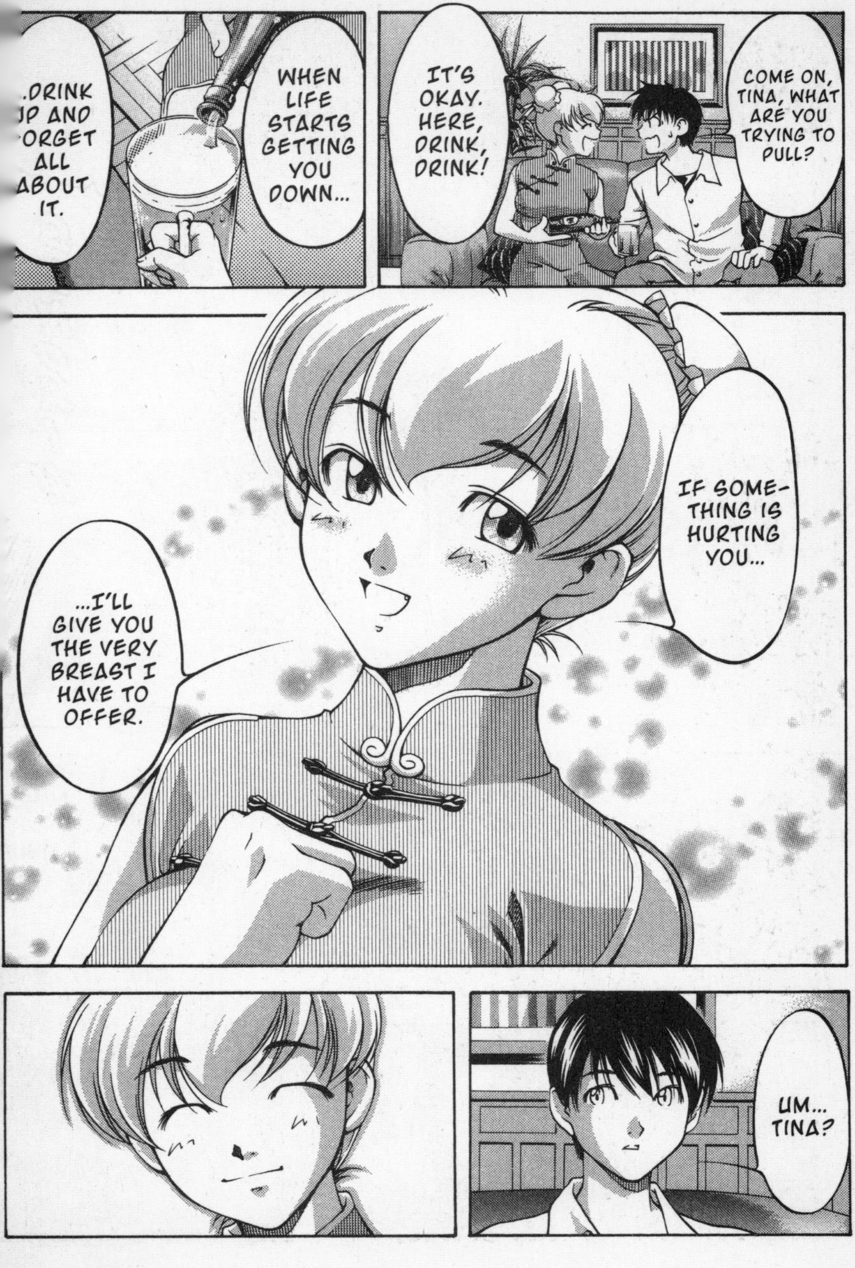
COME ON, TINA, WHAT ARE YOU TRYING TO PULL?
IT'S OKAY. HERE, DRINK, DRINK!
WHEN LIFE STARTS GETTING YOU DOWN...
.DRINK UP AND FORGET ALL ABOUT IT.
IF SOME-THING IS HURTING YOU...
...I'LL GIVE YOU THE VERY BREAST I HAVE TO OFFER.
UM... TINA?

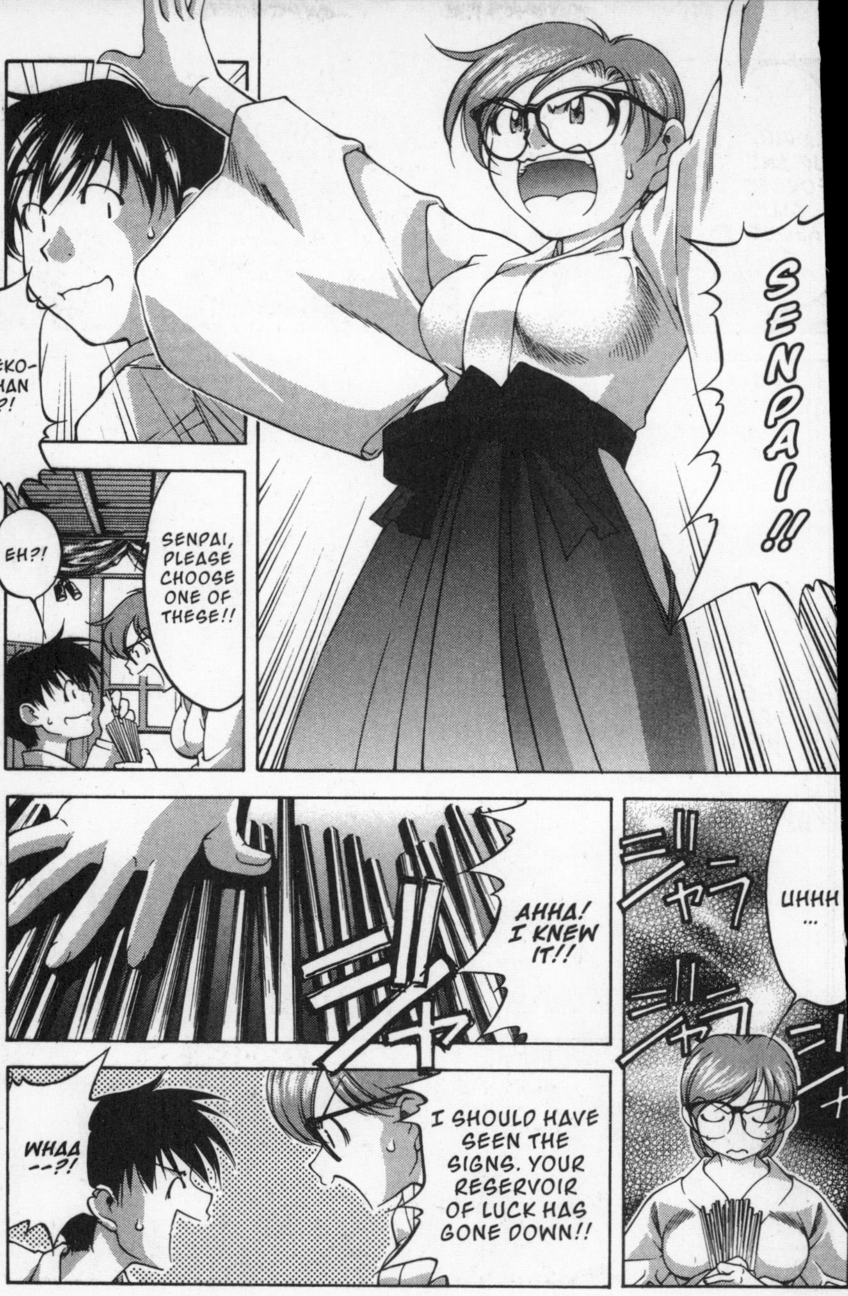
SENPAI!!
TAEKO-CHAN?!
SENPAI, PLEASE CHOOSE ONE OF THESE!!
EH?!
UHHH...
ジャラ
ジャラ
AHHA! I KNEW IT!!
I SHOULD HAVE SEEN THE SIGNS. YOUR RESERVOIR OF LUCK HAS GONE DOWN!!
WHAA--?!

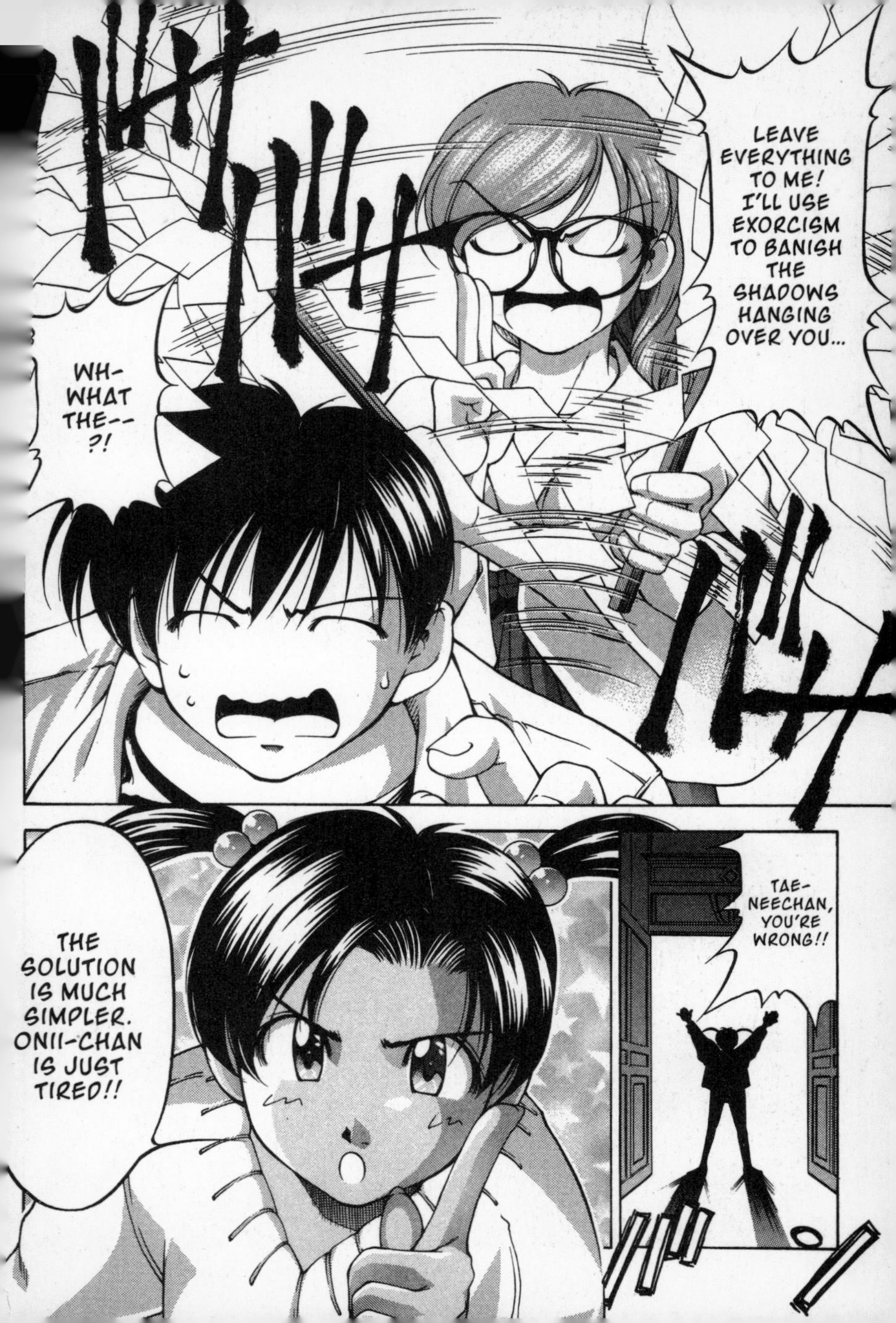
LEAVE EVERYTHING TO ME! I'LL USE EXORCISM TO BANISH THE SHADOWS HANGING OVER YOU...
WH- WHAT THE-- ?!
TAE-NEECHAN, YOU'RE WRONG!!
THE SOLUTION IS MUCH SIMPLER. ONII-CHAN IS JUST TIRED!!

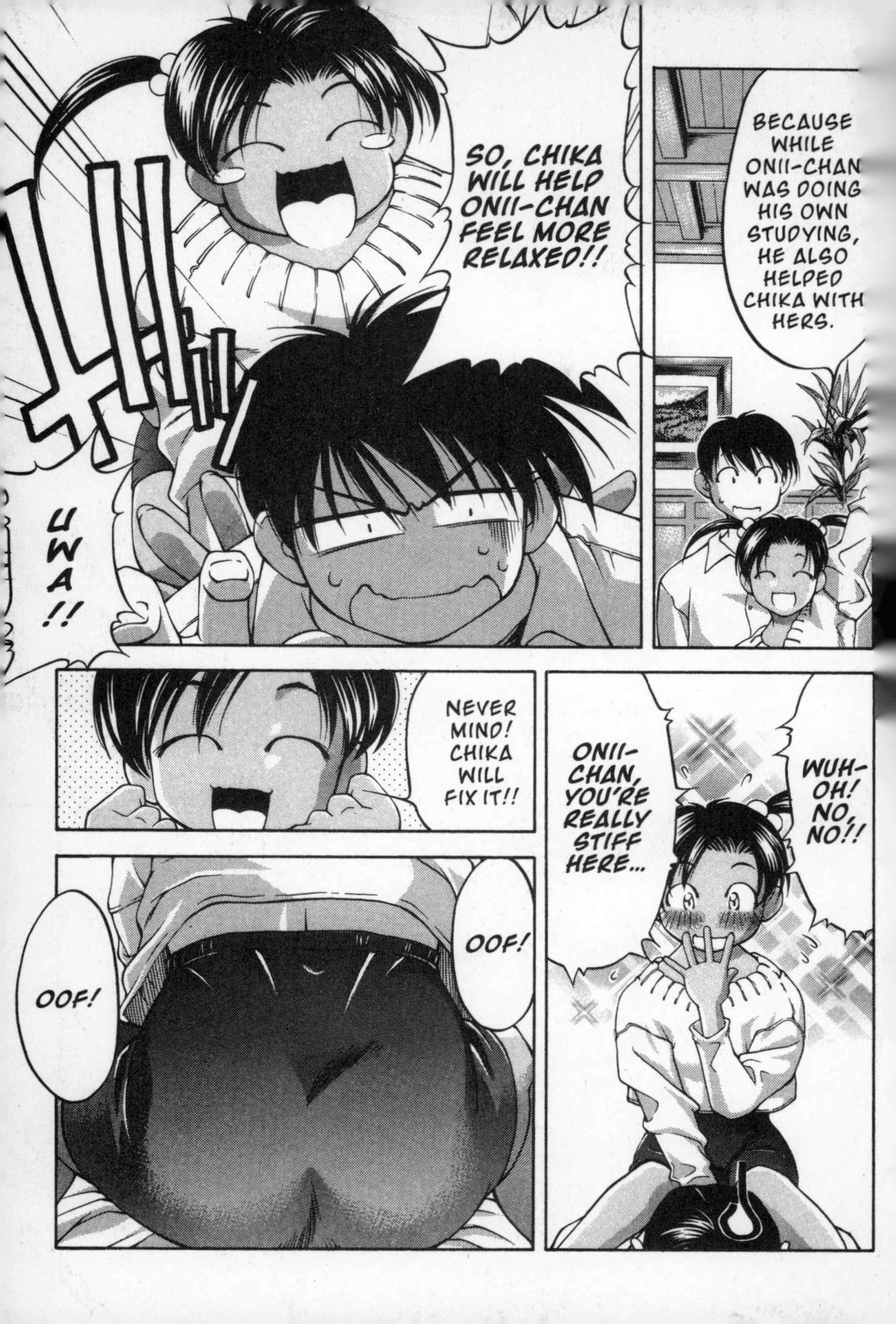
BECAUSE WHILE ONII-CHAN WAS DOING HIS OWN STUDYING, HE ALSO HELPED CHIKA WITH HERS.
SO, CHIKA WILL HELP ONII-CHAN FEEL MORE RELAXED!!
UWA!!
WUH-OH! NO, NO!!
ONII-CHAN, YOU'RE REALLY STIFF HERE...
NEVER MIND! CHIKA WILL FIX IT!!
OOF!
OOF!

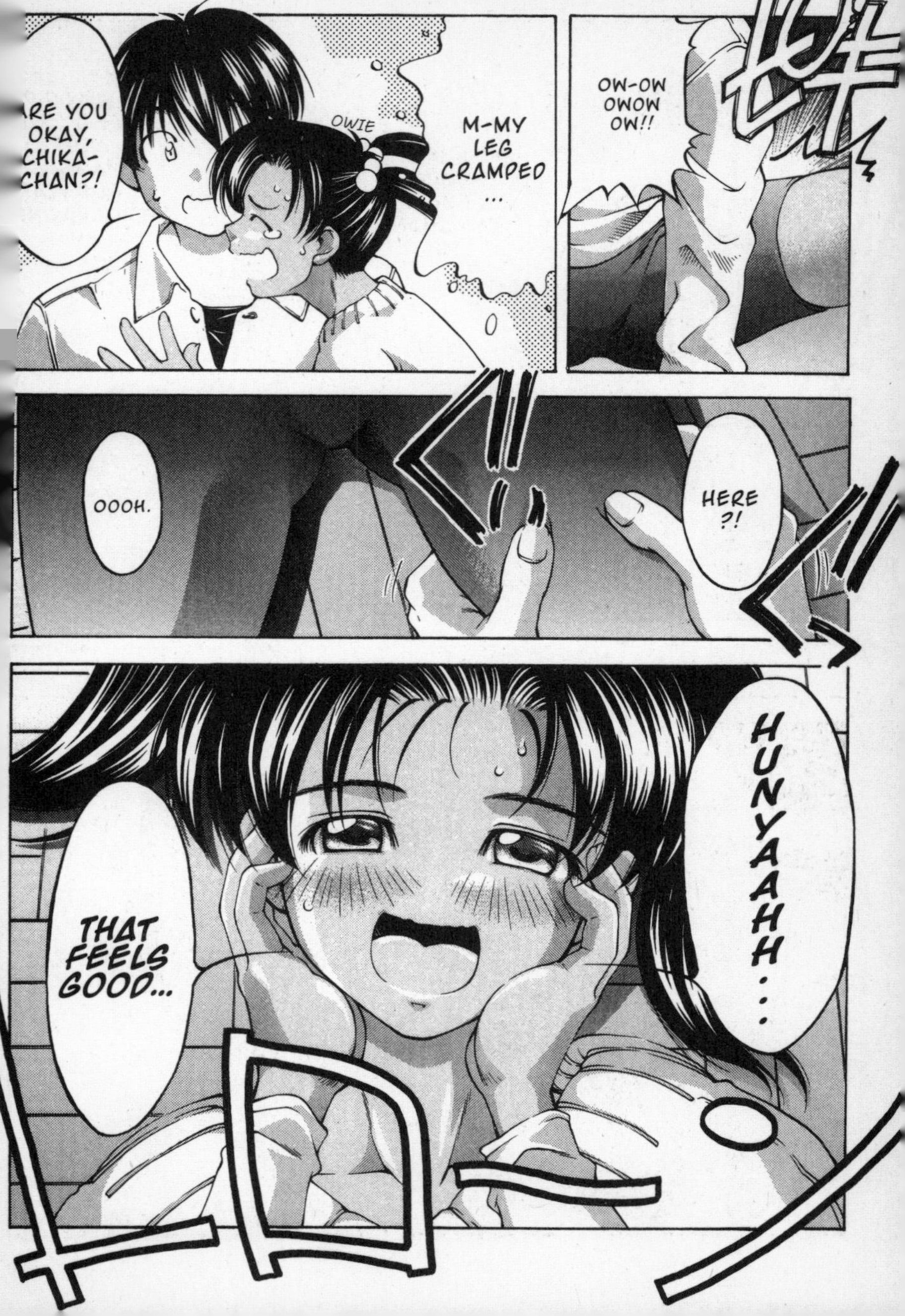
OW-OW OWOW OW!!
M-MY LEG CRAMPED ...
OWIE
ARE YOU OKAY, CHIKA-CHAN?!
HERE ?!
OOOH.
HUNYAAHH...
THAT FEELS GOOD...

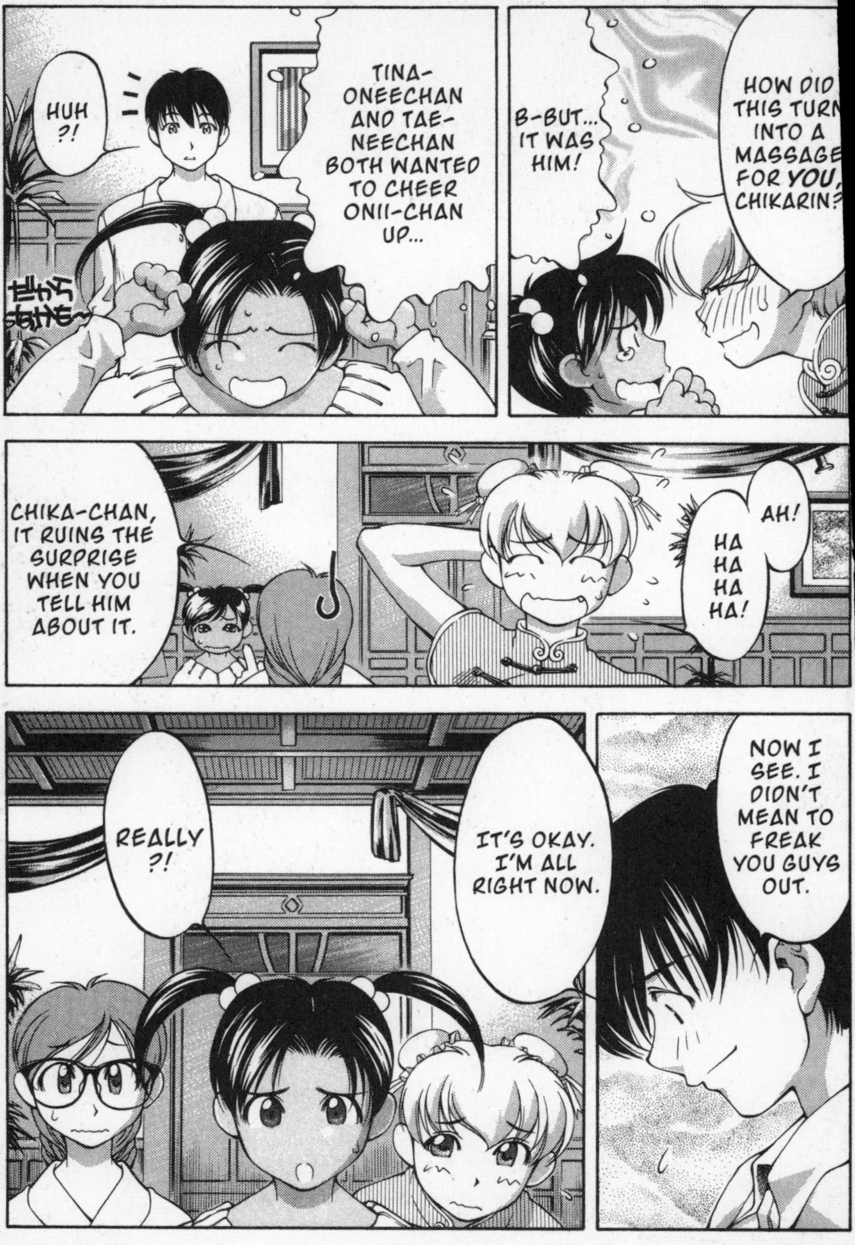
HOW DID THIS TURN INTO A MASSAGE FOR *YOU*, CHIKARIN?
B-BUT... IT WAS HIM!
TINA-ONEECHAN AND TAE-NEECHAN BOTH WANTED TO CHEER ONII-CHAN UP...
HUH?!
AH! HA HA HA HA!
CHIKA-CHAN, IT RUINS THE SURPRISE WHEN YOU TELL HIM ABOUT IT.
NOW I SEE. I DIDN'T MEAN TO FREAK YOU GUYS OUT.
IT'S OKAY. I'M ALL RIGHT NOW.
REALLY?!

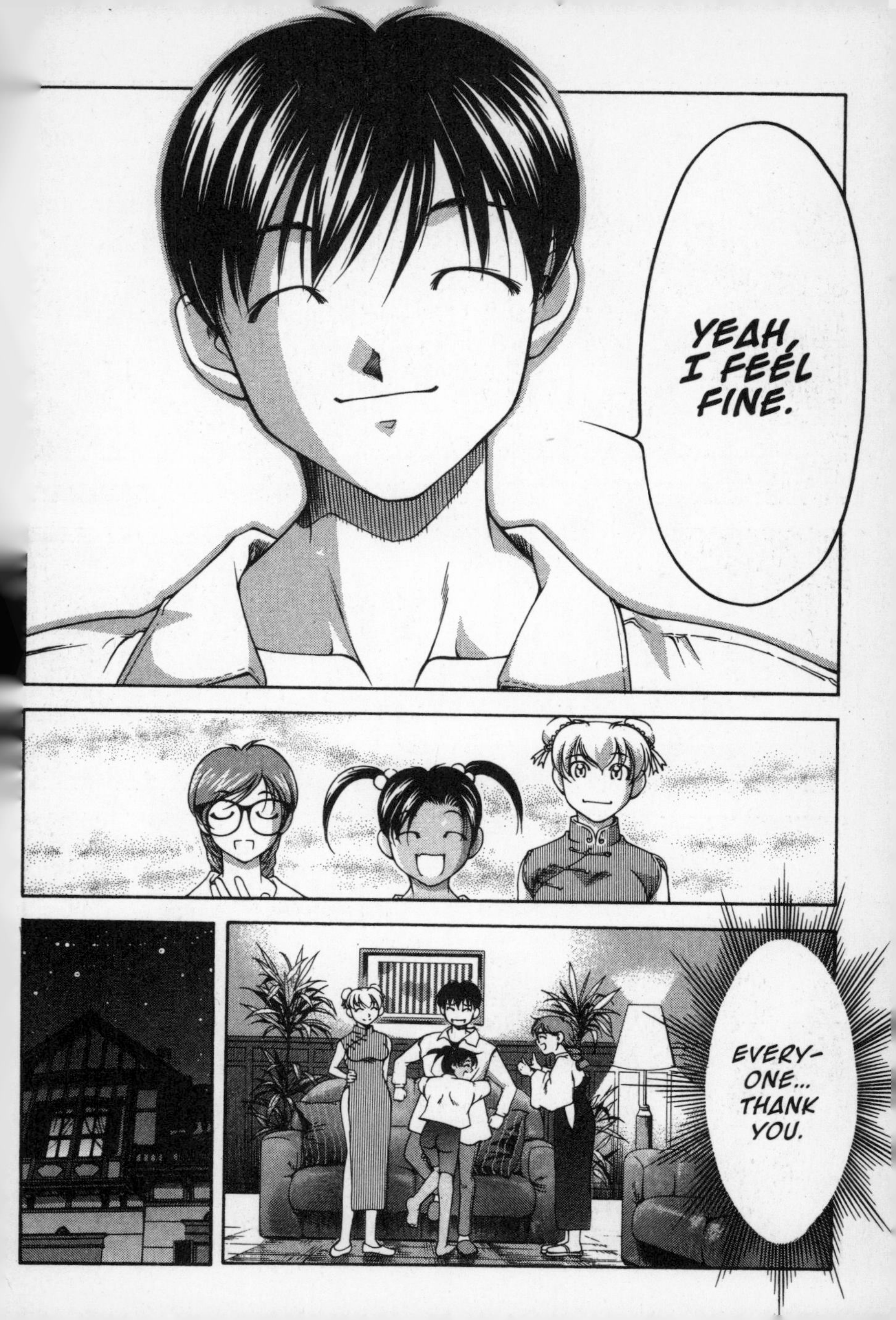
YEAH, I FEEL FINE.
EVERY-ONE... THANK YOU.

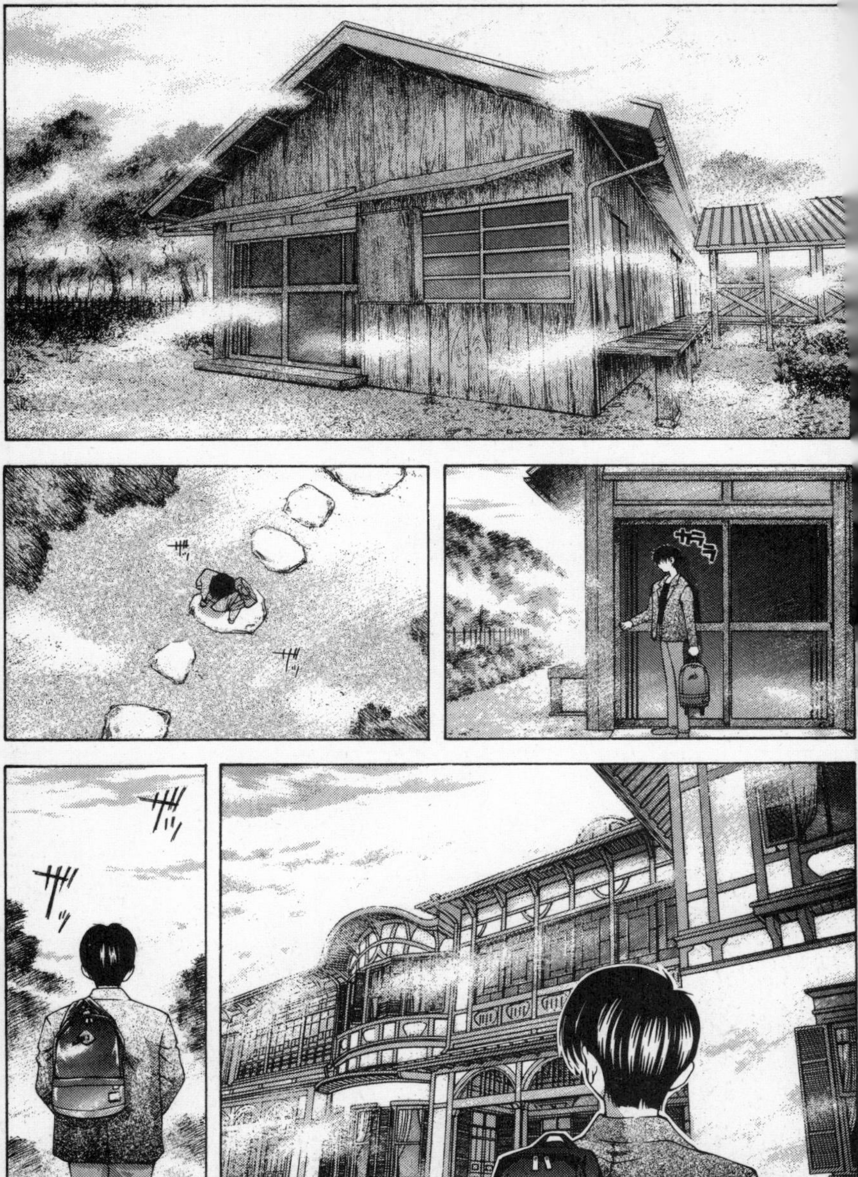
サララ
ザッ
ザッ
ザッ
ザッ

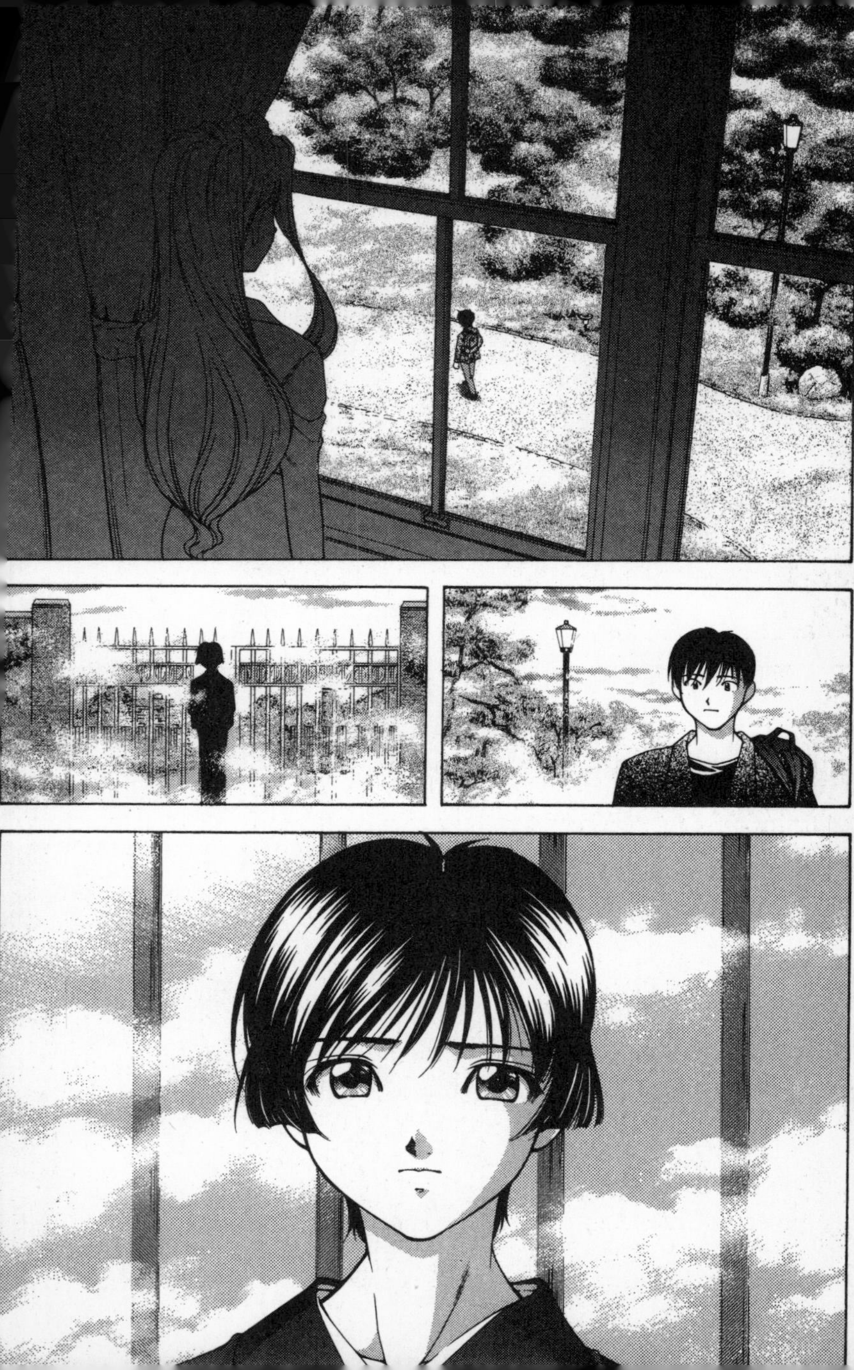

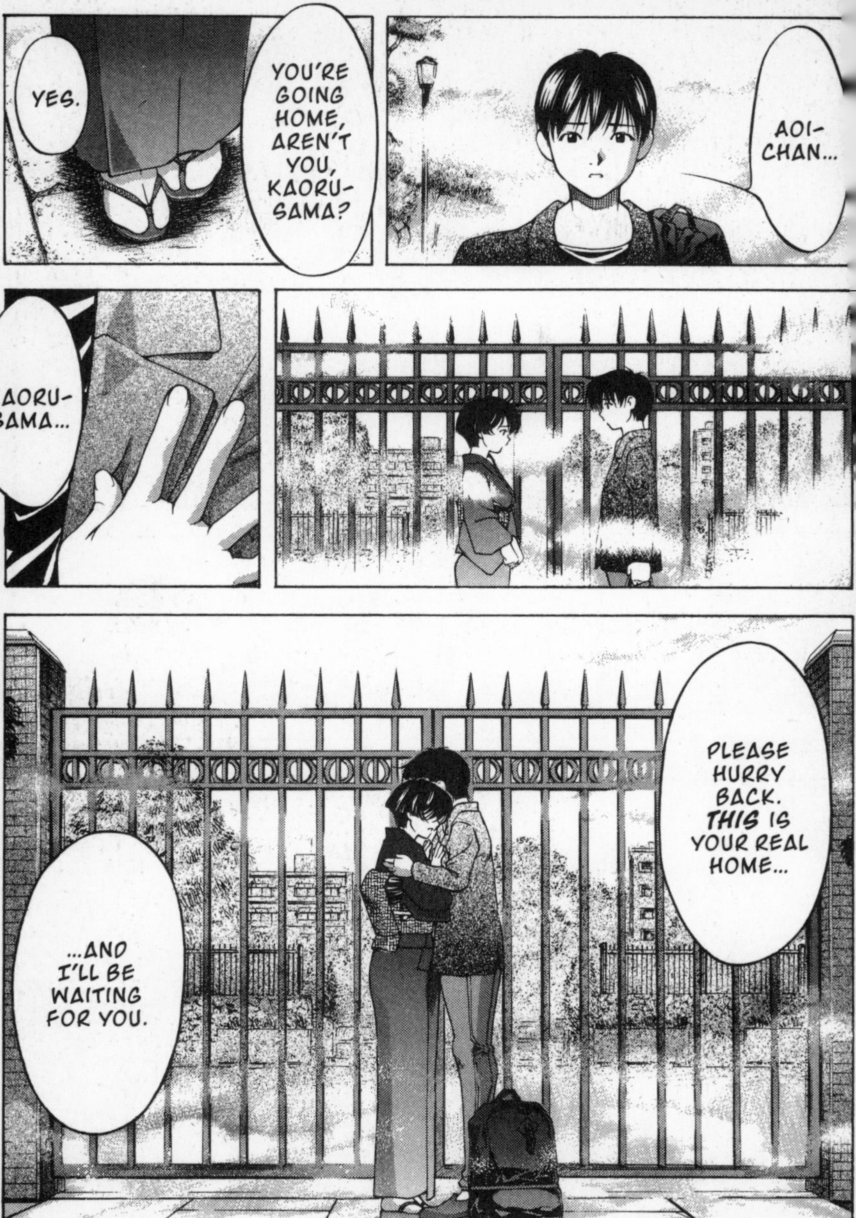
AOI-CHAN...
YOU'RE GOING HOME, AREN'T YOU, KAORU-SAMA?
YES.
KAORU-SAMA...
PLEASE HURRY BACK. THIS IS YOUR REAL HOME...
...AND I'LL BE WAITING FOR YOU.

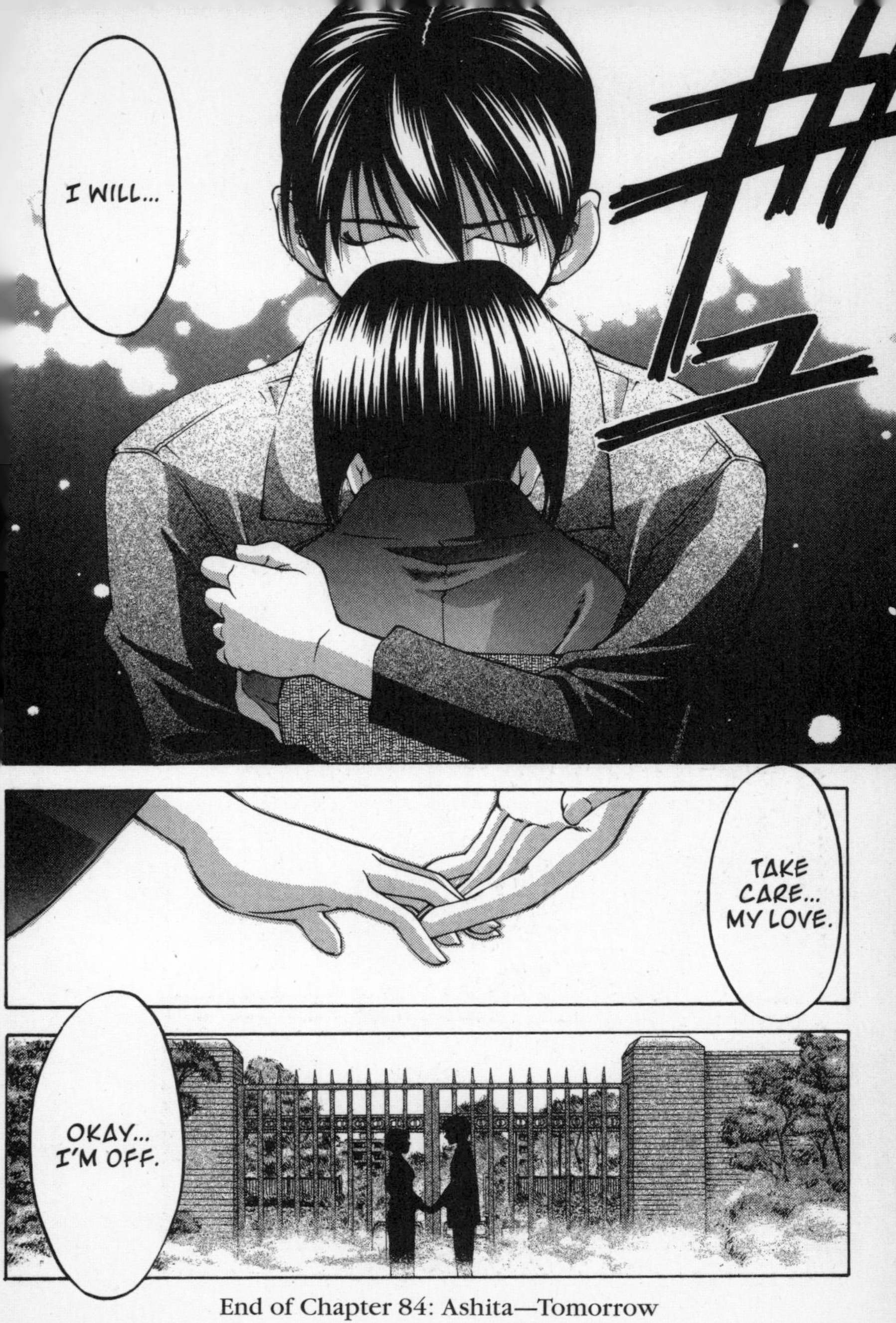
I WILL...
TAKE CARE... MY LOVE.
OKAY... I'M OFF.

End of Chapter 84: Ashita—Tomorrow

Ai-Ao Theatre, Part 23: Ai-Ao Game

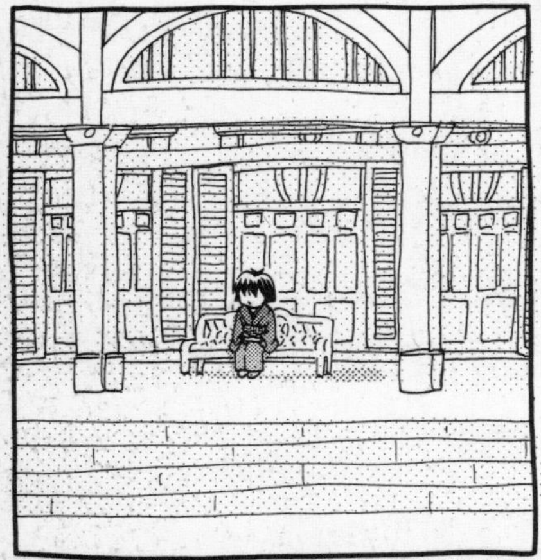

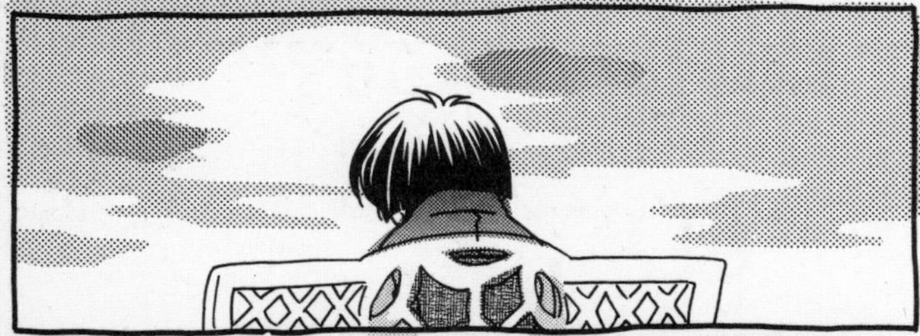

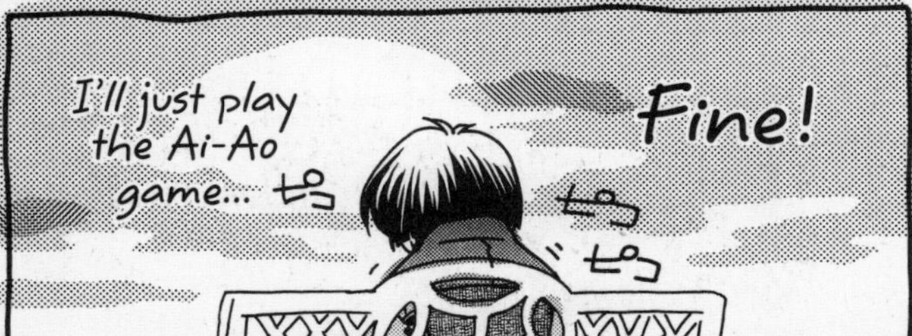
Fine!
ピコ
ピコ
I'll just play the Ai-Ao game...
ピコ

ASSIST THANKS

Jun Siozaki

Sisikura sama

Sono Yosihiro

Syunichi Fujiwara

Tomohiro Horie

Hidenori Iwanaga

Hiroaki Satou

Yosimi Nanjou

Miyuki

PC OPERATOR

Masataka Sibue

EDITOR

Syouichi Nakazawa
〈HAKUSENSHA〉

PRODUCE

Kou Fumizuki
〈Studio Little Cotton〉

NEXT TIME IN

藍より青し

AI YORI AOSHI

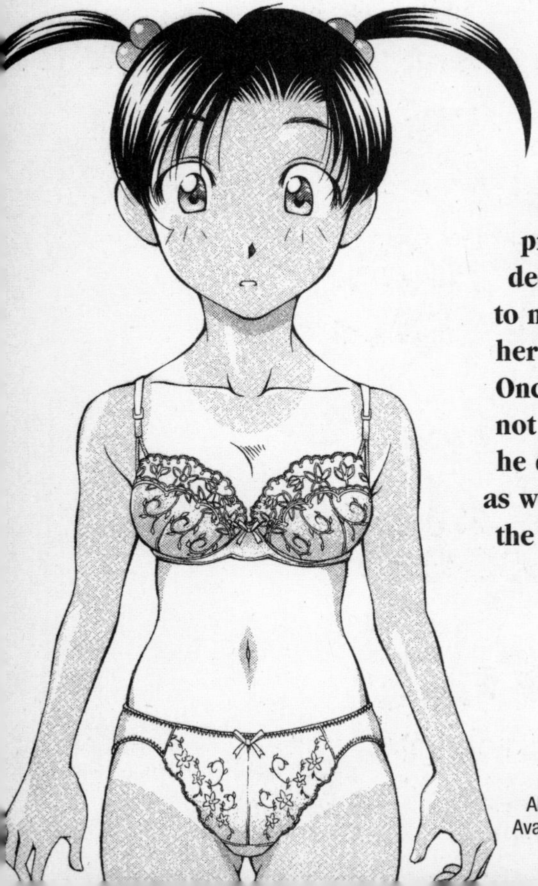

Despite her family's protests, Aoi Sakuraba decides that she is going to marry Kaoru Hanabishi, her love of eighteen years. Once he realizes that she's not working for his family, he decides it's a good idea as well. What obstacles must the two overcome in order to be together?

Ai Yori Aoshi Vol. 11—
Available December 2005

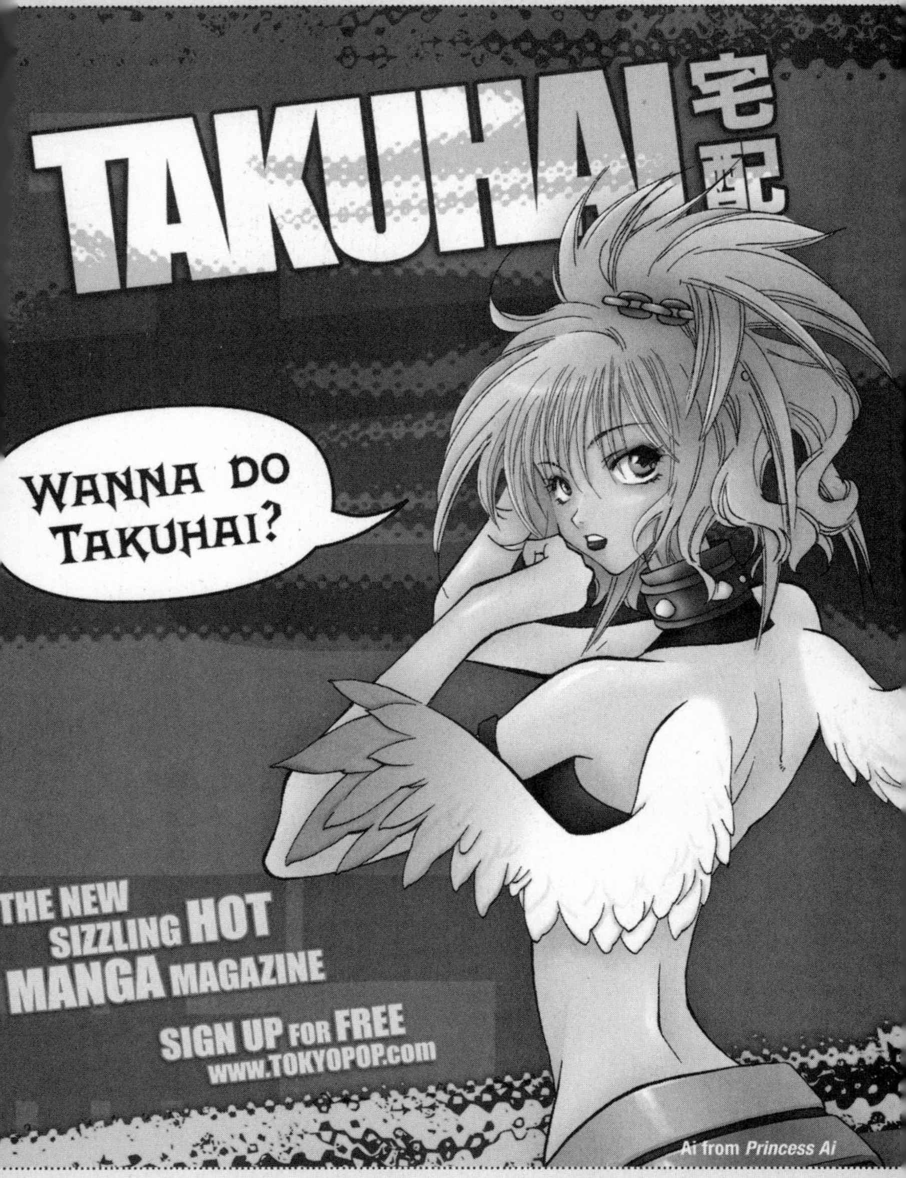
TAKUHAI 宅配
WANNA DO TAKUHAI?
THE NEW SIZZLING HOT MANGA MAGAZINE
SIGN UP FOR FREE
WWW.TOKYOPOP.com

Ai from *Princess Ai*

TOKYOPOP SHOP

WWW.TOKYOPOP.COM/SHOP

HOT NEWS!
Check out the
TOKYOPOP SHOP!
The world's best
collection of manga in
English is now available
online in one place!

GIRLS BRAVO

RIZELMINE

WAR ON FLESH

War on Flesh
and other hot
titles are
available at
the store that
never closes!

• LOOK FOR SPECIAL OFFERS
• PRE-ORDER UPCOMING RELEASES
• COMPLETE YOUR COLLECTIONS

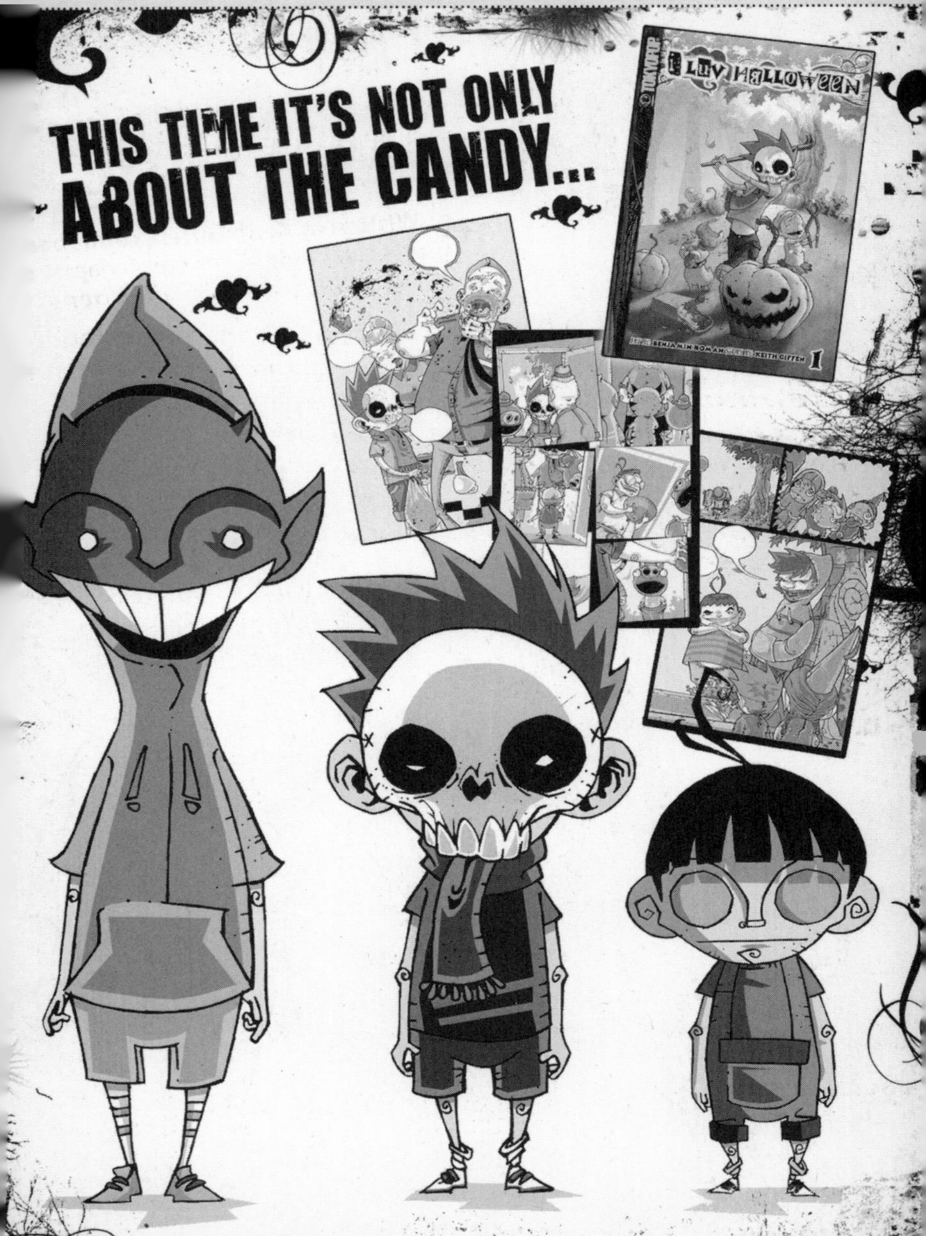
THIS TIME IT'S NOT ONLY ABOUT THE CANDY...
I LUV HALLOWEEN
TOKYOPOP
BENJAMIN ROMAN
KEITH GIFFEN
1

Written by Keith Giffen, comic boo
pro and English language adapter
Battle Royale and *Battle Vixens*.

Join the misadventures of a group of particularly disturbing
trick-or-treaters as they go about their macabre business on
Halloween night. Blaming the apples they got from the first
house of the evening for the bad candy they've been receiv-
ing all night, the kids plot revenge on the old bag who
handed out the funky fruit. Riotously
funny and always wickedly shocking—
who doesn't *love* Halloween?

OT
OLDER TEEN
AGE 16+

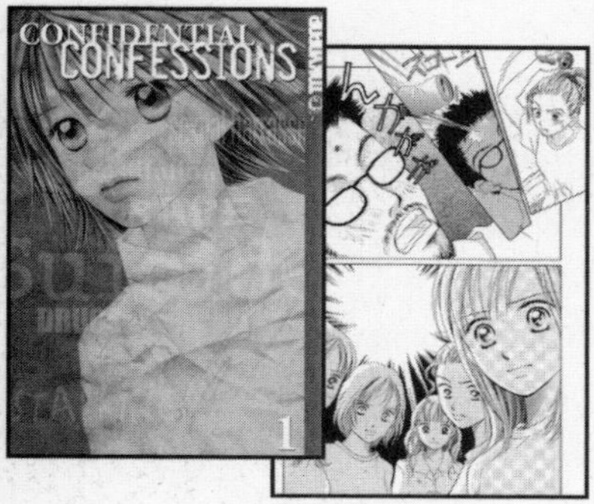

CONFIDENTIAL CONFESSIONS
1

BY REIKO MOMOCHI

CONFIDENTIAL CONFESSIONS

If you're looking for a happy, rosy, zit-free look at high school life, skip this manga. But if you're jonesing for a real-life view of what high school's truly like, *Confidential Confessions* offers a gritty, unflinching look at what really happens in those hallowed halls. Rape, sexual harassment, anorexia, cutting, suicide...no subject is too hardcore for *Confidential Confessions*. While you're at it, don't expect a happy ending.

~Julie Taylor, Sr. Editor

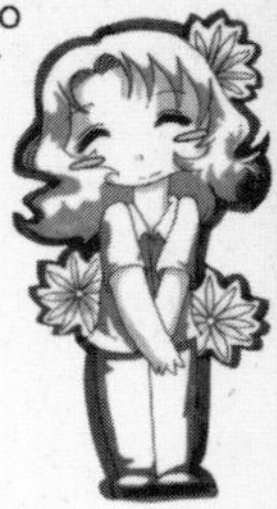

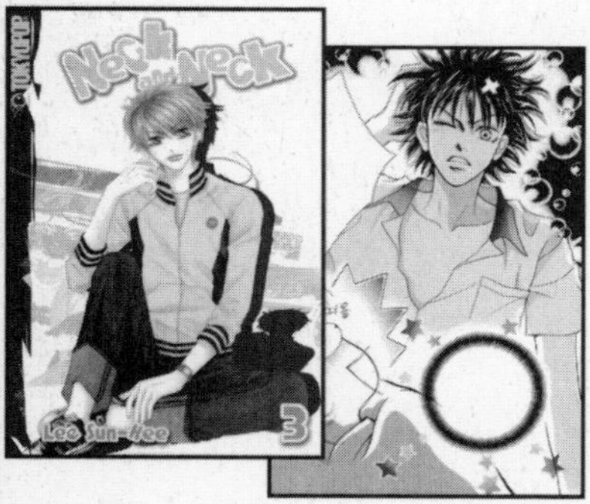

Neck and Neck
Lee Sun-Hee
3

BY LEE SUN-HEE

NECK AND NECK

Competition can bring out the best or the worst in people...but in *Neck and Neck*, it does both! Dabin Choi and Shihu Myoung are both high school students, both children of mob bosses, and each is out to totally humiliate the other. Dabin and Shihu are very creative in their mutual tortures and there's more than a hint of romantic tension behind their attacks. This book's art may look somewhat shojo, but I found the story to be very accessible and very entertaining!

~Rob Tokar, Sr. Editor

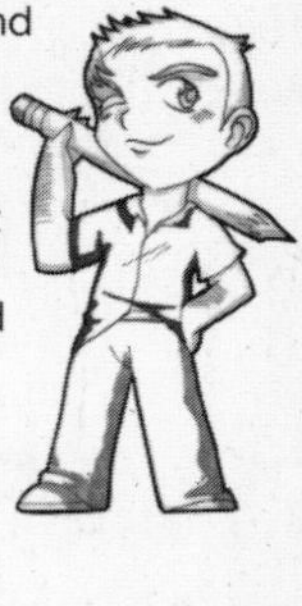

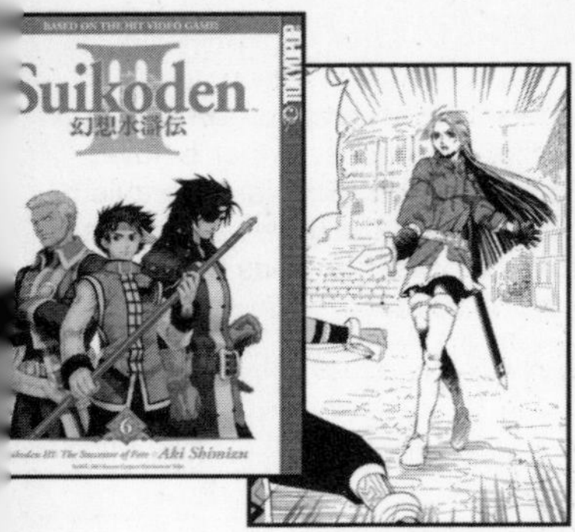
BASED ON THE HIT VIDEO GAMES
Suikoden III
幻想水滸伝
Aki Shimizu

BY AKI SHIMIZU

SUIKODEN III

I'm one of those people who likes to watch others play video games (I tend to run into walls and get stuck), so here comes the perfect manga for me! All the neat plot of a great RPG game, without any effort on my part! Aki Shimizu, creator of the delightful series *Qwan*, has done a lovely, lovely job of bringing the world of Suikoden to life. There are great creatures (Fighting ducks! Giant lizard people!), great character designs, and an engaging story full of conflict, drama and intrigue. I picked up one volume while I was eating lunch at my desk one day, and was totally hooked. I can't wait for the next one to come out!

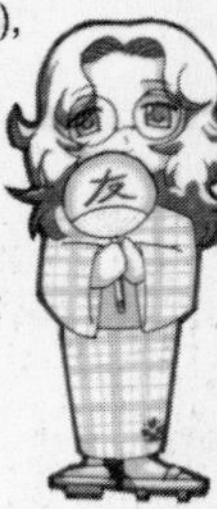

~Lillian Diaz-Przybyl, Editor

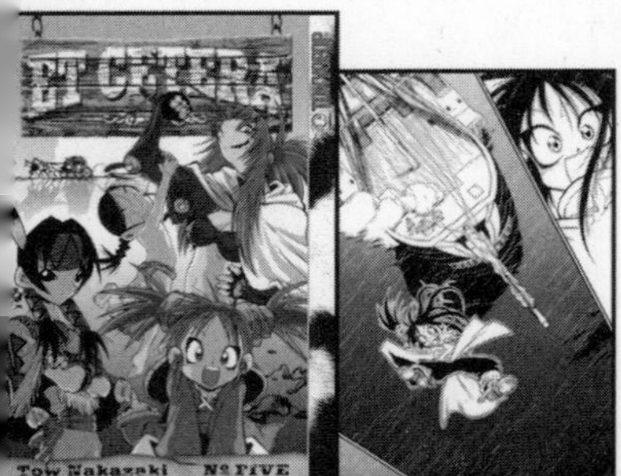
Tow Nakazaki
Nº FIVE

BY TOW NAKAZAKI

ET CETERA

Meet Mingchao, an energetic girl from China who now travels the deserts of the old west. She dreams of becoming a star in Hollywood, eager for fame and fortune. She was given the Eto Gun—a magical weapon that fires bullets with properties of the 12 zodiac signs—as a keepsake from her grandfather before he died. On her journey to Hollywood, she meets a number of zany characters...some who want to help, and others who are after the power of the Eto Gun. Chock full of gun fights, train hijackings, collapsing mineshafts...this East-meets-wild-West tale has it all!

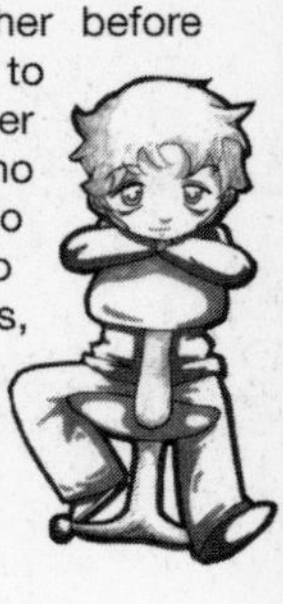

~Aaron Suhr, Sr. Editor

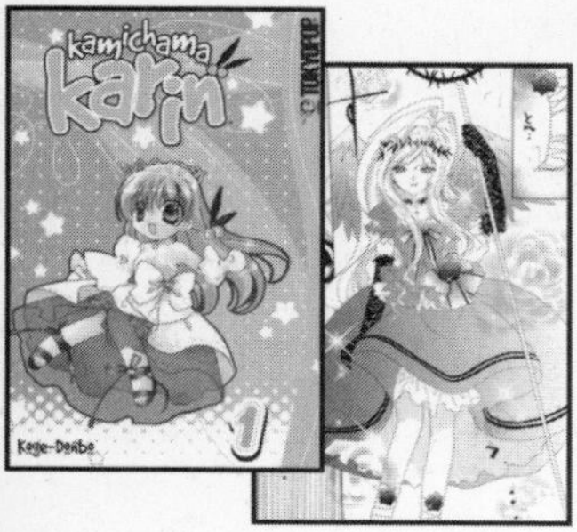
kamichama karin
Koge-Donbo
1

KAMICHAMA KARIN

BY KOGE-DONBO

Karin is an average girl...at best. She's not good at sports and gets terrible grades. On top of all that, her parents are dead and her beloved cat Shi-chan just died, too. She is miserable. But everything is about to change—little does Karin know that her mother's ring has the power to make her a goddess!

From the creator of *Pita-Ten* and *Digi-Charat!*

Y
YOUTH
AGE 10+

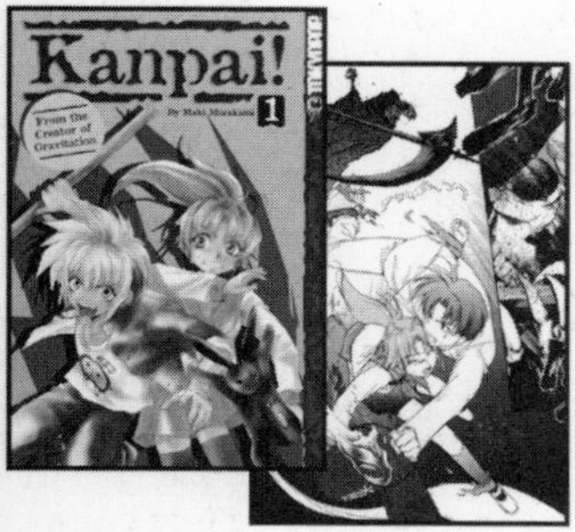
Kanpai!
By Maki Murakami
1

KANPAI!

BY MAKI MURAKAMI

Yamada Shintaro is a monster guardian in training—his job is to protect the monsters from harm. But when he meets Nao, a girl from his middle school, he suddenly falls in love...with her neckline! Shintaro will go to any lengths to prevent disruption to her peaceful life—and preserve his choice view of her neck!

A wild and wonderful adventure from the creator of *Gravitation!*

T
TEEN
AGE 13+

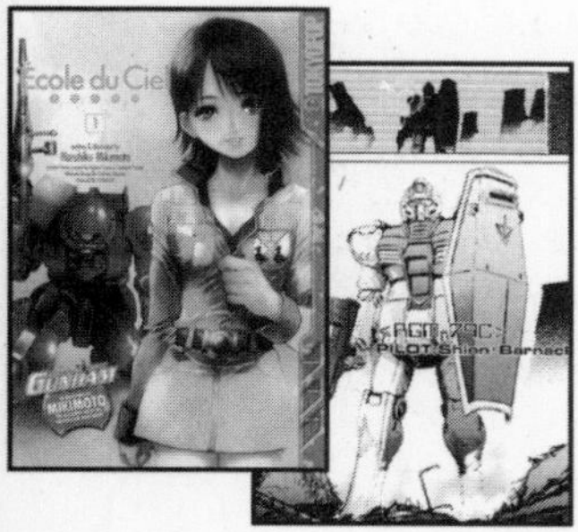
École du Ciel
1
MIKIMOTO

MOBILE SUIT GUNDAM ÉCOLE DU CIEL

BY HARUHIKO MIKIMOTO

École du Ciel—where aspiring pilots train to become Top Gundam! Asuna, daughter of a brilliant professor, is a below-average student at École du Ciel. But the world is spiraling toward war, and Asuna is headed for a crash course in danger, battle, and most of all, love.

From the artist of the phenomenally successful *Macross* and *Baby Birth!*

T
TEEN
AGE 13+

LAZIN' BARRELS

ing may look harmless and naïve, but he's really an excellent fighter and a wannabe
ounty hunter in the futuristic Wild West. When he comes across a notice that advertises
reward for the criminal outfit named Gold Romany, he decides that capturing the
-girl gang of bad guys is his ticket to fame and fortune!

IN-SEO PARK HAS CREATED ONE WILD TUMBLEWEED TALE FILLED WITH ADVENTURE GALORE AND PLENTY OF SHOTGUN ACTION!

© MIN-SEO PARK, DAIWON C.I. Inc.

FOR MORE INFORMATION VISIT: WWW.TOKYOPOP.COM